Freedom of Information Handbook

Related titles available from Law Society Publishing:

Data Protection Handbook
General Editor: Peter Carey

Design Law: Protecting and Exploiting Rights
Margaret Briffa and Lee Gage

Drafting confidentiality Agreements (2nd Edition)
Mark Anderson and Simon Keevey-Kothari

Execution of Documents: A Practical Guide
Mark Anderson and Victor Warner

Insolvency Law Handbook
Vernon Dennis

Technology Outsourcing: A Practitioner's Guide
General Editor: John Angel

Titles from Law Society Publishing can be ordered from all good legal bookshops or direct from our distributors, Marston Book Services (tel. 01235 465656 or email **law.society@marston.co.uk**). For further information or a catalogue, email our editorial and marketing office at **publishing@lawsociety.org.uk**.

FREEDOM OF INFORMATION HANDBOOK

General Editors: Peter Carey and Marcus Turle

The Law Society

Crown copyright material is reproduced with the permission of the Controller of Her Majesty's Stationery Office

ISBN 10: 1–85328–968–X
ISBN 13: 978–1–85328–968–2

Published in 2006 by the Law Society
113 Chancery Lane, London WC2A 1PL

Typeset by J&L Composition, Filey, North Yorkshire
Printed by Antony Rowe Ltd, Chippenham, Wiltshire

Contents

About the editors and contributors

EDITORS

Peter Carey is a Consultant Solicitor with Charles Russell in London, where he is Head of the Information Law Team. After gaining a Masters degree in International Business Law in the United States in 1993, Peter spent six years as a Senior Lecturer at the College of Law, the UK's leading legal education provider. Peter has established a reputation as one of the UK's leading data protection and privacy experts. He has written the UK's leading book on data protection (*Data Protection: – a practical guide to UK and EU law*, Oxford University Press) and is the editor of the journal, *Privacy & Data Protection*. Peter advises commercial organisations of varying sizes on all aspects of information law compliance. His clients include a major water utility, several charities, a global telecommunications services provider, one of the world's largest medical data suppliers, local authorities and several e-commerce companies.

Marcus Turle is a solicitor at Field Fisher Waterhouse in London and one of the founder members of FFW's Privacy and Information Law Group. A technology lawyer whose practice focuses on outsourcing, procurement and e-commerce, Marcus also specialises in the legal regulation of information. This includes freedom of information, data protection, information security and interception, confidentiality and human rights. Marcus has worked closely with central and local government on freedom of information, including advising on the information law aspects of the national DNA database and the government's proposed national identity card scheme. He also advises banks, consultancy firms and the health sector. Marcus edits *Freedom of Information*, the only legal journal available dedicated to this area.

CONTRIBUTORS

Patricia Barratt graduated from Jesus College, Cambridge with a degree in Classics in 1984 before working for a Greek law firm in Piraeus for several years. She trained in law at Chancery Lane College of Law, and qualified as a solicitor with Clifford Chance in 1991. In 1992 she joined Clifford Chance's newly established Public Policy Group, headed by Richard Thomas, the current Information Commissioner. She has extensive experience of advising on all aspects of parliamentary and public policy related work with particular expertise in parliamentary procedure, freedom of information and standards of conduct in public life, including advice on corruption and political donations. She is currently a member of the Law Society's Law Reform Board and travels regularly to Brussels for meetings of the European Services Forum Policy Committee. She also sits on the Law Society's GATS working group, and is on the Editorial Board of the *Freedom of Information* journal, to which she is a regular contributor. She has spoken frequently on freedom of information, and is the co-author of the Clifford Chance guide to the Freedom of Information Act.

Carolyn Bigg is an Assistant Solicitor at Charles Russell LLP, specialising in non-contentious commercial, information technology and communications law. She is a member of Charles Russell's dedicated freedom of information and data protection teams. Carolyn is currently advising a number of companies and not-for-profit organisations on data protection law and practice, in particular in the field of e-commerce, as well as several public authorities and private contractors on the impact of the Freedom of Information Act 2000. Carolyn was educated at Gonville and Caius College, Cambridge and qualified as a solicitor in 2003. She regularly contributes articles to the Charles Russell data protection and freedom of information microsites, as well as a number of publications.

Anna-Marie Harty is an associate at Herbert Smith, practising in the areas of information law (with particular emphasis on freedom of information and data privacy) and intellectual property. Anna-Marie is the Convenor of Herbert Smith's cross-firm Information Law Group. She is a graduate of Trinity College, Dublin (LL.B.Ger) and the University of Wuerzburg, Germany (LL.M) and has contributed articles on various aspects of information law to leading publications.

Jeremy Ison is a commercial litigator at Clifford Chance, where he qualified in 1997. He has handled corporate disputes in a range of industries, representing airlines, banks, energy suppliers and apparel manufacturers among others. In addition, much of his work has a media slant and he advises both claimants and defendants pre- and post-publication in relation to libel and contempt. Formerly the editor of *Media Law Review*, co-published by Clifford Chance and the Periodical Publishers Association, he has also authored articles on defamation and freedom of information. His regulatory experience includes a secondment to the Broadcasting Standards Commission where he worked on fairness and privacy cases, and he has brought and defended complaints for clients before several content regulators, such as the Advertising Standards Authority.

Brian Jones joined Herbert Smith as a consultant in 2000 following a career in which he taught administrative law and environmental law at a number of universities in the UK and in Australia. Between 1994 and 2000 he was Professor of Environmental Liability at De Montfort University in Leicester. He has published extensively in both subject areas: his most recent book being a co-authored work on *Environmental Liabilities* (Shaw and Sons, 2004).

He was involved in the late 1990's in several consultancy projects, advising governments in EU accession countries about requirements for harmonisation with EU environmental law. Since 1992 he has been editor of the bi-monthly professional journal *Environmental Liability*. He was recently appointed an Honorary Professor in the Department of Law, University of Wales, Aberystwyth.

Brian works closely within Herbert Smith with the environmental law, planning law, public law and IP groups. He is a member of the editorial board of the *Freedom of Information* journal.

Keith Mathieson is a partner specialising in media law at London solicitors Reynolds Porter Chamberlain. He has taken a close interest in the new freedom of information legislation and its application to the media. RPC is well known for its representation of media organisations in the defence of libel and other claims. Its clients include national and regional newspaper publishers, magazine publishers, book publishers, broadcasters, independent production companies, journalists and media liability insurers. As well as advice on freedom of information issues, Keith's practice encompasses all legal aspects of free speech, including defamation, copyright, privacy and reporting restrictions. Keith is a member of the Editorial Board of *Freedom of Information* journal.

Christopher Rees is Partner and Head of IT and e-commerce at Herbert Smith. He has 20 years' experience of the IT industry and advises on all types of IT-related issues. His practice covers system supply, outsourcing, M&A and corporate transactions for IT-centred businesses, e-commerce and internet related issues of all kinds. He has a particular interest in the protection and use of content (database ownership and data privacy). He acts for both suppliers and users to retain a balanced view of transactions and facilitate resolution of disputes.

He also has an interest in the developing field of information law. He is a regular writer and lecturer on the subject of data privacy and information law.

Christopher has been ranked in the top three of the world's IT lawyers in the two last surveys conducted by Euromoney (*Euromoney,* 'Best of the Best').

Andrew Sharpe is an Associate Solicitor at Charles Russell LLP, practising information technology, intellectual property and telecommunications law. Andrew has lectured widely on freedom of information and data protection law, including conducting tailored training onsite at clients' premises. He has advised companies, public authorities and not-for-profit organisations on all aspects of data protection, freedom of information and communications legislation. He has written on data protection and privacy issues for *Privacy & Data Protection* and also on issues relating to the new freedom of information regime for the *Freedom of Information* journal.

Prior to qualifying as a solicitor in 1999, Andrew was a Royal Air Force engineering officer. He was one of the first Data Protection Officers in the RAF, responsible for the introduction of data protection operating procedures and compliance upon the introduction of RAF data protection policies under the Data Protection Act 1984.

Hugh Tomlinson QC, is a founder member of Matrix Chambers with a wide ranging practice covering media and information, commercial law, human rights, civil liberties and public law. He is a well known author and lecturer. His books include the leading practitioner's work on human rights, *The Law of Human Rights* (Oxford University Press, 2nd Edition, 2006)(with Richard Clayton) and, as editor, *Privacy and the Media: The Developing Law* (Matrix, 2002). He regularly acts as a Council of Europe expert on media and privacy issues. Hugh is a member of the Editorial Board of *Freedom of Information* journal.

Antony White QC of Matrix Chambers practises in media and information law, commercial law and arbitration, employment law and public law. He appeared for the claimant in *Naomi Campbell* v. *MGN Ltd* [2003] QB 633 (CA) and [2004] 2 AC 457 (HL) which was the first successful High Court claim against a media defendant under the Data Protection Act 1998. He is the co-author of *Privacy and the Media* (Matrix, 2002).

Foreword

Open government is good government. The traditional culture of unnecessary secrecy is starting to erode.

The Freedom of Information Act 2000 and the Environmental Information Regulations 2004 have been fully in force for only a few months but already their effects have been deeply felt throughout the whole of the public sector and in many parts of the private sector too. As the independent Information Commissioner it is my office's responsibility to enforce the Act and Regulations, as well as to promote good practice. We received around 1,000 complaints in relation to FOI requests in the six months from 1 January 2005. Many of these arose from unfamiliarity with the new laws and were relatively straightforward to resolve. Other complaints raise complex and difficult issues, often engaging public interest considerations, and require detailed and careful evaluation.

So a body of decisions is beginning to take shape which can be expected to grow very quickly, and which is likely to inform and direct policy and practice in this area. But I should like to emphasise that these decisions will not necessarily constitute legally binding precedents, and that each complaint must continue to be dealt with on a case-by-case basis on its own merits. The starting point must always be the legislation itself and I would urge all those involved in making FOI decisions, in using FOI to gain access to information, and in advising on FOI issues, to gain a close familiarity with the detailed provisions of the Freedom of Information Act and the EIRs as well as with other important pieces of legislation, including in particular the Data Protection Act 1998. My office has issued a large number of short 'Awareness Guidance' Notes on relevant procedural and technical aspects. While these have no legal effect, I would recommend them as a further aid to implementing and interpreting the Act. The Department for Constitutional Affairs and the Department for Environment, Food and Rural Affairs have also issued extensive guidance and FOI officers should of course take note of the statutory Codes of Practice made under the Act.

This book, written by legal professionals with expertise in freedom of information, aims to draw together the various threads of legislation, guidance and experience. Intended as a practical handbook for practitioners, I am sure it will prove an invaluable tool in navigating this important new regime.

Richard Thomas
UK Information Commissioner
July 2005

Table of Cases

Table of Statutes

Table of Statutory Instruments

Tables of treaties, conventions and European legislation

TREATIES AND CONVENTIONS

EUROPEAN LEGISLATION

CHAPTER 1

Introduction and background to the law

Patricia Barratt, Clifford Chance

1.1 INTRODUCTION

Did the UK government ignore or influence its own legal advice on the legality of going to war with Iraq? Did Conservative leader, Michael Howard, try to help Mohamed Al Fayed obtain a British passport? How did the Conservative government handle the Black Wednesday crisis in 1992, when Sterling exited from the European Exchange Rate Mechanism? Did the UK government condone overseas bribery by UK companies in the late 1970s? The list of questions that requesters hope the Freedom of Information Act will help to resolve is endless and highly political. Since information is power, it is hardly surprising that the current government, in its application of the Freedom of Information Act 2000 (FOIA), has been accused of political chicanery and of misusing the Act for its own political ends in the run up to the general election in May 2005. At the time of writing, it is arguable that the FOIA has blown up in the government's face, with the stated aims of increasing trust in government and public participation in the political debate further off than ever and the newspapers having a field day with allegation and counter allegation.

The FOIA undoubtedly has a political side, but it has also a very real practical application for a very large number of people, and not just those who work in the 115,000 public authorities to which the Act applies. Public sector expenditure, not just that of central government, seems likely to attract unprecedented scrutiny as a result of the Act, with private sector contractors also deeply affected. Grant funding, planning permission applications, development plans, government-compiled statistics, lobbying efforts, public procurement details, departmental meeting minutes, public service contracts – these are all potentially accessible under the Act.

It could be argued that a number of different developments made the Act almost inevitable. Perhaps the most influential of these is the creation and growth of the Internet. With such a huge range of information from all sources already easily accessible to anyone using the Internet, and with few, if any, effective mechanisms for blocking the dissemination of information via that route, a government seeking to protect information that others want

1

is frequently going to be fighting a losing battle. The *Spycatcher* case (*A-G v. Guardian Newspapers (No.2)* [1990] AC 109) had already shown the limits of the government's power to restrain publication of information, but the Internet multiplies this problem to the nth degree with websites accessible from anywhere in the world and publication immediate. Also, with information access regimes becoming increasingly common in other countries, the UK was on the back foot in terms of international legal comparators. Sweden, famously, has had a form of freedom of information legislation in place since 1776. New Zealand has had a freedom of information act since 1962, the United States since 1966 (strengthened in 1982), Australia since 1982 and Ireland since 1997.

1.2 THE CODE OF PRACTICE ON ACCESS TO GOVERNMENT INFORMATION

The Conservative government, resisting calls for legislation, introduced the voluntary Code of Practice on Access to Government Information (the Code) in April 1994 (revised in January 1997), since then often described as one of government's best kept secrets. It fell under the remit of the Parliamentary Commissioner and only applied to organisations under her jurisdiction. This meant that any complaints about how requests were dealt with under the Code had to be approached in the same way as other complaints about, for example, maladministration by government departments, in other words, via a Member of Parliament. This cumbersome mechanism, coupled with the lack of real powers on the part of the Information Commissioner, kept the number of requests under the Code down, and its influence on public sector culture minimal, save within a few better informed and more progressive central government departments.

Decisions of the Ombudsman, as the Parliamentary Commissioner is also known, are, however, useful, because the UK Information Commissioner has said he would expect to have regard to decisions of the Ombudsman. So, in these early days, while there are still relatively few indications about how the FOIA will be enforced in the UK, these decisions are an invaluable resource (readers are referred to the periodical, *Freedom of Information*, as a resource for keeping up to date with developments – **www.foij.com**).

The Code came into force on 4 April 1994 (and was revised in 1997), setting out common standards applicable to all government departments responding to requests for disclosure of information, new procedures enabling those requesting the information to seek internal review of decisions not to disclose, and a new mechanism for external review of such decisions by the Parliamentary Ombudsman. In the opening paragraph of the Code, under the heading 'Purpose', it clearly stated that: 'The approach to release of information should in all cases be based on the assumption that information should be released except where disclosure would not be in the public interest, as specified in Part II of this Code.'

A number of MPs later argued for the inclusion of such an assumption – a presumption in favour of disclosure – on the face of the Act. However, amendments to this effect were rejected by the government. The Code also set out three aims:

- to improve policy-making and the democratic process by extending access to the facts and analyses which provide the basis for the consideration of proposed policy;
- to protect the interests of individuals and companies by ensuring that reasons are given for administrative decisions, except where there is statutory authority or established convention to the contrary; and
- to support and extend the principles of public service established under the Citizen's Charter.

However, the aims are immediately qualified by the need:

- to maintain high standards of care in ensuring the privacy of personal and commercially confidential information; and
- to preserve confidentiality where disclosure would not be in the public interest or would breach personal privacy or the confidences of a third party, in accordance with statutory requirements and Part II of the Code.

The main concerns of the private sector and businesses providing information to government under commercial contracts, grant applications, or other submissions, were therefore explicitly addressed, to some extent, the focus of the Code resting squarely on releasing genuinely official information, rather than simply information held by officials.

As part of this voluntary regime, the Chancellor of the Duchy of Lancaster undertook to report annually on the progress of the Code. In his report (*Open Government: Code of Practice on Access to Government Information, 1995 Report*) on the first full year of the Code's operation, 1995, he said that 1,353 requests for information had been recorded for that year (compared to over 7,000 requests recorded for the first three months of the operation of the FOIA). Code requests were narrowly defined as requests that specifically mentioned the Code; those for which a charge or standard fee was imposed; or those in respect of which information had been refused under one of more of the exemptions set out in the Code.

The Code only applied to those government departments and bodies which fell within the jurisdiction of the Parliamentary Commissioner (these are set out in Sched.2 to the Parliamentary Commissioner Act 1967). The Code provided that complaints about the way in which a request had been handled should be made first to the department or body concerned. Only after this should the complaint be referred, via an MP, to the Ombudsman. Guidance on this internal review stage may prove relevant to reviews carried out under the

Act: according to the *Guidance on Interpretation of the Code* (2nd edition, Part I, para.72), internal reviews should be a 'single stage process', though this advice has clearly not been followed by a number of public authorities which have set up two-tier, and in some cases, three-tier FOIA appeal procedures. Further:

> The aim should be to ensure that the applicant has been fairly treated under the provisions of the Code, that any exemptions have been properly applied and that charges are reasonably and consistently applied. It is good practice for such review to be conducted by someone not involved in the original decision.

The Code, thought by many to give superior rights of access to information than the Act, nevertheless suffered from a lack of profile, poor enforcement mechanisms and a limited application. It was made obsolete on 1 January 2005 when the FOIA right of access was finally introduced, four years after the Act was passed.

1.2.1 Lessons to be learned from the Code

Decisions on the application of the Code made by the Parliamentary Commissioner are only precedents insofar as the Information Commissioner chooses to follow them. From a legal point of view they are not binding. There are differences in wording between the exemptions in the Code and the exemptions in the Act which further limit the usefulness of Code decisions as precedents. Nevertheless the Information Commissioner has indicated that he expects all public authorities to take decisions of the Parliamentary Commissioner into account when making decisions on disclosure of requests for information.

> In a UK context, it will also be important to consider any decisions made by the Parliamentary Ombudsman when considering complaints under the Open Government Code. Although the Code is not statutory and applies to a much smaller number of public authorities, the public interest test applied by the Ombudsman is identical to that required under the Act. Summaries of cases considered by the Ombudsman under the Code can be found on the Ombudsman's website (at **www.ombudsman.org.uk/pca/document/aoi03nj/index.htm**).
> (Information Commissioner's Office, *Freedom of Information Awareness Guidance No.3, The Public Interest Test*)

Public authorities must therefore be familiar with these decisions, and those requesting information may also find valuable material there to substantiate their arguments for or against disclosure.

The Parliamentary Ombudsman published regular reports summarising her investigations into complaints under the Code. Her last annual report (*Access to Official Information: Investigations Completed July 2003–June 2004, HC*

701), published in June 2004, contained decisions on a range of issues, from briefings for Ministers, meetings between Ministers and trade associations, a National Audit Office report, information about the awarding of a contract and the publication of a Ministerial Direction. A further report, looking at more than 10 years of the operation of the Code, was published in June 2005. To reiterate, the Information Commissioner may choose not to follow these decisions but there is likely to be considerable adverse criticism of any decision which appears to row back from the position under the non-statutory Code.

The first reported case (A.21/03) in the 2004 report makes very interesting reading. It dealt with a request made to the Cabinet Office (and 17 other government departments) on 6 and 10 June 2002 for details of any contact between Ministers and representatives of a particular trade association since a specified date and in particular, the number of meetings that had taken place, the number of letters exchanged and the number of representations made by Ministers on behalf of the trade association to other parties.

Only one department provided the information requested: the Department for Culture, Media and Sport replied that there had been no contact between departmental Ministers and the trade association, and that Ministers had made no representations on behalf of the trade association. Eleven departments, including the Cabinet Office, refused to supply the information requested. The Cabinet Office (on 12 September 2002, three months after the request) claimed that the information was exempt under Exemptions 7(*b*) and 13 of the Code: that the release of the information sought would harm the proper and efficient conduct of the department and would constitute an unwarranted disclosure of commercial confidences which would harm the competitive position of a third party. (These exemptions correspond roughly to the exemptions set out in sections 36 and 43 respectively of the FOIA.) They also considered that the public interest in disclosure did not outweigh the harm which would result from such disclosure. This reply drew on central guidance issued by the Lord Chancellor's Department (as it was then) on 13 August 2002 to the effect that departments should regard information relating to contact between Ministers and officials and representatives of outside organisations as exempt under the Code, based on the application of the exemptions mentioned above.

When the applicant asked for an internal review of the refusal to disclose, further central guidance was issued confirming that it should not be the normal practice to release details of meetings with outside interests, and the refusal to disclose was repeated.

The applicant appealed to the Ombudsman, who found that the stated exemptions did not apply, and that the Cabinet Office was not justified in withholding the information requested. She recommended that the Permanent Secretary supply the information and issue revised guidance to the Department for Constitutional Affairs to enable it to advise the other departments to whom requests for release of information had been addressed. The Ombudsman also criticised the Cabinet Office for the way in which it had dealt with the request (the officials had failed to locate and identify the information requested before deciding whether to disclose it), and for delays in providing information to the Ombudsman's office.

The Cabinet Office confirmed that it would now provide the information requested to the applicant. This decision is of direct relevance to the request made under the FOIA by the *Guardian* newspaper to the Department for Culture, Media and Sport, for information about meetings between Ministers, officials, and representatives of the gaming industry prior to the introduction of the Gambling Bill into Parliament. The public interest test (a slightly different test under the Code than under the Act) was not engaged in the Ombudsman's case because she held that the exemptions could not apply.

If the Information Commissioner were to follow the Ombudsman in finding that Exemptions 36 and 43 did not apply to this request (and no further Exemptions were applicable), then again there would be no reason to consider the public interest test and the Commissioner should, in theory, order disclosure.

In other reported investigations, the Ombudsman recommended that background briefings for Parliamentary Questions should be released, but agreed that they could be edited so as to omit opinions and advice the disclosure of which might harm the frankness and candour of internal discussion (Exemption 2 under the Code, s.35 of the FOIA).

Interestingly, the Ombudsman was also asked to adjudicate on the Cabinet Office's refusal to supply copies of all documents drawn up by the Attorney General giving advice on the legality of military intervention in Iraq. The Ombudsman found that Exemption 4(*d*) of the Code relating to legal professional privilege (s.42 of the FOIA) applied and that the refusal to disclose the information requested was justified. She noted that the exemption in the Code was an absolute exemption and therefore she did not have to consider the public interest in disclosure. This, of course, is in direct contrast with the position under the FOIA, since the section 42 exemption is subject to the public interest test. The Ombudsman's decision in this instance, therefore, can be only of limited value as a precedent. Of course, the leak of the papers has meant that we will not see a formal decision on whether the statutory exemption of legal professional privilege has been effectively waived by publication of a summary of the advice, or on whether there was a greater public interest in publishing the information than in withholding it.

Other investigations included in the report deal with:

- the Ministry of Defence's refusal to provide information about accidents involving nuclear weapons;

- a refusal by the Department for Education and Skills to provide information about a decision to discontinue a procurement exercise relating to the electronic registration of schools;
- a refusal by the Foreign and Commonwealth Office and the Department of Trade and Industry to provide reasons why a company's application for funding under the Export Market Research Scheme had been refused;
- the Department of Health's refusal to provide information about the award of a contract to supply a stock of smallpox vaccine;
- a refusal by the Higher Education Funding Council for England to provide information about issues of financial probity and corporate governance;
- the Department of Trade and Industry's refusal to release a Ministerial Direction; and
- HM Treasury's refusal to provide details of external meetings attended by the Chancellor of the Exchequer, Treasury Ministers and special advisers.

1.3 HISTORY AND DEVELOPMENT OF THE LEGISLATION

Despite the existence of the Code, there was still strong pressure to introduce a statutory regime enabling access to public sector information. The Labour Manifesto in 1997, promising such a regime, said:

> Unnecessary secrecy in government leads to arrogance in government and defective policy decisions. The *Scott Report* on arms to Iraq revealed Conservative abuses of power. We are pledged to a Freedom of Information Act, leading to more open government, and an independent National Statistical Service.
> (New Labour, *Because Britain Deserves Better*
> Labour Party Manifesto 1997, M/029/97)

Further, in December of the same year, the newly elected Labour government presented a White Paper (*Your Right to Know – The Government's Proposals for a Freedom of Information Act*, Cm 3818, December 1997) to Parliament, setting out radical proposals for a new statutory right to obtain information from public authorities.

In introducing the White Paper, the Prime Minister said that 'The traditional culture of secrecy will only be broken down by giving people in the United Kingdom the legal right to know' (Cm 3818, Preface). (The sound bite would not, of course, be so effective if one were to add 'subject to 23 legal exemptions and over 400 statutory bars.')

The White Paper was considered by a House of Commons Select Committee, which welcomed the proposals and, a report (*Third Report of the Select Committee on Public Administration: Your Right to Know – The Government's Proposals for a Freedom of Information Act*, HC (1997–98)

7

398-I) published in May 1998, said that a Freedom of Information Act would 'help to begin to change for good the secretive culture of the public service'. The report, in addition to making 44 recommendations and observations, also found the proposals for increased access to information, if implemented in their White Paper form, would have three purposes and effects. They would:

- make it easier for members of the public to find out what information government holds about themselves;
- make it easier for politicians, journalists and members of the public to hold the government to account by making government cover ups more difficult;
- make it easier for members of the public to participate in an informed way in the discussion of policy issues, and improve the quality of government decision making because those drafting policy advice know that they must be able, ultimately, to defend their reasoning before public opinion.

The White Paper was followed by a consultation paper (*Freedom of Information: Consultation on draft legislation*, May 1999, Cm 4355) containing a draft Freedom of Information Bill, which was subject to pre-legislative scrutiny by committees of both Houses of Parliament, as well as to public consultation. The House of Commons Select Committee on Public Administration welcomed the draft Bill, but warned of 'serious deficiencies which, if not remedied, will undermine the potential' (House of Commons Select Committee on Public Administration, *Freedom of Information Draft Bill*, Third Report of Session 1998–99, 570-I, published 29 July 1999). Among its specific recommendations for remedying these deficiencies, it called for a purpose clause with a clear presumption in favour of disclosure on the face of the Bill, for the public interest in disclosing information to be balanced against the harm in so doing, for the right of access to apply as broadly as possible and exemptions drawn as narrowly as possible with a more demanding harm test, and for enforceable rights of access to information.

The House of Lords Committee looking at it said that the single most important amendment required to the draft Bill was one which would give the Information Commissioner 'a public interest override power in clause 44 to overrule a ministerial decision under clause 14, and to order disclosure' (House of Lords Select Committee, *Draft Freedom of Information Bill – First Report*, HL97, published 27 July 1999). It also called for the Long Title of the Bill to be amended from the neutral 'make provision about the disclosure of information' to the purposive 'facilitate the disclosure of information'.

After this very long lead-in period, with examination from no fewer than three parliamentary committees, the Bill was finally introduced into the House of Commons on 18 November 1999, though not to universal acclaim. Critics of the Bill argued that the proposals had been significantly watered down since the draft Bill, and complained that the views of the committees had not been taken on board sufficiently. Once the Act had received Royal Assent on 20 November 2000, there was further criticism of the long delay in implementing it, despite the Lord Chancellor's announcement:

> The Act will be fully implemented by January 2005, 11 months before the timetable set out in the Act itself. The publication scheme provisions will be implemented first, on a rolling programme, starting with central government in November 2002. ... the individual right of access to information held by all public authorities, including government departments, will be implemented in January 2005.

1.4 THE COURTS AND ACCESS TO INFORMATION

As recently as 1989, the Official Secrets Act 1911 prevented government officials or contractors from revealing any information learned in the course of carrying out their duty to any person unless authorised. The comprehensive nature of this prohibition – which applied to any information regardless of whether there was any justification for protection against disclosure or not – was gradually eroded by a series of court cases. In *R.* v. *Peter Anthony Galvin* (1988) 86 Cr App R 85 the Court of Appeal was asked to decide whether documents already in the public domain should be excluded from the parameters of the prohibition. Although the Court found that the wording of the legislation would not permit this interpretation, it found that no breach of the prohibition had occurred because the document in question had been so widely distributed that there had been implied authorisation for those in possession of it to use it as they saw fit. In 1990, the House of Lords (*A-G* v. *Guardian Newspapers (No.2)* [1990] AC 109, the *Spycatcher* case) held that an injunction would only be granted where the Crown could show that disclosure of the material in question would be likely to damage the public interest. Since the information (in the form of a book, *Spycatcher*) was already published worldwide and therefore no longer secret, the courts would not grant a continuing injunction against disclosure.

A new Official Secrets Act replaced the 1911 statute in 1989, and restricted the prohibition against disclosure to information about security, defence, international relations and law enforcement.

At the same time, the continually growing power of the courts to look at administrative decision making through judicial review proceedings, meant that the relevant decision-making bodies were forced to disclose to the courts background information relevant to the decision-making process. Fairness in the exercise of administrative powers, Lord Mustill said (*R.* v. *Secretary of State for the Home Department, ex p. Doody* [1994] 1 AC 531) required that those affected by decisions should be informed of the matters relevant to the decision and be given the opportunity to make representations.

Case law on the tort of breach of confidence, vital to an application of the section 41 exemption in the FOIA for information provided in confidence, also continues to develop from the statement of basic principles set out in the landmark case of *Coco* v. *AN Clark Engineers Ltd* [1969] RPC 41. This will be explored further in Chapter 4 dealing with exemptions.

1.5 FREEDOM OF INFORMATION IN OTHER JURISDICTIONS

The Information Commissioner has said he will consider decisions from other jurisdictions that have freedom of information laws, and will aim to remain in line with them as far as reasonably possible (though this, of course, imports no obligation on him to do so in any particular circumstance). This opens up a huge resource of potential precedents for anyone making decisions on access requests or seeking disclosure. Clearly, the decisions are more likely to be influential if the underlying legislation is similar to the FOIA. Decisions in the United States, Ireland, Canada, Australia and New Zealand are therefore likely to be the most influential in this regard due to the closer similarities in the legislation itself, as well as the common language. This whistle-stop tour of global freedom of information laws does not aim to be comprehensive, but rather to identify a few areas of agreement and of disagreement.

Many other jurisdictions have legislation on access to information. The Foreign and Commonwealth Office has published a table[1] with an alphabetical list of 53 countries that have such legislation, from Albania to Zimbabwe. Thirty other countries are said to be in the process of introducing access to information legislation. The oldest legislation (in Sweden) dates back over 200 years, whilst many other countries have adopted legislation within the last decade. In addition, there are various freedom of information laws and codes which apply to international organisations or political groupings. A variety of factors has led to their introduction, including the creation of the Information Society and the expansion of the Internet, pressure from the international community, the transition of countries to democracy, public demand following campaigns by civil society, and political scandals relating to health and the environment.

While ostensibly sharing a common goal of improving public access to information held by public bodies, the codes vary widely in their content and approach as well as in their effectiveness. There follows a discussion of some of the typical features of access to information regimes and consideration of how they are dealt with in different jurisdictions.

1.5.1 Bodies to which freedom of information applies

Since the drive for freedom of information springs from a desire to improve transparency and accountability in government, it is clear that the legislation must apply to government bodies. Depending on the type of government, this may include local or regional government. The courts, legislative assemblies and the security and intelligence services are normally exempt from application of the legislation.

US legislation only applies to organisations that are controlled by the federal government. State governments, municipal corporations, the courts and Congress are not subject to the regime. In Canada, the right to information applies to records 'under the control' of a 'government institution'. Irish legislation, like the FOIA, lists bodies to which it applies in a Schedule to the Act: the list includes local authorities, health boards, government departments and other public sector organisations, but does not extend to voluntary hospitals, schools, universities, the police force, a range of government agencies, and commercial state-funded enterprises.

The South African law, the Promotion of Access to Information Act 2000, goes further in providing a right for individuals and government bodies to obtain information from private sector entities where this is necessary to enforce people's rights – a separate Part of the Act is entitled 'Access to Records of Private Bodies'. The UK legislation, of course, gives the Secretary of State the power to designate certain private sector entities as public authorities for the purposes of the FOIA.

1.5.2 The right of access

The right of access is frequently to 'information', but sometimes to 'documents' or 'records'. Where documents are specified, these are sometimes defined to include mechanical or electronic records. The use of the term 'information' is thought to be more flexible. Often, requests must be made in writing and a response deadline of 20 or 30 days is common, though there are usually provisions enabling the deadline to be extended in given circumstances.

1.5.3 Proactive publication

Another common feature of freedom of information legislation is a requirement that government agencies publish information or documents proactively. This is reflected in the UK legislation in the duty on public authorities to maintain Publication Schemes. In the United States, each agency must publish a large amount of agency-specific information, including a description of the organisation of the agency, the internal reports of the agency, its regulations for reviewing information that it holds, statements of the general

11

methods or agency procedures, and other sources of data that could be useful to the public.

The Indian regime includes a requirement that public bodies publish information on their structure and duties, relevant facts concerning important decisions and policies, reasons for their decisions to those affected by such decisions, and background facts prior to initiation of projects.

In Ireland, public bodies are required to publish information relating to their structure, functions, duties, descriptions of records, and the internal rules, procedures, practices, guidelines and interpretations of the agency.

1.5.4 Exemptions

Not surprisingly, very similar exemptions are found in many of the access to information laws. In some cases certain exemptions are mandatory, i.e. prohibitions on disclosure, in contrast with the FOIA where exemptions, whether they are absolute or qualified, are to be applied at the discretion of the authority to which the request is addressed (with the exception of the exemption for statutory bars).

The most common exemptions concern the protection of national security and international relationships, personal privacy, commercial confidentiality, law enforcement and public order, information received in confidence and internal discussions. Privacy, protecting internal decision making, and national security tend to attract the highest level of protection. The United States has an unusual exemption covering geological or geophysical information, including information about wells and, in the wake of 9/11, has recently created new exemptions, for 'critical infrastructure information', and all information held by the Office of Homeland Security.

It is common for a harm test to be incorporated into the exemptions, i.e. that the information is only exempt if harm, or substantial harm, would result from disclosure. Many laws include a public interest test requiring the public interest in withholding the information to be balanced against the public interest in disclosure.

1.5.5 Charging

The level of fees charged for requests is a critical factor in the effectiveness of any freedom of information regime. Where fees are too high, access to information is placed outside the reach of ordinary people. US charging provisions distinguish between requests for educational or journalistic purposes, and those for commercial purposes. Agencies may charge commercial interests 'reasonable standard charges' in respect of their costs of searching for, reproducing and reviewing the information requested. Requests for educational or journalistic purposes attract only duplication fees. Where requests fall outside these two categories, reasonable standard charges may be made for document search and duplication. Documents are to be provided at no charge, or at a reduced charge:

> if disclosure of the information is in the public interest because it is likely to contribute significantly to public understanding of the operations or activities of the government and is not primarily in the commercial interest of the requester
> (The Freedom of Information Act 1966, s.552(a)(4)(A)(iii))

Ireland recently amended its freedom of information charging regime (the Freedom of Information (Amendment) Act 2003) to allow the government to impose fees for requests and appeals. The Irish Information Commissioner, Emily O'Reilly, in a report (Irish Information Commissioner, *Review of the Operation of the Freedom of Information (Amendment) Act 2003*, June 2004) into the impact of the charges for making freedom of information requests introduced by the Minister for Finance in July 2003, found that overall usage of the Act had fallen by over 50 per cent while requests for non-personal information had declined by 75 per cent.

Japanese law provides for a request fee and a disclosure fee, which must be within the limit of actual expenses and in accordance with government regulations. These fees may be reduced or waived in cases of economic hardship or for other 'special reasons'.

Costs of appealing refusals are also important since otherwise the legislation cannot be enforced. The Irish legislation now provides for payment of €75 in respect of internal reviews and €150 for reviews by the Information Commissioner.

1.5.6 Third party rights

There has been considerable criticism of the FOIA for its failure to provide rights for third parties whose interests are affected by the disclosure of information. Many access to information laws require the public body to which the request has been made to notify third parties, and to give them the right to make representations. The United States is the best known example, though in fact no right of action is afforded by the Freedom of Information Act – a more general right, which would permit an affected third party to bring an action to prevent disclosure, is provided by the Administrative Procedure Act 1946 (see *Chrysler Corp* v. *Brown*, US Supreme Court 441 U.S. 281 (1979)).

The South African legislation requires the public authority to 'take all reasonable steps to inform a third party to whom or which the record relates of the request' within 21 days. The third party has a statutory right to make written or oral representations as to why the request should be refused, and the public authority is under an obligation to give 'due regard to any representations made by a third party' (the Promotion of Access to Information Act 2000).

In Japan, a public body which has received a request for certain types of information (as specified) must notify the third party concerned and give him an opportunity to provide a written opinion, before making a decision to disclose (unless the third person's whereabouts are unknown). If the third party opposes disclosure, the public body, when making a decision to disclose, must immediately notify him in writing of the decision to disclose being made, the reason for it, and the date of implementation of disclosure, which must be at least two weeks later (the Law Concerning Access to Information held by Administrative Organs 1999, Art.13).

Canada also provides statutory rights for third parties to be notified of an intended decision to disclose specified information, to be given the opportunity to make representations and to be notified of the public body's decision on disclosure following consideration of the representations. The third party may apply to the Federal Court of Canada to seek an order against disclosure.

1.5.7 Appeals and enforcement

In most jurisdictions, where a decision by a public body on disclosure of information is challenged the first step will be an internal review by the public body concerned. If the results of the review are still unsatisfactory to the applicant, there will usually be a right to appeal the internal review decision to a third party. In the best enforcement regimes this will usually be an independent Information Commissioner or Ombudsman.

The Canadian Information Commissioner receives complaints and can investigate and issue recommendations but does not have the power to issue binding orders. He, or the applicant, can seek review of a refusal to disclose in the Federal Court of Canada. In Ireland, the Office of the Information Commissioner is able to make binding decisions which can be appealed on a point of law. The Ministry of Justice has the power to issue certificates preventing the release of information.

Japan has an Information Disclosure Review Board within the Cabinet Office, consisting of 12 members approved by both Houses. Cases are referred to the Board by the head of the body that has made the decision under dispute. Decisions of the Board may be appealed to the courts. In South Africa, the Human Rights Commission oversees the functioning of the Act, earlier proposals to create an Open Democracy Commission and specialised information courts having failed to make it to the statute book. While this has advantages in placing access to information alongside human rights enforcement, the Commission has reported that its work on information rights is hampered by a lack of funding.

The United States lacks a central regulator of information rights, the district courts having exclusive jurisdiction in relation to decisions under the Freedom of Information Act. The courts will normally consider all the issues of the case and will look at the procedures followed by the agency in trying to locate the requested information, but have no power to order disclosure where an exemption applies. Each of the individual states has legislation on access to government records, and some states also have information commissions which review decisions.

In most countries there is a final level of appeal to the national courts.

1.5.8 Application in the United Kingdom

Within the UK, the FOIA applies to England, Wales and Northern Ireland. Separate legislation in Scotland, the Freedom of Information (Scotland) Act 2002, applies to public authorities that operate solely in, or with regard to, Scotland, and is enforced by a separate Scottish Information Commissioner. Likewise, the Scottish Executive has issued its own Code of Practice on Access to Scottish Executive Information. The Scottish legislation is very similar, but not identical, to the FOIA, and is not specifically addressed in this publication. Further divergence between the two regimes may develop as a result of differences in approach by the two Information Commissioners.

1.6 OTHER UK LEGISLATION ON ACCESS TO INFORMATION

Probably the most significant pieces of UK legislation in this area, prior to the Freedom of Information Act, were the Data Protection Acts of 1984 and 1998.[2] Although one of the main purposes of data protection legislation is the antithesis of freedom of information – to protect information and keep it confidential – the data protection legislation also introduced an important right for individuals to have access to information held about themselves, initially in the form of electronically processed data, but extended by the 1998 Act to apply also to non-electronic records that are held in a structured form. Chapter 8 looks more closely at the data protection legislation and how it interacts with the FOIA, but the basic rule is simple enough to understand (if not to apply): information to which the Data Protection Act applies will be exempt from disclosure under the FOIA. Anyone receiving a request for information must therefore be able to determine whether the information is personal information and whether disclosure of the information would contravene any of the data protection principles (as set out in the Data Protection Act 1998).

Also of importance are the Environmental Information Regulations. Originally introduced in 1992, these Regulations, which also implement an EU Directive (EU Directive 2003/4/EC on public access to environmental information), provide access to information about the environment held by public bodies. Lacking any effective enforcement mechanism, and not widely publicised, they have not had a significant impact, but the new Regulations (Environmental Information Regulations 2004, SI 2004/3391), brought into force on the same date as the FOIA, on 1 January 2005, and to be enforced by the Information Commissioner, are expected to be much more effective. The definition of environmental information for the purposes of the Regulations is very wide, and includes elements of the environment, such as land, water, biological organisms, etc., as well as measures and activities which affect these, and information on the state of human health and safety. If information falls within the remit of the Environmental Information Regulations, then a request for such information must be treated in accordance with the procedures set out in the Regulations, and not in the FOIA. Just to make life more difficult, the exemptions in the Regulations are similar to, but by no means the same as, the exemptions in the FOIA. The Regulations are dealt with in more detail in Chapter 9.

In addition to these major pieces of legislation, there is a patchwork of smaller pieces of legislation which has, over the past decade, incrementally improved public access to official records. A number of these were drafted by the Campaign for Freedom of Information, and started life as Private Member's Bills. Where there exists a separate statutory right to information, it is likely that the section 21 exemption in the FOIA (for information reasonably accessible otherwise than by an access request) will apply.

One of these statutory rights was introduced by the Local Government (Access to Information) Act 1985, which amended the Local Government Act 1972 (by inserting Part VA) to provide rights of access to council meetings, reports and papers. (Limited rights existed previously in the form of the Public Bodies (Admission to Meetings) Act 1960.) There are specific exemptions for a number of types of personal information, as well as for contractual terms, and expenditure in relation to contracts for the acquisition of property or the supply of goods and services.

The Access to Personal Files Act 1987 (now repealed) gave the public the right to see manually held social work and housing records about themselves. The Access to Medical Reports Act 1988 provided the right for applicants to see reports produced about them by doctors for an employer or insurance company. The Access to Health Records 1990 provided wider access to information on individuals' medical records, though this was largely superseded by the Data Protection Act 1998.

The Environment and Safety Information Act 1988 gives people the right to see enforcement notices issued following breaches of environmental protection legislation.

In June 1995 a Code of Practice on openness in the National Health Service came into force.

1.7 THE INFORMATION COMMISSIONER – ENFORCING THE REGIME

Chapter 10 examines closely the legal enforcement mechanisms of the FOIA. This short section does not aim to duplicate that, but attempts rather to look at the policy approach the Information Commissioner is taking vis-à-vis its dealings with government departments, as evidenced by a recent agreement.

In February 2005, the Department for Constitutional Affairs and the Information Commissioner signed a Memorandum of Understanding[3] (MoU), the stated purpose being 'to promote good standards of co-operation between Departments and the Commissioner'. Following criticism of the content of this MoU in the press, the Information Commissioner, writing in the *Guardian* (Media, Letters, 4 April 2005) denied that it skewed the complaint process in the government's favour, and said that the key commitment in the MoU was that government departments provide all relevant information in relation to a valid complaint swiftly. He confirmed that, in relation to relevant information, the MoU 'sets out a number of corresponding undertakings from my office – such as keeping it secure and not disclosing it improperly to others'.

The signing of the MoU could be viewed as simply following in the footsteps of the Parliamentary Ombudsman. In an attempt to address 'a lack of knowledge within departments about the Code, unacceptable delays in responding to my Office and, in some cases, a lack of cooperation with my investigations', the Ombudsman had initiated discussion with the Cabinet Office and the Department for Constitutional Affairs, resulting in a Memorandum of Understanding, published by the Cabinet office on 22 July 2003. This Memorandum of Understanding[4] (the PCA MoU) set out timescales and procedures departments were expected to adhere to in their dealings with the Ombudsman. In particular, departments were required to:

- respond in full within three weeks of receipt of the Ombudsman's statement of complaint;
- reply to the draft investigation report within three weeks;
- contact the PCA as soon as possible if these timescales were not going to be met;
- provide all relevant papers as quickly as possible; and
- avoid citing new exemptions following receipt of the draft report.

While the majority of commitments specified in the PCA MoU are ones entered into by government departments, the Ombudsman in turn stresses that she will not disclose the information provided to her by the department, and that the decision on whether or not to disclose the information remains that of the department. Although she may use background information supplied to her in her report, she 'will only identify officials or disclose information which would otherwise be exempt under the Code (such as internal advice or consultation) to the extent that it is necessary to do so to make sense of the investigations or conclusions'.

The commitments in the MoU entered into by the Information Commissioner with the Department for Constitutional Affairs are far more extensive. There must be a suspicion that, rather than being a tool to increase acceptance by, and cooperation with, public bodies in their duties in relation to access to information, as the PCA MoU undoubtedly was, it was instead driven by a realisation on the part of the Department for Constitutional Affairs that the Information Commissioner himself is subject to the freedom of information regime and could be asked to disclose information he holds. Under the provisions of the Act, he would have to decide whether any exemptions applied, and whether there was a public interest in disclosure. There is a statutory prohibition on disclosure by the Information Commissioner or his staff of any information obtained by them for the purposes of the Act, and which 'relates to an identified or identifiable individual or business' (Data Protection Act 1998, s.59), unless the disclosure is made with 'lawful authority'. There will be lawful authority for a disclosure which is, among other things, 'necessary in the public interest'. These provisions appear to leave the Information Commissioner a considerable amount of discretion.

The Information Commissioner undertakes in the MoU to:

- contact the relevant department when he receives an application under section 50 of the FOIA, as soon as practicable and in any event within 10 working days;
- provide the department with details of the complainant's application;
- request all relevant information and invite comment; and
- aim to establish a single channel of communication.

He also agrees not (normally) to serve an Information Notice under section 51 of the FOIA on any government department unless he believes that relevant information is being withheld from him or that there has been undue delay in providing the information requested, and to inform the department in advance where he does intend to serve an Information Notice.

These are administrative matters designed to make enforcement of the Act a cooperative, rather than a confrontational, act. This cooperative approach is further enhanced by the obligations entered into by the Information Commissioner in relation to the disclosure of information provided to him. While the PCA MoU mentions in passing the fact that the Ombudsman will not disclose information provided to her, the MoU contains nine numbered paragraphs (9–17) headed 'Obligations in relation to information provided in accordance with this MoU', which set out a range of procedures designed to protect information provided.

Paragraph 9 states that the Commissioner:

will not disclose to the Complainant or to any third party any information provided to him by a government department either under the terms of this MoU, or as a result of serving a notice under section 50 or 51 of the FOI Act unless:

- the Department consents to the disclosure, or
- subject to paragraph 26, all appeal proceedings have been exhausted.

While the Information Commissioner's position is undoubtedly different from that of public authorities holding information provided to them from private sector companies, the MoU does make a strong contrast with the guidance issued to government departments, which are told not to accept such provisions from private sector companies. The statutory Code of Practice[5] states, at para.26:

> It is highly recommended that public authorities take appropriate steps to ensure that such third parties, and those who supply public authorities with information, are aware of the public authority's duty to comply with the Freedom of Information Act, and that therefore information will have to be disclosed upon request unless an exemption applies.

Further, at paras.34 and 35:

> Where there is good reason, as recognised by the terms of the exemption provisions of the Act, to include non-disclosure provisions in a contract, public authorities should consider the desirability where possible of making express provision in the contract identifying the information which should not be disclosed and the reasons for confidentiality. Consideration may also be given to including provision in contracts as to when consultation with third parties will be necessary or appropriate before the information is disclosed.
>
> Similar considerations will apply to the offering or acceptance of confidentiality obligations by public authorities in non-contractual circumstances. There will be circumstances in which such obligations will be an appropriate part of the acquisition of information from third parties and will be protected by the terms of the exemption provisions of the Act. But again, it will be important that both the public authority and the third party are aware of the limits placed by the Act on the enforceability of expectations of confidentiality, and for authorities to ensure that such expectations are created only where to do so is consistent with their obligations under the Act.

Clearly (and not unreasonably), government departments want certainty that if they provide information to the Information Commissioner he will not then disclose it in response to a request under the Act. In some other jurisdictions, the prohibition on disclosure of information provided as part of an investigation into whether such information should be disclosed or not by the Information Commissioner's counterpart is more stringent – in Japan a sentence of one year's hard labour could be the penalty for such disclosure.

Government departments undertake to:

- provide all relevant information as quickly as possible and in any event within 20 working days of being contacted by the Information Commissioner, unless otherwise agreed;
- provide any additional relevant information subsequently requested by the Information Commissioner as quickly as possible and in any event within 10 working days;

- provide all information requested including any redacted information; and
- inform the Information Commissioner, giving reasons, where they are not able to provide the information within the time periods.

It is, however, most unlikely that the Information Commissioner would ever be minded to disclose information provided to him in the context of an investigation. There are clearly a number of exemptions which would almost certainly apply to any information held by the Commissioner, including sections 30, 31, 36 and 41. The MoU also contains a get-out clause, stating that 'nothing in this MoU shall operate to restrict or otherwise inhibit the exercise of the Commissioner's or Department's powers and duties under the FOI Act or the EIRs'.

Perhaps then, the significance of this MoU will be as a precedent for agreements between private sector companies and public authorities, given that it has been created by the two authorities with lead responsibility for implementing and enforcing the Act. The Information Commissioner has indeed publicly stated that he hopes public authorities will follow the approach taken in the MoU.

1.8 FREEDOM OF INFORMATION – THE FUTURE

The FOIA is still very much in its infancy – a toddler walking with uncertain steps. The first months have brought cries of sham from the media, as well as the release of genuinely interesting and previously jealously guarded information. At the time of writing, the internal review processes for the first access refusals to be challenged have been completed and investigations commenced by the Information Commissioner. The results of these investigations – and their final outcomes – will be key to the future of the freedom of information regime in this country. After initial hesitation, the Information Commissioner has put the results of some of these investigations on his website in the form of Decision Notices.[6]

The past few years have also seen moves in other jurisdictions to increase limitations on access to information, most obviously in the United States as a direct consequence of the terrorist attacks of 11 September 2001. The Department of Homeland Security, created in response to these attacks, has a blanket Freedom of Information Act exception for everything it produces, whether it involves national security or not. There is also a new exception for 'protection of voluntarily shared critical infrastructure information'. The Ashcroft Memorandum,[7] issued a month after the attacks, also marked a cultural change in the administration's approach to freedom of information, changing the presumption from one of openness, to one of protection:

As you know, the Department of Justice and this Administration are committed to full compliance with the Freedom of Information Act (FOIA) 5 U.S.C. §552 (2000). It is only through a well-informed citizenry that the leaders of our nation remain accountable to the governed and the American people can be assured that neither fraud nor government waste is concealed.

The Department of Justice and this Administration are equally committed to protecting other fundamental values that are held by our society. Among them are safeguarding our national security, enhancing the effectiveness of our law enforcement agencies, protecting sensitive business information and, not least, preserving personal privacy . . . I encourage your agency to carefully consider the protection of all such values and interests when making the disclosure determinations under the FOIA.

It is essential to reach the correct balance in any freedom of information regime between the rights of the public to have access to public sector information in the interests of accountability and transparency, and the need to protect sensitive information, disclosure of which could be damaging to either the public interest, or to legitimate private sector concerns. The FOIA has already brought about a radical change in the law and practice on access to government information, but whether the correct balance has been achieved will only be revealed over time, and through a continuous dialogue between all the many players involved – the information applicants (including the media), public authority decision makers, third party information providers, Department for Constitutional Affairs officials responsible for issuing guidance, Ministers with the right to veto release, the Information Commissioner's Office, the Information Tribunal and the courts.

NOTES

1 Appendix C, *Freedom of Information – Getting it Right*, Issue 3, September 2004. It states that the information is taken from David Banisar: *Global Survey: Freedom of Information and Access to Government Record Laws Around the World* (at **www.freedominfo.org**).

2 These implemented Council Directive (EC) 95/46 on the protection of individuals with regard to the processing of personal data and on the free movement of such data.

3 *Memorandum of Understanding (MoU) between the Secretary of State for Constitutional Affairs (on behalf of government Departments) and the Information Commissioner, on co-operation between government Departments and the Information Commissioner in relation to sections 50 and 51 of the Freedom of Information Act 2000 (the 'FOI Act') (including ss.50 and 51 as applied, as amended, by Regulation 18 of the Environmental Information Regulations 2004)*, signed 24 February 2005.

4 *Memorandum of Understanding on co-operation between government Departments and the Parliamentary Commissioner for Administration of the Code of Practice on Access to Government Information*, Cabinet Office, Propriety and Ethics Team, July 2003.

5   Code of Practice (Freedom of Information Act 2000, s.45), Guidance to public authorities as to the practice which it would be desirable for them to follow in connection with the discharge of their functions under Part I of the Freedom of Information Act 2000.
6   News of the most significant Decision Notices will appear in *Freedom of Information* journal (**www.foij.com**).
7   Memorandum for Heads of all Federal Departments and Agencies from John Ashcroft, Attorney General, 12 October 2001.

CHAPTER 2

Publication Schemes

Patricia Barratt, Clifford Chance

S.19 (1) A publication scheme must:

    (a) specify classes of information that the public authority publishes or intends to publish;

    (b) specify the manner in which information of each class is, or is intended to be, published; and

    (c) specify whether the material is, or is intended to be, available to the public free of charge or on payment.

. . .

    (3) In adopting or reviewing a publication scheme, a public authority shall have regard to the public interest in allowing public access to information held by the authority and in the publication of reasons for decisions made by the public authority.

Publication Schemes could certainly prove to be a powerful vehicle for greater openness, depending on how much public authorities choose to include in them.

(The House of Commons Select Committee on Public Administration in the report on its pre-legislative scrutiny of the draft Bill[1])

2.1 BACKGROUND

Publication Schemes, called 'a sort of Cinderella' by Richard Thomas, the Information Commissioner in his evidence to a Parliamentary Select Committee,[2] are an often overlooked element of the freedom of information regime. Requesters and practitioners, and certainly the media, focus on the requests for information under section 1 of the FOIA, and the nature of the exemptions. This ignores the fact that, for the first time, all public authorities are legally required to publish information proactively and that a great deal of valuable information is now available directly through Publication Schemes. However, there are a number of reasons why they are outshone by their more forward sister. They were brought in in waves (see below), before the main section 1 access right, and without the publicity surrounding the section 1 right. Also, the FOIA's requirements in relation to Publication Schemes are stated in very generalised terms. So, while there are specified classes of information which are entirely removed from the ambit of the FOIA by absolute exemption (e.g. all information directly or indirectly supplied by, or relating to, bodies dealing with security matters (s.23), or information contained in court records (s.32)), there are no specified classes of information which must be included in a Publication Scheme. Some may say this is a deliberately inclusive approach: everything must go in, apart from that which is exempt. Others, more cynical, might argue that this lack of even basic minimum content requirements means that the schemes are meaningless.

For public authorities subject to the FOIA, and for those seeking information under the FOIA, however, Publication Schemes are likely to be the starting point. The staged way in which the FOIA has been implemented means that public authorities will have been required to produce and maintain a Publication Scheme a considerable time (up to two years) before requests under the FOIA could be made. This will therefore have been most authorities' first experience of the new regime. The old Code on Access to Government Information (Code of Practice on Access to Government Information, second edition 1997) included a voluntary commitment on the part of central government departments and the public bodies which were signatories to make certain types of information available. This information included the facts and analysis of the facts behind major policy proposals and decisions, explanatory material on departments' dealings with the public (including rules, procedures, internal guidance to officials and administrative manuals), reasons for administrative decisions, and information about the operation of public services, though it was subject to the exemptions set out in Part II of the Code. There was no structural framework to the provision of this information and only limited enforcement capability: those seeking information would generally begin by making a request in writing to the relevant authority.

Under the FOIA, however, the first port of call should be the authority's Publication Scheme, and its public website. Any information accessible through the Publication Scheme, or the authority's website, is automatically exempt from disclosure by the authority in response to requests (see below). While the authority does not have to supply the information requested by way of a section 1 request, because of the duty to provide advice and assistance (s.16) it should ensure that the requester knows how to, and is able to, access the information. Guidance[3] from the Information Commissioner's Office (ICO) states that although inclusion of information in a Publication Scheme will mean it does not have to provide that information in response to a section 1 request, '. . . it would still be necessary for the authority to direct the requester to its publication scheme'.

2.2 IMPLEMENTING THE PUBLICATION SCHEME PROVISIONS

To facilitate processing of submissions by the ICO, the provisions relating to Publication Schemes were brought into force a considerable time before the main right of access, and implementation of these provisions was staggered according to the type of public authority, with central government departments the first to jump (or to be pushed). The Information Commissioner published a table showing three dates for each type of authority: the date from which he would accept submissions, the final deadline for submission of the Publication Scheme, and the date by which public authorities were required to have adopted and be operating an approved Publication Scheme. From this date, public authorities were required to make the information contained in their Publication Schemes available to the public in accordance with the terms of the Schemes. Table 2.1 below includes a further column for the date on which the Information Commissioner's approval expires.

Table 2.1 Publication Scheme dates

Sector	Submissions accepted from	Final deadline for submissions	Scheme must be active by	Approval expires
Central government	1 July 2002	30 September 2002	30 November 2002	30 November 2006
Local government	1 October 2002	31 December 2002	28 February 2003	29 February 2007
Police and Prosecuting bodies	1 February 2003	30 April 2003	30 June 2003	30 June 2007
Health Service	1 June 2003	31 August 2003	31 October 2003	31 October 2007
Education (except for maintained nursery schools), remaining NDPBs and publicly owned companies	1 October 2003	31 December 2003	29 February 2004	29 February 2008
Other public authorities and maintained nursery schools	1 February 2004	30 April 2004	30 June 2004	30 June 2008

25

Publication Schemes are initially approved for a period of four years (although the Information Commissioner reserves the right to vary this for particular Publication Schemes, if appropriate).

2.3 WHAT IS A PUBLICATION SCHEME?

Section 19 of the FOIA requires all public authorities to whom the FOIA applies to 'adopt and maintain' a Publication Scheme, which must be approved by the Information Commissioner. The Publication Scheme must set out the classes of information that the authority publishes, or that it intends to publish, and the manner in which it publishes each class of information. It must also state whether the information is freely available or whether there is a charge. In adopting a scheme, the public authority must have regard to the public interest in allowing public access to information held by the authority, and the publication of reasons for decisions made by the authority.

Described, more prosaically, by the ICO as 'a guide detailing types of information which are to be made routinely available' (*Publication Schemes: Approval documentation*, April 2003) the purpose of the schemes 'is to ensure a significant amount of information is easily and routinely available'. They are also intended 'to encourage organisations to publish more information proactively and to develop a greater culture of openness'.

The Publication Scheme provisions mirror similar requirements set out in the information access laws of a number of other jurisdictions, including the United States, Australia and New Zealand. In the United States the relevant provisions are known as the 'reading room' requirement (s.552(a)(2) Freedom of Information Act 1966), and they require public bodies subject to the US Act to publish information falling within specified categories, including rules of procedure and a description of all forms and papers produced, as well as statements of policy and legal rules of general applicability. Amendments to the 1966 Act introduced the electronic reading room concept, requiring records created after 1 November 1996 to be made available by electronic means, as well as records released in response to a request which 'the agency determines have become or are likely to become the subject of a subsequent request for substantially the same records'. The Canadian Access to Information Act 1982 requires the designated Minister to publish a bulletin, updated at least once a year, containing 'a description of all classes of records under the control of each government institution in sufficient detail to facilitate the exercise of the right of access under [the] Act'. In New Zealand, under comparable provisions contained in the Official Information Act 1982 (s.20), the Ministry of Justice is required to publish a separate list for each department and organisation subject to the Act, a general description of the categories of documents held by it, a description of the manuals containing policies by which decisions are made, as well as the name of the officer to whom requests for information should be sent. Specified documents are publicly available as of right. Irish legislation (the Freedom of Information Act 1977) requires each public body to prepare and publish a reference book giving a description of the classes of records held by it, including the rules, procedures, etc. used by the body for the purposes of any enactment or scheme administered by it, as well as any details that might be reasonably necessary in order to exercise the right of access.

2.4 CLASSES

As described above, many access to information laws require public authorities to publish lists consisting of classes or categories of information that are publicly available. It is also usual for such legislation to contain some indication of what that means in practice, by specifying types of documents or records that must be included. The UK legislation provides no such indication, the only requirement being that the authority has regard to the public interest in allowing access to information and in publishing reasons for decisions.

The White Paper, *Your Right to Know*,[4] harbinger of the Act, stated that:

> Experience overseas consistently shows the importance of changing the culture through requiring active disclosure, so that public authorities get used to making information publicly available in the normal course of their activities. This helps to ensure that FOI does not simply become a potentially confrontational arrangement under which nothing is released unless someone specifically asks for it.
>
> We believe it is important that further impetus is given to the pro-active release of information. So, the Act will impose duties upon public authorities to make certain information publicly available, as a matter of course. These requirements will be consistent with the other provisions of the Act – including its harm and public interest tests. They will be broadly along the lines of those in the Code of Practice, namely:
>
> - facts and analysis which the government considers important in framing major policy proposals and decisions;
> - explanatory material on dealings with the public;
> - reasons for administrative decisions to those affected by them;
> - operational information about how public services are run, how much they cost, targets set, expected standards and results, and complaints procedure.

However, this requirement to publish specified types of information was not reflected in the draft Bill. The House of Commons Select Committee on Public Administration in the report[5] on its prelegislative scrutiny of the draft Bill argued in favour of a clearer definition of classes, and for the inclusion, on the face of the FOIA, of a requirement to publish internal guidance (paras.46 and 47):

Good schemes might provide, for example, for the publication of departmental manuals, rules and internal guidance . . ., the routine publication of government contracts (contract price, unit prices, performance standards), and the publication of all information which has been the subject of previous Freedom of Information requests.

We recommend that the obligation to publish information be strengthened in the Bill. It should specify more clearly the type of information that authorities will be required to publish. In particular authorities should be obliged to publish internal manuals and guidance as a matter of statutory duty.

There was a further attempt[6] to amend the Bill as it went through Parliament so as to require all public authorities to publish (subject to applicable exemptions):

any manuals, instructions, precedents and guidelines used by the officers or employees of the authority, for the purpose of –

(a) interpreting any enactment, or
(b) administering any scheme for which the authority is responsible, and to make adequate reference to the existence of such information in its publication scheme.[7]

This was intended broadly to replicate wording in the Open Government Code,[8] which required authorities:

to publish or otherwise make available, as soon as practicable after the Code becomes operational, explanatory material on departments' dealings with the public (including such rules, procedures, internal guidance to officials and similar administrative manuals as will assist better understanding of departmental action in dealing with the public) except where publication could prejudice any matter which should properly be kept confidential under Part II [the Exemptions] of the Code.

It was also claimed that such a provision was present 'in every English language freedom of information law throughout the world'.[9]

The government resisted the amendment, however, on the basis that, while it might be an appropriate requirement for some public authorities, the reach of the legislation was much broader than that of the Code, and included many very small entities, such as doctors' surgeries and dental practices for whom such a requirement could be overly burdensome, and inappropriate. Although a number of ways round this problem were suggested, the government maintained its position that the best way to regulate Publication Schemes was to require authorities to have their Scheme approved by the Information Commissioner, or adopt a model Publication Scheme.

What is meant by 'classes' is therefore left, to some extent, to the interpretation of the individual authority. But only to some extent, because of the requirement that each scheme be approved by the Information

Commissioner, who is also able to approve model Publication Schemes (see below). The Information Commissioner has said[10] he does not intend to be prescriptive with regard to the description of classes, but that it is important that the way in which classes are described has 'meaning both for those seeking to obtain information from the authority and those within the authority responsible for creating and managing information'.[11] The classes must be relevant to each particular authority or type of authority, but must not be determined by authorities 'according to their own internal needs or historical filing systems, where these would not support the principle of "reasonable accessibility" for the purposes of the Act'.[12]

The ICO recommends that public authorities consider whether consultation with relevant users or user groups might be helpful in identifying or developing classes of information for inclusion in the Publication Scheme. Public bodies are warned not to restrict the content of their Publication Scheme to information about the services they provide, but are specifically told to include information about their own internal structures, at least in outline, information about their decision-making processes and information about how key appointments are made, in order to fulfil their obligations under section 19(3)(b).

Since all information falling within the classes listed in the Publication Scheme must be published, it is tempting for public authorities to define the classes very narrowly, or to exclude particular types of classes entirely, in order to avoid the situation where the classes might be held to include information which would otherwise be exempt. The Information Commissioner has said he would not support such a restrictive approach.[13]

To avoid the problem of including exempt information, the Information Commissioner recommends that the description of a class should be set out 'in such a way that it excludes information which might be covered by an exemption. . . . The requirement to publish information in accordance with the scheme . . .' it goes on to say '. . . can therefore be met by the public authority because the exempt information has never fallen within the ambit of the scheme'.

The Financial Services Authority's (FSA) Publication Scheme includes a good example of a class – 'Dear CEO' letters – the extent of which is

Class D12	Dear CEO letters
This class comprises	Selected letters sent by the FSA to the chief executive of groups of regulated firms, where the FSA has judged that open publication is consistent with its objectives.
Note	This class does not include letters where the FSA judges that disclosure would unnecessarily damage market confidence.

restricted by a note, so that the FSA can retain discretion over which letters are to be published.

Where the public authority holds a lot of information which would be covered by exemptions, the ICO recommends that it states this in its Publication Scheme, and should outline the nature of the exempt information it holds and the exemption that applies. The Office of Fair Trading follows this advice, with a separate section in its Publication Scheme devoted to setting out all the exemptions that may apply as well as its position on the exemption most relevant to it (s.44 – where there is a statutory bar on disclosure). The section, headed 'What we may not disclose', states:

> The Act sets out exemptions to the right of access for certain types of information. Information on these exemptions is available on the Information Commissioner's website **http://www.informationcommissioner.gov.uk/eventual.aspx?id=6452**
> The OFT will rely on these exemptions where, for example:
>
> 1. There is a statutory bar on disclosure or disclosure would be incompatible with a European Community obligation or constitute contempt of court (an absolute exemption – section 44). Part 9 of the Enterprise Act 2002 prohibits certain authorities, including the OFT, from disclosing information which is not in the public domain and relates to the affairs of an individual or the business of any undertaking and is obtained in the course of carrying out certain of their statutory functions. It is a criminal offence to disclose such information in circumstances where disclosure is not permitted by Part 9 of the Enterprise Act. Disclosure of such information is permitted in certain limited circumstances. **We will not normally be able to disclose details of complaints about a particular trader for instance.**
>   There are certain circumstances when we are permitted to disclose information despite the Part 9 restriction:
>   - with the consent of all those concerned;
>   - to help either our statutory functions or those of another enforcer or public body;
>   - for the purpose of a Community obligation; or
>   - to help investigations leading to criminal proceedings (or certain kinds of civil or criminal proceedings if disclosure is to an overseas public authority).
>
> 2. The information has been obtained from any other person or public authority where disclosure would constitute an actionable breach of confidence (an absolute exemption – section 41).
>
> 3. We consider disclosure is not in the public interest and a qualified exemption applies. The following are qualified exemptions under the Act:
>   a) the OFT intends to publish the information and it is reasonable to withhold it until it is published (section 22)
>   b) disclosure may be prejudicial to the economic interests of the UK or any part of the UK or the financial interest of any government body (section 29)
>   c) disclosure would be prejudicial to someone's commercial interests (section 43)

    d)   information is held for purposes of a criminal investigation or criminal proceedings (section 30)

    e)   information is held for the purpose of an investigation (including non-criminal investigations) or criminal proceedings and relates to the obtaining of information from a confidential source (section 30(2))

    f)   disclosure would be likely to prejudice specified matters such as the prevention and detection of crime, the administration of justice and the exercise by the OFT of its functions for any purpose specified in section 31(2) such as:

- investigations to find out whether any person has complied with the law or
- is responsible for any conduct which is improper
- or for checking whether regulatory action is justified (section 31)

    g)   information relates to policy formulation or development and ministerial communications. We will consider whether disclosure is in the public interest (section 35)

    h)   the information would or would be likely to prejudice the effective conduct of public affairs (section 36).

4.   The information is personal data related to an individual and disclosure to a third party would contravene the Data Protection Act (section 40).

The Information Commissioner's Guidance on Publication Schemes[14] advises public authorities to make it clear where exemptions might apply to information falling within a class. For example, the class 'staff policies' would be likely to include the Staff Handbook:

> Whereas the majority of the handbook might be information that can easily be made public, it may well contain some exempt information. The amount of information that would be exempt may be very limited and so it would be unhelpful to exclude the whole book from the class. The Commissioner intends to adopt an approach that would allow a scheme to accommodate such a situation. Although considering in advance whether an exemption might apply to material covered by their scheme may mean extra work at this stage, there are clearly long-term savings to be gained by the authority, once the right of access becomes available.

The important point is that where a class includes information from documents that also contain exempt information this is made clear when defining that class. Hence the definition of staff policies given above may be refined as follows:

> internal policies which collectively establish the procedures that should be followed and conduct that is expected by members of the authority's staff in the performance of their duties. Some of the material in this class is derived from documents which we consider to contain exempt information. Where this occurs the material will clearly show where information has been withheld and explain what exemption has been applied and why. Typically information may be withheld if its release would compromise the health and safety of staff or national security.

It is interesting to note also the approach of the Department for Constitutional Affairs (DCA) to this issue in dealing with the inclusion of decisions of the Information Commissioner within its Publication Scheme:

Class: Decisions.

Definition: Decisions of the Information Commissioner in relation to the Freedom of Information Act and Data Protection Act 1998, and the Parliamentary Ombudsman in relation to the Code of Practice on Access to Government Information, relating to the Department for Constitutional Affairs. Some of the material in this class is derived from documents that we consider to contain exempt material. Where this occurs the material will clearly show where information has been withheld and explain what exemption has been applied and why. Typically information may be withheld if it constitutes personal data.

Format available: Hard copy from DCA.

DCA Guidance,[15] while stressing these should not be considered as recommended classes of information sets out some kinds of information which all departments and NDPBs should consider for inclusion in their Publication Schemes. These are:

1. *Guidance to staff* – including rules, procedures, internal guidance to officials and similar administrative manuals that assist better understanding of the organisation's interaction in dealing with the public, plus internal guidance to officials on implementing/operating the FOIA, the Environmental Information Regulations (EIR) and the DPA.
2. *Background to policy* – facts and analysis of the facts the government considers relevant and important in framing major policy proposals and decisions.
3. *Management information* – full information about how public services are run, how much they cost, who is in charge and what complaints and redress procedures are available; full and, where possible, comparable information about what services are being provided, what targets are set, what standards of service are expected and the results achieved. Information about the mission, objectives and functions of the authority; organisation of the authority; information about board meetings ('This may include the agendas and minutes of the meetings and associated papers or summaries where appropriate'); targets for standards of service and financial performance as well as results

achieved and comparable information; sources of income and how effectively money is raised and spent.

4. *Public consultation* – the guidance advises authorities to follow the Cabinet Office guidelines on consultation. 'Responses submitted in confidence should have that confidence respected if the information submitted is properly confidential'.

5. *Departmental circulars* – it is probable that some circulars should be included.

6. *Information placed in the Libraries of the Houses of Parliament* – departments and non-departmental public bodies (NDPBs) are advised to consider whether these should be included.

7. *Decisions* – including decisions of the ICO relating to the organisation, decisions of other bodies relating to the organisation and decisions made by the department where the decision affects a significant number of interested parties, or where it sets a precedent or is likely to have ramifications for the future handling of similar cases. The guidance uses as an example the Charity Commission, which, it says, is making more information available in relation to its decisions, particularly when there is considerable public interest.

8. *Speeches* – keynote speeches by Ministers and senior officials should be made available.

9. *Legislation and related information* – the legal framework within the public authority including a description of the relationship between the legislation and the department's structure and functions; details of legislation or Codes of Practice that give rights of access to information; texts of international treaties, conventions and agreements should be accessible if not provided elsewhere.

10. *Procurement, grants, loans and guarantees* – departments and NDPBs are encouraged to be as open as possible when considering making available information in relation to procurement, grants, loans and guarantees. In particular, the publication of procurement and supplier policies should be considered for publication as should the details of contracts awarded. Departments and NDPBs should also consider the provision of information on specific projects including notification of bidding opportunities, decision criteria, contract performance standards, results of regular performance reviews, and results achieved where appropriate. They should also consider including information on the awarding of grants, loans and the provision of guarantees, as well as background information on schemes they administer; an account of how grants have been dispensed under a particular scheme, including overall funds dispensed, and an assessment of the benefit of the scheme in terms of its objectives should be considered. The publication of details of guarantees such as the recipient, purpose and amount should

be considered, subject to protecting legitimate personal and commercial confidentiality.

11. *Information required to be published under other legislation* – in particular information accessible under the EIR, Environmental Impact Assessments and Departmental Sustainable Development Strategies where appropriate.

12. *Research reports; risk and impact assessments, etc.* – appropriate guidance on the publication of scientific research from the Office of Science and Technology and on risk assessment should be followed when considering the content of a Publication Scheme. Regulatory impact assessments are also likely to be accessible.

13. *Information disclosed under the Freedom of Information Act 2000* – if of general interest should be included.

Despite its non-prescriptive approach to classes, the ICO has issued a guide to classes,[16] augmenting the guidance already issued in *Guidance and Methodology* and *Approval Documentation*. Among the aims of the guide was 'to help clarify what a class of information is and some of the considerations a public authority should take into account when constructing or defining classes' (para.3.1). A definition suggested by responses to the Information Commissioner's consultation on schemes was '. . . a group of information having one or more common characteristics'. Perhaps the most obvious interpretation would be categories such as minutes of meetings, consultation documents, internal guidance notes or staff policies. The ICO uses as its main example a sectoral heading, 'Recruitment', saying:

> if a public authority chose to use 'recruitment' as a class of information then the expectation would be that all information held in connection with the recruitment process would be available through the publication scheme. This would clearly not be appropriate, not least because much of the information that might fall under that heading would be personal data held on application forms, the disclosure of which may breach the Data Protection Act 1998.

It suggests breaking down 'Recruitment' into separate classes, such as vacancies, induction and job descriptions, with a further definition of each class, including any limitations or potential exemptions.

2.5 APPROVAL BY THE INFORMATION COMMISSIONER

'The judgment about what is appropriate in an individual publication scheme is a matter not for the Government but for the Information Commissioner', said a Home Office Minister, David Lock, during the passage of the Bill through Parliament.[17]

All Publication Schemes must be approved by the Information Commissioner, and the ICO produced guidance[18] on how to obtain approval. The public authority must submit two documents: a Publication Scheme text document, and a completed approval questionnaire. These can be submitted in hard copy, or electronically. There is a different process where authorities wish to adopt a Model Publication Scheme.

The Information Commissioner set out specifications which he said must be clearly identifiable in the Publication Scheme and which must be set out in the text document:

1. *Information about the identity of the public authority operating the scheme, including a brief description of the authority's responsibilities and an explanation of the purpose and aims of the scheme:*

   Full title of the public authority operating the publication scheme.
   Job title at senior level that contains responsibility for the scheme on behalf of the organisation.
   Job title and name of the individual with responsibility for maintaining the scheme on a day to day basis.
   A list of all agencies, if applicable, contained within the publication scheme along with clearly and easily identifiable access routes and information relating the agencies.
   Statement explaining the purpose and aims of a publication scheme (this can either be the ICO's own standard statement, or a statement drafted by the authority for its own purposes – the ICO's standard statement is reproduced below).

2. *Classes of information the public authority publishes, or intends to publish:*

   List and definitions of all classes of information contained within the scheme, in an easily identifiable manner.
   List of all classes which are to be published at a later date, with timescales, and reasons for delays.
   Any classes that could contain information which may be subject to exemptions should be clearly identified as such and the reasons given.
   Overview of approach used in determining which classes are to be included.

3. *Manner in which the information of each class will be, or is intended to be, published:*

   For each class a list of formats available and from where that information can be obtained.

4. *Whether the material is, or is intended to be, available to the public free of charge or on payment:*

   Indication of whether a class includes chargeable material (this relates to charges for materials available within the publication scheme, not charges made for individual access requests made under section 1, FOIA).

The ICO's standard statement as to the purpose of the Publication Scheme – which authorities may use as a component of their response to Question 1 – is as follows:

The Freedom of Information Act 2000 (FOIA) received Royal Assent on 30 November 2000. It gives a general right of access to all types of recorded information held by public authorities, sets out exemptions from that right and places a number of obligations on public authorities. A 'public authority' is defined in FOIA, and includes but is not restricted to, central and local government, non-departmental public bodies (NDPBs), the police, prosecuting bodies, the health service, and schools, nurseries, colleges and universities. The general right of access to the information held by a public authority is provided for under section 1 of the Act. Any person wishing to exercise this right, which will not come into force until January 2005, will have to make a written request to the public authority. Any person who makes such a request must be informed whether the public authority holds that information and, subject to exemptions, supplied with that information.

However, the Act provides another mechanism for gaining access to information. Every public authority is required to adopt and maintain a publication scheme. A publication scheme is a guide detailing types of information which are to be made routinely available. This guide should provide the public with a simple means of obtaining information and reduce the need for public authorities to respond to requests made under section 1.

A publication scheme must set out the classes of information contained within the scheme, the manner in which the information is intended to be published, and whether or not a charge will be made for the information. The purpose of a scheme is to ensure a significant amount of information is easily and routinely available. Schemes are intended to encourage organisations to publish more information proactively and to develop a greater culture of openness.

Once a public authority has prepared a scheme and approval for the scheme has been given by the Information Commissioner, the scheme is adopted by the public authority. On adopting a publication scheme the public authority is committed to making the information contained within the scheme routinely accessible, and to reviewing the scheme periodically.

The approval questionnaire asked the following questions, in order to assess a public authority's compliance with the FOIA s.19(3) and, in particular, whether the scheme has regard to the public interest:

(1) What exercises, consultations and initiatives did you carry out in order to assess what information is of public interest and so should be included in your publication scheme? Please give specific details.

(2) How does your scheme provide access to records of the decisions taken by your authority together with the information upon which those decisions were based and the decision making process? Please give specific examples.

(3) Have you considered frequently asked questions and specific areas of interest when determining your classes of information? Please give specific details.

(4) Have you made information available within your scheme that has not previously been made available under other information regimes? If yes, please give details of new information. If no, please give reasons why no new information is to be made available.

(5) Have you decided not to include in your scheme any information which has been made available by you in the past? If yes, please give specific details.

(6) What steps have been taken to produce your publication scheme in alternative formats and languages so that it is accessible to individuals with disabilities, those who do not have English as their first language or those in disadvantaged communities? Please give specific examples.

With some 115,000 public authorities now subject to the FOIA, according to government pronouncements, the ICO clearly had a mountainous task, even taking into account the staggered introduction of the requirement to adopt Publication Schemes and the existence of model schemes.

In giving evidence before a Select Committee, the Deputy Information Commissioner said that:

> given the size of the task, it was not possible for us to cross check each and every instance of that [whether the Scheme put information into the public domain that was not there before]. The way we approached the approval of publication schemes was very much getting all public authorities, if you like, on to a first base.[19]

The Parliamentary Select Committee highlighted this in its report:

> However, the sheer number of schemes approved in the time available meant that these schemes were apparently assessed in terms of their form, not their content. That is, the ICO staff did not have time to check what the publication schemes actually contained, but rather how they were structured.[20]

Approval is normally for a period of four years, though the Information Commissioner has the power to approve schemes for a different period and may also revoke his approval (see below).

2.6 MODEL PUBLICATION SCHEMES

To cut out duplication and to spare small public authorities the burden of devising a Publication Scheme from scratch, the FOIA permits the use of Model Publication Schemes. The ICO has indicated that Model Publication Schemes are appropriate where 'a large number of public authorities all perform very similar functions'.[21] Section 20 provides that the Information Commissioner may approve Model Publication Schemes for public authorities falling within particular classes. The Model Publication Schemes may be drafted by the Information Commissioner, or by 'other persons'. If there is a Model Publication Scheme for a particular class, then a public authority which falls within that class and which adopts the Model Publication Scheme does not need to get the approval of the Information Commissioner for its scheme. If the public authority has changed the Model Publication Scheme, however, then it will need to get the approval of the Information Commissioner in relation to those changes. If the Information Commissioner refuses to approve a proposed Model Publication Scheme, on the application of any person he must give a statement of reasons for his refusal to the applicant. Similarly, if the Information Commissioner refuses to approve any modifications that a public authority has made to the Model Publication Scheme, he must give a statement of reasons for his refusal to the public authority.

The Information Commissioner may provide that his approval of a Model Publication Scheme expires at the end of a specified period (s.20(3)). He also has the power to revoke his approval for a Model Publication Scheme though he must issue a notice of revocation giving a six months' notice period before the approval is revoked. The notice must include a statement of the Information Commissioner's reasons for revoking the approval.

The Information Commissioner has approved Model Publication Schemes for classes of public authorities in a number of sectors including local government, the health sector and education. In local government there are model schemes for District Drainage Commissioners, Fire Authorities, Internal Drainage Boards, Parish and Town and Community Councils, Parish Meetings, Passenger Transport Authorities and Port Health Authorities. In the health sector there are Model Publication Schemes for Acute Trusts, Ambulance Trusts, Community Health Councils, Dentists, GPs, Health and Social Services Boards, Mental Health Trusts, Opticians and Optometrists, Pharmacists, Primary Care Trusts, Strategic Health Authorities and Trust Agencies and Councils (NI). In some cases there are different Model Schemes for Wales, Northern Ireland and England (Scotland, of course, is subject to its own, different, legislation on access to information).

Although there is no legal requirement for authorities adopting a Model Scheme to make any submission to the ICO, in practice it is common for some kind of notification to be made. Under some of the Model Schemes the public authority is requested to complete a Declaration Form and submit it to the Information Commissioner with contact details of the person responsible for maintaining the Publication Scheme and who should be contacted if any issues arise. The Declaration Form for Acute Trusts, for example, includes the statement that the signatory has adopted the relevant Model Publication Scheme and an additional option for adopting Optional Class, Archives Deposit.

The Model Publication Schemes in the healthcare sector were developed by the NHS FOI Project Board, which also produced guidance notes outlining the information that is expected under each heading. The other Model Schemes were developed by representative bodies in the relevant sector.

Approval is time limited. For example, public authorities in the health sector were required to have adopted approved Publication Schemes by 31 October 2003. The Information Commissioner's approval of the Model Schemes is for a four-year period from that date, expiring on 31 October 2007.

Guidance from the ICO on Model Publication Schemes[22] points out that, in order to fulfil its obligations under the FOIA, a public authority needs to do more than simply sign and return the Declaration Form. It must also make the Publication Scheme available and must publish information in accordance with it. It has a further obligation to review the Scheme on a regular basis.

2.7 ACCESSING PUBLICATION SCHEMES

In addition to the statutory requirement that all public authorities maintain and adopt a Publication Scheme, each public authority is also required to 'publish its publication scheme in such manner as it thinks fit' (s.19(4)). There was some debate over this wording as the Bill passed through Parliament, one MP identifying this as a dangerous loophole.[23] Continuing, Mr Maclennan MP pointed out that this wording leaves the manner of publication of an authority's Publication Scheme entirely up to the authority, with no provision for review by the Information Commissioner:

> An authority could publish its scheme in an obscure form, which could make it extremely difficult to inspect. There could be a single copy, which could be held in the office of a chief executive and made available for perusal only by appointment and at an unacceptably high cost.

The Minister (Mr Mike O'Brien, then Parliamentary Under Secretary of State for the Home Department) responded by saying that a requirement to have the Information Commissioner's approval for the manner of publication would be unnecessary since:

> It is in the authority's interest to publish the scheme and make it widely available, as one of the scheme's effects would be to reduce the number of requests under clause 1 and reduce the burden on the authority.

The Minister also thought that making the manner of publication subject to the ICO's approval would be unnecessarily bureaucratic and entail considerably more work for the Commissioner.

Although the Information Commissioner does not have statutory authority over the manner of publication, he has stated his view,[24] as follows:

> Web access is not sufficiently universal to render it the sole means by which a scheme is delivered. Though a scheme may be intended to supply information primarily on the Internet, a hard copy must exist for those who do not have Web access. The hard copy guide must explain how to access information, and procedures should be in place to facilitate requests for information by phone and mail. A hard copy guide does not need to replicate all of the Web content; it does not need to list every document in the scheme, but it should give a clear description of how the scheme is structured, and state where documents covered by the scheme can be accessed.
>
> Due attention must be paid to making the scheme accessible to people with disabilities. The guide should be available to all who request it and, in normal circumstances, authorities should not charge users for copies of it. It may also be appropriate to have the hard copy scheme placed in, or distributed to, a range of outlets according to the nature of the authority, in order to demonstrate openness.

Many Publication Schemes are easily accessible online. A dedicated NHS website, for example, lists around 3,000 Publication Schemes with direct links to the individual schemes. Public authorities will frequently have a direct link to the Publication Scheme from their home page.

Good Publication Schemes should include details of how to access information where the applicant has special requirements, for example, by offering to make the information available, where possible, in a variety of formats such as Braille, audio, or in a language other than English.

Information which falls within one of the classes in a Publication Scheme does not have to be directly accessible from the Publication Scheme, and does not have to have been published already. For example, an authority may include as a class: Minutes of Committee [X]. It will then be required to publish all minutes of Committee [X] but may, as a matter of policy, publish such minutes after a specified period, whether that be one day, or three months. The Scheme should also spell out how long the information in each class will be kept in accordance with the authority's policy on retention of documents.

2.7.1 Principle of reasonable accessibility

There is no obligation on public authorities to provide information in response to a section 1 request where the information is 'reasonably accessible to the applicant' by other means (FOIA, s.21). The FOIA specifies that information may be reasonably accessible even where the information is not freely available but is subject to a charge. It also specifically provides that this exemption (which is an absolute exemption) does apply where the information is available in accordance with the authority's Publication Scheme. If a payment is required this must be specified in, or determined in accordance with, the Scheme.

In some cases, however, the fact that payment is required may result in the information not being reasonably accessible. Guidance issued by the Information Commissioner[25] suggests, for example, that where a public authority is asked for information contained in its annual report, or other long report, it may not be reasonable to require the applicant to purchase a copy of the report if the request is only for a small amount of the information contained in it.

2.8 CHARGING FOR INFORMATION IN PUBLICATION SCHEMES

The fact that information falls within a class of information in a public authority's Publication Scheme means that the public authority is committed to publishing that information, but does not mean that the information must be made available without charge. Indeed, the FOIA requires public authorities to spell out in the Publication Scheme which information is available free of charge, and which information is subject to charges. There are no provisions regulating how much public authorities may charge for information under the Publication Scheme – the Freedom of Information and Data Protection (Appropriate Limit and Fees) Regulations 2004, SI 2004/3244 only apply to requests made under the section 1 access right, and not to information provided under a Publication Scheme.

However, the FOIA does not give public authorities the power to charge for providing information outside the fees regime set up for section 1 access requests. If a public authority were to attempt to charge for information where statutory authority did not exist, that authority could be acting *ultra vires*. There may be situations in which a public authority has the power to charge but only on a cost recovery basis, whereas in other cases there may be authority to make a specified profit margin.

Within the FOIA regime, the only sanction available in the case of public authorities which attempt to over charge for information contained in the Publication Scheme is the nuclear option of revocation of approval by the Information Commissioner, though doubtless there would be a dialogue prior to such a step being taken.

The ICO's guidance[26] to completing the Model Publication Scheme for Acute Trusts states:

> Much of the information covered by the model schemes will be available at no charge. However where charges are to be levied in respect of the provision of information, this needs to be indicated to scheme users by the inclusion of the £ sign within the relevant class. The circumstances in which charges may be levied are set out in the model scheme.

The Model Scheme itself says:

> For the most part, we will charge you only for hard copies or copying onto media (e.g. CD ROM). Some information is available free, but for others there may be a charge. The charges will vary according to how information is made available. Charges are as follows:
>
> a) Via the Trust's website – free of charge, although any charges for Internet service provider and personal printing costs would have to be met by the individual.
> For those without Internet access, a single print-out as on the website would be available by post from . . . or by personal application at Trust Headquarters . . . However, requests for multiple printouts, or for archived copies of documents which are no longer accessible or available on the web, may attract a charge for the retrieval, photocopy, postage etc. We will let you know the cost and charges that will have to be paid in advance. We will not provide printouts of other organisations' websites.
> b) Leaflets and brochures – free of charge for leaflets or booklets on, for example, services we offer to the public. A list is available from ....

c) 'Glossy' or other bound paper copies, or in some cases a CD Rom, video or other mediums, are charged for as in our publication lists available from
....

d) E-mail – will be free of charge unless it says otherwise.

The charges will be reviewed regularly.

There is a separate paragraph dealing with Crown copyright.

Ordnance Survey, which publishes a vast quantity of commercial information, has similar wording; the section on Crown copyright and reuse of information is included under the Fees heading:

> The printed hard copy items in the publication scheme are free unless otherwise stated and can be ordered from the Customer Contact Centre, Ordnance Survey, Romsey Road, Southampton, SO16 4GU, phone: 08456 05 05 05, fax 023 8079 2615 or by personal application at the same address. Send your request to them, giving the full title of the publication and stock code number (see publications table).
>
> The other items in the scheme are electronic documents in, for example, Word or .pdf, and can be downloaded free of charge from the web site.
>
> To read .pdf documents you will need Adobe® Acrobat Reader®, which is free and available from Adobe.
>
> Requests for multiple printouts, or for archived copies of documents that are no longer available on the web, will attract a charge for the cost of retrieval, photocopy, postage and so on. We would let you know this at the time of your request (the charge would be payable in advance).
>
> Glossy or other bound paper copies, or in some cases a CD-ROM, video or other mediums, are charged as in our publication list available from Customer Contact Centre (address as detailed above).
>
> If you wish to reuse or reproduce our publications, for example, commercially or for circulation for education and similar purposes, you will in most cases need to apply for a copyright licence for this. Ordnance Survey is a Crown body and our information is subject to Crown copyright administered by Her Majesty's Stationery Office [now Office of Public Sector Information (OPSI)]. For HMSO [now OPSI] Guidance Notes on a range of copyright issues, see the [OPSI] website or write to Intellectual Property and Legal Department, Ordnance Survey, Romsey Road, Southampton, SO16 4GU.

The DTI's Publication Scheme makes it clear that it will follow Treasury Guidance on charges (*Charges for Information: When and How – Guidance for Government Departments and other Crown Bodies*) where it makes a standing charge for a publication. It also points out that the DTI, its Agencies and British Trade International (BTI) operate a number of schemes providing information, as part of a paid service, derived from a range of sources held by the DTI, its Agencies or BTI as well as information not already held in recorded form.

Much of the material listed on the DTI's Publication Scheme is freely available on the Internet. Other material listed is available on subscription, e.g. under 'Contracts Awarded' it lists:

Class:	For contracts issued under EU procurement priority services regime above £100,410 and those let under the EC Residual Services above £123,000:
	• Nature of contract
	• Identity of winning contractor
	Price of contract or range of bids received (subject to considerations of commercial confidentiality)
Format available:	Web format; hard copy 'Official Journal of the European Communities' and 'Government Opportunities' (need to subscribe)
Hard copy available from:	DTI Procurement Unit
Includes chargeable material:	Subscription cost

The DTI's *Monthly Bulletin of Indices: price adjustment formulae for construction contracts* is similarly included in the Publication Scheme. It can be ordered at cost from the DTI Publications Orderline.

The fact that information is only available from a subscription service, or on payment of the cost price, does not preclude that information from being included in the Publication Scheme.

Guidance from the Information Commissioner's Office[27] on charges under Publication Schemes states that the level of charges made by a public authority for the provision of information in its Publication Scheme should be 'compatible with the principle of promoting public access to the information held by public authorities'. It also points out that the general public will easily be able to compare charging regimes across similar organisations.

While the guidance warns public authorities against including information in a Publication Scheme with the intention of charging for information that was previously provided free, it recognises that the public authority may be entitled to reserve the right to levy a charge as a concomitant of its assumption of a legal commitment to provide access in place of a previous policy of providing information on a purely discretionary basis.

2.9 PUBLICATION SCHEMES FOR COMPANIES DESIGNATED UNDER SECTION 5

The government is reported to have said that it will start the process of designating companies under section 5 after the general election and once the new Parliament is sitting. A company may be designated under section 5 if it:

(a) appears to the Secretary of State to exercise functions of a public nature, or
(b) is providing under a contract made with a public authority any service whose provision is a function of that authority.

There is no provision in the FOIA for any derogation from the effect of sections 19 and 20 and therefore designated companies will also have to adopt and maintain a Publication Scheme, whether bespoke or model, which will have to be approved by the Information Commissioner. The designation will only relate to the functions performed by the company which are public functions and, similarly, the company's Publication Scheme will only need to list classes of information relevant to those functions.

2.10 THE INFORMATION ASSET REGISTER AND THE PUBLIC SECTOR INFORMATION DIRECTIVE

Derived from a consultation exercise into Crown copyright (and announced in the White Paper, *The Future Management of Crown Copyright*, Cm 4300, 1999), the idea of an Information Asset Register (IAR) was intended to be a one-stop shop for potential reusers of government-generated or government-held information.

In practical terms, it is an online catalogue of unpublished information resources, accessible to anyone with Internet access, on **www.inforoute.hmso. gov.uk**. It is supposed to contain details of all information held by all government departments and other Crown bodies, focusing on unpublished information.

Anyone accessing the Register currently is likely to encounter mixed results. A search intended to locate the Civil Aviation Authority's flight paths (aviation flight paths), for example, threw up seven results, none from the CAA, including one for the Scottish Aphid Database (SAD(!)), which consists of 'records of daily (or weekly) catches of aphids from 4 Rothamsted suction traps located at 4 sites within Scotland'. Under the potentially vast category heading, Business Practice and Regulation, there are only four entries, three of which are Annual Reports for the Food Standards Authority in different years.

The development of the IAR should receive a dramatic boost, however, as a result of the Public Sector Information Directive (the Directive), implemented in the UK by the Re-use of Public Sector Information Regulations 2005 (SI 2005/1515), which introduce a statutory obligation on public sector bodies to provide access to details about reusable information held by the public sector. A recital to the Directive claims:

Public sector information is an important primary material for digital content products and services and will become an even more important content resource with the development of wireless content services. Broad cross-border geographical coverage will also be essential in this context. Wider possibilities of re-using public sector information should inter alia allow European companies to exploit its potential and contribute to economic growth and job creation.[28]

Article 9 provides for the creation of information asset lists:

Practical arrangements
Member States shall ensure that practical arrangements are in place that facilitate the search for documents available for reuse, such as assets lists, accessible preferably online, of main documents, and portal sites that are linked to decentralized assets lists.

The Regulations implement this Article by requiring public sector bodies to ensure that a list of significant documents available for reuse is made available to the public, preferably by electronic means and, as far as reasonably practicable, with an electronic search capability.

The main thrust of the Directive is to ensure that, where public sector information is available for reuse, it is made available on terms that are fair, reasonable and not anticompetitive. It does not require any information actually to be made available for reuse, and even the requirement on the creation of asset lists is sufficiently vague and non-prescriptive to allow considerable room for manœuvre.

Nevertheless, while the Public Sector Information Directive could be seen as less ambitious than the Information Asset Register initiative which predates it, in terms of what it requires of the Asset Register, the fact that it will be on a statutory footing should make a substantial difference to the project.

An OPSI Guidance Note, *Information Asset Register and Freedom of Information – a co-ordinated response to information access*, is intended to explain how the IAR, and specifically departmental IARs, 'should contribute usefully to Freedom of Information Publication Schemes and the broader management of information requests under FOI'.

Government departments will be required to produce both a freedom of information Publication Scheme for the purposes of the FOIA and an Information Asset Register for the purposes of the public sector information regime (PSI). The guidance says that information that departments have left out of their Publication Scheme because, for example, it could not be made widely available without considerable cost, or there is thought to be limited interest in it, 'should already be included in departmental IARs, which detail information that may be of interest, yet is not published' (para.15). The guidance also states that the existence of the IAR will make it simpler for departments to identify where information requested is held and so will facilitate the management of information requests, whether or not covered by the FOIA or the EIR.

The main area of overlap, therefore, between the two regimes, is the respective requirements to produce a list of information held by the public authority, albeit according to differing criteria. It is clear that it would not be possible to combine the two information schemes, although there have been calls to do so, in order to avoid duplication of effort. Publication Schemes are intended to be a means of making more information available proactively and, in most cases, free of charge. The IAR is, however, a scheme to facilitate the commercial reuse of public sector information. Despite HMSO's cheerleader tones, the divergent aims of these two schemes give rise to a tension and even, potentially, a conflict of interest between them. This tension is perhaps more apparent in the underlying principles than will be the case in practice: requests for access to information under the PSI will typically be in relation to large collections of information as opposed to the much more targeted requests for discrete 'bits' of information which would be appropriate under the FOIA. Further, the PSI entails no obligation to supply the information requested, unlike the statutory obligation under the FOIA to provide information unless subject to an exemption. The other major difference is that information requested under the PSI is intended for reuse, while information accessed under the FOIA, including by way of Publication Schemes, will generally be subject to restrictions on reuse.

2.11 REVIEW OF PUBLICATION SCHEMES

Each public authority is required (under s.19(1)(c)) to review its Publication Scheme 'from time to time'.

The best Publication Schemes, of course, change on a daily basis, with new material being added. The Lord Chancellor, Lord Falconer, announced in December 2004 that where information disclosed in response to an access request was likely to be of wider interest, then it should be published simultaneously online. Some departments, for example, the DCA, provide a separate listing from their website for such information, the DCA's link being called 'Information released under the Freedom of Information Act 2000 since 1 January 2005'. It would make sense for this to be included as a separate class within a Publication Scheme, with the information also being available under the relevant heading, if there was one.

The review requirement is not, however, merely a requirement to update the Publication Scheme so as to give access to the most recent components of a specified class. Rather it is a requirement to consider whether the nature of the classes and the structure of the Scheme are still appropriate, taking into consideration the public interest both in allowing access to information held by the authority, and in the publication of reasons for decisions made by the authority.

Where any changes are made to a Publication Scheme as a result of a review (or otherwise) these must be notified to the Information

Commissioner. His approval will be required where it is proposed to remove classes of information.

A survey[29] carried out by the ICO in relation to the experience of local authorities and freedom of information found that 'Formal reviews of the publication schemes have been reported by the majority of local authorities in England, with most conducting them on a six monthly or annual basis'.

A further finding was that:

Local authorities have approached the task of developing and reviewing publication schemes in the right spirit, although some may need to think of more regular reviews particularly in the light of patterns of individual requests for information.

The survey also found that local authorities engaging in best practice carried out a review of their Publication Schemes every six months.

A number of Publication Schemes make no mention of the review process, failing even to mention the statutory requirement (including the ICO's Publication Scheme). The Department of Trade and Industry, when asked about the lack of provisions on review in its Publication Scheme, confirmed that it added material to the Publication Scheme continually on an ad hoc basis. Questioned further, it said it had had a formal review in July 2004 and would 'probably' have another review in the summer of 2005. Table 2.2 shows some different approaches to the review requirement adopted by a random sample of 10 public authorities, selected to present a spread of different categories of authorities. The fact that some Publication Schemes make no reference to a review does not, of course, mean that no review mechanism exists. The findings are as at 24 March 2005 and are the result of an examination of the Publication Schemes only.

In his evidence to the Select Committee on Constitutional Affairs,[30] the Information Commissioner said 'We have plans to put pressure on selected public authorities to upgrade their publication schemes'. He did not say which authorities he had in mind, but if he expected to implement these plans before the expiry of the four-year period, i.e. outside the formal approval procedure, then it is likely that he expected the upgrading to take place within the review process. From a first base position, then, authorities are encouraged by the Information Commissioner to improve the availability of information under their Publication Schemes as part of the ongoing review process required by the FOIA.

Table 2.2 Public authority Publication Scheme review policies

Public authority	Review policy
Metropolitan Police Service	*Reviewing and Updating the Publication Scheme* New material will be added to the Scheme regularly and brought to the attention of users on the Internet through the What's New Page . . . We are committed to expanding the amount of information in this Scheme and ensuring that you can find, request, and receive information easily.
Bank of England	We aim to formally review our scheme in June 2005.
Redditch and Bromsgrove Primary Care Trust	The Publication Scheme was published in October 2003. It was revised in July 2004. Its next revision date is October 2004.
Wigan Council	No reference.
Office of Communications	*Approval and review* The scheme was approved by the Information Commissioner for a period of four years until 29 February 2008. The scheme will therefore be formerly [*sic*] reviewed in February 2008. Our website is updated daily and we will regularly review the scheme to ensure it is up to date and provides as much information as possible.
Royal Mail Group	We will continue to update the material shown in the Annex to this scheme and review it annually, or as directed by the Information Commissioner.
Environment Agency	The statutory requirement to maintain and develop the Scheme means that we must take stock of what information we make available and what, in the public (and therefore environmental) interest we intend to make available in the future . . . We shall publish information in accordance with the scheme, and shall monitor and review its operation in order to develop the scheme in the light of public comment and feedback.
Lancashire Combined Fire Authority and Lancashire Fire and Rescue Service	The Publication Scheme is a 'living' document and will be updated on a regular basis.
Peak District National Park Authority	This publication scheme is part of an ongoing process aimed at improving the openness and accessibility of the National Park Authority.
Kingston University London	No reference.

2.12   ENFORCEMENT

The obligation to adopt, maintain and review Publication Schemes is a statutory duty on the public authorities who are subject to the FOIA. Failure to do so is a matter, in the first instance, for the Information Commissioner. He has stated that his policy is to secure compliance by a process of educating and advising public authorities. However, where compliance cannot be achieved by this informal route he will consider exercising his formal enforcement powers set out under sections 50–56 of the FOIA. Where the Information Commissioner's Office is satisfied that a public authority has failed to comply with any of the requirements of the FOIA, including the requirements on Publication Schemes, it may serve an Enforcement Notice requiring the authority to comply. If the public authority fails to comply with the Enforcement Notice the Information Commissioner's Office may certify that fact in writing to the High Court. The Court may then deal with the public authority as if it had committed a contempt of court. The procedures for enforcement are set out in much more detail in Chapter 10 on enforcement, but it is worth noting that the Information Commissioner's very first foray into enforcement of the FOIA has been in relation to Publication Schemes.

When the relevant deadlines for submission of Publication Schemes had passed, a small minority of public bodies had not established Publication Schemes. One of these was Allerdale Borough Council, which was required to submit its Scheme to the Information Commissioner for approval by 31 December 2002, and to have the Scheme active by 28 February 2003. The Information Commissioner therefore served a Preliminary Enforcement Notice (which warns the authority that legal action will be taken if the problem is not resolved). The Information Commissioner has indicated that he would expect this notice to be effective in resolving the problem in a majority of cases, his experience being that most public bodies are keen to co-operate and that delays in setting up a Publication Scheme were usually due to administrative problems rather than to any reluctance to implement the legislation. However, Allerdale, alone of the bodies on whom Preliminary Enforcement Notices were served, did not respond to the notice.

The Information Commissioner then took enforcement proceedings against the Chief Executive Officer of Allerdale Borough Council for contempt of court, with the aim, the ICO has said, of seeking compliance, rather than of punishing. The Information Commissioner believed that Allerdale would immediately comply once proceedings were served. However, the Council failed to respond to the claim form and to a number of letters, and no one from the authority appeared at the Directions Hearing. Nothing was heard from Allerdale until the day of the actual hearing.

The case was transferred from Macclesfield County Court to Chester Crown Court because of the statutory requirement in the FOIA (s.54) that proceedings must be before a High Court judge. The case is unreported but the ICO has indicated that, on the day of the hearing (in spring 2004), a representative from Allerdale Council explained that it had now implemented a Publication Scheme. The judge therefore dismissed the case. No explanation was given for the delay, or indeed the earlier failure to respond.

Lessons were learned from the case, though: the Information Commissioner had issued proceedings against the CEO of Allerdale Council, rather than the Council itself. This issue was raised by Allerdale at the last minute at the hearing and it was eventually agreed by all parties that the FOIA required the Information Commissioner to initiate proceedings against the Council directly and not against the CEO in person. However, this procedural irregularity had no direct bearing on the result of the case. Moreover, if Allerdale had not established a Publication Scheme by the day of the hearing then the Information Commissioner would no doubt have requested that the claim form be amended so that proceedings were issued against the Council.

There are lessons to be learned for those subject to the provisions of the FOIA, too – that the Information Commissioner will not shy away from enforcement action where he deems it necessary to ensure compliance with the FOIA. The Information Commissioner's role in the shaping of the still amorphous freedom of information regime is critical. If Publication Schemes are still the Cinderella of the freedom of information regime, only the Information Commissioner has the magic wand to make a dazzling transformation.

NOTES

1   House of Commons Select Committee on Public Administration, *Freedom of Information Draft Bill*, Third Report of Session 1998–99, 570-I, published 29 July 1999.
2   House of Commons Constitutional Affairs Committee, *Freedom of Information Act 2000 – progress towards implementation*, First Report of Session 2004–05, HC 79-II, published 7 December 2004.
3   *Publication Schemes, Guidance and Methodology*, Information Commissioner's Office, April 2003, para.5.8.
4   *Your Right to Know, the Government's proposals for a Freedom of Information Act*, Cm 3818, 11 December 1997 (paras.2.17 and 2.18).
5   House of Commons Select Committee on Public Administration, *Freedom of Information Draft Bill*, Third Report of Session 1998–99, HC 570-I, published 29 July 1999.
6   Amendment No.65 tabled by Mr Maclennan MP, Standing Committee B (Pt 8), 20 January 2000.
7   House of Commons Standing Committee B, 6th sitting, 20 January 2000, Part I.

8   Code of Practice on Access to Government Information, second edition 1997.
9   House of Commons Standing Committee B, 6th sitting, 20 January 2000, Part I.
10   *Publication Schemes, Guidance and Methodology*, Information Commissioner's Office, April 2003, First section, Guidance, para.6.2.
11   *Ibid.*, para.6.3.
12   *Ibid.*, para.6.5.
13   *Ibid.*, para.6.8.
14   *Freedom of Information Act 2000: Preparing for Implementation, Publication Schemes: A Practical Guide: Part I 'Classes'*, April 2003, paras.4.4 and 4.5.
15   *Freedom of Information Act 2000 – Publication Schemes: Central Government and Non-Departmental Public Body Guidance*, July 2002.
16   *Freedom of Information Act 2000: Preparing for Implementation, Publication Schemes: A Practical Guide: Part I 'Classes'*, Information Commissioner's Office, April 2003.
17   Standing Committee B, Part 2, col.189, 20 January 2000.
18   *Freedom of Information Act 2000: Preparing for Implementation, Publication Schemes: Approval Documentation*, Information Commissioner's Office, April 2003.
19   House of Commons Constitutional Affairs Committee, *Freedom of Information Act 2000 – progress towards implementation*, First Report of Session 2004–05, HC 79-II, published 7 December 2004.
20   House of Commons Constitutional Affairs Committee, *Freedom of Information Act 2000 – progress towards implementation*, First Report of Session 2004–05, HC 79-I, 7 December 2004.
21   Information Commissioner's Guidance Note, attached to the Model Publication Scheme for Acute Trusts.
22   *Ibid.*
23   Mr Maclennan MP, Standing Committee B (Pt 7), 6th sitting, 20 January 2000, Part I.
24   *Publication Schemes, Guidance and Methodology*, Information Commissioner's Office, April 2003, Second section, Methodology, paras.6.4 and 6.5.
25   Freedom of Information Act Awareness Guidance No.6, *Information Reasonable Accessible to the Applicant by Other Means*.
26   Information Commissioner's Guidance Note, attached to the Model Publication Scheme for Acute Trusts.
27   Awareness Guidance, *Charging under Publication Schemes*, October 2003.
28   Recital 5, Directive 2003/98/EC of the European Parliament and of the Council of 17 November 2003 on the reuse of public sector information.
29   The Information Commissioner, *Freedom of Information Act 2000 Survey Findings: Principal Local Authorities*, February 2004.
30   House of Commons Constitutional Affairs Committee, *Freedom of Information Act 2000 – progress towards implementation*, First Report of Session 2004–05, HC 79-II, published 7 December 2004.

CHAPTER 3

The right of access

Andrew Sharpe and Carolyn Bigg, Charles Russell

3.1 INTRODUCTION

The introduction of the Freedom of Information Act 2000 (FOIA) has sparked an unprecedented level of awareness amongst the media and the public in accessing documentation and information held about them, their community and about local and national issues and causes.

This chapter aims to provide practical guidance first to members of the public as to how to make an effective request for information under the FOIA, and secondly to public authorities on how to respond to requests for information under the FOIA. Broadly we will consider the formalities and practicalities of making and responding to requests for information, as well as the type of information that is available by means of the public's right of access under the FOIA.

An individual's right of access to information in fact goes far wider than that prescribed under the FOIA. While interest since 1 January 2005 has naturally focused on rights granted under the FOIA, there are also a number of other statutory rights of access to certain information. These may in fact prove more relevant and useful to an individual in obtaining a required piece of information, particularly as certain of these rights are to information held by private individuals and organisations. In addition, a public authority may need to deal with a request for information asking for mixed types of information.

Accordingly, in addition to considering rights of access under the FOIA, in this chapter we will also consider an individual's right of access to information under the Data Protection Act 1998 and will also refer to the Environmental Information Regulations 2004 (EIR) (which are covered in more detail in Chapter 9) and other statutory rights of access to information (which include rights to medical and educational records and financial information relating to companies).

The FOIA was intended to enhance, rather than replace, existing information regimes. Indeed, information is exempted from disclosure under the FOIA if it is available to applicants by other means (s.21). Therefore, an individual may only be able to access information by means of these other statutory rights.

3.1.1 Initial considerations for an individual wishing to make a request for information

The first consideration in relation to any request for information should be: 'Under what statutory access right should I make my request?' The answer will depend on:

- *the nature and focus of the information desired*: we have identified below the type of information that may be disclosed under each statutory regime; and
- *the organisation that holds the desired information*: certain information rights only oblige public authorities to disclose information, whereas others apply equally to public and private bodies. We have identified below to whom each statutory right of access applies.

3.1.2 Initial considerations for a public authority responding to a request for information

Equally on receipt of a request for information a public authority's first consideration must be: 'What is the nature of the information requested?' The answer to this question will identify the statutory access regime under which the public authority must respond to that request. We have identified in this chapter the type of information that may be disclosable under each statutory regime, together with the costs and formality involved in responding to each type of request.

If a request for information comprises a mix of environmental information, personal information relating to the individual requesting the information and other information, then a public authority must separate out the requests and deal with each element separately under the EIR, the Data Protection Act 1998 and the FOIA as appropriate.

The following flowchart (Figure 3.1) provides a process for a public authority or others to follow when dealing with a request for personal data.

The flowchart at Figure 3.2 provides a useful summary to both applicants and public authorities (or other bodies to whom requests for information may be made under the various statutory access regimes) as to which regime should be applied to specific requests for information.

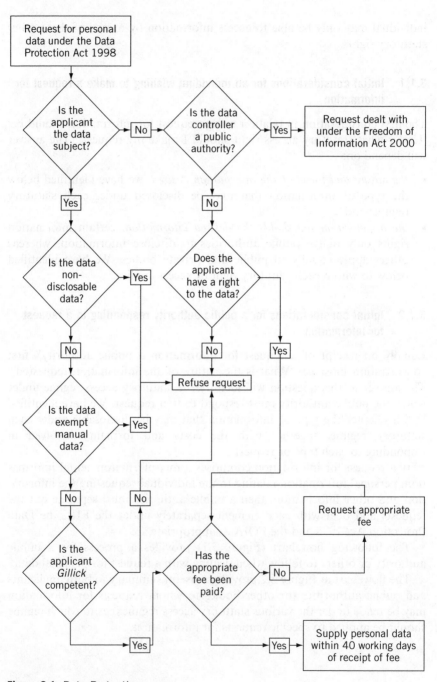

Figure 3.1 Data Protection access

3.2 FREEDOM OF INFORMATION ACT 2000

3.2.1 What information can be accessed?

The FOIA provides a right of access to the general public to information held by public authorities. The information is disclosable via Publication Schemes and requests for information (subject to a number of important exemptions).

Any information in the possession of, or held on behalf of, a public authority (as defined) is potentially disclosable under the FOIA regime, provided it is held for the purpose and interest of the public authority (see section 3.2.4). Information held by public authorities will comprise information created (solely or partly) by or on behalf of the public authority but also may include information received from third parties, regardless of whether or not that third party was aware that such information may be disclosable under the FOIA. This could include information provided to a public authority by a private sector body, such as correspondence from a private contractor providing services to a public authority, or information about individuals, such as education and benefits records. Examples of information requests reported in the first half of 2005 include requests relating to high profile, national issues such as the Iraq war, Black Wednesday, pay reviews for public sector workers and public enquiries; historical records including previously classified information relating to state secrets; and, at a local level, more detailed performance data from local hospitals and schools.

Information is potentially disclosable regardless of the format of the information (for example, whether it is electronically stored, a hard copy, an audio recording or a graph), and includes handwritten notes, opinions and historical data. It is important to bear in mind that, unlike access regimes in other jurisdictions, the FOIA provides a right of access to information rather than to documentation. Therefore, while a specific document, or part thereof, may be exempt from disclosure, some or all of the information contained within that document may be disclosable, perhaps by way of a summary or by redacting the remainder of the document. The FOIA also only covers information that is recorded. Therefore, information which may be in the knowledge of an employee of a public authority, but which is not, or is no longer, recorded in a permanent form will not be disclosable.

Certain information is excluded or exempted from disclosure under the FOIA:

- personal data about the applicant, disclosure of which is covered by the access regime under the Data Protection Act 1998 (see section 3.3);
- environmental information, which is disclosable under the EIR (see section 3.4);
- information which is because of its subject matter or nature is subject to an exemption under Part II of the FOIA. These exemptions are considered in detail in Chapters 4 and 5. For example, information is exempted

from disclosure under the FOIA if it is available to applicants by other means (s.21), as is information which is intended for future publication by the public authority (s.22); and

- there are a number of procedural limitations on disclosure set out in Part I of the FOIA, which are discussed in section 3.2.4 of this chapter.

A number of existing Acts of Parliament have been amended so as to permit disclosure of information under the FOIA that would otherwise have been prohibited or restricted.[1]

Publication Schemes

The first port of call for any potential applicant under the FOIA should be a public authority's Publication Scheme. Any individual, company or other organisation may request a copy of the information included within a Publication Scheme (FOIA, s.19).

As described in Chapter 2, a variety of information, and particularly frequently requested information, will be increasingly available via public authorities' Publication Schemes. The advantages to a potential applicant of making use of this resource are:

- the information will be quickly and easily accessible (as Publication Schemes must be), often on the public authority's website;
- the information will often be available via the Publication Scheme free of charge;[2] and
- public authorities are under no obligation to provide information in response to an information request where that information is already available under the authority's Publication Scheme (FOIA, s.21). Therefore, checking the Publication Scheme first may save the need to go through the process of submitting an information request.

Information requests

The general principle of the FOIA is that any person making a request for information to a public authority is entitled (subject to a number of exceptions and exemptions):

(a) to be informed in writing by the public authority whether or not it holds information of the description specified in the request; and

(b) if it does hold the information, to have that information communicated to him (FOIA, s.1(1)).

We have set out in the next section practical guidance to enable a potential applicant to make a request for information under the FOIA, and in section 3.2.4 we consider how, and when, the public authority should respond to the information request.

3.2.2 The request

Who can make an information request?

A request can be made by any individual, partnership, unincorporated body or company, whether or not they are UK national or resident, and regardless of the purpose of the application.

To whom can a request be made?

The FOIA grants a right of access to individuals to information held by or on behalf of a public authority, both as defined in the FOIA (ss.3(1) and (2)).

The definition of public authorities in the FOIA includes public bodies listed in Schedule 1 to the FOIA (as amended by various secondary legislation (ss.3(1)(*a*)(i) and 4)), certain authorities designated by the Lord Chancellor (ss.3(1)(*a*)(ii) and 5) and all companies that are publicly owned.[3] For example, this definition will encompass central government and local authorities, the Houses of Parliament, NHS trusts and health authorities, schools and other educational institutions, the police and the armed forces, as well as executive agencies. As the number of public authorities caught by the FOIA is continuously expanding, it is advisable to check the consolidated list of public authorities maintained by the Department for Constitutional Affairs (DCA) (**www.foi.gov.uk/coverage.htm**). Some of the bodies listed may only be caught by the FOIA in relation to certain information (for example, the BBC is liable to disclose all information except that held for the purpose of journalism, art or literature).

Unlike other rights of access, information requests cannot be submitted to organisations in the private sector, even if they perform public functions. However, a proposal by the DCA to widen the definition of public authority to include private organisations that perform a public function was under consultation at the time of writing.

Information requests should be addressed to the relevant public authority which the potential applicant believes holds the desired information, either where the public authority has the information in its own possession, or where the information is held for that public authority by another person (FOIA, s.3(2)). The reasons for which a public authority holds information will be relevant, as information which is merely held on behalf of a third party (for example, for preservation or security reasons), where the public authority itself has no interest in the information, will not be disclosable under the FOIA. This will obviously depend on the circumstances in question but, for example, information belonging to a minister about party political matters, or a purely personal email sent by an employee of a public authority, which are stored on the authority's computer system will not be deemed to be held by the public authority for the purposes of the FOIA.

Formality of the request?

(i) *Legal formality:* the information request must be made in writing, which includes requests by letter, fax or email, and must include details of the name and address of the applicant (FOIA, ss.8(1)(*a*) and (*b*) and 8(2)). The request should also describe in as much detail as possible the required information (FOIA, s.8(1)(*c*)).

(ii) *Practical guidance on how to make a request more effective:*

- Provide contact details, or else the public authority cannot respond to, and indeed is not required under the FOIA to deal with, the request.
- Requests may be submitted in English or Welsh. If requests are made in other foreign languages, the public authority may ask the applicant to resubmit the request in English or Welsh; otherwise, the public authority is not obliged under the FOIA to respond to a request in other languages.
- A public authority must provide assistance to enable a written request to be submitted if an applicant is unable to do so (see 'Advice and assistance' later in this section). Some public authorities may also provide standard request forms to assist an applicant to make a request.
- Explain the nature and scope of the information desired as clearly as possible. It will be easier for a public authority to respond to a request which focuses on the specific information sought, rather than a general request for information on a wider topic. Therefore, if possible refer to a specific document containing the information (for example, a report or minutes of a meeting); otherwise, give examples of the type of documentation that may include the information or an indication of when the information may have been originally documented.
- The request need not refer expressly to the FOIA, but mentioning this in a request may assist the public authority in identifying and responding appropriately.
- If the information is required urgently, ask the public authority to respond in a shorter timescale than that prescribed in the FOIA (see section 3.2.4, 'Timescale for response'). Although the public authority is not obliged to respond quicker than 20 working days from the day after the date of receipt of the request, the Code of Practice suggests it is good practice for the authority to try to respond promptly,[4] which may be within a quicker timescale.
- An applicant is entitled to request that the information be provided in a convenient form or format, but bear in mind that this should be reasonable (see section 3.2.4, 'Format for response'). Note also that

requesting a particular form or format should not be used as a way of avoiding paying for published information.

- An applicant does not have to disclose why he or she wants the information, even if asked by the public authority.
- Public authorities may refuse to answer a request altogether on the grounds that it is repetitious or vexatious (i.e. does not have any genuine or serious value or intention, is designed to be disruptive, cause annoyance or harassment, or is manifestly unreasonable).[5] Otherwise, a public authority should treat requests made as part of an organised campaign in the same way as individual requests.
- Ensure that the information requested is not already available as part of the public authority's Publication Scheme – this will save time and effort. In any event the public authority need not respond in these circumstances. Information that is requested repeatedly is likely to have been included in the authority's Publication Scheme.
- It may be sensible to submit a separate request for more controversial information or older materials which are likely to have been stored away. This way a public authority should be able to provide more straightforward data promptly and can deal separately with the more problematic request.

To whom should the request be sent?

Requests for information under the FOIA can be made to any employee (or agent) of a public authority. However, directing requests to the appropriate person or department within a public authority is likely to bring a quicker and more focused response.

Each public authority (and certainly larger public authorities) should have appointed a nominated officer to deal with, and to advise on, requests for information under the FOIA. A public authority should publish its procedures for dealing with requests for information (or for assistance), including details of an address, email address and telephone number of the person to whom requests for information should be directed (Access Code of Practice Part II, para.5). If this information is not easily available, it is recommended that a request for information is sent to the relevant public authority's head of legal or to the relevant head of the public authority (for example, the Minister or head of the executive agency or local authority), so as to ensure that the request reaches the appropriate person without undue delay.

If an information request is made to an authority that holds the information on behalf of another public authority, the recipient public authority may either decide to deal with the request in consultation with the authority that actually holds the information, or may redirect the request as soon as possible to the originating authority, bearing in mind its duty to provide reasonable assistance and advice to applicants (Access Code of Practice Part III, paras. 16–24).

Advice and assistance

A public authority is obliged to provide advice and assistance to applicants, and to those considering making a request for information, so far as it is reasonable to do so (pursuant to its responsibilities under FOIA, s.16(1)), and in accordance with the Codes of Practice (see section 3.2.4) (FOIA, s.16(2) and Foreword to the Access Code of Practice, para.13).

The duty to provide assistance is wide ranging and covers all stages of making and responding to a request, including the type of information that may be accessed under the FOIA, how to formulate a clear and focused request, other sources of the information desired, and the progress of a submitted request. Public authorities should be prepared to explain why they are asking for additional information in relation to a request or proposed request (Access Code of Practice Part II, para.9). The key is for a public authority to be flexible and to provide appropriate advice and assistance in the circumstances having liaised with the applicant.[6] The public authority should not ask why the applicant or potential applicant is requesting the information, although an applicant is free to disclose this information.[7]

Other than a public authority's right to request further information from an applicant in order to locate and/or identify information requested (where an extension of time for responding to the request is available – see section 3.2.4, 'Timescale') (FOIA, ss.1(3) and 10(6)), a public authority will not be entitled to an extension to the standard 20 working day response period to provide all other advice and assistance once a request has been made.

The advice and assistance must be provided free of charge (unless it is provided as part of clarification of a request for information already submitted, in which case fees may be chargeable as set out in section 3.2.3), and should be provided in any appropriate or reasonable media or format. Public authorities should also be aware of their obligations under other Acts of Parliament (such as disability and race discrimination legislation and Welsh language legislation) when providing advice and assistance (Foreword to the Access Code of Practice, para.14). Any employee of a public authority may provide advice and assistance. It is good practice for a record of the advice or assistance to be kept by the public authority, in case it is later queried.

3.2.3 Fees

Publication Schemes

A public authority's Publication Scheme should state whether or not the authority will charge to provide a copy of information made available as part of the scheme (FOIA, s.19(2)(*c*)). If a charge is payable, the amount of the charge should also be stated within the scheme. VAT will be payable on any fees charged for information made available under a public authority's Publication Scheme.[8]

Information requests

Fees chargeable under the FOIA are subject to an 'appropriate limit' (FOIA, s.12). This has been defined by subsequent secondary legislation (the Fees Regulations),[9] and fees will not be charged for FOIA information requests as long as the public authority will spend less than £450 in complying with the request, or £600 in the case of requests to central government departments.[10] Therefore, public authorities must comply with any requests that fall within these limits free of charge, although they may charge applicants for disbursements incurred in providing the information (for example, photocopying or postage costs) if it is reasonable to do so.[11]

If a public authority estimates that it will spend more than these prescribed amounts, it need not comply with an information request (FOIA, s.12(1) and (2)), and must generally notify the applicant of this.[12] However, it may offer to do so if the applicant first pays the relevant cost (or even free of charge, at the authority's discretion) (FOIA, s.13). The information as to the cost payable should be provided to the applicant in a fees notice (FOIA, s.9(1)). The amount of fees payable must be subject to a maximum, specified in the fees notice (FOIA, ss.9(4)(*b*) and 13(2)), which should be calculated in accordance with the Fees Regulations.[13] If an applicant refuses to pay any notified charge, or if the cost of complying with a request is likely to be high, a public authority should consider whether it can make available any information that may be of interest to the applicant free of charge or for a lesser fee.[14]

The Fees Regulations provide guidance for public authorities in estimating the likely cost of compliance with any information request.[15] The costs to be taken into account are limited to those which the public authority reasonably expects to incur in undertaking certain specified activities in response to the request, namely determining whether the information is held, locating and retrieving the information, and extracting the information from other documents. The public authority cannot take into account any costs incurred in considering whether the exemptions apply to the information.[16]

VAT will not be payable on the amount of any fees if the public authority is the only possible source of the information requested.[17]

3.2.4 The response

A public authority should have in place a system to ensure the efficient processing of, and advising on, requests for information submitted under the FOIA. While any employee of a public authority can respond to a request for information, public authorities are advised to nominate an officer to deal with these requests. Nonetheless, public authorities are also advised to ensure that staff who deal with members of the public, or who provide information as part of their role, can identify information requests and are familiar with the requirements of the FOIA and other good practice guidance.[18]

The DCA has published two codes of practice (the Codes of Practice) (pursuant to its responsibilities under FOIA, ss.45 and 46), which provide guidance to public authorities on desirable practice in discharging their functions under Part I of the FOIA (the Access Code of Practice),[19] and also in relation to records management.[20] The Codes are available at **www.foi.gov.uk/codepafunc.pdf** and **www.foi.gov.uk/codemanrec.pdf** respectively. The Information Commissioner (pursuant to his powers under FOIA, ss.47 and 48) and the DCA have also published a number of useful guidance notes (available on their websites), to assist public authorities in dealing with various aspects of the FOIA.

Dealing with a request – initial considerations

It is recommended that a public authority acknowledges receipt of all requests received (or at least those that cannot fully and quickly be responded to), to inform applicants that the request is being dealt with and also as means of keeping track of the progress of compliance with the request.[21] All requests should also as a matter of course be logged by a public authority on receipt for monitoring purposes.[22]

On receipt of a request for information the public authority must:

- *Consider whether a request for information is reasonable (not vexatious):* public authorities may refuse to answer requests altogether on the grounds that they are repetitious or vexatious (see section 3.2.2) (FOIA, s.14).
- *Consider whether the request is specific enough for the public authority to respond to it:* if a request does not describe the information desired in sufficient detail, a public authority may ask for further information or clarification to enable it to respond to a request. If the public authority requests further information from the applicant in order to identify and locate the information requested, the time limit for compliance (see

'Timescale for response' below) will not commence unless and until the date the further information is received from the applicant (FOIA, ss.1(3) and 10(6)).

Where a public authority decides that a request is potentially voluminous (and so may exceed the appropriate limit) it must ask the applicant as soon as possible to focus the request, and must assist the applicant in doing this.[23] However, if the information request is not ambiguous, but just potentially time consuming and expensive, the public authority will still have to respond within the time limit for compliance (see below) from the day following receipt of the information request.

If, once initial assistance has been provided, the applicant is still unable to describe the information requested, or focus the request, in a way that would enable a public authority to identify and locate it, a public authority is not expected to seek further clarification and should just disclose what it can and then explain in a refusal letter why it cannot take the request further.

- *Determine whether or not it holds the information requested:* this is considered in section 3.2.2.

  As a matter of good practice, a public authority should notify or even consult with third parties related to, or with an interest in, the information requested, as to disclosure or whether any exemptions apply, and whether additional explanatory materials should accompany the information to be disclosed (Access Code of Practice Part IV, paras.25–30). However, in most circumstances the views of such third parties are not ultimately binding on the public authority.

- *Estimate whether or not a charge is payable:* if the cost of responding to a request is estimated to be less than the appropriate limit, the public authority must comply with the request. If the cost is likely to be higher than the appropriate limit, it need not comply with the information request or may choose to do so either free of charge or on payment of a fee by the applicant (see section 3.2.3).

Nature of response

If, having taken into account the initial considerations, a public authority is required to deal with the information request, the general principle of the FOIA is that any person making a request for information to a public authority is entitled:

(a) to be informed in writing by the public authority whether or not it holds information of the description specified in the request (the duty to confirm or deny) (FOIA, s.1(1)(*a*) and (6)); and

(b) if that is the case, to have that information communicated to him (FOIA, s.1(1)(*b*)), in each case in the timescale set out in 'Timescale for response', and in the format set out in 'Format for response' both later in this section.

However, each of these rights to information is subject to a number of exceptions and exemptions (see section 3.2.1 and Chapters 4 and 5) (FOIA, s.2). If a public authority relies on an exemption under the FOIA so as either not to confirm or deny to an applicant whether it has the requested information or so as not to disclose to an applicant information that it has confirmed that it holds, the public authority must explain this in a refusal notice (as set out in 'Format for response' later in this section).

Timescale for response

As a general rule, public authorities have 20 working days from the day after the date of receipt to comply with a request for information (FOIA, s.10(1) and (6)), and must respond promptly, which may mean a shorter response time if the information is easily accessible.[24]

Where a fee is payable under a fees notice, the time limit for compliance will not restart until the fee has been paid (FOIA, s.10(2)) and, if it is not paid within three months of the date of the fees notice, the public authority may assume that the applicant no longer wants the information (FOIA, s.9(2)).

Where it is reasonable to do so, a public authority may inform an applicant that it requires an extension to the 20 working day standard response time in order to consider the public interest test in relation to a qualified exemption (FOIA, s.10(3)) (for details of the public interest test see Chapter 5). The public authority should give the applicant written notice of the anticipated additional time required (FOIA, s.17(2)) (the estimated time must be reasonable and justifiable). Any non-exempt information, or any refusal of a request where information is subject to an absolute exemption, must still be disclosed within the initial 20 working days. Public authorities should nevertheless aim to respond within the initial 20 working days even where the public interest test is to be considered.[25]

Subsequent secondary legislation,[26] which also came into effect on 1 January 2005, also allows public authorities in certain circumstances a longer maximum period of time than is normally provided to comply with information requests:

- where the information is held outside the UK a public authority must respond to the request within 60 working days following the date of receipt of the request;[27]
- information requests to a public records office in relation to information wholly or partly contained in a public record (i.e. information transferred to the National Archives by another public authority) must be complied with within 30 working days following the date of receipt of the request;[28]

- where the information must be obtained from a member of the armed forces on active operation, a public authority must apply to the Information Commissioner for an extension of time (which will normally be no more than 60 working days following the date of receipt of the request) and must then respond within the specified time;[29] and
- information requests to the governing body of a maintained school or a maintained nursery school must be complied with within 60 working days following the date of receipt or the 20th working day following the date of receipt, disregarding any working day which is not a school day, whichever is the earlier.[30]

However, in each of these circumstances, the extension of time granted to public authorities to comply is subject to the overriding obligation to comply promptly with all information requests.

The period of time within which a public authority must respond to a request for information commences on the day after the date of receipt of the request for information. In effect, this is the date that the request is received by any person within or on behalf of the public authority, and not necessarily the date when the request is received by the authority's nominated FOIA officer or the appropriate person for dealing with the request. Therefore, the public authority should ensure that it has in place an adequate system to ensure that all requests for information are promptly identified and passed to the relevant FOIA officer (or appropriate person) as quickly as possible. It is also good practice to ensure that there is a back-up system to deal with requests in the event that the nominated officer, or any other addressee of a request for information, is absent.

If the public authority requests further information from the applicant in order to identify and locate the requested information, the time limit for compliance will not commence unless and until the date the further information is received from the applicant (FOIA, ss.1(3) and 10(6)).

If a request has been transferred from, or referred by, another public authority, the request will be deemed to be received by the public authority on the date that it actually receives the transferred request (i.e. ignoring the period of time in which the transferring public authority received and considered the request) (Access Code of Practice Part III, para.22).

Format for response

A response either confirming or denying that a public authority has the information requested should be in writing and, provided it is reasonable, in the format requested by the applicant. In considering whether or not it is reasonable to comply with the applicant's requested format, the public authority must consider all the relevant circumstances, including the cost (FOIA, s.11(2)). If it is unreasonable, the public authority must state why, and provide the confirmation or denial in a format that is reasonable in the circumstances (FOIA, s.11(3) and (4)).

Where the applicant has specified that he would like the information to be made available in a preferred form or format, the information should be made available in that form or format (for example, in electronic or hard copy, large print, Braille, audio version, database, in Welsh, as a summary or digest, or alternatively an opportunity to inspect the original) (FOIA, s.11(1)) unless:

- the information is already:

    - publicly available (for example, if the information is already made available as part of the public authority's FOIA Publication Scheme); and
    - easily accessible to the applicant in another form or format (taking into account, for example, whether the applicant has access to the Internet, the applicant's location, mobility and any disability, and also considering whether the applicant would have to pay for any alternative means of accessing the information); or

- it is unreasonable in the circumstances for the public authority to make the information available in the requested form or format (FOIA, s.11(3) and (4)). For example, if the amount of work required to provide the information in the form or format requested would be excessive, or if creating the specified form or format may damage the original document.

It may be appropriate for public authorities to contact the applicant to determine whether the proposed alternative form or format is appropriate to them, especially if the cost of providing their preferred format is likely to be expensive, and also to explain the options available for providing the information.

The FOIA provides a right of access to information, not to documentation and so only part of a document may be disclosable, with the remainder of the document redacted, or else only extracts or a summary of the document could be provided.

Any notice either confirming or denying whether the public authority holds the requested information should also give details of the public authority's FOIA complaints policy, and the applicant's right to appeal to the Information Commissioner (FOIA, s.17(7)). Any disclosure of information should also give this information.

If a public authority relies on an exemption or a procedural limitation under the FOIA so as either to refuse to confirm or deny to an applicant whether it has the requested information, or to disclose information to an applicant that it has confirmed that it holds, the public authority must explain this in a written notice to the applicant. The written notice must specify the exemptions or limitations relied upon and the reason(s) why it believes the exemption or limitation applies (FOIA, s.17(1)). If the public authority has applied the public interest test in relation to qualified exemptions, the written notice should also state the public authority's reasons for the public interest in non-disclosure outweighing the public interest in disclosure (FOIA, s.17(3)). The duty to give reasons in these circumstances, however, will not apply if this itself would involve disclosure of exempt information (FOIA, s.17(4)).

Any notice of refusal either to confirm or deny and/or to disclose information should also give details of the public authority's FOIA complaints policy, and the applicant's right to appeal to the Information Commissioner (FOIA, s.17(7)).

3.2.5 What if not satisfied with a response?

Chapter 10 considers the procedure for making complaints to a public authority under the FOIA, and the appeals process to the Information Commissioner if such complaints are not handled to the applicant's satisfaction.

3.3 PERSONAL INFORMATION

Under the FOIA, access to personal information by the subject to the information is subject to an absolute exemption (see Chapter 4) (FOIA, ss.2 and 40). This section, therefore, summarises how a person may obtain access to information about himself or herself.

3.3.1 Data Protection Act 1998[31]

Background

The Data Protection Act 1998 (DPA) essentially regulates the processing of 'personal data', which is given a particular meaning at section 1(1) of the DPA. However, despite being in effect since 24 October 1998, the scope of this definition continues to cause problems. These problems most commonly occur when a processor of personal data has to deal with a request for that personal data and other information to which the subject of that data has a right. In particular, the landmark case of *Durant* v. *Financial Services Authority* [2003] EWCA Civ 1746 was a case arising out of a challenge to a processor of personal data and its unwillingness to disclose data relating to an individual who had made a request for that information under the DPA. The case has determined what is meant by 'relevant filing system', which, as described below, is an important component of the personal data definition.

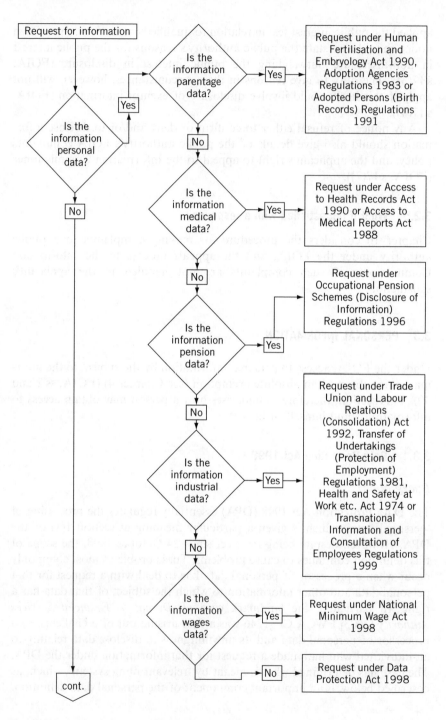

Figure 3.2 Summary of access regimes

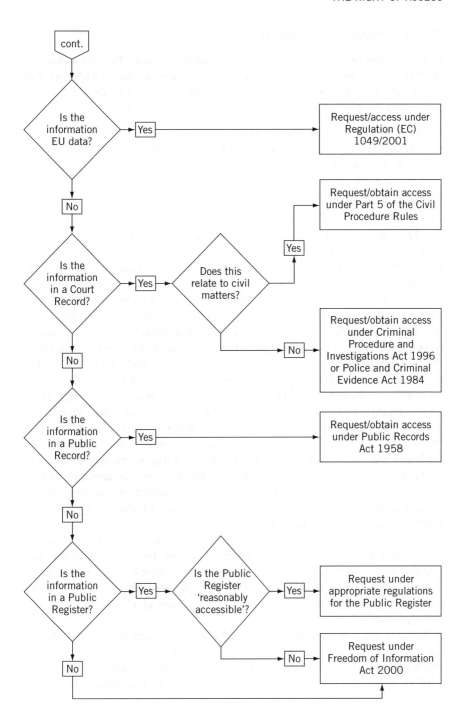

Figure 3.2 Summary of access regimes – *cont.*

What information can be accessed?

Personal data is any information on a living individual (the data subject as defined in the DPA) which is stored by reference to a unique identifier that can be matched back to the data subject by the processor of the data, where those data are of a private or biographical nature and are:

- contained in computerised records; or
- manual data held in a relevant filing system, where a relevant filing system is one that allows a user of the system to readily find and process any particular personal data on the data subject; or
- in the case of public authorities (as defined in the FOIA), any other manual records.

The DPA provides, at section 7, a right of access to the applicant to personal data processed relating to him or her and certain other information relating to the processing of those personal data, subject to a number of important exemptions listed in Part 4 of the DPA, such as the total exemption from section 7 where processing is for the purposes of national security (DPA, s.28), or subject to parliamentary privilege (DPA, s.35A), or is information available by or under enactment (DPA, s.34). The introduction of all manual records within the scope of personal data for public authorities (as defined in the FOIA, s.68) (DPA, s.1(1)(e)), and amendments introduced by the FOIA, have required some rather specific exemptions to cover certain public authorities' manual data. For example, manual data not held in a relevant filing system relating to the appointments or removals, pay, discipline, superannuation or other personnel matters of any person in relation to service in any of the armed forces or any office or employment under the Crown or any authority are exempt from section 7 (DPA, s.33A(2)), as are personal data in relation to negotiations between a public authority and the applicant (DPA, s.37 and Sched.7, para.7), and personal data processed for the purposes of management forecasting or management planning of the public authority (DPA, s.37 and Sched.7, para.5).

Some of the exemptions from section 7 are only partial, such as the exemptions to the obligation to disclose certain types of personal data relating to social work, health and education,[32] which in general exempt disclosure of the personal data where the disclosure would cause serious harm to the physical or mental health or condition of the applicant or any other person.

Certain other individuals have a right to access personal data of which they are not the direct data subjects, being principally those with parental responsibility or some similar authority to conduct the affairs of another, such as guardians or trustees appointed under the Mental Health Act 1983.

The DPA includes as a total exemption disclosures of information that is available to the public by or under another enactment (other than the FOIA) (DPA, s.34 mirroring FOIA, s.21). These other enactments are considered in section 3.3.2.

The request

A request can be made by any individual or, in the case of a child, a parent or guardian or any other person with parental responsibility for that child (see Children Act 1989, s.3), whether or not they are UK or EU citizen or resident, and regardless of the purpose of the application. The DPA does not state at what age a child can exercise his or her rights under the DPA, and so the common law on the capacity of the child as ruled by the House of Lords in *Gillick* v. *West Norfolk and Wisbech Area Health Authority* [1986] AC 112 has to be considered.[33]

The DPA grants a right of access to individuals to information processed by a data controller, both as defined in the DPA.

'Processing' is given a wide definition in the DPA, including merely holding the relevant personal data. A 'data controller' is the person who determines how any particular personal data are to be processed. Therefore, persons who only process data as directed by a third party, or data processors as they are confusingly defined in the DPA, need not respond to the access request, but may merely refer the request to the proper data controller.

The subject access request must be made in writing, which includes requests by letter, fax or email. The request can be refused until the appropriate fee is paid to the data controller. In addition, the data controller can refer back to the data subject if the request is not made in sufficient detail to enable the data controller to identify the personal data the controller may or may not be processing.

As with all requests discussed in this chapter, the applicant for the information, here being personal data, will have a greater chance of succeeding if the request is as specific as possible. In general the courts, in determining whether a holder of information properly exercised its obligations under the relevant statutory regime, are not willing to support the use of the relevant regime for general applications of 'fishing expeditions'.[34]

There is no legal requirement for the request to be sent to any particular individual or officer of a data controller. However, if the data controller is notified to the ICO, then the notification details in the Public Register (accessible online at **www.informationcommissioner.gov.uk**) will include the contact details for the data controller's data protection contact. Where the data subject has received a fair processing notice, then this may have given the contact details of the data controller's data protection representative, if there is/was one. Otherwise a request could be sent for the attention of the Data Protection Officer at the data controller.

Fees

The DPA provides that a data controller is entitled to charge for responding to a subject access requests, subject to certain limits.[35] Data subjects making standard subject access requests may only be charged a maximum of £10, but this can rise to £50 for access to certain medical and education records (these are defined terms in the DPA (s.1(1) and Sched.6)).

The response

The Information Commissioner has published a number of useful guidance and practice notes, to assist data controllers in dealing with subject access requests (see **www.informationcommissioner.gov.uk/eventual.aspx?id=87**).

Under section 7 of the DPA a data controller of any personal data must reply to an applicant with the following information, unless an exemption applies in respect of some or all of the following:

- whether personal data of which that applicant is the data subject are being processed by or on behalf of that data controller;
- if that is the case, a description of:
  - the personal data of which that individual is the data subject;
  - the purposes for which they are being or are to be processed;
  - the recipients or classes of recipients to whom they are or may be disclosed;
  - the information constituting any personal data of which that individual is the data subject;
  - any information available to the data controller as to the source of those data; and
  - where the processing by automatic means of personal data of which that individual is the data subject for the purpose of evaluating matters relating to him such as, for example, his performance at work, his creditworthiness, his reliability or his conduct, has constituted or is likely to constitute the sole basis for any decision significantly affecting him, the logic involved in that decision taking.

Data controllers have 40 working days in nearly all cases to comply with a subject access request (DPA, s.7(10)). The time limit for compliance will not commence until any fee payable in connection with the information request has been paid (DPA, s.7(2)(*b*)).

Provided the disclosure by the data controller complies with the requirements of section 7, then there is no prescribed format for any disclosures under the DPA.

What if not satisfied with a response?

The data subject has rights under section 7 to apply to a court to obtain a court order ordering disclosure by the data controller. Alternatively, the data subject can at any time lodge a complaint with the Information Commissioner, who may then use his powers to commence an investigation under the DPA to request of the data controller its reasons for not fulfilling the subject access request. Failure to respond or an inadequate response to the Information Commissioner may lead to further enforcement steps being taken by the Information Commissioner under the DPA.

3.3.2   Other access to personal information

Parentage data

For the purposes of the flowchart in Figure 3.2, parentage data means data relating to the parentage of an applicant or other person under the Human Fertilisation and Embryology Act 1990 (HFEA) or under the Adoption Act 1976.

The Human Fertilisation and Embryology Authority maintains a register of information relating to:

- the provision of treatment services (as defined in the HFEA) for any identifiable individuals so treated;
- the keeping of gametes of any identifiable individuals or of an embryo taken from any identifiable woman; or
- details of any identifiable individual who was or may have been born as a result of the provision of treatment services (HFEA, s.31).

Any person aged 18 or over may by notice to the Human Fertilisation and Embryology Authority make a request for any information held by the Authority on him or her, which the Authority must disclose if the person was or may have been born as a result of treatment services (HFEA, s.31(4)). The information must include information as to the true genetic parents of the applicant, where requested. Up until 1 April 2005, the Authority could not be required to give information on the identity of any gametes donor or persons from whom an embryo had been taken. However, such information will be disclosable to any persons born as a result of treatment services provided on or after this date.[36]

In addition, a person under 18 may by notice to the Authority inform it of a person the applicant wishes to marry (the intended spouse in the terms of the HFEA) and request that the Authority confirm that the applicant and the intended spouse are not or not likely to be related. Before responding, the Authority must ensure that the minor has had the opportunity to receive proper counselling about the implications of the Authority complying with the request.

Some of the information relating to treatment services will be held by persons licensed under the HFEA to provide the treatment services. Provisions are included in the HFEA to place restrictions on such licensed persons from disclosing this type of registrable information, with the notable exception of information disclosed on an application for access to health records (HFEA, s.33).

The following procedures apply to access under the Adoption Act 1976. As soon as an adoption agency has made an adoption order, it must disclose whatever information it considers appropriate about the adopted child to the adopters, charging them to share this information with the child when appropriate, but no later than the child's 18th birthday.[37]

In addition, the agency must provide access to its records to certain persons, as set out in the appropriate regulations, including a child's guardian or reporting officer for the purposes of the guardian or officer discharging their statutory duties.[38]

The birth records of an adopted child must also be disclosed to that adopted child on its request to the Registrar General of births, marriages and deaths, provided that the Registrar General has complied with his duty to inform the applicant about the counselling services available to the applicant, so that the applicant can obtain a certified copy of the record of his or her birth.[39] Applicants adopted after 11 November 1975 must have attended an interview with a counsellor before the information is released. Applicants adopted before 12 November 1975 need not attend a counselling session. The relevant regulations set out a prescribed form for the application,[40] and provide for the payment of a prescribed fee, but no fee has yet been prescribed.

Having obtained information to enable their birth parents or blood relatives to be traced, adopted persons had no method before 1989 of knowing whether those parents or relatives would welcome contact. For this reason, the Registrar General maintains a register, the Adoption Contact Register. However, this register is not open to inspection or access. Each of the adopted persons who want to contact their birth parents or relatives or those parents or relatives must apply to be included in the register. If the Registrar General discovers a match between the parties, he must forward the relevant contact details to the adopted person; no information is forwarded to the parent or relative other than the knowledge that their details have been so forwarded (Adoption Act 1976, s.51A).

Medical data

For the purposes of the flowchart in Figure 3.2, medical data means information contained in medical reports, as that term is defined in the Access to Medical Reports Act 1988, and data making up a health record, as defined in the Access to Health Records Act 1990.

Access under the Access to Medical Reports Act 1988 is as follows. Any person may obtain a copy of a medical report on him or her, which is or has been supplied for employment or insurance purposes by a medical practitioner (Access to Medical Reports Act 1988, s.2). A third party can, for purposes connected with employment or insurance, obtain a medical report only with the consent of the data subject, who can insist that a copy of the report be provided to him or her before it is disclosed to the third party (Access to Medical Reports Act 1988, ss.3 and 4). However, the medical practitioner can withhold the report where its disclosure would be likely to cause serious harm to the physical or mental health of the data subject or any others; would indicate the practitioner's intentions in respect of the data subject; or would reveal the identity of a third party who has supplied information for the medical report, unless that third party has consented to the disclosure (Access to Medical Reports Act, s.7).

Access under the Access to Health Records Act 1990 is as follows. Any patient and certain representatives of a patient may make an application in writing for the patient's health records to the holder of the record (Access to Health Records Act 1990, s.11). A health record is defined as information relating to the physical or mental health of a patient made by or on behalf of the health professional (as defined in the DPA) in connection with the care of the patient, other than information to which the patient is, or could be but for an exemption, entitled to access under the DPA. However, only those parts of the record made on or after 1 November 1991 are subject to the right of access, together with such earlier parts of the record as are necessary to make the parts made on or after 1 November 1991 intelligible (Access to Health Records Act 1990, ss.1(1), 5(1), 11 and 12(2)). However, an exemption to disclosure of the same nature as for medical reports, described above, may apply (Access to Health Records Act 1990, s.5(1)).

Persons other than the patient who can obtain access to a health record include:

- a person authorised in writing by the patient (Access to Health Records Act 1990, s.3(1));
- in England and Wales, a person having parental responsibility for the patient where that patient is a child and disclosure is in the patient's best interests, provided that if the patient is *Gillick* competent in the opinion of the holder of the health record and the patient has not consented to such access, it must be refused (Access to Health Records Act 1990, ss.4 and 5);

- a person appointed by a court to manage the affairs of a patient incapable to manage them;[41] or
- where the patient has died, the patient's personal representatives or any person who may have a claim arising out of the patient's death (Access to Health Records Act 1990, s.3(1)).

However, the holder of the records can withhold information that in the holder's opinion the patient would not have expected to have been disclosed (Access to Health Recoreds 1990, s.5(3)).

Disclosure of the health records must be made within 21 days of a request, where the records were created within 40 days of the request, or otherwise within 40 days. If any part of the record is unintelligible without an explanation, this must also be given with the disclosure. The cost of making of copies and postage costs can be charged to the applicant (Access to Health Records Act 1990, s.3(2)).

Pension data

Trustees of certain occupational pension schemes have a number of statutory duties in respect of obtaining accounts audited by auditors to the schemes, the auditors' statements and valuations by an actuary of the assets and liabilities of the schemes, together with the actuary's statement concerning such aspects of the valuation as prescribed in the relevant regulations.[42] The trustees are required to make copies of these documents available to members and prospective members of the scheme and their spouses, persons connected with the application of the scheme and qualifying or prospectively qualifying for its benefits or, independent trade unions recognised for the purposes of collective bargaining in relation to members or prospective members of the scheme. Any of these persons can apply for a copy of the latest documents, free of charge, which must be supplied with two months of the request.[43]

Industrial data

For the purposes of the flowchart in Figure 3.2, industrial data means information disclosable to trade union representatives under the Trade Union and Labour Relations (Consolidation) Act 1992, the Health and Safety at Work etc. Act 1974 or the EC Council Directive on the establishment of European Works Councils.

Access under the Trade Union and Labour Relations (Consolidation) Act 1992 is as follows. Employers who recognise independent trade unions for the purposes of collective bargaining have certain statutory duties to disclose to the representatives of the relevant unions on their request information relating to all stages of the collective bargaining and which is information without which the representatives would be materially impeded in carrying on the collective bargaining or which good industrial relations practice would dictate should be disclosed for the purposes of collective bargaining (Trade Union and Labour Relations (Consolidation) Act 1992, s.181). Pursuant to its powers under the Trade Unions and Labour Relations (Consolidation) Act 1992, the Advisory, Conciliation and Arbitration Service (ACAS) has produced a Code of Practice on Disclosure of Information to Trade Unions for Collective Bargaining Purposes,[44] which sets out the types of information a union representative should expect, under the headings pay and benefits, conditions of service, manpower, performance and financial. As may be expected, the duty to disclose on the employer is qualified; the employer is not required to disclose information, for example, which would cause substantial injury to its undertaking for reasons other than its effect on the collective bargaining.

A trade union can complain to the Central Arbitration Committee if it believes an employer has failed to disclose to its representatives that which it is required to disclose in accordance with these statutory requirements. Ultimately, the Central Arbitration Committee has the power to impose terms and conditions of employment on recalcitrant employers (Trade Union and Labour Relations (Consolidation) Act 1992, ss.183–185).

Access under the Health and Safety at Work etc. Act 1974 is as follows. Employers have a statutory duty under the Health and Safety at Work etc. Act 1974 to allow trade union appointed safety representatives on reasonable notice to inspect and take copies of any document relevant to the workplace that the employer is required to keep by any statutory provision, except a document consisting of a health record of an identifiable individual.[45]

Access under the Transnational Information and Consultation of Employees Regulations 1999 is as follows. The regulations implement in the UK the EC Directive on the establishment of European Works Councils for the right to information and consultation of employees in Community-wide undertakings.[46] Whilst the regulations do not provide employees or their representatives express rights to demand information, by triggering the establishment of a European Works Council,[47] the employees gain indirect rights to information. If any information is not provided by the central management of the relevant undertaking on the grounds that it is confidential or exempt (as it would seriously harm the functioning of or would be prejudicial to the undertaking or group of undertakings concerned), the European Works Council can appeal to the Central Arbitration Committee for a declaration as to whether the information was properly withheld or an order for the disclosure of the information or relevant document.

Wages data

Employers have a statutory duty to maintain records in the prescribed form in connection with the National Minimum Wage Act 1998.[48] A worker may require his or her employer upon written request to produce the relevant records and may inspect those records and copy any part of them, where the worker believes on reasonable grounds that he or she is or may be being, or has or may have been, remunerated at less than the national minimum wage rate and for the purposes of establishing the actual position. The employer must comply within a reasonable time, not being longer than 14 days unless agreed between the worker and the employer.

If an employer does not allow access to records, the worker may make a complaint to an employment tribunal. If the worker's complaint is in time (within three months of the expiry of the 14 days referred to above) and the tribunal finds that the worker's underpayment complaints are well founded, then it can award the worker a sum equal to 80 times the hourly rate of the national minimum wage at the date of the award for the underpaid hours.

3.4 ENVIRONMENTAL INFORMATION

The Environmental Information Regulations 2004, SI 2004/3391 (the Regulations)[49] also came into force on 1 January 2005,[50] and broadly grant rights of access to environmental information held by or on behalf of public authorities (including some non-public bodies carrying out a public function). Environmental information (which is defined widely by the Regulations) is exempted from disclosure under the FOIA, s.39. Therefore, requests for such information, and consideration as to whether or not such information must be disclosed or withheld, must be made under the Regulations. Other statutory provisions provide more limited rights of access to environmental information, but the wider right of access provided by the Regulations takes precedence.[51]

Chapter 9 considers the rights of access granted by these Regulations, and how to make and respond to a request for environmental information. It is worth noting that, while the right of access to environmental information and the procedures for making and responding to requests for environmental information under the Regulations are similar to those provided by the FOIA, there are some key differences, which are highlighted in Chapter 9.

3.5   OTHER STATUTORY RIGHTS OF ACCESS TO PUBLIC AUTHORITY INFORMATION

In the excitement over the FOIA, it should not be forgotten that there are numerous other statutory regimes that give the public rights of access to information held by public authorities. Information available under other Acts of Parliament include, for example,

- public records held at the National Archives;[52]
- registration records relating to rights over land held by local authorities and HM Land Registry;[53]
- records of registered intellectual property rights;[54]
- records relating to incorporated companies;[55] and
- records regarding licensed premises.[56]

Such legislation may prescribe the form for any requests and the form and timescales for the public authority response, and may include an appeals procedure, which varies from those provided by the FOIA. There is also a great deal of information that is available to the public upon inspection of the relevant records, such as the indices kept for the registrations of births, marriages and deaths in England and Wales kept by the Registrar General or superintendent or other registrars.[57] Access to these inspection-only records can be made under the FOIA.

In addition to information held by public authorities, the European Commission has a track record of ensuring that wherever possible, all European Union information is readily available to citizens of the Union. The key document to prescribe access to European Union information is Regulation (EC) 1049/2001 regarding public access to European Parliament, Council and Commission documents.[58] Under the Regulation the European Parliament, Council and Commission are required to provide the widest possible access to documents held by them (including received by them) in all areas of activity of the European Union. As with the FOIA, however, there are a number of exceptions that permit the institutions to refuse access (Regulation (EC) 1049/2001, Art.4). The Regulation expressly states that it is without prejudice to copyright in any document, so that an applicant's right to reproduce or exploit released documents may be limited (Regulation (EC) 1049/2001, Art.16). For political documents the Regulation includes a public interest test in familiar terms. Each of the institutions has also put in place institution-specific procedures detailing their policies and practices for granting public access to their documents.

3.6 CONCLUSION

While the FOIA has certainly widened the scope of information made available to the public, additional rights of access to information available under other statutory regimes should also be considered.

It should be noted that there is a distinction between receiving information from public authorities (and other organisations, depending on the relevant statutory regime) and the reuse of that information by the person that requested it. The statutory rights of access to information discussed in this chapter do not automatically grant recipients of information the right to reproduce or reuse documentation supplied under these statutory regimes, and certainly not in a way that would infringe copyright.[59] Normal rules governing reuse of copyright works still apply, which means that charges may be applied for the reuse of the materials provided in addition to the fees paid (or payable) for the supply of the materials. The Office of Public Sector Information (OPSI) has issued guidance on this area in relation to information disclosed by public authorities that is subject to Crown copyright.[60] For example, a fee may be payable to OPSI for a licence to reuse materials provided by a government body for a commercial purpose. Further, the EU Directive on the reuse of public sector information[61] was implemented in the UK on 1 July 2005, and this also entitles public authorities to charge for the reuse of documentation provided to the public.

NOTES

1   Freedom of Information (Removal and Relaxation of Statutory Prohibitions on Disclosure of Information) Order 2004, SI 2004/3363.
2   The Publication Scheme should set out whether or not the public authority is going to charge to provide a copy of the information.
3   FOIA, s.3(1)(*b*); 'publicly owned' is as defined in FOIA, s.6
4   Paragraph 1 of the Office of the Information Commissioner's *Freedom of Information Act Awareness Guidance No.11.*
5   FOIA, s.14; Access Code of Practice Part II at para. 15; and para.2 of the Office of the Information Commissioner's *Freedom of Information Act Awareness Guidance No.22.*
6   Access Code of Practice Part II, para.7 and Office of the Information Commissioner's *Freedom of Information Act Awareness Guidance No.23*, para.1.
7   Office of the Information Commissioner's *Freedom of Information Act Awareness Guidance No.23*, para.2.
8   Department for Constitutional Affairs' *Guidance on the Application of the Freedom of Information and Data Protection (Appropriate Limit and Fees) Regulations 2004*, para.6.
9   Freedom of Information and Data Protection (Appropriate Limit and Fees) Regulations 2004, SI 2004/3244, made pursuant to FOIA, ss.9(4) and 12(4).

10 Freedom of Information and Data Protection (Appropriate Limit and Fees) Regulations 2004, SI 2004/3244, reg.3

11 Department for Constitutional Affairs' *Guidance on the Application of the Freedom of Information and Data Protection (Appropriate Limit and Fees) Regulations 2004*, para.3.4.

12 FOIA, s.17(5). Any such notice should also give details of the public authority's FOIA complaints policy, and the applicant's right to appeal to the Information Commissioner (under FOIA, s.17(7)).

13 Freedom of Information and Data Protection (Appropriate Limit and Fees) Regulations 2004, SI 2004/3244, reg.7, FOIA, s.9(4)(*c*).

14 Access Code of Practice Part II paras.13 and 14 and Office of the Information Commissioner's *Freedom of Information Act Awareness Guidance No.23*, para.14.

15 Freedom of Information and Data Protection (Appropriate Limit and Fees) Regulations 2004, SI 2004/3244, regs.4, 5 and 6; pursuant to FOIA, ss.9(3) and 12(5).

16 Department for Constitutional Affairs' *Guidance on the Application of the Freedom of Information and Data Protection (Appropriate Limit and Fees) Regulations 2004*, para.2.3.

17 *Ibid.*, para. 6.

18 Office of the Information Commissioner's *Freedom of Information Act Awareness Guidance No.23* (para.5) and Foreword to the Access Code of Practice, para.15.

19 The Secretary of State for Constitutional Affairs' Code of Practice on the discharge of public authorities' functions under Part I of the FOIA issued under FOIA, s.45.

20 The Lord Chancellor's Code of Practice on the management of records issued under FOIA, s.46.

21 Office of the Information Commissioner's *Freedom of Information Act Awareness Guidance No.11*, para.3.

22 Chapter 6 of the Department for Constitutional Affairs' Procedural Guide.

23 Office of the Information Commissioner's *Freedom of Information Act Awareness Guidance No.11*, para.4.

24 *Ibid.*, para.1.

25 *Ibid.*, para.7.

26 Freedom of Information (Time for Compliance with Request) Regulations 2004, SI 2004/3364; made pursuant to FOIA ss.10(4) and (5).

27 Freedom of Information (Time for Compliance with Request) Regulations 2004, SI 2004/3364, reg.6.

28 *Ibid.*, reg.4.

29 *Ibid.*, reg.5.

30 *Ibid.*, reg.3.

31 This section gives a summary of the data subject access regime in the Data Protection Act 1998. For a full analysis of the data subject access provisions, see the sister publication to this book, Peter Carey (ed.), *Data Protection Handbook*, Law Society, 2004.

32 DPA, s.30, as detailed in the relevant orders (the Data Protection (Subject Access Modifications) (Social Work) Order 2000, as amended, the Data Protection (Subject Access Modifications) (Health) Order 2000 and the Data Protection (Subject Access Modifications) (Education) Order 2000).

33 The case concerned capacity of a child to consent to medical treatment, but the subsequent test of maturity and understanding, or '*Gillick* competence' test, can be applied to other situations.

34 See *Durant* v. *Financial Services Authority* [2003] EWCA Civ 1746, [2004] FSR 573, *Johnson* v. *Medical Defence Union* [2004] EWHC 2509 (Ch) and *Smith* v. *Lloyds TSB Bank plc* [2005] EWHC 246 (Ch).

35 Data Protection (Subject Access) (Fees and Miscellaneous Provisions) Regulations 2000, SI 2000/191 as amended.

36 Human Fertilisation and Embryology Authority (Disclosure of Donor Information) Regulations 2004, SI 2004/1511, reg.3.

37 Adoption Agencies Regulations 1983, SI 1983/1964, reg.13A.

38 *Ibid.*, reg.15.

39 Adoption Act 1976, s.51 (as amended); and the Adopted Persons (Birth Records) Regulations 1991, SI 1991/1981.

40 Adopted Persons (Birth Records) Regulations 1991, SI 1991/1981, reg.2 and Scheds.1 and 2.

41 Appointed by a Court of Protection under the Mental Health Act 1983 and the Court of Protection Rules 2001, SI 2001/824 (as amended).

42 Pensions Act 1995, s.41; the Occupational Pension Schemes (Disclosure of Information) Regulations 1996, SI 1996/1655 (as amended); and the Stakeholder Pension Schemes Regulations 2000, SI 2000/1403 (as amended).

43 Occupational Pension Scheme (Disclosure of Information) Regulations 1996, SI 1996/1655, regs.6(1) and (2); and Stakeholder Pension Schemes Regulations 2000, SI 2000/1403 (as amended), reg.18.

44 Employment Protection Code of Practice (Disclosure of Information) Order 1998, SI 1998/45.

45 Health and Safety at Work etc. Act 1974, s.2; and Safety Representatives and Safety Committees Regulations 1977, SI 1977/500 (as amended).

46 Transnational Information and Consultation of Employees Regulations 1999, SI 1999/3323, implementing EC Council Directive 94/45 (as amended).

47 This is triggered by a written request of at least 100 employees or their representatives in at least two undertakings or establishments in at least two different member states, where the undertaking has at least 1,000 employees with at least 150 in two or more member states.

48 National Minimum Wage Act 1998, s.9; and National Minimum Wage Regulations 1999, SI 1999/584 (as amended).

49 The Regulations are made under powers set out in (i) the FOIA, s.74; and (ii) the European Communities Act 1972.

50 Environmental Information Regulations 2004, SI 2004/3391, reg.1.

51 Guidance to the EIR Code of Practice, para.3.11.

52 Under the Public Records Act 1958.

53 Under the Commons Registration Act 1965, Land Charges Act 1972, Local Land Charges Act 1975 and the Land Registration Act 2002.

54 Under the Registered Designs Act 1949, Patents Act 1977 and Trade Marks Act 1994.

55 Under the Companies Act 1985.

56 Under the Licensing Act 2003.

57 Births and Deaths Registration Act 1953, ss.30–32; and Marriage Act 1949, ss.64 and 65; and see the range of online information available from National Archives at **www.nationalarchives.gov.uk**.

58 Regulation (EC) 1049/2001 of the European Parliament and of the Council of 30 May 2001 regarding public access to European Parliament, Council and Commission documents, OJ L 145/43 31 May 2001.

59 Draft Guidance to the EIR Code of Practice, para.6.35.

60 OPSI Guidance Note No.19 Freedom of Information Publication Schemes, (**www.opsi.gov.uk/advice/crown-copyright/index.htm**).

61 Directive 2003/98/EC of the European Parliament and of the Council of 17 November 2003 on the reuse of public sector information, OJ L 345, 31/12/2003 pp.90–96.

CHAPTER 4

Freedom of information – exemptions

Marcus Turle, Field Fisher Waterhouse

4.1   INTRODUCTION

As we have seen, the FOIA establishes a new statutory right of access to information held by more than 100,000 public authorities across England, Wales and Northern Ireland. The right is retrospective, applies to all information regardless of format, origin or degree of accessibility, and is available to anyone, anywhere in the world.

Importantly, however, while the entitlement to information under the FOIA is very wide, it is not unlimited. The law recognises that certain areas of government need to retain some measure of secrecy and that freedom of access to information imposes an administrative burden which, beyond a certain point, should justifiably be limited. It also seeks to balance the legitimate interests of those whose commercial and confidential information merits protection. A person making a request is therefore not entitled to have any information whatsoever – the FOIA confers a general right to know, but with exemptions. Lawyers continue to argue about whether the exemptions are too wide. Amid all the talking, one thing is clear: the application of the exemptions is critical to the operation of the FOIA and will ultimately determine whether the law works, and how effectively.

A deal of responsibility for ensuring the exemptions are properly used lies with the Information Commissioner, whose role as data watchdog now extends to freedom of information as well. The Information Commissioner has said that his office will be 'independent, robust and responsible' in policing the FOIA. He says:

> Our independence, means that we can be robust in ensuring that information is released where the new law requires. This involves a presumption in favour of disclosure . . . we must be responsible in our approach, recognising that greater openness should strengthen, not undermine, effective government.
> (Both quotes from **www.informationcommissioner.gov.uk/cms/DocumentUploads/ 1105%20Information%20Commissioner%20welcomes%20new%information% 20rights.pdf**.)

This is encouraging, since we must expect that the operation of the FOIA will depend in significant part on the attitude of civil servants. A rigorous approach by the Information Commissioner is essential to encouraging the public sector to embrace the spirit as well as the letter of the legislation. At the time of writing, there is reason to be optimistic.

Commentary and analysis of all the exemptions is set out below, and in Chapter 5.

4.2 THIRD PARTY INFORMATION

As the FOIA applies to all information which a public authority holds regardless of its provenance, the question arises: what about information originating outside the authority itself? Authorities will hold a large amount of information in the form of correspondence, contracts, invoices, tenders, technical data and all sorts of other material which was authored or otherwise provided by external organisations, but which will still be FOIA accessible by virtue of being held in the authority's files.

For anyone in the private sector doing business with government, this should be ample reason to read on. In effect, the law pre-1 January 2005 is now turned on its head. Much information which the law might then have protected will now, by law, be open to public access. What is more, the FOIA neither imposes an obligation on public authorities to notify or to consult third parties before disclosing information relating to them, nor does it provide any statutory mechanism for preventing disclosure. Assessment of the exemptions, and the decision whether or not to apply them, is entirely at the discretion of the public authority.[1] Some suppliers may try to protect themselves using contractual provisions which require the customer to notify and consult before disclosing, but since the buck stops with the authority regardless of what the contract says, most will be reluctant to accept any contractual provisions which attempt to control their FOIA processes (unless, presumably, the supplier is prepared to give a properly compensating indemnity).

This leaves suppliers with limited options. Any pre-emptive challenge to an authority's application of the FOIA will be contingent on the supplier knowing a request has been made. The best advice to suppliers must therefore be to do everything to ensure their customers tell them when a request comes in. Suppliers can try putting contractual obligations on customers to this effect, but the key to risk management will be a close working relationship between the supplier's and the customer's teams. Customer liaison should be geared to ensuring the customer's information handling process functions to meet its own legal obligations, but also allows the supplier to mitigate the risk of sensitive information finding its way into the public domain. If there is disagreement over a document, then the ultimate sanction for the supplier would be an injunction preventing disclosure.

Without some kind of early warning system, customers will simply disclose information without the supplier knowing. In this case, there are only really two ways to go: either the supplier takes it on the chin, or it can sue for damages on the ground the information was disclosed unlawfully. This of course is a long way short of satisfactory, not least because litigation carries uncertainty of outcome, and further cost.

For individuals disputing disclosure, the options will usually be slightly different. The Information Commissioner is obliged to investigate complaints about the way authorities handle requests, and a person may ultimately sue or apply for judicial review.

4.3   TYPES OF EXEMPTION

There are two types of exemption to the right of access, described in FOIA, ss.2(1) and (2). These are:

(a)   absolute exemptions; and
(b)   exemptions which might apply:

  (i)   if disclosure would prejudice certain interests (which are set out in the FOIA); and/or
  (ii)   for reasons of public interest.

The exemptions in (b), above, are known as qualified exemptions, because they can only apply where the public interest permits (see Chapter 5 for an analysis of the public interest test) and, in some cases, where exemption is necessary to protect a specific interest (such as, for example, national security).

Of the 23 exemptions in the FOIA, only eight are absolute. These are listed in section 2(3). They are:

(a)   information accessible to the applicant by other means (s.21);
(b)   security matters (s.23);
(c)   court records (s.32);
(d)   parliamentary privilege (s.34);
(e)   prejudice to the effective conduct of public affairs (so far as this relates to information held by Parliament) (s.36);
(f)   personal information (except to a limited extent, where the exemption is qualified (see further, Chapter 5)) (s.40);
(g)   confidential information (s.41); and
(h)   other legal prohibitions on disclosure (s.44).

The qualified exemptions are examined in Chapter 5.

4.4   ABSOLUTE EXEMPTIONS

The absolute exemptions apply to all information which falls within each of the categories listed above. In other words, the exemptions apply to whole classes of information. In assessing whether an absolute exemption applies, the only question is whether the information falls within one of the categories. If it does, then it is exempt. There is no test of public interest or prejudice.

If an absolute exemption applies, then the public authority does not have to disclose the information and may not even have to say whether it holds it. It is though, required to tell the applicant which exemption it thinks applies, and why.

Each of the absolute exemptions is considered below.

4.4.1   Information accessible to the applicant by other means (s.21)

The purpose of this exemption is to ensure that public authorities do not become the natural first choice source for information which the applicant can get elsewhere. The FOIA does not cut across existing legal regimes which provide access to information, nor does it provide alternative means of access to information which is already freely available through commercial publishing operations or existing publicly funded provision. The FOIA is designed to supplement rather than duplicate the ordinary circulation of information to the public through the commercial electronic and print media and through existing library and archive services.

Provided the information requested is reasonably accessible by other means (FOIA, s.21(1)) then the exemption will apply. Information is reasonably accessible if (for example):

- it is made available in accordance with the authority's Publication Scheme (FOIA, s.21(3)) (in effect, an authority is not obliged to answer individual requests for information if it already makes that information generally available to everyone); or
- it is available by virtue of other legislation (FOIA, s.21(2)(b)), e.g., information which is accessible under the subject access rules in the Data Protection Act or information about the environment which is available under the Environmental Information Regulations 1992.

Note that information may still be reasonably accessible (and therefore exempt under this section) even though it is only available on payment of a fee (FOIA, s.21(2)(b)), e.g. under the subject access regime in the Data Protection Act. Of course, where the cost of obtaining information by other means would be excessive, that might preclude use of the exemption. Some factors to consider when assessing whether information is readily accessible are as follows.

- Is it is available to purchase through commercial outlets, or is it out of print?
- Is it mass produced in a large print run, or distributed only through scarce or specialist outlets?

- Is it available over the Internet or through a public library?
- How easily can it be identified? Has it been catalogued or indexed?
- Is it ephemeral or has it been archived?
- Is it subject to onerous conditions of access or subsequent use?

Note, however, that there is a subjective element to the exemption, in the sense that the information must be reasonably accessible to the applicant. Consider the following points.

- Are any legal access rights available to the particular applicant (for example, Access to Health Records Act 1990, s.3, which provides that the holder of a health record shall allow access to the health record of a deceased person on application by that person's personal representative, by supplying them with a copy or an extract)?
- Does the applicant have access to otherwise closed or private sources of information, by virtue of some particular quality, entitlement or qualification?
- Does the applicant possess enhanced skills or resources which may bring otherwise inaccessible information within reach (e.g., research, technical or linguistic skills)?
- Is the applicant disadvantaged in some way (e.g., because of disability or educational or economic circumstances) which might render information inaccessible which would otherwise be readily accessible to the general public?

Information will not be exempt by virtue of its availability under other legislation if the relevant statutory obligation is only to make the information available for inspection.[2]

Importantly, this exemption does not apply to the requirement to confirm or deny, so even if the exemption means an authority does not have to make information available, it is still required to say whether or not it holds it.

Where an authority does rely on this exemption, it should try as a matter of good practice to point the applicant to where, by other means, he can obtain the information requested.

Public archives and public records

Information held in public archive or by the Public Records Office may be FOIA exempt under section 21 if the information requested is catalogued and included in the relevant authority's Publication Scheme (or its parent authority's Publication Scheme).

The Public Services Quality Group of the National Council on Archives has produced a *Standard for Access to Archives*, providing guidance on what constitutes an acceptable level of service for archive repositories, including availability to the public. Where a personal visit to an archive is not practicable, some alternative should be made available, such as a paid research service or reference to a list of professional researchers.

4.4.2 Security matters (s.23)

This exemption covers all information originating from or relating to one of the security services. Section 23 states that:

(1) Information held by a public authority is exempt information if it was directly or indirectly supplied to the public authority by, or relates to, any of the following bodies:

- the Security Service (i.e. MI5);
- the Secret Intelligence Service (i.e. MI6);
- the Government Communications Headquarters (i.e., GCHQ) (and this includes any unit or part of a unit of the armed forces which is required by the Secretary of State to assist GCHQ in carrying out its functions);
- the special forces;
- the Tribunal established under section 65 of the Regulation of Investigatory Powers Act 2000;
- the Tribunal established under section 7 of the Interception of Communications Act 1985;
- the Tribunal established under section 5 of the Security Service Act 1989;
- the Tribunal established under section 9 of the Intelligence Services Act 1994;
- the Security Vetting Appeals Panel;
- the Security Commission;
- the National Criminal Intelligence Service; and
- the Service Authority for the National Criminal Intelligence Service.

(2) A certificate signed by a Minister certifying that the information to which it applies was directly or indirectly supplied by, or relates to, any of the above bodies shall, subject to section 60 (which governs appeals against certificates), be conclusive evidence of that fact.

The exemption also applies to the duty to confirm or deny, to the extent that confirming or denying would involve disclosure of any exempt information (whether or not already recorded). It will therefore be appropriate in many cases for a department neither to confirm nor deny the existence of the information requested. It may equally be appropriate to rely on the exemption even where the department does not hold the information.

Application of the exemption in practice

The first part of the exemption refers to information directly or indirectly supplied by one of the security bodies, so the question of whether or not this applies will turn on the source rather than the content of the information requested. For this part of the exemption, the content of the information is irrelevant.

Insofar as the application of the exemption turns on the second part of it (i.e. whether information relates to any of the security bodies), it will be capable of covering a wide range of subject matter, whether of a policy, operational or administrative nature.

In relation to any particular item of information, it will be a question of fact whether it falls within section 23 or not. Where the origin of information is unclear, the exemption should be applied with care, and if possible after consultation with the author.

The FOIA does not specify how remote from the original source information needs to be before it ceases to be indirectly supplied by or related to one of the security bodies. As such, if it is possible to trace a discrete piece of information back through each transmission to its original source, then this would seem to be sufficient, however many hands it has passed through and even if the wording has changed along the way.

The section 23 exemption applies to all records, regardless of their age, including historical records, except that for historical records held by the National Archives or the Public Record Office of Northern Ireland, section 23 ceases to be an absolute exemption after 30 years.

Ministerial certificates

Ministerial certificates require the signature of either a Cabinet Minister, the Attorney-General or the Advocate General. It is not necessary to have a certificate to rely on section 23, but a certificate will normally reinforce a department's position in any legal proceedings, and determine the forum for hearing an appeal (the Information Tribunal rather than the Information Commissioner). As such, certificates are primarily relevant to enforcement proceedings and need not be served until such proceedings commence. Serving a certificate when answering a request will normally be premature and might involve unnecessary work, although departments should consider the need for a certificate at a reasonably early stage to take account of the time needed to prepare one.

Although section 23(2) provides that it is conclusive evidence that information falls within this exemption where it is certified as such by a Minister, this can still be challenged under section 60. Further, section 23 also only permits Ministers to certify specific information – which precludes the preparation of certificates in expectation of future requests.[3]

Interaction with other exemptions

The security matters exemption may overlap with a number of other exemptions: namely, national security (s.24), defence (s.26), international relations (s.27) and the economy (s.29). There is nothing to prevent a department claiming exemption under several, or indeed all, these heads, if appropriate.

It is worth remembering, however, that except for national security, the other exemptions do not provide for ministerial certificates. Further, all of them are qualified exemptions and therefore subject to the public interest. This could give rise to procedural difficulties if an applicant challenges their efficacy. If, for example, a department claimed exemption under both the section 23 (security matters) and section 26 (defence) exemptions, then the route for appeal would be:

- an appeal to the Information Tribunal under section 60 against the section 23 certificate, by either the applicant or the Commissioner;
- a challenge by the applicant to the Commissioner on the balance of the public interest (although this may be adjourned pending the outcome of any section 60 appeal);
- a challenge by the applicant to the Commissioner on the s.26 exemption, although again, it may be appropriate for the Commissioner to adjourn this pending hearing of the section 60 appeal.

4.4.3   Court records (s.32)

Information contained in court records and other similar documents is absolutely exempt from FOIA disclosure. In essence, the exemption covers:

- any document served on or by a public authority; and
- documents held or created by a court, or a person conducting an inquiry or arbitration

in each case, for the purposes of proceedings.

Documents served on or by a public authority

This covers documents created by the parties to litigation and will include information contained in:

- claim forms and statements of defence;
- committal documents in criminal proceedings;
- witness statements, medical and other experts' reports and exhibits;
- skeleton arguments;
- standard disclosure lists;
- public interest immunity applications and certificates;
- allocation questionnaires or pre-trial checklists (listing questionnaires);

- notices of a payment of money into court made pursuant to Part 36 of the Civil Procedure Rules;
- application notices;
- applications under sections 76 and 78 of the Police and Criminal Evidence Act 1984;
- trial bundles;
- response to a Request for Further and Better Particulars (Civil Procedure Rules Part 18); and
- any other documents which are placed before a court for the purpose of a decision or ruling.

Where an authority is party to litigation, documents provided to it by the other parties under their disclosure obligations will normally be exempt. However, the exemption will not extend to information contained in exempt documents if the information is also held by the public authority in another form. So, for example, if an authority is litigating over a contract, the contract will not be exempt (assuming the authority holds a copy in its files) just because that contract is included in the authority's statement of case. This is because the opening line in section 32 reads 'Information held by a public authority is exempt information if it is held *only* by virtue of being held in [court documents etc.]' (FOIA, s.32(1)) (author's italics).

In practical terms, this means that information will usually only be susceptible to the section 32 exemption where it is known to the public authority solely because it is contained in documents served on the authority by another party in litigation, or where it is held by the authority solely because it was recorded in connection with litigation.

Documents held or created by a court

For the purposes of section 32, a court includes a tribunal or other body exercising the judicial power of the State. As well as the civil and criminal courts (comprising magistrates' courts, county courts, the Crown Court, the High Court and the Court of Appeal), this includes the Judicial Committees of the House of Lords and the Privy Council, and the judicial functions of coroners. It would probably exclude the European Court of Justice and the European Court of Human Rights, which are not UK domestic courts. Proceedings includes any inquest or post mortem.

This part of the exemption would cover information contained in documents such as:

- judgments and orders of the court which have not been published;
- notebooks of judges, tribunal members, coroners and other judicial officers;
- notices of hearings;
- summaries prepared by judicial assistants; and

- court or tribunal internal memoranda and correspondence which relate to particular proceedings.

The point about the section 32 exemption is that there are separate and specific regimes for access to information held by courts and tribunals, designed to give those bodies control over the information they hold. Special rules set out a comprehensive code governing the disclosure of court records and documents served in the course of proceedings. For example, Rule 5.4 of the Civil Procedure Rules deals with access to court documents in civil proceedings in county courts, the High Court and the Court of Appeal.[4] For certain types of proceedings (such as in the family court, where children need to be protected), only limited classes of persons may access court documents. the FOIA does not exist to provide indirect access to these records. The greater public interest is considered to lie in preserving the courts' own procedures for disclosure, and the section 32 exemption therefore functions to ensure that the courts can continue to control this.

There is a distinction, of course, between the courts themselves – which are not public authorities under the FOIA – and the government departments responsible for organising the court and tribunal systems (i.e. the Court Service and the Northern Ireland Court Service) – which are. Information held by the latter is accessible under the FOIA in the normal way, as is information held by the police, the Legal Services Commission and the Legal Services Ombudsman.

Documents held or created by a person conducting an inquiry

Inquiries will be subject to the FOIA unless they are legally independent of the sponsoring department. A public authority may therefore hold information which falls within section 32 either because it conducted an inquiry itself or because it was the inquiry's sponsoring department. However, there is a very important limitation on the application of the exemption to inquiries. The exemption can only apply where an inquiry has statutory constitution or is set up under Royal Prerogative (even if a judge heads the proceedings). This might include:

- inquiries which are required to be held by specific statutory provision;
- a discretionary inquiry or hearing designated by an order under section 16(2) of the Tribunals and Inquiries Act 1992 (the relevant order is the Tribunals and Inquiries (Discretionary Inquiries) Order 1975, as amended);
- an inquiry set up by the exercise of a statutory power (e.g. under section 250 of the Local Government Act 1972 or section 81 of the Children Act 1989);
- any inquiry to which the provisions of the Tribunals of Inquiry (Evidence) Act 1921 apply.

There are numerous examples of specific inquiries set up under an enactment.[5] Examples of inquiries which would normally fall outside the scope of section 32 are:

- departmental 'leak' inquiries;
- Lord Butler's review of the intelligence published prior to the invasion of Iraq on weapons of mass destruction;
- Sir Michael Bichard's inquiry arising from Ian Huntley's murder of Soham schoolgirls Holly Wells and Jessica Chapman;
- Lord Penrose's inquiry into Equitable Life; and
- Lord Philip's inquiry into BSE.

Documents held or created by a person conducting arbitration

Arbitration is defined by reference to Part 1 of the Arbitration Act 1996, which applies only where there is a written arbitration agreement. Arbitration involves an impartial, independent third party hearing both sides (usually in private) and issuing a final and legally binding decision to resolve the dispute.

The exemption would normally apply to information contained in, for example:

- notes taken by an arbitrator;
- written decisions or reports of the arbitration;
- a written arbitration agreement that is created by a person conducting an arbitration;
- internal correspondence between persons involved in the conduct of an arbitration; and
- a letter from a person conducting an arbitration requesting further evidence.

4.4.4 Parliamentary privilege (s.34)

Information is exempt where necessary to prevent infringement of parliamentary privilege. Similarly, the duty to confirm or deny does not apply if or to the exent that exemption is required for the same reason.

It is outside the scope of this book to discuss at length the nature of parliamentary privilege. It is sufficient for our purposes to note that while parliamentary privilege is not intrinsically regarded as a reason for secrecy, it is deemed a form of immunity applying to the House of Commons and House of Lords which is necessary for them to function independently, without external interference. The most significant privilege is the right of freedom of speech and proceedings in Parliament, which effectively means that MPs and peers cannot be sued or prosecuted for anything they say in debates or proceedings. As it applies to the FOIA, it means that no external authority can adjudicate on Parliament's right to withhold information where that right is exercised on grounds of parliamentary privilege.

Both the House of Commons and the House of Lords are public authorities for the purposes of the FOIA (individual MPs and peers are not) and both have Publication Schemes. Information included in these Publication Schemes will be exempt under section 21. For the most part, the exemption will apply to information generated and held by the Commons or Lords which are unpublished, such as:

- committee reports and report drafts;
- memoranda submitted to committees, and draft memoranda;
- internal papers prepared by the Officers of either House directly related to the proceedings of the House or committees (including advice of all kinds to the Speaker or Lord Chancellor or other occupants of the Chair in either House, briefs for the chairmen and other members of committees, and informal notes of deliberative meetings of committees);
- papers prepared by the Libraries of either House, or by other House agencies such as the Parliamentary Office of Science and Technology, either for general dissemination to Members or to assist individual Members, which relate to, or anticipate, debates and other proceedings of the relevant House or its committees, and are intended to assist Members in preparation for such proceedings;
- correspondence between Members, Officers, Ministers and government officials directly related to House proceedings;
- papers relating to investigations by the Parliamentary Commissioner for Standards;
- papers relating to the Registers of Members' Interests; and
- bills, amendments and motions, including those in draft, where they originate from Parliament or a Member rather than from Parliamentary Counsel or another government department.

As well as information generated and held by the Commons or Lords themselves, section 34 could extend to information held elsewhere (for example, by central government departments) if related to parliamentary proceedings. If so, then the department concerned must consult with the appropriate House authorities before disclosing. Importantly, although it is open to a department to refuse disclosure on section 34 grounds, only the House authorities can conclusively certify the exemption (as permitted by s.34(3)). Since any person breaching privilege may be punished by Parliament, failure to engage the exemption where it applies may result in serious sanctions. Departments should normally therefore seek advice from the relevant officials to ensure that privilege is asserted (and duly certified) where it is proper to do so.[6] Particular care should be taken with requests for information contained in:

- any of the unpublished working papers of a select committee of either House, including factual briefs or briefs of suggested questions prepared by the committee staff for the use of committee chairmen and/or other members, and draft reports (most likely to be held by a department where a Minister is or has been a member of such a committee);
- any legal advice submitted in confidence by the Law Officers or by the legal branch of any other department, to the Speaker, a committee chairman or a committee, or any official of either House;
- drafts of motions, bills or amendments which have not otherwise been published or laid on the Table of either House;
- any unpublished correspondence between Ministers or department officials on the one hand, and any member or official of either House on the other, relating specifically to proceedings on any Question, draft bill, motion or amendment, either in the relevant House or in a committee; and
- any correspondence with or relating to the proceedings of the Parliamentary Commissioner for Standards or the Registrar of Members' Interests in the House of Commons.

Much information which is privileged is now routinely published by Parliament itself anyway, and this goes well beyond the record of proceedings. It includes internal administrative documents and even individual Members' expenditure against parliamentary allowances. Information published in this way does not cease to be privileged (it remains Parliament's decision whether or not to continue publication) but disclosure of published information cannot be taken as infringing parliamentary privilege in a way which would engage the section 34 exemption (although the information may be eligible for exemption under section 21, being reasonably accessible to the applicant other than under the FOIA).

Note that section 34 is not intended to enable the withholding of information which would be disclosable but for its being contained in parliamentary papers. So, while the draft of a memorandum responding to a select committee report may itself be privileged, factual information included in it may not be. The factual information would normally have to be disclosed unless it cannot be extracted without revealing what else is in the draft report.

There will also be a range of information which is not published by Parliament but which is also not related to parliamentary proceedings and therefore not protected by parliamentary privilege. The best examples of this are:

- papers prepared by the Libraries of either House or other House agencies, intended to provide general or specific background information on matters not currently under examination or expected or planned to be considered in formal proceedings of either House or their committees;
- Members' correspondence and other communications not specifically related to proceedings of either House or of one of its formally consti-

tuted committees (correspondence between a Member and a Minister about a constituency issue that is not the subject of proceedings is not privileged, but correspondence about a draft motion, amendment or Question is privileged);

- the deliberations of parliamentary bodies established by statute (although if they are discussing matters relating to the preparation of formal proceedings in Parliament, those deliberations may well be privileged);
- meetings of political parties and other committees.

4.4.5 Prejudice to the effective conduct of public affairs (s.36)

This is actually a qualified exemption (see Chapter 5), except in relation to information held by the House of Commons or House of Lords, where it is absolute, presumably for reasons of parliamentary privilege. A detailed analysis of section 36 is set out in Chapter 5.

4.4.6 Personal information (s.40)

The exemption relating to personal data is covered in detail in Chapter 8, which deals with the FOIA and the Data Protection Act 1998 (DPA). In summary, the FOIA now extends the meaning of personal data in the DPA (as it applies to public authorities) to include unstructured manual files (previously, the DPA only covered electronic records and manual records held in structured filing systems – and this is still the case for the private sector).

The rules for dealing with requests for personal data depend on who is making the request – i.e. whether the requestor is the data subject himself, or a third party. There are also some special rules in the FOIA designed to reduce the administrative burden which requests for information are likely to place on public authorities.

- *Subject access requests – i.e. requests made by the data subject himself:* subject access requests are absolutely exempt from the FOIA because they are covered by the regime in section 7 of the DPA. Any request for personal data made by the data subject can therefore be treated as a subject access request under section 7 of the DPA (although note that public authorities' obligations under section 7 of the DPA will now also apply to unstructured manual files).
- *Requests for personal data by third parties:* these requests *do* fall within the FOIA regime, but the obligations vary. The rules are complex, but, in a nutshell, information which is protected from disclosure under the DPA cannot be obtained using the FOIA.

4.4.7 Confidential information (s.41)

Information which a public authority obtained from outside the organisation (including from another public authority) is exempt from disclosure if disclosure would be an actionable breach of confidence. Public authorities are also not obliged to confirm or deny possession of confidential information to the extent that this would in itself be an actionable breach of confidence.

Importantly, the exemption cannot apply to an authority's own confidential information (although it can still apply to information which is confidential to an authority's officers and staff) because section 41 refers to information 'obtained by the public authority *from another person*' (author's italics). Further, although government departments are treated as separate entities for FOIA purposes (FOIA, s.81(1)) a government department cannot claim section 41 exemption on the grounds that disclosure of information would be actionable by another government department (because the government cannot sue itself). The same applies between Northern Ireland departments, but not between a Northern Ireland department and a UK department.

What is confidential information?

The legal rules which define confidentiality are continually developing. It is outside the scope of this book to explore the law of confidence in detail. In essence, information can only be confidential if:

- it has the necessary 'quality of confidence' about it (trivial information will not be confidential);
- it was imparted in circumstances importing an obligation of confidence (information in the public domain will not be confidential); and
- disclosure of it would be detrimental to the party wishing to keep it confidential.

Importantly for FOIA practitioners, however, even if these conditions are met, an action for breach of confidence will fail (and therefore the exemption will not apply) if disclosure is in the public interest. This is known as the public interest defence to an action for breach of confidence and derives from common law, not the FOIA. So, although the FOIA exemption for confidential information is absolute (i.e. not subject to a public interest test), if a public authority judges that a breach of confidence will not be actionable because the authority has a public interest defence to a claim, then the authority would normally have to disclose that information notwithstanding its confidentiality.

In practice, information with some commercial value which is not easily available from other sources is likely to be confidential, as is information which an individual would consider confidential (e.g. a staff appraisal, salary details, etc.). Three important factors must be assessed whenever a public authority is applying section 41:

- whether or not information is protected by confidentiality will depend largely on the circumstances in which it was obtained and whether, at the time, the authority expressly agreed to keep it confidential (there are guidelines in the Lord Chancellor's Section 45 Code of Practice (see below) on when an authority should agree to confidentiality restrictions);
- special considerations apply if the information in question is personal data; and
- if information is disclosed in breach of a duty of confidence, then the authority may be liable to a claim for damages; if, on the other hand, information is withheld when it should be disclosed, sanctions under the FOIA may apply. The application of section 41 must therefore be approached with care, and legal advice sought where appropriate.

Lord Chancellor's Code of Practice

The overriding purpose of freedom of information is to ensure openness and transparency in the public sector. It will therefore be apparent to readers that sweeping confidentiality restrictions on information held by public authorities are necessarily incompatible with the FOIA. The Lord Chancellor's Code of Practice issued under FOIA, s.45 (referred to here as the Section 45 Code of Practice) sets out guidance on when public authorities should accept information in confidence, and also on when to consult third parties where an authority plans to disclose their confidential information.

In relation to information provided to a public authority by a third party:

- the public authority should only accept that information is in confidence where possession of the information is necessary in connection with the authority's functions and where it would not otherwise be provided;
- the public authority should not agree to hold information in confidence unless the information is genuinely confidential; and
- the public authority should only agree to express confidentiality provisions where these are capable of justification to the Information Commissioner.

Although the Section 45 Code of Practice does not have the legal force of the FOIA itself, it nevertheless has considerable clout. The Information Commissioner has a duty to promote its observance, and a legitimate expectation that authorities will comply with it. The courts will also normally refer to the Code when determining any question of compliance.

When considering whether to agree to hold information in confidence, here are some useful pointers:

- consider the nature of the interest to be protected and whether it is really necessary to hold information in confidence to protect that interest;

- consider whether it is possible to agree a limited duty of confidentiality, for example by clearly stating the circumstances in which the authority would disclose information;
- if the information will only be provided on condition that it is kept confidential, how important is the information in relation to the authority's functions?
- consider the nature of the person from whom the information is to be obtained and whether that person is also a public authority to whom the FOIA and the Section 45 Code of Practice applies (departments must be particularly cautious about agreeing to keep information confidential where the supplier of the information is also a public authority).

The Section 45 Code of Practice also deals with consultation with third parties where an authority cannot disclose third party material without risking a breach of confidence. The Code says that:

- where disclosure cannot be made without consent (e.g. because this would in itself be a breach of confidence) the authority should consult the third party with a view to getting its consent to disclose, unless this is not practicable (for example because the third party cannot be located or because the costs of consulting would be disproportionate); and
- if the authority believes the cost of consulting to be disproportionate, then it should consider what is the reasonable course of action in light of the requirements of the FOIA and the circumstances of the request.

In essence, if the authority has consent to disclose, then it will not be able to rely on section 41. If the authority notifies a third party of its intention to disclose and the third party objects, the authority may still disclose if it chooses, and the third party can only prevent disclosure by injunction (there is no mechanism under the FOIA for the third party to prevent disclosure). If the authority discloses without consulting at all, then the third party will have no redress under the FOIA. Its only remedy would be a claim against the authority for damages, perhaps with an injunction to prevent further disclosure.

The public interest defence to breach of confidence

When considering the application of section 41, an authority must assess whether a public interest defence to a claim exists. If so, then the exemption cannot apply. The following principles should be applied when assessing the likelihood and force of a public interest defence:

- where a duty of confidence exists, there is a general public interest in favour of keeping that confidence;
- there is no general public interest in the disclosure of confidential information in breach of a duty of confidence – in other words, for a public interest defence to arise, there must be a specific factor in favour of disclosure;

- there is a public interest in ensuring public scrutiny of the activities of public authorities, so, if disclosure would enhance this scrutiny, this will weigh in favour of disclosure; examples might be:
  - information revealing misconduct or mismanagement of public funds;
  - information demonstrating that a public contract is not providing value for money;
  - information which would correct untrue statements or misleading acts by an authority;
- on the other hand, where the interests of a private person (whether an individual or an organisation) are protected by a duty of confidence, the public interest in scrutiny of public authority information is unlikely to override that duty (although this will be less compelling where a substantial period of time has passed since the information was obtained, as a result of which the harm which would have been caused has depleted);
- the FOIA itself has no influence on the nature of any public interest which attaches to the disclosure of information – so the fact that the FOIA might require disclosure were it not for section 41 is irrelevant;
- public authorities must have regard to the interests of the person to whom the duty of confidence is owed, but the authority's own interests are not relevant; and
- the identity of the person requesting the information and the reason for the request are both irrelevant – the question is not whether disclosure to the applicant would be a breach of confidence, but whether disclosure to the public would be a breach (a request from a journalist or pressure group must be treated in the same way as a request from a person who is conducting historical research).

There is unlikely to be a public interest defence in cases where:

- the duty of confidence arises from a professional relationship;
- disclosure would affect the continued supply of important information (e.g. information from whistleblowers); or
- where disclosure would involve some risk to public administration or public or personal safety.

4.4.8 Other legal prohibitions (s.44)

Disclosures which are prohibited by other legal rules are also exempt from the FOIA. The FOIA does not cut across existing legal regimes which restrict access to information, nor does it provide alternative means of access to information which is expressly protected.[7]

There are three types of existing legal provisions which will apply in this context:

- disclosures prohibited by statute;
- disclosures which would be incompatible with EU law; or
- disclosures which would be a contempt of court.

The requirement to confirm or deny also does not apply to the extent that doing so is restricted by other legal prohibition.

It will be immediately apparent that the exemption applies to any disclosure which is a criminal offence, or subject to regulatory, public or civil law restriction. It does not, however, extend to disclosures which are unlawful at common law (except by reason of contempt of court), so the FOIA is no basis for avoiding a disclosure which might be a tort or breach of contract.[8]

There will be many bars to disclosure falling within this category, far too numerous to list here. The fundamental principle underlying the exemption is that the FOIA does not cut across other legal restrictions on disclosure. So, where disclosure is prohibited by the Official Secrets Act, the Data Protection Act or the Human Rights Act, for example, the FOIA will not compel a public authority to make information available. There are similarly many restrictions relating to tax and social security, and various prohibitions on disclosure of information obtained in the course of investigations by bodies such as the Equal Opportunities Commission, the Commission for Racial Equality and the Parliamentary Commissioner for Administration. Certain information obtained by regulators such as the Financial Services Authority and utilities watchdogs like Ofgem, Ofwat and Ofcom will also be exempt, although the application of the exemption will depend on the circumstances in which the information was obtained by the watchdog and the precise scope of its statutory powers.

NOTES

1   Part VII of the Lord Chancellor's Code of Practice issued under FOIA, s.45 makes it clear that consultation is good practice, but there is no requirement to consult.

2   For example, Commons Registration Act 1965, s.1 requires the keeping of registers of commons, and town or village greens. Section 3 provides that 'any register maintained under this Act shall be open to inspection by the public at all reasonable times'. Although this does not preclude the provision of copies on request, the obligation does not go beyond allowing inspection and would therefore not engage the FOIA, s.21 exemption. By contrast, the Trade Marks Act 1994, s.67(1), states that 'after publication of an application for registration of a trade mark, the registrar shall on request provide a person with such information and permit him to inspect such documents relating to the application, or to any registered trade mark resulting from it, as may be specified in the request ... any request must be made in the prescribed manner and be accompanied by the appropriate fee (if any)'. This meets all the requirements of FOIA, s.21(2)(b). The fact that payment of a fee may be required is irrelevant. Similarly, the Births and Deaths Registration Act 1953, s.33(1), provides that 'any person shall, on

payment of a fee . . . and on furnishing the prescribed particulars, be entitled to obtain from the Registrar General, a superintendent registrar or a registrar a short certificate of the birth of any person.'

3   Note however that certificates issued under s.24 (national security) *can* be general and prospective.

4   It allows anyone, on payment of a fee, to inspect and take a copy of a claim form which has been served, a judgment or order given or made in public, and, if the court gives permission, any other document. Where a person has the right to inspect a document without permission, a request can be made to the court staff. Where permission is required, application must be made to a judge.

5   The Bloody Sunday Inquiry (Tribunals of Inquiry (Evidence) Act 1921), the Marchioness Inquiry (Merchant Shipping Act 1995), and the Victoria Climbie Inquiry (Children Act 1989, NHS Act 1971, Police Act 1996), to name but three.

6   For the House of Commons, the relevant official is the Speaker of the House, for the House of Lords, it is the Clerk of the Parliaments. Each House asserts privilege over its own material.

7   At the time of writing, the DCA is engaged in a review of existing legislation to determine whether various statutory restrictions on disclosure of information are consistent with the FOIA. Where the DCA determines that restrictions are not consistent, the relevant statutes will be amended, using powers conferred by FOIA, s.75. Practitioners should therefore ensure they check up to date versions of any statutory provision where a restriction on disclosure may have existed in the past.

8   Breaches of common law are dealt with, where appropriate, by specific exemptions, such as those covering breach of confidence (s.41) and defamation (s.79).

CHAPTER 5

Qualified exemptions

Marcus Turle, Field Fisher Waterhouse

5.1 INTRODUCTION

Chapter 4 looked at the absolute exemptions, which protect whole classes of information falling within the various categories set out in the FOIA. The qualified exemptions are very different. The qualified exemptions apply:

- only where the public interest permits – that is to say, only if the public interest in withholding information outweighs the public interest in disclosing it (see Chapter 7 for a more detailed general consideration of the public interest test); and
- in some cases, only if disclosure would prejudice the interests described (such as, for example, the effective conduct of public affairs), and so for these exemptions the question arises not only of what interests they protect, but also the question of what prejudice means.

As noted, the public interest test applies to all the qualified exemptions. The prejudice test applies only to some. The prejudice-based exemptions relate to:

- national security (s.24);
- defence (s.26);
- international relations (s.27(1));
- relations within the UK (s.28);
- the economy (s.29);
- law enforcement (s.31);
- audit functions (s.33);
- the effective conduct of public affairs (s.36);
- health and safety (s.38); and
- commercial interests (s.43(2)).

The remaining qualified exemptions – for which only the public interest is relevant – relate to:

- information intended for future publication (s.22);
- international relations (s.27(2), which relates to information obtained from another state);

104

- investigations and proceedings conducted by public authorities (s.30);
- formulation of government policy (s.35);
- communications with Her Majesty, etc. (s.37);
- environmental information (s.39);
- personal information (s.40);
- legal professional privilege (s.42); and
- commercial interests (s.43(1), which applies only to trade secrets).

Section 5.3 lists the exemptions to which the prejudice test does not apply, whereas section 5.4 lists the exemptions to which it does.

5.2 APPLYING THE PUBLIC INTEREST TEST

The qualified exemptions operate on the basis that any disclosure of information falling within each category would be harmful and is therefore exempt *if* the public interest in maintaining the exemption outweighs the public interest in disclosing the information.

Public authorities are required to consider the balance of the public interest case by case. This means an authority cannot rely on rigid guidelines which may lead to specific categories of requests being rejected without allowing for the circumstances of each one. Chapter 7 looks in more general detail at the application of the public interest test, although it is addressed in relation to specific exemptions in this chapter.

The time limit for responding to a request to which a public interest exemption may apply is extended for 'such time as is reasonable in the circumstances' to allow authorities to decide where the balance of the public interest lies. However, even if an authority does think an exemption applies, it is still required to tell the applicant within 20 days that it is considering the exemption.

5.3 CATEGORIES TO WHICH THE PUBLIC INTEREST TEST (BUT NOT THE PREJUDICE TEST) APPLIES

Information falling within these categories will be exempt only if the public interest in withholding information outweighs the public interest in disclosing it.

5.3.1 Information intended for future publication (s.22)

Most public authorities are now proactive about releasing information independently of their FOIA obligations. The section 22 exemption is intended to facilitate this process by ensuring that individual requests do not dictate publication timetables or force publication prematurely (unless, of course, the public interest requires this). In effect, the exemption allows authorities to manage proactive publication according to the particular exigencies of preparation, administration and other circumstances. So, for example, where an authority has commissioned a report for which a publication date has been set, section 22 may allow it to withhold the content of the report until the 'official' publication date, provided it is reasonable to do so.

To qualify for the exemption, information must meet three conditions:

- it must be held by the authority with a view to its publication by the authority or by someone else at some future date (although the precise date need not have been determined);
- the intention to publish must exist at the time the FOIA request is made; and
- it must be reasonable in all the circumstances for the authority to withhold the information until the future date of planned release.

'Publication' means any information which is addressed to the public at large or any section of it. For most public authorities this will therefore include the scheduled publication of announcements, press releases, speeches, interviews and articles, email bulletins, information available online and information retrievable electronically, including books, journals, periodicals and newspapers. For central government it will also include consultation papers, White Papers and Green Papers, reports and responses to select committee reports. Publication of research and statistics may also be covered.

What does 'with a view to publication' mean?

Section 22 can apply whether or not the actual date of publication has been determined, and whether or not publication will be by the authority itself or by someone else. The requirement that information must *already* have been held with a view to publication at the time the request is made means only that an authority cannot avoid disclosing something (for example, because it might be embarrassing) by deciding *when it receives a request* that the information will be published at some future date.

Information which an authority intends to pass on to another organisation for publication by it would normally also engage the exemption, as, perhaps, would information held by an authority which it has no intention of publishing itself, but which it knows will be published by someone else. Naturally, it is not enough in these circumstances that a decision whether or not to publish is pending.

A view to publication must be current and continuing, and in this sense will cover draft documents whilst a document is the current draft. Once a draft has been superseded, however, information which is removed from the subsequent draft will not normally be section 22 exempt unless there remains a justifiable ground on which it can still be said to be held with a view to publication (although, of course, other exemptions may apply instead).

Applying the public interest test

In relation to section 22, disclosure is planned at some future date anyway, therefore the public interest in this context turns not on whether to disclose, but on *when* – that is, on whether it is reasonable to withhold disclosure until the intended future date.

The public interest in allowing public authorities to release information in a manner and form, and at a time, of their own choosing is important. In the general run of public affairs, publication is planned and managed according to prevailing circumstances and authorities should rightfully be able to make their own arrangements. Considerations relevant to assessing the public interest might therefore include:

- the nature of the proposed publication timetable itself (the more distant, contingent or indeterminate the prospective publication date, the less heavily it might weigh in favour of exemption and the less reasonable delay might be);
- possible detrimental effects of early/delayed publication – for example, if disclosure might damage a third party's private interests or give rise unnecessarily to public concern, then this might favour withholding;
- whether simultaneous disclosure is a consideration in itself – advanced disclosure to a freedom of information applicant may be unfair to others;
- pre-publication procedures – whether immediate disclosure would undermine consultation with, or pre-publication disclosure to, a particular person (it is normally good practice, for example, to disclose information about a complaint to the complainant or the subject of the complaint before publication);
- publication procedures – for example, the reports of public inquiries are often published under the protection of the Parliamentary Papers Act to avoid defamation or other civil action;
- previous undertakings – for example, where ministers have promised to inform Parliament first about certain information, or where family members should be informed first about matters relating to a relative.

5.3.2 International relations[1]

Section 27 is a prejudice-based exemption except insofar as it relates to confidential information which is obtained from a foreign State or an international organisation or international court. Information from these bodies is exempt irrespective of any question of prejudice (but still subject to the public interest test).

An international court is one established by a resolution of an international organisation of which the UK is a member, or by an international agreement to which the UK is a party. The International Court of Justice, European Court of Justice, International Criminal Court and European Court of Human Rights all qualify as international courts for FOIA purposes.

An international organisation is one whose members include two or more states. For these purposes, a state includes the government of any state, and any organ of government, such as a state's legislature and executive, and also territories outside the UK including Crown dependencies like Jersey and Guernsey, British Overseas Territories like Gibraltar, and territorial entities not necessarily recognised otherwise as states.

The UK itself need not be a member state for an organisation to qualify as an international organisation, so, as well as the United Nations and European Union, OPEC is covered, as is the Organisation of American States. The definition also extends to any organ of such an organisation, which would include, for example, the European Commission and European Parliament.

Confidential information is defined in section 27(3) as:

> information obtained ... at any time while the terms on which it was obtained require it to be held in confidence or while the circumstances in which it was obtained make it reasonable for the state, organisation or court to expect that it will be so held.

This allows for the possibility that a duty of confidence may arise by reasonable expectation or by express agreement. It is therefore wider than the section 41 exemption for confidential information generally, which reflects the common law position rather than the conventionally wider restrictions which parties agree by written contract. Also in contrast with section 41, section 27 is not conditional on a breach being actionable.

Applying the public interest test

Some examples of factors to consider when assessing the public interest as it relates to confidential information falling within section 27 are whether:

- disclosure would be contrary to international law (e.g. a breach of a treaty obligation);
- disclosure would undermine the UK's reputation for honouring its international commitments and obligations;
- disclosure is be likely to undermine the willingness of the state, international organisation or court that supplied the information to supply other confidential information in future (or would be likely to have such an effect on the willingness of states, international organisations or courts in general);

- disclosure is likely to provoke a negative reaction from the state, international organisation or court that supplied the information which would damage the UK's relations with them and/or its ability to protect and promote UK interests;
- disclosure is likely to result in another state, international organisation or court disclosing – contrary to the UK's interests – confidential information supplied to the UK; or
- the state, international organisation or court that supplied the confidential information has objected to its disclosure, and whether good relations with it are likely to suffer if the objection were ignored.

Authorities should also consider consulting the Foreign and Commonwealth Office when considering disclosing information which may affect the UK's international relations.

5.3.3　Investigations and proceedings (s.30)

In essence, section 30 serves to ensure that the FOIA cannot be used to circumvent the rules of disclosure governing criminal investigations and proceedings. There are two very separate exemptions within section 30 and each applies in distinct circumstances. The first, section 30(1), applies to information which has been held at any time for the relevant purposes – even if those purposes have since ceased to obtain. The second, section 30(2), focuses on the reasons for the acquisition of the information and applies only if it was obtained or recorded for purposes which are specified in section 30(3).

Section 30(1)

The section 30(1) exemption itself has three separate parts. The first (s.30(1)(*a*)) relates to information held relating to particular criminal investigations or proceedings[2] and applies to information which an authority has held at any time for an investigation which it has a duty to conduct in order to ascertain:

- whether a person should be charged with an offence; or
- whether a person charged with an offence is guilty of it.

The section 30(1)(*a*) exemption is primarily intended to cover information obtained by the police, National Criminal Intelligence Service or the Serious Fraud Office during the course of an investigation, and also information and evidence which leads to the bringing of charges, but it could also apply to criminal investigations conducted by organisations like:

- HM Revenue and Customs;
- the Department of Trade and Industry;
- the Department for Environment, Food and Rural Affairs;

- the Food Standards Agency;
- the Environment Agency;
- the Health and Safety Executive;
- the Financial Services Authority; and
- the Office of Fair Trading.

The section 30(1)(*b*) exemption applies to investigations which may lead to criminal proceedings which the authority has the power (but not necessarily the duty) to conduct. It is therefore relevant primarily to authorities with regulatory or investigatory functions who may conduct investigations with a view to deciding whether a person should be charged with a criminal offence.

Following on from section 30(1)(*b*), section 30(1)(*c*) applies to actual criminal proceedings which the authority has the power to conduct itself. The exemption will therefore apply to authorities such as the Crown Prosecution Service and any other public authority with prosecution functions.

Section 30(1) will not make exempt information which is unrelated to particular investigations or proceedings – such as statistics on conviction rates – but because it is not limited by time it will continue to apply to relevant information even after investigations and proceedings are finished (although, of course, the conclusion of proceedings may affect the application of the public interest test).

Section 30(2)

The section 30(2) exemption is not restricted to particular investigations or proceedings but is nevertheless quite narrow, being limited by two quite specific requirements.

First, it can only apply if the information in question was obtained or recorded for the purposes of the authority's functions in relation to one of four categories listed in section 30(2)(*a*)(i)–(iv). Secondly, the information must have come from confidential sources.

The authority's functions

Section 30(2) can only apply where information was acquired for the purposes of the authority's functions *relating to*:

(i) investigations of the type referred to in section 30(1)(*a*); or
(ii) criminal proceedings which the authority has power to conduct; or
(iii) investigations conducted under the authority's statutory or prerogative powers[3] for any of the specified purposes (see below); or
(iv) civil proceedings[4] brought by an authority, or on its behalf.

In relation to part (iii), the specified purposes are:

(a)   for ascertaining whether any person has failed to comply with the law;
(b)   for ascertaining whether any person is responsible for any conduct which is improper;
(c)   for ascertaining whether circumstances exist or may arise which would justify regulatory action in pursuance of any enactment;
(d)   for ascertaining a person's fitness or competence in relation to the management of bodies corporate or in relation to any profession or other activity which he is, or seeks to become, authorised to carry on;
(e)   for ascertaining the cause of an accident;
(f)   for protecting charities against misconduct or mismanagement (whether by trustees or other persons) in their administration;
(g)   for protecting the property of charities from loss or misapplication;
(h)   for recovering the property of charities;
(i)   for securing the health, safety and welfare of persons at work; and
(j)   for protecting persons other than persons at work against risk to health or safety arising out of or in connection with the actions of persons at work (FOIA, s.31(3)).

One effect of the wording of section 30(2) appears to be that, if an authority sets up an inquiry which may reveal illegality, but which the authority does not have express statutory or prerogative power to conduct, then the information obtained or recorded for that inquiry will not be exempt, even if obtained from confidential sources.

Confidential sources

Confidential sources will usually be informants or whistleblowers whose identity an authority would want to protect. It will not normally extend, however, to personnel working covertly to gather information, nor to information gathered using covert technology.

To engage section 30(2), the information itself need not be confidential, it is the relationship with the source which must be confidential. In practice, the personal information and confidential information exemptions may also apply to information obtained from confidential sources in which case sections 40 and 41 should be considered before looking at section 30(2). Examples of information likely to fall outside the sections 40 and 41 exemptions but within section 30(2) are:

- a diary with recorded appointments to meet an unnamed informer;
- details of surveillance and investigative techniques associated with the management of external confidential sources; and
- an indication that certain information has been obtained from an unnamed confidential source.

111

Applying the public interest test

At the heart of section 30 lies the importance to law enforcement of public confidence in the investigations and proceedings to which the exemption refers. Public confidence can obviously be fostered by transparency, but it also requires the processes themselves to deliver justice effectively. As the White Paper on Open Government (Cm 2290, 1993) stated:

> There should be no commitment to disclose information which would help potential lawbreakers and criminals, put life, safety or the environment in danger ... Investigation of suspected crime must normally be kept secret from the suspect and others. Witness statements, names and addresses of witnesses and reports from the police and others to prosecutors could, if disclosed other than as required by the courts, jeopardise law enforcement or the prevention or prosecution of crime, or be extremely unfair to a temporary suspect against whom (in the event) no real evidence existed. It is in the interests of both the individuals concerned and the integrity of the prosecution process that material relating to both live and completed prosecutions and to prosecutions which do not go ahead can be kept confidential.

In balancing public interest considerations, public authorities will need to consider the potential effects of a disclosure and the nature and seriousness of the matter being pursued.

The ability of the police, HM Revenue and Customs and other public authorities to obtain information in pursuance of their investigative processes is critical to the prevention and detection of crime and to the integrity and effectiveness of the criminal justice system. Certain disclosures, particularly in relation to confidential sources, could have extremely serious consequences, lead to serious risk of injury or loss of life and be damaging to the willingness of other individuals to supply information.

When considering the balance of the public interest, a weighty consideration will be the extent to which disclosing or withholding information would:

- promote or diminish the chances of a successful prosecution, bringing future charges or making arrests;
- promote or diminish the chances of a fair trial;
- be fair to those who have not been prosecuted, in cases where a decision has been taken not to proceed;
- assist or hamper the gathering of intelligence information from confidential sources such as informants, whistleblowers or calls to Crimestoppers;
- further the interests of justice through the participation of victims, witnesses, informants, suspects or offenders in investigations and proceedings – and either protect or endanger them as they do so;
- assist or impede other ongoing or future proceedings;
- prevent or facilitate the commission of crime.

5.3.4 Formulation of government policy (s.35)

The application of section 35 turns on the content of the information in question, and in particular whether it relates to the formulation or development of government policy.

The purpose of the exemption is to protect the internal deliberative process as it relates to policy making – in other words, to allow the government private thinking space where the threat of public exposure might otherwise compromise candid and robust discussions about policy. The exemption is intended to ensure that the FOIA does not deter policy makers from full and proper deliberation, where, for example, the prospect of disclosure might discourage the exploration of extreme options, the keeping of detailed records and the taking of hard choices, or where disclosure might prejudice good working relationships, the neutrality of civil servants and ultimately the quality of government.

However, the Information Commissioner's view is that the exemption can only apply where there is clear, specific and credible evidence that the formulation or development of government policy would be materially undermined by the threat of disclosure under the FOIA.

Government policy

'Policy' is not defined. According to the Information Commissioner, it will usually cover the development of options and priorities for ministers who determine which options should be translated into political action, and when.

The Modernising Government White Paper refers to policy as the process by which governments translate their political vision into programmes and actions, to deliver outcomes or desired changes in the real world.

Policy can be sourced and generated in various ways. For example, it may come from Ministers' ideas and suggestions, manifesto commitments, significant incidents (such as a major outbreak of foot and mouth disease), EU policies or public concern expressed through letters, petitions and the like. Proposals and evidence for policies may come from external legal advisers, stakeholder consultation, or external researchers, as well as civil servants.

Importantly, policy is unlikely to include purely operational or administrative matters, or decisions about individuals. For instance, decisions about applications for licences or grants are not likely to involve the formulation of policy, but rather its application. Similarly, in most cases, information about an individual's freedom of information application will not fall into the category of information relating to the formulation or development of policy.

Government policy is seen as distinct from departmental or other types of policy. This implies policy which has had Cabinet input or represents the collective view of Ministers or which applies across government. It also implies some political process. Departmental policy will frequently be derived from and be identical to government policy, but where departmental policy applies only to the internal workings of the department it would not be caught (for example, departmental policy about working hours or estate management).

'Formulation' and 'development' of policy

These terms do not have precise meanings.

'Formulation' suggests the output from the early stages of the policy process, where options are generated and sorted, risks are identified, consultation occurs and recommendations and submissions are put to a Minister.

'Development' is sometimes used interchangeably with formulation, but also goes beyond it. It may refer to the processes involved in improving on or altering existing policy, for example through piloting, monitoring, reviewing, analysing or recording the effects of existing policy. At the very least, formulation and development suggests something dynamic – in the sense that something must be happening to the policy. The exemption cannot apply to a finished product, or a policy which has been agreed, is in operation or has already been implemented.

Factors to consider when applying the exemption

The following questions may be relevant to the application of the exemption:

- Would release of the information in this particular case make civil servants less likely to provide full and frank advice or opinions on policy proposals? (Would it, for example, prejudice working relationships by exposing dissenting views?)
- Would the prospect of future release inhibit consideration and debate of the full range of policy options (for example, if on reflection some of them seem extreme)?
- Would the prospect of release lead to civil servants defending everything that is or has been raised during deliberation (in anticipation, for example, of certain things later being discounted)?
- Would the possibility of future release deter the giving of advice which is ill-considered, vague, poorly prepared or written in unnecessarily brusque or defamatory language? Would the prospect of release in fact enhance the quality of future advice? (If so, then this would weigh in favour of release.)
- Is the main reason for applying the exemption to spare a civil servant or Minister embarrassment? (If so, then the exemption is not appropriate.)

Applying the public interest test

Arguments against disclosure might include:

- the need to maintain the quality of government policy making by facilitating free and frank exchanges between civil servants and the thorough consideration of all policy options, however extreme, without inducing the need to defend them;
- the need to maintain the quality of records, working relationships and a neutral civil service;
- the fact that the particular circumstances of the case indicate that public participation in the policy is inappropriate.

Arguments in favour of disclosure might include that:

- public participation in the policy is appropriate (in the sense of permitting people to contribute to policy prior to a final decision). Note:

  - participation cannot be meaningful without access to relevant recorded information about how policy decisions are reached, what options are being considered and why some are excluded and others preferred;
  - without public participation in key policy decisions, certain individuals or groups will enjoy undue influence in the policy-making process;
  - a key driver for freedom of information is to provide access to information which will facilitate informed participation in the development of government proposals or decisions which are of concern to them;
  - information disclosed prior to a decision being taken will facilitate more informed public debate;

- accountability for government decisions (i.e. the need for government to explain why something has happened, or to demonstrate sufficient rigour in taking account of all relevant considerations, including addressing legitimate objections, or that it is keeping its word and delivering what it has promised). Note:

  - disclosure of information is desirable where it may expose wrongdoing, the fact that wrongdoing has been dealt with or dispels suspicions of wrongdoing;
  - access to information under the FOIA may facilitate objective assessment, particularly where information obtained direct from the civil service (as opposed to government press offices) has not been spun;
  - there will usually be a strong public interest in favour of disclosure where a policy decision is going to lead to large scale public expenditure;

115

– similarly, there will usually be a strong public interest in favour of disclosure where a policy decision involves departure from routine procedures or standard practice.

5.3.5 Communications with Her Majesty, etc. (s.37)

Section 37 relates to royal communications and honours. Information is exempt if it relates to:

• communications with Her Majesty, with other members of the Royal Family or with the Royal Household;[5] or
• the conferring by the Crown of any honour or dignity.

The duty to confirm or deny does not arise in relation to information which is exempt under section 37.

5.3.6 Environmental information (s.39)

Section 39 exempts information which an authority is obliged to make available in accordance with the Environmental Information Regulations 2004 (EIR), or would be obliged to make available but for an exemption in those Regulations.

The duty to confirm or deny does not apply to information which is exempt under section 39.

In essence, information which falls within the EIR must be processed in accordance with the EIR. The public interest test is applied by the EIR in the same way as it applies under the FOIA.

The EIR are dealt with in full in Chapter 9.

5.3.7 Personal information (s.40)

The section 40 exemption is for the most part an absolute exemption but there are limited circumstances in which it is only qualified. See Chapter 8 for a full analysis of the interaction between the FOIA and the Data Protection Act 1998.

5.3.8 Legal professional privilege (s.42)

Information which attracts legal privilege is FOIA exempt – subject to the public interest – from both the duty to disclose and the duty to confirm or deny (where this would in itself disclose information which is privileged).

Legal professional privilege (LPP) protects material from disclosure on the ground that a client must be sure that what he and his lawyer discuss in confidence will not be disclosed to third parties without his consent. Unfortunately, having been largely settled since the sixteenth century, the application of LPP has been significantly undermined following a Court of Appeal decision in *Three Rivers District Council* v. *The Governor and Company of the Bank of England* CA [2003] EWCA Civ 474 (*Three Rivers*). Widely criticised as artificial and impractical, it is fair to say the ramifications of the ruling have yet to be fully worked out. We are therefore in a state of considerable uncertainty. This is exacerbated by the FOIA's imposition of a public interest test in relation to LPP. This is another significant shift in the application of previously settled legal principles.

As a result of these changes to LPP, there are likely to be documents to which authorities would expect LPP to apply, but to which, in fact, LPP may not apply. Further, there may be documents to which LPP did apply at the time the document was produced, but to which privilege has later ceased to apply. In both cases, information which an authority would wish and expect to be FOIA exempt, will not be exempt (at least under section 42).

LPP is divided into two categories: legal advice privilege and litigation privilege.

Legal advice privilege

A communication is protected by legal advice privilege if it is made:

- confidentially; and
- between a client and his lawyer; and
- for the dominant purpose of seeking or giving legal advice or assistance.

Litigation privilege

A communication is protected by litigation privilege if it is made:

- confidentially; and
- for the dominant purpose of conducting or giving advice in relation to litigation, either pending or contemplated.

'Litigation' for this purpose covers adversarial proceedings. Adversarial proceedings are not defined, but include court proceedings and arbitration. Non-adversarial proceedings, such as inquiries or investigations, are excluded.

Unlike litigation privilege, legal advice privilege can only apply to communications passing directly between a lawyer and his client. Legal advice privilege cannot apply to correspondence between a lawyer and a third party, or between a client and a third party, even if the communication is for the purpose of obtaining information to be submitted to the client's lawyer.

The change to privilege introduced by the *Three Rivers* decision is that the Court of Appeal confined within narrow limits the persons who qualify as the client for the purpose of determining whether legal advice privilege applies. The *Three Rivers* case arose out of the collapse of BCCI following fraud on a vast scale perpetrated by its senior staff. The creditors and the liquidators of BCCI sued the Bank of England for misfeasance in public office in respect of its supervision of BCCI. The Bingham Inquiry was set up to consider whether the action taken by the UK authorities, including the Bank, had been appropriate and timely. Shortly after the inquiry was established, three Bank officials were appointed by the governor to deal with all communications between the Bank and the inquiry and with the Bank's solicitors in relation to the inquiry. They became known as the Bank's Inquiry Unit (BIU). The Bank received legal advice from its lawyers on every aspect of the presentation of its evidence and submissions to the inquiry. Preparatory work was carried out by the BIU including discussions with present and former Bank staff involved in the licensing or supervising of BCCI. The flow of factual information from the Bank to its lawyers was usually channelled through the BIU. Specific requests for factual matters to be investigated and reported to its lawyers were often made by its lawyers to the BIU who then delegated those fact finding tasks to others within the Bank. The Court of Appeal held that only the members of the BIU should be regarded as the client for the purpose of LPP.

The Bank submitted that communications from any employee should be treated as from the client because a company can only act through its employees. The Court of Appeal accepted that a company can only act through its employees but did not regard that as sufficient for determining whether privilege should apply. It said that 'information from an employee stands in the same position as information from an independent agent' and was thus not protected by legal advice privilege. Thus, not every employee of the client will be regarded as the client for the purpose of determining whether a document is protected by legal advice privilege.

The Court held that confidential internal documents prepared for the purpose of instructing lawyers are not protected by legal advice privilege because such documents are not in themselves a communication between lawyer and client, or a document evidencing such communication. The Court decided that legal advice privilege did not extend to documents prepared by the Bank's employees who were not part of the BIU:

- with the intention that they should be sent to and were in fact sent to the Bank's lawyers;
- which were said to have been prepared with the dominant purpose of the Bank obtaining legal advice but which were not in fact sent to the Bank's lawyers, whether or not prepared for submission to or at the direction of the Bank's lawyers, even if their effect was incorporated into documents which were sent to the lawyers;
- prepared otherwise than for the dominant purpose of obtaining legal advice but which were in fact sent to the lawyers.

118

The definition of 'client' has therefore become critical to determining whether a document is protected by legal advice privilege. Nevertheless, the Court of Appeal gave no guidance about how to determine who the client is. The client would seem to include in-house lawyers, senior officers whose duties include instructing the client's lawyers and those specifically appointed to communicate with the client's lawyers on particular matters.

Communications between an employer and his in-house lawyer where the lawyer is providing legal advice in his capacity as legal adviser will qualify for LPP, but where the lawyer acts in an administrative or executive capacity the communications will not be privileged.

Can privilege be lost?

Privilege can be lost where the underlying confidentiality in a document is lost or where the client waives the right to LPP in a document. Waiver of LPP for one document in a series of documents may, depending on the facts, also waive privilege in other related documents. The Court will ensure fairness and prevent a party from cherry picking and waiving privilege only in those documents which assist it. Waiver of privilege in respect of part of a document will extend to the entire document, unless the subject matter of the remaining part is completely different.

Partial waiver should be distinguished from redaction of a document whereby privileged material is edited out: disclosure of the unprivileged part of the document will not waive privilege in the privileged part.

What is 'legal advice' for the purposes of LPP?

Most – but not all – communications between a lawyer and client will qualify as advice for the purpose of LPP. Legal advice is not confined to telling the client the law, provided that the advice is directly related to the performance by the solicitor of his or her professional duty as legal adviser of the client.

In *United States of America* v. *Philip Morris Inc & Ors and British American Tobacco (Investments) Ltd (Intervener)* [2004] EWCA CIV 330, the Court of Appeal said that the leading modern authority on the practical application of the principles governing privilege is still *Balabel* v. *Air India* [1988] Ch 317. In that case Taylor LJ said (at 330–1):

> The test is whether the communication or other document was made confidentially for the purposes of legal advice. Those purposes have to be construed broadly. Privilege obviously attaches to a document conveying legal advice from a solicitor to client and to a specific request from the client for such advice. But it does not follow that all other communications between them lack privilege. In most solic-itor and client relationships, especially where a transaction involves protracted dealings, advice may be required or appropriate on matters great or small at various stages. There will be a continuum of communication and meetings between

the solicitor and client. Where information is passed by the solicitor or client to the other as part of the continuum aimed at keeping both informed so that advice may be sought and given as required, privilege will attach. A letter from the client containing information may end with such words as 'please advise me what I should do'. But, even if it does not, there will usually be implied in the relationship an overall expectation that the solicitor will at each stage, whether asked specifically or not, tender appropriate advice. Moreover legal advice is not confined to telling the client the law; it must include advice as to what should prudently and sensibly be done in the relevant legal context.

A little later (at 331–2) Taylor LJ said that the scope of the privilege had to be kept within justifiable bounds. He stated in relation to documents recording information or transactions or recording meetings that:

> Whether such documents are privileged or not must depend on whether they are part of that necessary exchange of information of which the object is the giving of legal advice as and when appropriate.

The House of Lords in another *Three Rivers* decision unanimously endorsed the approach of the Court of Appeal in *Balabel* v. *Air India* [1988] Ch 317, and in particular Taylor LJ's comments.

There will always be borderline cases in which it is difficult to decide whether or not the advice is given in a legal context. Much will depend upon whether it is reasonable for the client to consult the special professional knowledge and skills of a lawyer. However, there will normally be a relevant legal context when a client seeks advice from a lawyer.

Litigation privilege

The test for determining whether litigation privilege can be invoked in relation to any communication where litigation has not commenced, is whether there was a real likelihood that litigation was reasonably in prospect at the time when the communication was made. There must be a real prospect of litigation as distinct from a mere possibility, but the prospect does not have to be more likely than not. The requirement that litigation be reasonably in prospect is satisfied if the party seeking to claim privilege can show that he or she was aware of circumstances which rendered litigation between himself or herself and a particular person a real likelihood.

Applying the public interest test

The public interest in maintaining the legal privilege exemption will normally be substantial because legal privilege itself derives from the public interest in maintaining confidentiality between lawyer and client. The guidance from the DCA on section 42 underlines this. It notes that where legal privilege applies, the balance of the public interest will usually weigh in favour of disclosure only in exceptional circumstances.

There are a number of factors which, as a matter of principle, will weigh in favour of maintaining LPP in the face of an FOIA request for privileged information:

- decisions by public authorities must be taken in a fully informed legal context;
- authorities require legal advice for the effective performance of their operations and that advice must be given by lawyers who are fully apprised of the factual background;
- legal advisers must be able to present the full picture, which will include arguments in support of their final conclusions and arguments that may be made against these (it is in the nature of legal advice that it will set out the arguments both for and against a particular view, weighing up their relative merits, and highlighting perceived weaknesses in any position);
- without such comprehensive advice, authority decision making may be compromised because it would not be fully informed;
- disclosure of legal advice could materially prejudice an authority's ability to protect and defend its legal interests;
- disclosure might unfairly expose a legal position to challenge and diminish the reliance which may be placed on the advice; and
- even where litigation is not in prospect, disclosure of legal advice may carry a risk of prejudicing an authority in future litigation, and legal advice connected with one department could have wider implications for other departments.

Public interest factors weighing in favour of disclosing privileged information might include that:

- circumstances are such that the government would waive privilege if litigation were afoot;
- departments should be accountable for the quality of their decision making and this may require transparency in the decision-making process and access to the information on which decisions were made; and
- in some cases there may be a public interest in knowing whether or not legal advice was followed.

5.3.9 Commercial interests (s.43(1))

There are two separate qualified exemptions under section 43 which serve to protect the legitimate interests of business. Section 43(1) applies to trade secrets, for which there is no requirement to assess the prejudice which disclosure might cause, because this is inherent in the meaning of a trade secret. If information is a trade secret, then it will be exempt, subject to the public interest. The duty to confirm or deny does not arise if compliance would defeat the purpose of the exemption.

There is no definition of a trade secret, either in the FOIA or in English law generally. However, the essence of a trade secret is generally taken to comprise three elements (*Lansing Linde Ltd* v. *Kerr* [1991] 1 WLR 251):

- it must be specific information used in a trade or business;
- it must not generally be known – which usually means that the owner must have limited, or at least not permitted, its widespread publication; and
- it must be information which, if disclosed to a competitor, would be liable to cause real or significant harm to the owner.

In 1997, the Law Commission, seeking views on the criminalisation of trade secrets as part of a Consultation Paper, identified four categories:

- formulae for highly specific products;
- technological secrets;
- strategic business information; and
- collations of publicly available information, such as databases.

These categories have not, however, been formally drafted into protected categories.

An analysis of section 43(2), and the application of the public interest test to section 43 generally, follows later in this chapter.

5.4 PREJUDICE-BASED EXEMPTIONS

The public interest test applies to each of the exemptions set out below in the usual way. However, unlike the exemptions referred to already, for the following group of exemptions to apply, disclosure of information must, or must be likely to, give rise to the prejudice referred to in each category. The prejudice itself need not be serious or substantial – any prejudice is sufficient – but it must at least be likely; a mere possibility of prejudice will not suffice.

It is conceivable of course that disclosure of information to one person might be prejudicial, whereas disclosure to someone else would not be. If so, then the correct approach is to consider whether widespread public disclosure of the relevant information would cause prejudice. For example, disclosing information about the specification of British army rifles might be judged harmless if the requestor is a retired colonel living in Dorset, but highly dangerous if the applicant is known to have sympathies with insurgent groups in Afghanistan. If it is likely that disclosure of information to the first applicant might find its way into the hands of the second (e.g. because our retired officer posts it on the Internet), then this is clearly a factor to be built into the assessment of whether disclosure should be made.

An analysis of each of the prejudice-based exemptions follows.

5.4.1 National security (s.24)

Information which is not covered by the absolute exemption for security matters under section 23 will still be exempt if exemption is required to safeguard national security. The exemption applies also to the duty to confirm or deny.

Like section 23, section 24 also provides that certification by a Minister is conclusive evidence of exemption.

National security

The term 'national security' has never been defined in UK legislation, and both domestic and European courts have considered that the assessment of the threat to national security is essentially a matter for the executive. The courts here have accepted that it is proper to take a precautionary approach[6] – that is, it is necessary not only to consider circumstances where actual harm has occurred or will occur to national security, but also to consider preventing harm, or the risk of harm, occurring.

Despite the absence of a definition, it is possible to infer certain statements about the meaning of national security from case law and statute.[7] For example:

- the security of the nation includes its well being and the protection of its defence and foreign policy interests, as well as its survival;
- the nation does not refer only to the territory of the UK, but includes its citizens, wherever they may be, or its assets wherever they may be, as well as the UK's system of government; and
- there are a number of matters which UK law expressly recognises as constituting potential threats to, or otherwise being relevant to, the safety or well being of the nation, including terrorism, espionage, subversion, the pursuit of the government's defence and foreign policies, and the economic well being of the UK. However, these matters are not exhaustive. Government would regard a wide range of other matters as being capable of constituting a threat to the safety or well being of the nation. Examples include the proliferation of weapons of mass destruction and the protection of the critical national infrastructure, such as the water supply or national grid, from actions intended to cause catastrophic damage.

As common sense would suggest, national security is not the same as the interests of the government of the day. Official information that would be

123

embarrassing or inconvenient to the government if made public is not of itself a matter of national security.

As a qualified exemption, section 24 is contingent on two things. First, the test for reliance on the exemption is that non-disclosure should be required for the purpose of safeguarding national security. An authority must be prepared to demonstrate the need to withhold the information requested, and if steps could be taken to allow information to be disclosed while safeguarding national security in some other way, those steps will need to be considered. Secondly, even if exemption is required for this purpose, the exemption is also subject to the public interest.

Applying the public interest test

The public interest requires consideration of:

- whether, in all the circumstances of the case, the public interest in disclosing the information outweighs the public interest in withholding it; and
- if it is decided to withhold the information, whether the exemption from the duty to confirm whether or not the information is held is required for the purpose of safeguarding national security, and whether there is any overriding public interest in communicating the fact that a department holds the information, while not actually disclosing it.

In reality, of course, the public interest and the maintenance of national security are very closely allied. It is difficult in the abstract, therefore, to envisage circumstances where the former would override the latter. The circumstances would have to be fairly extraordinary, and presumably such that national security and the public interest were somehow in conflict.

5.4.2 Defence (s.26)

Section 26 makes information exempt if its disclosure would, or would be likely to, prejudice:

(a)   the defence of the British Islands or any colony; or
(b)   the capability, effectiveness or security of any relevant forces (meaning the armed forces and any forces co-operating with those forces).

This is a qualified exemption which turns not on the description of particular information but on the effects of disclosure. In every case, therefore, it is a question of assessing the risk of prejudice that disclosure may cause to the matters in (a) and (b), regardless of the content of the information, the kind of document in which the information is contained, or its source. In assessing prejudice, any prejudice is sufficient – it need not be significant, serious or substantial – but prejudice would normally have to be a likely consequence of disclosure, rather than a mere possibility.

Relevant examples falling within this exemption might be:

- defence policy and strategy, military planning and defence intelligence;
- the size, shape, organisation, logistics, order of battle, state of readiness and training of the armed forces;
- the actual or prospective deployment of those forces in the UK or overseas, including their operational orders, tactics and rules of engagement;
- the weapons, stores, transport or other equipment of those forces and the invention, development, production, technical specification and performance of such equipment and research relating to it;
- plans and measures for the maintenance of essential supplies and services that are or would be needed in time of conflict;
- plans for future military capabilities;
- plans or options for the defence or reinforcement of a colony or another country;
- analysis of the capability, state of readiness, performance of individual or combined units, their equipment or support structures; and
- arrangements for co-operation, collaboration, consultation or integration with the armed forces of other countries, whether on a bilateral basis or as part of a defence alliance or other international force.

Applying the public interest test

The public interest in avoiding prejudice to defence matters will be strong in most cases, so will outweigh the public interest in disclosure unless the harm or prejudice likely to result from disclosure would be trivial or minor.

There is at the same time widespread public interest in defence policy and the activities of the armed forces, so it is appropriate that the public should be able to understand how and why key decisions are taken. Where disclosure will inform debate, the public interest in disclosure will be weightier. Examples might include disclosure of information relating to:

- the safety of military personnel or loss of life;
- risks to the safety of civilians;
- the use of land or the environmental impact of military activity (for which section 39 may also be relevant);
- the factual and analytical bases used to develop defence policies; and
- the use of public funds.

Clearly the public interest will weigh against disclosure where this might undermine the conduct of a specific military operation or have an adverse impact on security or safety. Further, the disclosure of information in the face of an objection from an allied country, or in breach of a clear undertaking to preserve confidentiality, may well prejudice the UK's defence relations by restricting exchanges of information or by jeopardising military co-operation.

Related issues

Authorities which deal routinely with defence information will usually have their own specific clearance procedures for dealing with requests. Officials should always comply with such procedures because they will have been written to reflect the legal restrictions which apply to the organisation. The FOIA preserves all existing statutory prohibitions on disclosure, the breach of some of which is a criminal offence.

In many cases, it will also be appropriate for an authority to consult the Ministry of Defence before disclosing potentially exempt defence information.

5.4.3 International relations (s.27(1))[8]

Section 27 exempts from disclosure information which would, or would be likely to, prejudice:

- relations between the UK and any other state;
- relations between the UK and any international organisation or international court;
- the interests of the UK abroad; or
- the promotion or protection by the UK of its interests abroad.

Information, the disclosure of which is potentially covered by this exemption, spans a broad spectrum and could include, for example:

- reports on, or exchanges with, foreign governments or international organisations such as the EU, NATO, the UN, Commonwealth, World Bank or International Monetary Fund;
- information about the UK's activities relating to UK citizens or companies abroad, particularly their consular and commercial interests;
- information about other states' views or intentions provided in the course of diplomatic and political exchanges of views;
- details of inward and outward state visits and visits by Ministers and officials;
- information supplied by other states on diplomatic or other channels;
- discussion within the UK government on approaches to particular states or issues;
- information relevant to actual or potential cases before an international court; and
- details of the UK's position in multilateral or bilateral negotiations.

Applying the public interest test

The fundamental question when applying the public interest test under section 27 is whether the public interest in disclosure is outweighed by the damage or likely damage that would be caused to the UK's international relations, its interests abroad or its ability to protect and promote those interests.

For prejudice which is likely to be trivial – for example, where disclosure about the content of a discussion with a foreign official would be unlikely to provoke any significant negative reaction or have any significant detrimental effect on other states' willingness to have similar discussions with the UK in the future – then the public interest in disclosure is likely to prevail.

Correspondingly, for prejudice likely to be more serious – such as disclosure about the UK's attitude to an international issue of concern to a particular state which would provoke a strong negative reaction and could, for example, make it less likely that British companies would be awarded government contracts in future with that state – then the public interest in disclosing would have to be more specific and compelling to justify disclosure. The same would be true of a disclosure which would be likely to weaken significantly the UK's bargaining position in international negotiations, inhibit other governments' willingness to share sensitive information, or inhibit frankness and candour in diplomatic reporting.

5.4.4   Relations within the UK (s.28)

Section 28 will apply where disclosure would, or would be likely to, prejudice relations between any administration in the UK and any other such administration. The duty to confirm or deny does not apply to the extent that compliance would defeat the purpose of the exemption.

'Administration in the UK' means the UK government itself, and the various devolved administrations within the UK. These are:

* the Scottish administration;
* the Executive Committee of the Northern Ireland Assembly (which, at the time of writing, is suspended); and
* the National Assembly for Wales.

Local authorities and the Greater London Assembly are excluded, as are the Scotland, Northern Ireland and Wales Offices which are part of the UK government.

Section 28 applies – regardless of the nature or content of the information in question – where the effects of disclosure would, or would be likely to, prejudice relations between any of the administrations covered – that is, between the UK government and any of the devolved administrations, and also between any of the devolved administrations themselves.

In essence, there are now three devolved administrations within the UK, and the UK government represents UK interests in matters which are not devolved to Scotland, Wales or Northern Ireland. Policy responsibility for non-devolved matters is the responsibility of UK government Ministers and departments, and in these areas the Secretaries of State for Scotland, Wales and Northern Ireland are responsible for ensuring that the interests of those parts of the UK are properly represented and considered.[9]

Accordingly, there are two distinct circumstances in which section 28 might apply: where information requested under the FOIA has been obtained from or shared between administrations; and where information held by one administration could prejudice relations because that administration does not want other administrations to see it, or because other administrations would not want the information to be disclosed.

Information obtained from or shared between administrations

Under the terms of the Memorandum of Understanding between the UK administrations (MoU), all four are committed to the principle of good communication with one another, especially where one administration's work may have some bearing on the responsibilities of another. To enable each to operate effectively, they provide each other with policy information, including scientific and technical statistics, research results and, where appropriate, representations from third parties. Where necessary, they will in confidence:

- alert each other to relevant developments within their areas of responsibility, wherever possible prior to publication (although there are certain areas, notably national security and budget proposals, where prior notification is much less likely);
- give consideration to the views of the other administrations; and
- where appropriate, establish arrangements that allow for policies to be developed jointly between administrations.

The MoU also includes safeguards to ensure that information shared with other administrations is appropriately protected. In certain circumstances, this means that confidentiality is expected. In particular, the MoU provides that administrations will:

- state what restrictions there should be on information they share;
- treat information received in accordance with the restrictions they have agreed to respect;
- comply with the FOIA but in difficult cases refer back to the originator of the information; and
- accept that some information is subject to statutory or other restrictions and that there will be a common approach to the classification and handling of sensitive material.

An expectation of confidentiality will not be a conclusive demonstration of prejudice likely to result from disclosure, but it will be a relevant consideration.

Other information

There will be multifarious circumstances in which information shared between administrations might be prejudicial to relations if disclosed. Some examples might be:

- sensitive information about devolved matters which predate devolution, held by UK government departments but concerning devolved administrations;
- information held by devolved administrations relating to reserved or excepted matters;
- briefing or comments on another administration's plans or policies;
- an options analysis in an area of reserved policy which also includes an assessment of the operation of policy in a devolved area; and
- information about another administration which has come direct from a third party.

Note that, as with the other qualified exemptions, potential embarrassment is not enough to justify its use.

Applying the public interest test

The exigencies of open government have to be balanced with the political imperatives underlying the devolution settlement, namely trust, co-operation, information sharing and respect between the four administrations. The prospect of harming the effective functioning of the devolved relationships will be a significant factor in assessing whether to disclose information.

In weighing the public interest, it is important to consider the following:

- the wider public interest in freedom of information and any particular commitments given by administrations;
- the commitment to sharing information between the four administrations;
- the commitment to respecting confidential information shared between bodies;
- the nature and extent of prejudice to the relationships between administrations that might be caused by the disclosure of a particular piece of information;
- the importance of ensuring appropriate frankness and candour of discussion between administrations; and
- the extent to which other exemptions may be relevant.

The following are some examples where the public interest might favour withholding information:

- confidential briefings for UK Ministers provided for ministerial meetings;
- policy plans received from devolved administrations on a confidential basis which have not yet been announced;
- details of meetings between the four administrations the disclosure of which could impact on the effectiveness of such meetings;
- details of a sensitive UK negotiating position in the EU which, though reserved, impacts on devolved matters; and
- UK government assessments of politics and policies in the devolved administrations.

Examples where the public interest might favour disclosure are as follows:

- information which helps public understanding of the devolution settlement;
- information which would explain how decisions were taken (after an announcement has been made);
- details of negotiations which are no longer sensitive because of the passage of time; and
- cases where the administration which provided the information would have disclosed the information (even if a case can be made for non-disclosure).

5.4.5   The economy (s.29)

Information is exempt if disclosure would, or would be likely to, prejudice:

- the economic interests of the UK or any part of the UK;
- the financial interests of any administration in the UK.

The duty to confirm or deny does not arise to the extent that doing so would defeat the object of the exemption.

Economic interests

'Economic interests' include the central aim of government, to provide economic and financial management which supports the maintenance of a stable macroeconomic framework, maintains sound public finances and promotes UK economic prospects and productivity. Associated with these issues is the maintenance of a competitive financial services market, and efficient tax and benefits systems. The exemption exists in recognition of the instability and economic damage to the wider economy that could be caused by the disclosure of some information.

Financial interests

'Financial interests' means the efficient conduct of the financial aspects of government administration, to minimise the cost to the taxpayer. Public accountability necessitates that sufficient information is available to assess the probity and cost-effective nature of such dealings. This must be balanced against the damage to an administration's financial interests which might result if too much information is disclosed about its financial dealings, or if information is disclosed too soon after a particular event. This component of the exemption exists in recognition of the long-term cost to the taxpayer which could result from disclosure (premature or otherwise) of certain information.

The expression 'an administration in the UK' has the same meaning as in section 28.

The economic interests of the UK

This covers a considerable range of subject matter. It is likely that prejudice could result from disclosure of some of the following, where the information in question is sensitive:

- tax, national insurance and benefits policy;
- IMF loan programmes;
- financial stability discussions and support operations;
- firm-specific financial regulatory information;
- discussions with overseas financial authorities;
- analyses of macroeconomic policy;
- marketing trends, including interest rates and the framework of monetary policy and forecasts of government borrowing; and
- analyses of the effects of increases in public spending on wage and inflation pressures.

In most of these areas, the potential for prejudice is likely to turn on the timing of disclosure, particularly in cases where premature release could cause market instability.

The financial interests of an administration in the UK

Again, this covers a broad spectrum of subject matter. Examples of likely prejudicial disclosures include:

- allocation of gilts and Treasury bills at auctions/tenders to particular investors or market makers;
- government cash dealing and banking arrangements;
- UK reserves and foreign currency liabilities management and foreign exchange dealings;
- timing of large cash and stock transactions in the future;

- intended investment strategies;
- contracts details of PFI and PPP deals;
- auction bidding details (e.g. gilts, spectrum licences); and
- finances of public corporations.

Some examples of potentially prejudicial disclosures

These examples of potentially prejudicial disclosures are drawn from the DCA guidance on section 29. The list is only illustrative.

- information contained in Standing Committee and financial stability papers (of, for example, HM Treasury, the Bank of England, the Financial Services Authority);
- vulnerability assessments, for example of emerging market economies;
- gilt auctions – the size of offering at a gilt auction has a short-term but nevertheless significant sensitivity which could influence price and therefore the cost of borrowing for the government;
- budget information – release of budget information ahead of formal announcement, particularly in relation to tax and national insurance, might lead to pre-emptive action by companies and individuals, leading to a reduction in tax payable to the government;
- government cash flows and borrowing requirements – premature disclosure is likely to be market sensitive; and
- terrorism reinsurance – disclosure of information about claims could potentially prejudice the economic interests of a part of the UK.

Applying the public interest test

There is a legitimate public interest in the UK's economic policy, taxation and financial management, and release of some information will promote public understanding and informed debate (and, indeed, it has been government policy for some time to release information such as Monetary Policy Committee meeting minutes and the annual borrowing plans and gilt auctions calendar).

Some specific factors will weigh in favour of disclosure:

- the need to hold public authorities to account for their stewardship of public resources; and
- the objective of building public trust and establishing transparency in the operation of the economy so as to increase the credibility of economic policy decision makers and enhance the UK's reputation as a fair and honest business environment.

Factors weighing in favour of withholding information might include:

- where disclosure could result in financial instability within institutions or countries, either in the UK or abroad;
- where disclosure could pre-empt announcements on taxation, national insurance or benefits;
- where selective disclosure of the information could affect financial markets – financial regulation and government policy requires the transparent release of market sensitive data simultaneously to the whole market because this reinforces confidence in market integrity, thereby reducing the cost of capital in financial markets; selective or premature release of information undermines confidence in dealing in UK markets;
- where information has been obtained from confidential sources (e.g. overseas governments or regulators) and these would be damaged by disclosure and reduce the likelihood of information being made available in the future; and
- where the information consists of assessments of an institution's or economy's viability.

Authorities should consider consulting HM Treasury and/or other relevant government departments before releasing information which might fall within section 29.

5.4.6 Law enforcement (s.31)

The application of section 31 turns on the likely *effects* of disclosure rather than the source of the information or the purpose for which it is held – which are covered under section 30. As such, section 31 will only be relevant in cases where section 30 is not. This therefore excludes from section 31 most substantive information relating to an authority's own law enforcement functions. However, section 31 is a considerably broader exemption than section 30, because it is relevant to information which authorities hold for the law enforcement purposes of other bodies.

The exemption operates by reference to a list of law enforcement interests which might be prejudiced by disclosure of information. Some are very wide, others very specific. Information is exempt if its disclosure would, or would be likely to, prejudice:

(a) the prevention or detection of crime;
(b) the apprehension or prosecution of offenders;
(c) the administration of justice;
(d) the assessment or collection of any tax or duty or of any imposition of a similar nature;
(e) the operation of immigration controls;
(f) the maintenance of security and good order in prisons or in other institutions where persons are lawfully detained;

(g) the exercise by any public authority of its functions for any of certain specified purposes (see below);

(h) any civil proceedings which are brought by or on behalf of a public authority and arise out of an investigation conducted for any of the certain specified purposes by or on behalf of the authority exercising either prerogative powers or powers conferred by or under any enactment; or

(i) any inquiry held under the Fatal Accidents and Sudden Deaths Inquiries (Scotland) Act 1976 to the extent that the inquiry arises out of an investigation of the type referred to in paragraph (h) above.

The duty to confirm or deny does not arise to the extent that compliance would prejudice any of these matters.

As will be clear, paragraphs (a)–(f) stand by themselves and refer to a series of law enforcement interests which could be prejudiced by disclosure.

Paragraphs (g)–(i) can only apply in relation to the specified purposes set out below (FOIA, s.31(2)):

(a) to ascertain whether any person has failed to comply with the law;

(b) to ascertain whether any person is responsible for any conduct which is improper;

(c) to ascertain whether circumstances exist or may arise which would justify regulatory action in pursuance of any enactment;

(d) to ascertain a person's fitness or competence in relation to the management of bodies corporate or in relation to any profession or other activity which he is, or seeks to become, authorised to carry on;

(e) to ascertain the cause of an accident;

(f) to protect charities against misconduct or mismanagement in their administration (whether by trustees or other persons);

(g) to protect the property of charities from loss or misapplication;

(h) to recover the property of charities;

(i) to secure the health, safety and welfare of persons at work; and

(j) to protect persons other than persons at work against risk to health or safety arising out of or in connection with the actions of persons at work.

The prevention or detection of crime and the apprehension or prosecution of offenders

The above terms appear throughout English law and have no special meaning within the context of the FOIA. They may apply specifically or in general terms. Examples of circumstances in which potential prejudice (i.e. resulting from disclosure) may make the exemption bite are:

- intelligence about anticipated criminal activities (disclosure here has a high potential to prejudice the prevention or detection of the crime in question, and the apprehension of the alleged offenders);
- information relating to planned police operations, including specific planned operations, and policies and procedures relating to operational activity;
- information relating to the identity and role of police informers (to which a number of other exemptions are also likely to be relevant, including those under sections 30, 38, 40 and 41);
- information relating to police strategies and tactics in seeking to prevent crime (the disclosure of such information has a high potential to undermine legitimate police objectives carried out in the public interest);
- information disclosure of which would facilitate the commission of any offence; and
- information disclosure of which would prejudice the fair trial of any person against whom proceedings have been or may be instituted (to which, again, a number of other exemptions may also be relevant, particularly, with reference to section 44, in relation to disclosures which would breach Article 6 of the European Convention on Human Rights).

Applying the public interest test

Maintaining confidence in law enforcement and the criminal justice system is obviously crucial to the public interest, but it is a consideration which can weigh both for and against disclosure. Much is done through police and community consultation (and the media) to keep citizens informed about the ways in which the police carry out their responsibilities. On occasions, however, there will be some tension between this emphasis on openness and the need to maintain the confidentiality of specific operations or policies. Similar considerations will apply to other law enforcement bodies.

It is also important to be aware that prejudice may arise incrementally, as well as from a single disclosure. Clearly, disclosure of information on a single specific police operation designed to apprehend alleged offenders could be prejudicial. What, though, about disclosures of more general information relating to police strategies and tactics? Such disclosure may undermine legitimate police objectives and hamper future operational activity by limiting the value of those strategies and tactics once disclosed (or by providing valuable intelligence to perpetrators of crime).

Examples of specific considerations which might be relevant to this section include:

- the effects of crime on individuals – for example, it would not be in the public interest to disclose details of a surveillance operation and thus potentially compromise that operation, where the target was a person suspected of a series of violent assaults;

- the effects of crime on society – for example, it may not serve the public interest to disclose in advance the arrangements for an operation to combat graffiti and other criminal damage in a specific area; and
- the effects of crime on the economy – for example, it may be against the public interest to disclose specific police strategies for action against those failing to pay fines or other penalties.

The administration of justice

There is no definition of the administration of justice, but it should be interpreted broadly. In particular:

- the exemption does not only concern the operation of the courts – justice is administered through courts and tribunals, through arbitrators, and through alternatives to litigation;
- all categories of justice are included (criminal, civil, family or administrative), as are matters which may not fit into that classification or which are general in nature;
- justice may be administered by professional judges and adjudicators, or by lay magistrates or panel members, or by jurors;
- administration of justice need not imply an adversarial context – it includes non-contentious or uncontested business, and inquisitorial processes (such as inquiries and coroners' courts);
- ensuring public access to justice is part of the administration of justice; and
- the administration of justice may be prejudiced in an individual case, or by something happening to the general process by which justice is delivered.

In the normal course, the administration of justice could be prejudiced by disclosures relating to:

- the operation of the judicial appointments system;
- the ability of a judge to deliver justice effectively, fairly and fearlessly in a particular case;
- the ability of a judge, or of the judiciary, to deliver justice effectively in more general terms;
- the business of the running of the courts and tribunals (though other exemptions might also be relevant);
- the enforcement of sentences and the execution of judgments;
- the ability of litigants to bring their cases, or a particular case, to court;
- the prospects of a fair trial taking place;

- the effectiveness of relationships between different agencies involved in the administration of justice (for example, premature disclosure of plans to redistribute functions between different agencies could lead to a breakdown of co-operation);
- a range of other matters and systems that support the administration of justice (e.g. the operation of the legal aid system, or IT systems – disclosure of the security measures on computer systems would facilitate unauthorised access and thereby make them vulnerable to interference); and
- the maintenance of an independent and effective legal profession.

Applying the public interest test

Clearly, the public interest in the administration of justice is very high. However, in addition to this, there is a public interest in the separation of powers between courts and the executive. This effectively means that there is a public interest in the government acknowledging that the administration of justice is within the courts' particular domain, and in recognising that the courts are, constitutionally, the ultimate arbiters of the law.

As such, although the nature, degree and likelihood of prejudice to the administration of justice will be an essential part of weighing the balance of public interest, government recognition of the courts' position means that authorities should take particular care whenever concluding that the public interest in avoiding prejudice is outweighed. Circumstances where prejudice in a particular case is outweighed by the prevention of prejudice more generally might be one example of where the balance may lie in favour of disclosure. There may be other circumstances, particularly at the administrative margins of the administration of justice (as opposed to the judicial centre of the system), where the operational impact of a prejudicial disclosure is more diffuse, and considerations of administrative transparency weigh more strongly. Precisely because prejudice to the administration of justice encompasses such a wide range of circumstances, the specific factors relevant to individual cases may be particularly important to the operation of this exemption.

Tax

Taxes, duties and impositions of a similar nature includes:

- income tax;
- corporation tax;
- VAT;
- insurance premium tax;
- petroleum revenue tax;

137

- national insurance contributions;
- climate change levy;
- excise duties (for example, on tobacco, oil, beer, spirits and wine);
- motor vehicle duties;
- air passenger duty; and
- stamp duty.

Disclosures likely to be prejudicial to the assessment or collection of these levies include:

- details of plans to close tax loopholes;
- information held in relation to the tax affairs of companies or individuals;
- information which informs plans for future investigations;
- third party information which aids the collection of tax or duties; and
- details of strategies, investigative practices or even negotiating tactics used to assist in the collection of taxes or duties.

Applying the public interest test

There is a strong public interest in having stable and secure public finances. These are crucial to the stability and sustainable growth of the UK economy and to the delivery of resources to fund public services. An efficient and well administered tax system also improves the competitiveness of business and supports the government's social and welfare objectives. A central requirement of a modern and fair tax system is that everyone pays the proper amount of tax and receives the benefits to which they are entitled. Tax avoidance and evasion reduce the revenue available for delivering public services, and distort the incentives that the tax system aims to offer, unfairly shifting a greater tax burden on to honest and compliant taxpayers.

Of course, disclosure of information promotes public awareness of how taxes work, which helps make it simpler for individuals and business to pay taxes. Authorities should take into account the public interest in the proper administration of taxation both in general and in particular cases, and in the avoidance of disruption or distortion of markets, or of the successful delivery of tax policy objectives.

Operation of immigration controls

'Immigration controls' is not defined in the FOIA but it will obviously cover the physical immigration controls at points of entry into the UK, as well as the arrangements made (whether in or under legislation, or as a matter of policy or procedure) in connection with entry into, and stay in, the UK, including the investigation of offences relating to immigration.

Clearly, the disclosure of information would be prejudicial under this head if its release into the public domain would help people to evade immigration controls (although, as long as that is likely to be the consequence of release, the information itself need not be about immigration controls).

Examples of circumstances where disclosure might prejudice the operation of immigration controls include disclosure of:

- information about the extensive counterfeiting of travel documents of a particular country, on the basis of which travel documents issued by that country should be subjected to particular scrutiny. In this case, the disclosure of the information or the identity of the targeted country might be prejudicial because it could alert counterfeiters (and persons making use of their services) to use another country's travel documentation;
- information which would reveal an incidence of suspected illegal working which is to be investigated by the immigration service. In this case, the disclosure of the information about the proposed investigation might be prejudicial because it could alert employers of the illegal workers in advance and allow them to escape investigation; and
- information on proposed changes to visa regimes. The imposition or amendment of visa regimes usually takes place with little or no notice to the public. This is because visa regimes are generally introduced to prevent evasion or abuse of immigration controls by nationalities who, over time, have been shown to pose a higher risk of evasion or abuse than other nationalities when seeking to enter the UK. Therefore, the disclosure of information relating to visa regimes could, in some cases, prejudice the operation of immigration controls because it would encourage persons from the countries which are due to be affected to seek to enter the UK before the changes are introduced, thus avoiding the more stringent regime which has necessarily been developed.

Applying the public interest test

Immigration controls are important in order to regulate entry to and settlement in the United Kingdom, in which there is a clear public interest.

In the immigration context, there are a number of public interest considerations which may favour disclosure in the context of a particular request. There is a public interest in ensuring that there is public confidence in the operation of our immigration controls, and one way to ensure this is to keep the public informed of policies, developments, and proposals for the future, and the reasons underlying them. Linked with this is the public interest in ensuring that the public have access to correct information. Immigration is an emotive issue and inaccurate information should not be allowed to circulate uncorrected in the public domain.

It is in the public interest to provide information which confirms the performance of immigration control – for example, by providing statistics on the number of passengers and applications that are handled by the

Immigration and Nationality Directorate. There is also a public interest in establishing that the implementation of immigration control is carried out in accordance with the published statements and policies by providing, wherever possible, details of implementation of immigration control.

There is also a public interest in ensuring that those who are subject to immigration controls are aware of those controls and how they operate, as this may discourage such persons from seeking to enter the UK illegally.

Equally there are a number of public interest considerations which may, in the context of a particular request, favour non-disclosure. For example, there is a public interest in ensuring that:

- people are not able to evade or abuse our immigration controls in order to enter the UK illegally;
- the efficiency and integrity of our immigration controls are not undermined; and
- investigations into suspected immigration offences can be conducted effectively.

Maintenance of security and good order in prisons

'Security' and 'good order' are not defined in the FOIA but common sense suggests that 'security' will include everything related to the secure custody of detainees, the safety of the prison population, and the detection and prevention of activity (criminal or otherwise) prohibited under prison rules. It is likely that good order refers to measures intended to counter individuals' disobedience or concerted indiscipline, and which promote a safe and orderly prison regime. Note, however, that this exemption is intended to preserve not only security and good order in prisons but also in 'other institutions where persons are lawfully detained'. This includes young offenders institutions, secure hospitals, secure training centres, local authority secure accommodation and immigration detention and removal centres.

Since the exemption focuses on the effects of disclosure, information would presumably cause harm if its release would compromise security, lead to the breakdown of good order or impair an institution's ability to restore either.

A key aspect of this, therefore, is the need to ensure that changes to prison routine are introduced in a carefully managed way, with prisoner reaction being assessed and expectations managed so that when the change is introduced there is not an immediate adverse reaction that may put staff and prisoners at risk. Premature release of information about a potentially unpopular policy change could therefore be prejudicial. Hypothetical examples of information relevant to good order might be information about proposed changes in the home detention curfew (or tagging) policy, or incentives and earned privileges scheme, or information about changes in meal times or arrangements for visits.

An example of security-related information might be information detailing the times and routes of prisoner escorts, and information relating to good order may include, for example, the strategy for dealing with concerted prisoner indiscipline or the contingency plans for responding to other types of incident.

Conversely, information on physical security at a prison which is assessed as having little or no impact on the risk of prisoner escape if disclosed, might not be considered to prejudice security and should therefore be disclosed.

Applying the public interest test

There is a public interest in ensuring public confidence in the operation of the prison system, which may be achieved by informing the public of policies, developments and proposals for the future. The public interest is clearly not served, however, by releasing information which may aid prisoners to escape, may cause unrest, or may put anybody within an institution at risk.

Sections 31(1)(g), (h) and (i)

As noted above, these exemptions operate only where:

- disclosure would prejudice one of the processes in section 31(1)(*g*), (*h*) or (*i*); and
- that process is for one of the purposes listed in s.31(2); and
- the public interest allows.

The following paragraphs assess the application of each paragraph of section 31(1) in turn.

Section 31(1)(g) – functions of a public authority

'Functions' refers to an authority's powers and duties. These derive either from statute or from the royal prerogative, and the connected purposes in section 31(2) indicate that the provision is chiefly concerned with those systems operated by authorities to ensure that proper standards of conduct and safety are met. Notwithstanding this, though, section 31 does not limit the application of the exemption to particular central functions, since in reality very many authorities and departments exercise functions for the purpose of ascertaining whether any person has complied with the law (s.31(2)(*a*)), ascertaining whether any person is responsible for any conduct which is improper (s.31(2)(*b*)), ascertaining the cause of an accident (s.31(2)(*e*)), or securing the health, safety and welfare of persons at work (s.31(2)(*i*)).

141

Section 31(1)(h) – civil proceedings arising out of statutory or prerogative investigations

'Civil proceedings' certainly comprises non-criminal legal action before a court or tribunal, but it could stretch to include other proceedings such as, for example, some forms of regulatory enforcement proceedings. Much will depend on the terms of any regulatory regime, and on the particular circumstances involved.

The prejudice in question must be to the civil proceedings themselves, but there is no need to give that an artificially narrow interpretation. It is capable, for example, of applying to prejudice to the authority's position in such proceedings.

The proceedings must arise, directly or indirectly, out of an investigation. The investigation, in turn, must have been conducted for one of the specified purposes in section 31(2), though the same is not true for the proceedings themselves (even if, in practice, this will be likely). For example, having ascertained that someone has improperly disclosed sensitive information to journalists, a public authority may attempt to prevent publication of that material by a breach of confidence action.

The investigation must have been conducted either:

- by virtue of the royal prerogative (many investigations undertaken by government departments are undertaken under prerogative powers, because the residual source of their legal powers – where not expressly conferred by statute, for example – resides in the Crown; this is particularly the case regarding investigations in the context of the internal management of government departments); or
- by or under an enactment – that is to say, by virtue of provisions in an Act of Parliament or in an instrument made under powers contained in an Act (this will include, in particular, statutory regulations).

Both the civil proceedings and the investigation may be undertaken either by the authority itself, or by another body on the authority's behalf.

This provision has potential to overlap with section 31(1)(*c*) (the administration of justice) and with sections 32 (court records) and 42 (legal professional privilege). The general public interest considerations likely to be engaged are therefore those relating to the administration of justice and the proper conduct of legal proceedings.

Section 31(1)(i) – inquiries under the Fatal Accidents and Sudden Deaths Inquiry (Scotland) Act 1976

The 1976 Act provides for public inquiries to be held in respect of fatal accidents, deaths of persons in legal custody, sudden, suspicious or unexplained deaths, or deaths which occur in circumstances giving rise to serious public concern. As the Lord Advocate's powers to investigate deaths in Scotland under this legislation are wide-ranging, this provision will have relevance to UK government departments operating in Scotland in a wide variety of circumstances where a death occurs, even where the death does not occur in legal custody. For Whitehall departments, these will of course be in areas of reserved policy/operations, such as, for example, defence (deaths of MoD service personnel based in Scotland) or immigration (deaths of asylum seekers in Home Office detention in Scotland), and in such cases the relevant exemptions (s.26, s.31, etc.) may also apply.

Like section 31(1)(*h*), this provision is limited by the following factors:

- the prejudice must be to the inquiry;
- the exemption applies only to the extent that the inquiry arises out of an investigation;
- the investigation must have been conducted for one of the purposes specified in section 31(2); and
- the investigation must have been conducted under statutory or prerogative powers (although not necessarily under the 1976 Act itself).

Some statutes, which have their own provisions about inquiries into deaths, expressly allow for the disapplication of the 1976 Act, to prevent a death triggering two parallel statutory inquiries. Examples include section 14(7) of the Health and Safety at Work etc. Act 1974, and section 271(6) of the Merchant Shipping Act 1995. Such provisions will limit the application of this exemption.

The section 31(2) purposes most likely to be relevant to the investigations referred to in connection with the 1976 Act are:

- ascertaining whether any person has failed to comply with the law;
- ascertaining whether any person is responsible for any conduct which is improper;
- ascertaining whether circumstances which would justify statutory regulatory action exist; and
- ascertaining the cause of an accident.

5.4.7 Audit functions (s.33)

This exemption is intended to protect the effectiveness of the audit functions of certain public authorities. It applies where the disclosure of information would, or would be likely to, prejudice an authority's functions relating to (a) the audit of the accounts of other public authorities; or (b) the examination of the economy, efficiency and effectiveness with which other public authorities use their resources in discharging their functions (FOIA, s.33(1)). The duty to confirm or deny does not apply to the extent that doing so would defeat the purpose of the exemption.

While much of the information that an auditor holds could be disclosed and may indeed be prepared with a view to publication, there may be cases where disclosure would prejudice the audit function.

Disclosure might prejudice audit functions in the following ways:

- relations with audited bodies and audit third parties may be compromised – there may be information that originates from an audited body which, if disclosed, could harm relations between the auditors and that body, and so affect the ability of the auditors to carry out their functions effectively;
- disclosure may interfere with audit methods – in the interests of an audit's effectiveness, it may be important that details of the audit method, including, for example, the specific files that the auditor intends to examine, are kept from the audited body before the audit takes place. Disclosure of audit methods after an audit may also prejudice subsequent audits where, for example, an auditor intends to use the same method. Similarly, releasing information about how the auditing body derives its conclusions could also prejudice the audit function; and
- public reporting and scrutiny – before publication, many public sector auditors discuss their emerging findings and draft report with the audited bodies and other affected parties to ensure accuracy and completeness of the evidence on which they base their conclusions and recommendations. In the case of the National Audit Office (NAO), it may also be under a duty to inform Parliament first of the findings of its reports. If information from an audit were disclosed before official publication, this may preempt the proper reporting process and could lead to preliminary findings – which had not been fully tested – being given the same currency as fully tested conclusions. This may undermine the fairness of the audit process and create a misleading impression of both the auditor and the body being audited, possibly causing unwarranted damage to either reputation. In these circumstances the audit function would clearly be prejudiced.

Applying the public interest test

There is a strong public interest in ensuring that auditors can effectively carry out audits of public authorities. Much of the information that auditors produce is made available for the same general public interest reasons that support the principles of the FOIA. These include:

- making the reasons for a public body's decisions evident;
- enhancing the scrutiny and improving the accountability of public bodies;
- contributing to public debate; and
- increasing public participation in decision making.

The audit process facilitates the accountability and transparency of public authorities for decisions taken by them, which in turn facilitates accountability and transparency in the spending of public money. In general, most value for money audits lead to a public report with these express aims. There is therefore a clear public interest in protecting the effectiveness of the audit process. However, there is also a counter-balancing public interest in making available information which would lead to greater public confidence in the integrity of the audit process by allowing scrutiny, not only of the audited body, but also of the auditor's performance. In many cases the balance of the public interest will change over time, with the key issue likely to be whether the final report has been published.

Auditing departments and agencies must be aware of the confidentiality requirements of legislation that governs the particular bodies they audit. For example the external auditor of HM Revenue and Customs, the NAO, is bound by the Finance Act 1989, which makes it a criminal offence to disclose taxpayers' information.

5.4.8   The effective conduct of public affairs (s.36)

The section 36 exemption recognises the critical role in effective government of free and frank discussion. However, section 36 can only apply in cases where the information in question is not exempt under section 35 (although the two may be claimed in the alternative). It is therefore likely that section 36 will tend to apply to areas which do not relate to policy – such as management, delivery and operational functions. Further, section 36 exempt information need not relate to government Ministers. It can include any advice and discussion taking place at official level.

The fundamental difference between sections 35 and 36 is that the latter turns on the effects of disclosure rather than the nature of the information itself. In other words, section 36 can apply irrespective of what the information is, if disclosure:

> would, or would be likely to . . . *inhibit* the free and frank provision of advice . . .
> or the free and frank exchange of views for the purposes of deliberation . . . or
> would otherwise *prejudice*, or would be likely to prejudice, the effective conduct of
> public affairs (author's italics).

Importantly, section 36 is contingent on the reasonable opinion of a qualified person, which means that it can only apply with the authority of one of the officials listed in section 36(5). This indicates that section 36 must be used with great deliberation.

What do 'advice' and 'exchange of views' cover?

There is very little guidance on what is meant by these terms. Advice can be internal (e.g. from officials to Ministers) or external (e.g. from third parties).

145

It includes any advice whether made by an authority, or to it. Any exchange of views is limited only by having to be for the purposes of deliberation. This will include processes of decision making, opinion forming or evaluation, but is likely to exclude casual or trivial exchanges.

The term 'inhibit' does not feature elsewhere in the FOIA. It suggests a suppressive effect, in other words a situation where communications would be less likely to be made, or would be made in a more reticent or circumscribed fashion, or would be less inclusive.

In considering its effects, it may be relevant to consider whether disclosure may:

- make it more likely that the person offering advice will be unwilling to do so in future;
- inhibit that person from offering unwelcome advice;
- make it more likely that the person being advised will not ask for advice in future;
- have a similar inhibiting effect on other people in future;
- make it more likely that advice will be given that is materially different because of the possibility of disclosure;
- make people less likely to engage in discussion (whether oral or written) as part of the deliberative process;
- distort or restrain that discussion; or
- result in pressure being brought to bear on officials to provide particular advice.

What does the 'effective conduct of public affairs' cover?

This provision deals with situations which fall outside the other specific circumstances covered by section 36. Little guidance is available so far, but during debates on the Bill, Lord Falconer explained that it is intended to cover residual cases which cannot be foreseen, but where it is necessary to withhold information in the interests of good government. It is a broadly expressed residual exemption, therefore a clear justification would have to be provided when seeking to rely on it (and it is also subject to ministerial authorisation).

In relation to statistical information only, information which an authority holds is exempt if disclosure:

- would prejudice the free and frank provision of advice; or
- would prejudice the free and frank exchange of views for the purposes of deliberation; or
- would otherwise prejudice the effective conduct of public affairs.

This exemption can only be applied to non-statistical information if the authority is authorised by government to exercise discretion.

5.4.9 Health and safety (s.38)

Section 38 exempts information if its disclosure would, or would be likely to, (a) endanger the physical or mental health of any individual; or (b) endanger the safety of any individual (FOIA, s.38(1)). 'Endanger' connotes risk of harm rather than harm itself.

The following are some examples of disclosures with an evident potential for the kind of endangerment to which this exemption applies:

- those which would allow individuals, groups or firms to be identified or located and consequently targeted and attacked for their beliefs or practices, including work in controversial scientific areas;
- disclosure of plans and policies relating to the accommodation of individuals, or groups of individuals, where disclosure could lead to their being threatened or harassed (e.g. asylum seekers);
- disclosure of information about negotiations with kidnappers, where disclosure could endanger the safety of hostages; and
- disclosure of sensitive or graphic information about deceased individuals which could cause serious distress to particular individuals such as family members, particularly if they were not previously aware of the details.

Of course, information relating to health and safety may often be environmental information within the meaning of the EIR. If such information is environmental information, exemption from the FOIA under section 39 must be claimed and the disclosure of that information should be considered under the EIR.

Applying the public interest test

It is never in the public interest to endanger the health and safety of any individual. However, more generally, details to be considered will include:

- the size of the risk involved, the likelihood of the outcome in question, and the extent to which steps might be taken to reduce or manage that risk;
- the nature and seriousness of the resulting outcome were that risk to materialise;
- the possibility that disclosure would help to protect the health or safety of other individuals; and
- the possibility that the anticipated danger could be prevented or managed by other, reasonable, precautions.

There is a public interest in disclosing information in order to reduce the potential danger to people and to increase their personal freedom by making them aware of various risks and enabling them to take appropriate action. A certain level of trust is necessary if the recommendations and information supplied by departments with specific responsibilities to inform the public of health and safety issues are to be acted upon. This trust may be enhanced by a high level of disclosure.

Other statutes and policies

There may be legal prohibitions on disclosing information which would endanger an individual's health or safety. The most relevant examples include the Rehabilitation of Offenders Act 1974 and section 28 of the Health and Safety at Work etc. Act 1974. It is important to be alert to the possibility of such information being environmental information within the meaning of the EIR, in which case, exemption from the FOIA under section 39 is the necessary route.

5.4.10 Commercial interests (s.43(2))

The section 43 exemption has already been addressed as it applies to trade secrets (FOIA, s.43(1)). As a separate point, section 43(2) provides a more general category of exemption for commercially sensitive information if the disclosure of information would, or would be likely to, prejudice someone's commercial interests (including the authority's own). The duty to confirm or deny does not arise if compliance would defeat the purpose of the exemption.

Commercial interests are wider than trade secrets and apply – theoretically, at least – to any activity related to the business, trade or profession of any person or organisation. An organisation's commercial interests might, for example, be prejudiced where a disclosure would be likely to:

- damage its business reputation or the confidence that customers, suppliers or investors may have in it;
- have a detrimental impact on its commercial revenue or threaten its ability to obtain supplies or secure finance; or
- weaken its position in a competitive environment by revealing market sensitive information or information of potential usefulness to its competitors.

Examples of information the disclosure of which may have particular potential to damage commercial interests include:

- research and plans relating to a potential new product;
- product manufacturing cost information;
- product sales forecast information;
- strategic business plans, including, for example, plans to enter, develop or withdraw from a product or geographical market sector;
- marketing plans, to promote a new or existing product;
- information relating to the preparation of a competitive bid;

- information about the financial and business viability of a company; and
- information provided to a public authority in respect of an application for a licence or as a requirement of a licence condition or under a regulatory regime.

Importantly, section 43(2) can apply to an authority's own commercially sensitive information as well as to such information held by the authority relating to outside organisations.

Prejudice to a third party's commercial interests

Public authorities will hold a great deal of information which falls within section 43(2) because disclosure would cause commercial damage to third parties.

Third party commercially sensitive information will come into the possession of public authorities in a number of ways, for example:

- as a result of legal, regulatory or licensing requirements;
- in the course of policy development – for example, information obtained, usually voluntarily, to inform and influence the development of policy, or changes to law or regulation;
- through providing support for business – for example, information provided by a company or trade association to a public authority to obtain advice, help with a specific project, and/or financial assistance; and
- through contracts, for example for products, services or research.

Authorities may also procure commercial information as a product of their own research, for example when conducting assessments of product performance and financial viability. They will hold commercial information on various products and services in their role as purchasers.

Areas of particular sensitivity

Certain areas of activity in which all authorities are involved are likely to carry particular risks in relation to commercially sensitive information.

One such area is procurement. All public authorities buy goods and services, and a great deal of information which changes hands during the procurement process will be commercially sensitive. Some examples of information to which section 43 is most likely to apply include:

- *information relating to general/preliminary procurement activities:* for example, market sounding information; information relating to programme, project and procurement strategies; and contextual information about the authority, its business objectives and plans;

- *information relating to supplier selection:* e.g. qualification information for potential bidders; information about requirements including specifications; details of the qualification process; and details of qualified bidders;
- *information relating to contract negotiation and award:* e.g. bids; papers about capabilities of bidders, evaluations of bids, negotiating briefs and recommendations; the contract; information about successful bid and bidder; and information about other bids and bidders; and
- *information relating to contract performance and post-contract activities:* e.g. information about implementation; information about performance; information about contract amendments with supporting papers; and information which may be provided and reviewed by third parties (e.g. consultants/auditors).

The requirements of the public procurement regime should also be taken into account in relation to the possible disclosure of information. The EC Public Procurement Directives, implemented in the Public Works Contracts Regulations 1991, the Public Services Contracts Regulations 1993 and the Public Supply Contracts Regulations 1995, recognise that the interest of suppliers in sensitive information supplied by them in a procurement must be respected and that both the interest of suppliers and the public interest may mean that certain information relating to a contract award is withheld from publication.

The new Consolidated Public Procurement Directive (2004/18/EC), yet to be implemented in the UK, continues to recognise these interests and prohibits the disclosure of information which suppliers have designated as confidential in a procurement, except as provided by the Directive and by national law.

When considering likely public interest considerations; there are lessons to be learned from overseas.

Experience of the enforcement of access to information legislation in Ireland is instructive in this area, although care should be taken not simply to read across from the Irish experience, as the freedom of information regime is similar but not identical. The picture in Ireland tends to support the view that the public interest in the disclosure of procurement-related information is not sufficiently strong to override the harm that may be done to commercial interests before the award of the contract. However, the public interest in making information available after the award of the contract – such as the total tender price and evaluation details of the successful tenderer, along with information about the fee rates and other details necessary to understand the nature of the services contracted – was found to be much stronger.

A second area is public authorities' commercial interests in the disclosure or publication of information. FOIA obligations to disclose information apply to copyright information as well as to other information. However, the commercial effects of disclosure on the copyright holder (including the authority itself if it is the copyright owner) should be considered, where relevant, in relation to section 43. Of course, copyright protection in a work will continue to subsist even if information is disclosed under FOIA. A copyright holder may therefore enforce its copyright against any successful the FOIA applicant who then sought to exploit that information in breach of the copyright.

Applying the public interest test

There is a public interest in protecting the commercial interests of both the private sector (which plays an important role in the general health of the economy) and the public sector (whose commercially related functions need in any event to be exercised in the wider context of the public interest).

Conversely, there is a general public interest in the disclosure of commercial information in order to ensure that:

- there is transparency in the accountability of public funds;
- there is proper scrutiny of government actions in carrying out licensing functions in accordance with published policy;
- public money is being used effectively, and that departments are getting value for money when purchasing goods and services;
- departments' commercial activities, including the procurement process are conducted in an open and honest way; and
- business can respond better to government opportunities.

Factors that might weigh in favour of the public interest in withholding information in this area include:

- where disclosure would make it less likely that companies or individuals would provide the department with commercially sensitive information in the future and consequently undermine the ability of the department/ agency to fulfil its role;
- where disclosure would be likely to prejudice the commercial interests of the department by affecting adversely its bargaining position during contractual negotiations which would result in the less effective use of public money;
- where disclosure would, as a consequence, make it more difficult for individuals to be able to conduct commercial transactions or have other dealings with public bodies which are not typical commercial transactions – for example, where an organisation obtains a grant or financial assistance from a public authority – without fear of suffering commercially as a result. It would not, for example, be in the public interest to disclose information about a particular commercial body if that information was not

151

common knowledge and would be likely to be used by competitors in a particular market to gain a competitive advantage.

NOTES

1 See also section 5.4.

2 Criminal proceedings include proceedings before a court martial or a standing civilian court.

3 There are very many investigations carried out under either statutory or prerogative powers, too numerous to cover in full here. Some examples are inquiries under the Health and Safety at Work etc. Act 1974, s.14 and investigations under the Financial Services and Markets Act 2000, s.169. As a rule, most investigations carried out by statutory bodies will be statutory investigations, and investigations carried out by central government departments will be either statutory investigations or carried out under prerogative powers.

4 'Civil proceedings' is not defined but will certainly include legal proceedings which are not criminal proceedings, before a court or tribunal. It is possible that in some cases the phrase might have a wider meaning, perhaps including certain forms of statutory regulatory enforcement action.

5 The Royal Household is not defined but can be taken to mean those individuals who are authorised to act on behalf of a member of the Royal Family (such as their employees, agents and servants, and including members of the Private Offices of each of the Royal Family) in the carrying out of public, official and constitutional affairs. Contractors who supply to the Royal Household (e.g. holders of Royal Warrants) do not form part of it. Certain members of the government Whips' offices in both Houses of Parliament are formally members of the Royal Household (senior government Whips in the Commons are designated the Treasurer and Comptroller of the Household; the Vice Chamberlain also serves as a senior government Whip; junior government Whips in the Lords are Lords and Baronesses in Waiting). The activities of these individuals as government Whips are not covered by s.37.

6 The House of Lords judgment in the appeal of Shafiq Ur Rehman against deportation, Secretary of State for the Home Department (11 October 2001 [2001] UKHL 47).

7 e.g. Security Service Act 1989, Intelligence Services Act 1994, Radioactive Substances Act 1993, Water Industry Act 1991, Control of Pollution Act 1974, Offshore Safety Act 1992, Town and Country Planning Act 1990.

8 See also section 5.3.

9 Details of the relationships between the administrations, and their respective responsibilities, is set out in Cm 5240, an inter-administration Memorandum of Understanding. A summary of the terms of the MoU is available at **www.foi.gov.uk/guidance/exguide/sec28/annex_a.htm**.

CHAPTER 6

Implications for the private sector

Hugh Tomlinson QC, Matrix Chambers

6.1 INTRODUCTION

It has been widely recognised that freedom of information legislation is likely to have a substantial impact on the private sector.[1] Although the Freedom of Information Act 2000 (FOIA) only places duties of disclosure on public authorities, it potentially allows any applicant to have access to any information held by the public sector. Any information which has been provided[2] to public authorities[3] by businesses is potentially disclosable to *any* applicant.[4] This includes a huge range of information about the activities of the private sector. The information will have come into the hands of public authorities for a wide variety of reasons, such as through the process of taxation, or as a result of regulation or direct commercial relationships between public and private sectors.

As many commentators have pointed out, the FOIA represents both a threat and an opportunity for the private sector. The threat is that commercially sensitive material will be made available to competitors or the media with potentially adverse consequences. The opportunity is for the private sector to obtain a huge range of commercially valuable information at extremely modest cost.[5]

The threat of public disclosure of private sector confidential commercial material is the most immediate issue. Private bodies provide a wide range of sensitive information to public authorities. The threats of disclosure could include matters such as the following:

- when a business wins a government contract, that competitors will learn the price and contractual levels of performance and might be able to find the results of performance reviews;
- when a business loses a bid, that competitors may be able to discover details of the bid;
- when a private body has been the subject of a regulatory investigation or inquiry, that competitors or the media might be able to discover details.[6]

Private bodies must take steps to protect confidential commercial information from disclosure. It is clear that marking a document confidential will no longer be a guarantee that the public (including business competitors and the media) will be prevented from gaining access to it. It is necessary to consider a wide range of carefully targeted measures to provide as much protection as possible for information which has been or will be given to public authorities.

The opportunities arising from the FOIA are less immediate but potentially of even greater importance. Material held by public authorities provides the private sector with a huge information resource – available at modest cost. Using this resource involves detailed analysis of the kinds of commercially useful information which might be held by public authorities and the making of focused requests aimed at obtaining disclosure of information which can be put to commercial use.

In an examination of the impact of the FOIA on the private sector, this chapter will address the four main areas detailed below:

- *FOIA exemptions and the private sector:* this section deals with the operation of the exemptions in the FOIA which are likely to be relevant when commercially important information is held by public authorities, focusing, in particular, on the confidentiality and commercial interests exemptions in sections 41 and 43 of the FOIA.
- *FOIA requests and the supplier of information:* the position of private bodies in relation to FOIA requests for information which they have supplied to public authorities is considered, in relation to both consultation and express contractual provision.
- *Practical steps for protecting information:* the risks faced by private bodies are examined together with practical steps which might be taken to protect information from disclosure under the FOIA.
- *Making use of the FOIA:* this section covers the opportunities available for private bodies to obtain information under the FOIA.

6.2   FOIA EXEMPTIONS AND THE PRIVATE SECTOR

6.2.1   Introduction

Section 1 of the FOIA creates a general right of access to information held by public authorities. This includes information held by another person on behalf of the authority (FOIA, s.3(2)(*b*)), but it does not, however, include information held by a public authority on behalf of another person (s.3(2)(*a*)). By virtue of section 1(1), any person who requests information (this means 'information recorded in any form', FOIA, s.84) from a public authority is entitled (a) to be informed in writing by the public authority whether it holds information of the description specified in the request; and (b) if it does, to have that information communicated to him.

The above right is, of course, subject to a series of exemptions. Some of these are absolute: if information falls into one of the categories of information which is absolutely exempt from disclosure, then the public authority has no duty to disclose under the FOIA. (It may, however, be entitled to disclose the information voluntarily.) There are seven absolute exemptions:

- section 21: information accessible by other means;
- section 23: information supplied by or relating to bodies dealing with security matters;
- section 32: information contained in court records;
- section 34: where exemption from the duty of disclosure is required to avoid an infringement of parliamentary privilege;
- section 40: where the information constitutes personal data of which the applicant is the data subject;[7]
- section 41: where disclosure of the information would constitute an actionable breach of confidence;
- section 44: where disclosure is prohibited by statute.

Other exemptions are qualified – they are subject to a test of prejudice and/or public interest. If the information falls into any of these categories, a balancing exercise must be undertaken to determine whether, in all the circumstances of the case, the public interest in excluding the duty to confirm or deny, or in maintaining the exemption, outweighs the public interest in disclosing whether or not the public authority holds the information or in communicating the information. There are 16 qualified exemptions:

- section 22: information intended for future publication;
- section 24: information required for the purpose of safeguarding national security;
- section 26: information the disclosure of which would be likely to prejudice defence;
- section 27: information the disclosure of which would be likely to prejudice international relations;
- section 28: information the disclosure of which would be likely to prejudice relations between administrations within the UK;
- section 29: information the disclosure of which would be likely to prejudice the economic interests of the UK or the financial interests of any administration within the UK;
- section 30: information held for the purpose of criminal investigations and proceedings and investigations conducted by public authorities;
- section 31: information the disclosure of which would be likely to prejudice law enforcement;
- section 33: information the disclosure of which would be likely to prejudice the exercise of audit functions;
- section 35: information relating to the formulation of government policy;

- section 36: information the disclosure of which would be likely to prejudice the effective conduct of public affairs (this is sometimes described as hybrid exemption);
- section 37: information relating to communications with Her Majesty and in relation to honours;
- section 38: information the disclosure of which would be likely to prejudice health and safety;
- section 39: information which is subject to disclosure under the EIR;
- section 42: information in relation to which a claim to legal professional privilege could be maintained;
- section 43: information which constitutes a trade secret or the disclosure of which would be likely to prejudice commercial interests.

It should be noted that a request is for information and not documents. This means that one document may contain some pieces of information which are non-exempt, some which are subject to an absolute exemption and some which require the application of a public interest test.

All these exemptions are potentially relevant to the private sector. Commercially sensitive information may be covered by a whole range of possible exemptions. In most cases, however, the interest being protected by the exemption is of the nature of a public one which the public authority is likely to be careful to protect. For example, it seems likely that a public authority holding sensitive information about defence systems will rely on the exemption in section 26. However, in two cases, the exemption is protecting a private interest. In such a case, private bodies will wish to take steps to ensure that such interests are being properly protected by public authorities. The exemptions in question are those concerning confidential information (s.41) and information which constitutes a trade secret or whose disclosure is likely to prejudice commercial interests (s.43). The operation of these two exemptions is likely to be vital to the private sector. They will be considered in the next three sections.

6.2.2 The confidential information exemption[8]

Introduction

The FOIA is designed to protect confidential information which private bodies have supplied to public authorities from disclosure to applicants. Section 40 provides:

(1) Information is exempt information if –

   (a) it was obtained by the public authority from any other person (including another public authority), and

(b) the disclosure of the information to the public (otherwise than under this Act) by the public authority holding it would constitute a breach of confidence actionable by that or any other person.

(2) The duty to confirm or deny does not arise if, or to the extent that, the confirmation or denial that would have to be given to comply with section 1(1)(a) would (apart from this Act) constitute an actionable breach of confidence.

The term 'actionable breach of confidence' is not defined but it appears to mean a claim which would be upheld by the courts (not merely a claim that is arguable).[9] In other words, information is exempt only if it can be shown that a disclosure by the public authority would, in the circumstances – and putting the FOIA to one side – be an actionable breach of confidence. The public authority and, if there are appeals, the Information Commissioner, the Information Tribunal and the High Court will have to decide whether or not an action for breach of confidence by the supplier of the information would have succeeded.

The importing of the common law concept of breach of confidence into the FOIA makes the assessment of the applicability of the section 41 exemption an extremely difficult exercise.[10] The precise limits of breach of confidence are still being explored in case law and public authorities will, inevitably, approach the issue in different ways. As a result, it will be very difficult to predict whether, in a given case, the exemption will protect a particular piece of information. An essential first step is the analysis of the requirements for establishing an actionable breach of confidence as explained in the case law.

Requirements for breach of confidence

There are now four[11] requirements for an actionable breach of confidence:[12]

- the information must have the necessary quality of confidence about it;
- the information must have been imparted in circumstances importing an obligation of confidence;
- there must be an actual or threatened misuse of this information;
- there must be no countervailing public interest favouring disclosure.

In order to satisfy the first requirement, the information must have the necessary quality of confidence. The basic attribute of confidentiality is inaccessibility – the information must not be common knowledge (*Saltman Engineering* v. *Campbell Engineering* (1948) 65 RPC 203, 215). Information which is in the public domain cannot be confidential. In a well-known passage in the *Spycatcher* case in the House of Lords, Lord Goff said:

> . . . the principle of confidentiality only applies to information to the extent that it is confidential. In particular, once it has entered what is usually called the public

domain (which means no more than that the information in question is so generally accessible that, in all the circumstances, it cannot be regarded as confidential) then, as a general rule, the principle of confidentiality can have no application to it.

(*Attorney-General* v. *Guardian Newspapers (No.2)* [1990] 1 AC 109 at 282).

The Court of Appeal has recently offered the following definition of confidential information:

> information will be confidential if it is available to one person (or a group of people) and not generally available to others, provided that the person (or group) who possesses the information does not intend that it should become available to others.
> (*Douglas* v. *Hello! (No.6)* [2005] 3 WLR 881).

Confidentiality does not depend on the establishment of absolute secrecy. This is another way of saying that the question as to whether a particular item of information is in the public domain is not an all or nothing one. As was said in *Franchi* v. *Franchi* [1967] RPC 149, 153: 'It must be a question of degree depending on the particular case, but if relative secrecy remains, the plaintiff can still succeed'.

The concept of relative secrecy has not been fully analysed in the authorities but a number of points are clear, as follows:

- The fact that information is known to a small number of people does not mean that it is no longer confidential (see, e.g. *Franchi* v. *Franchi* [1967] RPC 149, 152).
- Information which is only accessible by carrying out specialist research which requires background knowledge and the expenditure of time may still be confidential.[13] So, in *Attorney-General* v. *Greater Manchester Newspapers, The Times*, 7 December 2001[14] it was held that information which was accessible in a specialist part of a public library to a person with specialist knowledge was not in the public domain.
- The fact that the public can only obtain a particular item of information on the payment of a fee or subject to some other restriction does not mean that the information is confidential.[15]
- Information is not confidential if it is generally available to the public, for example, in the press or from public records.

In relation to the second requirement, the law imposes a duty of confidence whenever a person receives information he knows or ought to know is fairly and reasonably to be regarded as confidential.[16] Although in the vast majority of cases, this duty will arise out of some transaction or relationship between the parties this is not necessary to establish the duty. It is now recognised that this second requirement need not be met if it is plain that the information is confidential (*Douglas* v. *Hello! (No.6)* [2005] 3 WLR 881).

In order to satisfy the third requirement, there must be an actual or threatened use of the information for a purpose other than that for which it was imparted to the confidant (see generally *Coco* v. *AN Clark (Engineers) Ltd* [1969] RPC 41). There is no need for the claimant to show specific detriment (at least when the claim for breach of confidence is brought by a private individual) (*Cornelius* v. *De Taranto* [2001] EMLR 329).

The fourth requirement has been expressed in a number of ways in case law. Whilst considering the *Spycatcher* case Lord Goff said:

> although the basis of the law's protection of confidence is that there is a public interest that confidences should be preserved and protected by the law, nevertheless that public interest may be outweighed by some other countervailing public interest which favours disclosure. This limitation may apply, as the learned judge pointed out, to all types of confidential information. It is this limiting principle which may require a court to carry out a balancing operation, weighing the public interest in maintaining confidence against a countervailing public interest favouring disclosure
>
> (*Attorney-General* v. *Guardian Newspapers (No.2)* [1990] 1 AC 109, 282)

This is sometimes referred to as a public interest defence but might, more properly, be seen as an element of the tort.

The weighing or balancing exercise referred to by Lord Goff takes on different forms in different kinds of cases, considered below:

- In some cases the public interest in disclosure will simply outweigh the public interest in preserving confidentiality. This was once known as the iniquity defence but is now recognised as being more general.
- This principle has been held to justify disclosure of suspected criminal conduct (*Malone* v. *Metropolitan Police Commissioner* [1979] Ch 344), disclosure of fraudulent business practices (*Gartside* v. *Outram* (1857) 26 Ch 113), alleged corruption by a local authority (*Preston Borough Council* v. *McGrath, The Times*, 19 May 2000), dangerous medical practices which endanger the public (*Schering Chemicals Ltd* v. *Falkman Ltd* [1982] 1 QB 1), dangerous medical hazards (*W* v. *Egdell* [1990] 1 Ch 359), information about cults (*Hubbard* v. *Vosper* [1972] 2 QB 84 (in relation to a book about Scientology)) and information concerning the functioning of the Intoximeter device (*Lion Laboratories* v. *Evans* [1985] QB 526 (this case established that the justification of the disclosure of confidential information did not depend on establishing an iniquity)).
- In the case of a disclosure of private information to the media, it is necessary to carry out a balancing exercise between privacy and freedom of expression (*Campbell* v. *MGN* [2004] AC 457).
- In the case of the disclosure of information concerning the expenditure of public money, there are strong freedom of expression arguments in favour of disclosure although the public interest must be assessed on the basis of proportionality considerations arising under Article 10(2) of the European Convention on Human Rights.[17]

- In the case of commercial information, it appears that the public interest in the free flow of commercial information[18] means that commercial and industrial confidentiality only attaches to:

> specific information which an enterprise needs to keep confidential in order to protect its competitive position, not general knowledge of business organisation or methods.
>
> (*R*. v. *Secretary of State for Transport, ex p. Alliance against the Birmingham Northern Relief Road* [1999] Env LR 447, 475)

The fourth requirement means that although section 41 contains an absolute exemption, there is substantial opportunity for the person making the request to raise, and the public authority to consider, public interest arguments in favour of disclosure, particularly where there is any suggestion that the information relates to actual or potential wrongdoing.

The person making the request for disclosure can raise public interest arguments based on government openness but these can only be general arguments and cannot be based on the FOIA itself. This is because the test as to whether information falls within the section 41 exemption is whether a disclosure otherwise than under the FOIA would constitute an actionable breach of confidence. In other words, what must be considered is whether, but for the FOIA, the disclosure of the information would have been a breach of confidence. This appears to have the result that the public interest in open access to information underlying the FOIA is not a relevant consideration and the definition of confidentiality cannot be influenced by the terms of the FOIA itself.[19]

6.2.3 The trade secrets exemption

Trade secrets are protected by a qualified exemption. By section 43(1), information is exempt information if it constitutes a trade secret. The FOIA does not define trade secret and the English courts have not sought to provide any comprehensive definition of the term[20] or to define the precise difference between this and confidential business information. The definition usually cited is that set out in *Lansing Linde Ltd* v. *Kerr* [1991] 1 WLR 251:

> information which, if disclosed to a competitor, would be liable to cause real (or significant) harm to the owner of the secret. I would add first, that it must be information used in a trade or business, and secondly that the owner must limit the dissemination of it or at least not encourage or permit widespread publication.

It is suggested that a useful working definition is that adopted by Australian courts in the freedom of information context:

- something used or usable in trade;
- used for the benefit of the owner's business; and
- not in the public domain (*Searle Australia* v. *Public Interest Advocacy Centre* (1992) 108 ALR 163).

This appears to be wide enough to cover anything which a private body does which is unique to it, which gives it a competitive edge and which is not generally known. It potentially covers not just product-related information but also working practices and approaches.[21]

It is plain that the notion of trade secret includes not only secret formulae for the manufacture of products but also innumerable other pieces of information, such as technical knowledge and experience associated with manufacture of particular goods, and information relating to sales, prices and customers which would be of advantage to competitors.

If a public authority is of the view that information does constitute a trade secret then the duty to disclose and the duty to confirm or deny do not apply if public interest in maintaining the exemption outweighs public interest in disclosing the information (FOIA, s.2(2)(*b*)). The public interest in maintaining this exemption would involve consideration of matters such as the maintenance of intellectual property rights and the need to protect the flow of commercial secrets to public authorities.[22]

It is of the essence of a trade secret that it is confidential: if it is in the public domain it loses its quality of secrecy. It is difficult to see how the conditional exemption in section 43(1) adds anything to the absolute exemption in section 41.

6.2.4 The prejudice to commercial interests exemption[23]

If the disclosure of information is prejudicial to commercial interests then it is covered by a qualified exemption. By section 43(2), information is exempt information if its disclosure 'would, or would be likely to, prejudice the commercial interests of any person (including the public authority holding it)'.

The government expressed the view during parliamentary debate that 'prejudice' means prejudice which is actual, real or of substance.[24] It is suggested that there must be some specific evidence of prejudice, going beyond the general assertion that adverse consequences could follow from disclosure.[25] It should be noted that the commercial interests of the public authority are also covered by this exemption.

If a public authority is of the view that disclosure of the information would be likely to prejudice commercial interests then the duty to disclose and the duty to confirm or deny do not apply if the public interest in maintaining the exemption outweighs the public interest in disclosing the information (FOIA, s.2(2)(*b*)). It has been suggested that, given the private nature of the interest being protected, it is likely to be difficult to show a public interest in maintaining the exemption without bringing in interests already protected under sections 41 and 43(1).[26] It seems likely that this exemption will be of limited practical importance.

6.2.5 Operation of similar exemptions in other jurisdictions

Some indication of the way in which these types of exemption may be operated in practice can be found in cases from other jurisdictions which have similar freedom of information legislation.[27] It should, of course, be borne in mind that the statutory provisions are worded differently in different jurisdictions, but nevertheless, the policy considerations are similar. Provided it is used with care, foreign case law can provide valuable guidance to the approach which the English courts are likely to take to FOIA exemptions designed to protect the commercial interests of the private sector.

The following examples are types of commercial information which have been held to be disclosable under freedom of information legislation in other jurisdictions:

- detailed invoices paid by the government (showing detailed breakdowns of prices and services) – the Irish Information Commissioner accepted that the information might be useful to competitors and could damage the telecommunications company's business but took the view that there was a significant public interest in ensuring that public bodies obtained value for money and in ensuring maximum openness in relation to the use of public funds (*Eircom plc* v. *Department of Agriculture and Food* [2000] ICIE 1);
- total costs figures included in the original tender of a company which successfully tendered for a government contract for aircraft maintenance, disclosed under the Canadian freedom of information legislation (*Proxamis Systems* v. *Minister of Public Works and Government Services (Canada)* (2002) 116 ACWS (3d) 470);
- tender prices in relation to a contract for Irish army vehicles. Although disclosure of the tender prices could prejudice the commercial position of the tenderers, this was outweighed by the advantages in terms of openness and accountability (*Henry Ford and Sons* v. *The Office of Public Works* [1999] IEIC 12);
- the names of bidders for the purchase of public land and the amount of each bid (*Center for Public Integrity* v. *Department of Energy* (25 March 2002, US District Court, DC)).

However, it has been recognised that businesses that are unsuccessful as a result of a tender have different expectations of confidentiality than successful ones, and disclosure of unsuccessful tender prices has been refused (*Raytheon* v. *Department of Navy* 731 F Supp 1097 (1989)). Outside the area of prices, the courts in other jurisdictions have been much more willing to protect the confidentiality of commercial information, such as:

- commercial plans, project proposals and values contained in submissions by companies wishing to participate in US trade missions (*Judicial Watch v. United States Department of Commerce* 83 F Supp 2d 105 (1999));
- descriptive shipping codes which revealed the nature, cost, profit margin and origin of shipments.[28]

6.2.6 Summary

In summary, the effect of these exemptions is that a public authority should not disclose information which has been supplied to it by a private body if:

- such disclosure would constitute a breach of confidence (s.41);
- the information is a trade secret (s.43(1)); or
- disclosure of the information would be likely to prejudice the private body's commercial interests (s.43(2)).

In practice, there is a high degree of overlap between the three exemptions.[29] For example, any detailed financial information supplied by a private body in a procurement context is likely to fall within both section 41 and section 43(2). It is highly likely that any information which will be exempt under section 43 would also be confidential information and, therefore, exempt under section 41 in any event.

Whether or not a particular piece of information falls within one of these exemptions is a fact sensitive question which will depend on matters such as:

- the precise nature of the information: to what extent is it in the public domain, and how commercially sensitive is it?
- the circumstances in which the information was supplied to the public authority: whether, for example, it was made clear at the time that the private body regarded the information as confidential;
- when the information was supplied: other things being equal it is likely that commercial sensitivity will diminish over time and information supplied, say, five or 10 years ago is much less likely to be exempt than information supplied in relation to a current contract;
- whether there are any public interest considerations: for example, in general there is a public interest in knowing how public money is spent – this may mean that public authorities will disclose global figures for sums paid under supply contracts, but not the detailed breakdown of these figures.

6.3   FOIA REQUESTS AND THE SUPPLIER OF INFORMATION

6.3.1   Introduction

The private body which has supplied confidential information or trade secrets to a public authority has no statutory right to be consulted when an applicant asks for disclosure of this information. In other words, in contrast to some other jurisdictions, there are no formal reverse freedom of information procedures: the supplier of information has no formal status under the FOIA. Under the statute, it is the public authority alone which must deal with the complex analysis required to determine whether the section 41 or 43 exemptions apply.

There are, however, two potential ways in which a private body can protect its position in relation to FOIA requests for information which it has supplied to a public authority. These are:

- by making representations to the public authority in a process of consultation with the public authority;
- by reliance on express provision in its contracts with the public authority.

6.3.2   Consultation

Although there is no statutory right for the supplier of information to be consulted before information is disclosed, the Section 45 Code of Practice makes it clear that consultation should take place where the views of the third party may assist the public authority to determine whether an exemption applies or where the public interest lies (para.35).

Paragraph 27 of the Section 45 Code provides that:

> In some cases it will be necessary to consult, directly and individually, with [those who supply public authorities with information] in order to determine whether or not an exemption applies to the information requested, or in order to reach a view on whether the obligations in section 1 of the Act arise in relation to that information. But in a range of other circumstances it will be good practice to do so; for example where a public authority proposes to disclose information relating to third parties, or information which is likely to affect their interests, reasonable steps should, where appropriate, be taken to give them advance notice, or failing that, to draw it to their attention afterwards.

This provision places public authorities under a public law obligation to consult with the suppliers of information. This obligation is enforceable in judicial review proceedings in the Administrative Court.

Where information appears to be confidential it is likely that public authorities will consult the suppliers of information as a matter of course. If a request for information is refused by the public authority the applicant has four levels of appeal: internal, Information Commissioner, Information

Tribunal and High Court. The supplier of information must be aware of the progress of any appeal against a decision to refuse information with a view to intervening if its interests are adversely affected.[30]

If the request for information is accepted by the public authority then the body whose information is released has no right of appeal under the FOIA. It would, however, have two potential remedies:

- an application for judicial review of the public authority's decision to release the information;
- a High Court action for breach of confidence against the public authority.

6.3.3 Contractual provisions

Introduction

Public authorities cannot contract out of the FOIA. They may be obliged to disclose information in response to requests even if they have agreed not to do so (see later in this section). Nevertheless, the terms of contracts with private bodies may be highly relevant to the disclosure decisions which public authorities will have to make.

Many private bodies seek to impose contractual confidentiality obligations on public authorities. The Section 45 Code makes it clear that public authorities must consider these clauses with care before agreeing to them. Paragraph 32 states that:

> When entering into contracts with non-public authority contractors, public authorities may be asked to accept confidentiality clauses, for example to the effect that information relating to the terms of the contract, its value and performance will not be disclosed. Public authorities should carefully consider the compatibility of such terms with their obligations under the Act. It is important that both the public authority and the contractor are aware of the limits placed by the Act on the enforceability of such confidentiality clauses.

However, the Section 45 Code makes it clear that there are circumstances in which the preservation of confidentiality between public authority and contractor is appropriate, and must be maintained, in the public interest (para.33). It suggests that where there is good reason to include non-disclosure provisions in a contract, public authorities should consider the desirability where possible of making express provision in the contract identifying the information which should not be disclosed and the reasons for confidentiality.

Confidentiality clauses

Confidentiality clauses obviously have an important role to play in the freedom of information context. They are particularly helpful if they clearly

165

identify the information that may be exempt. Although information covered by a clause will not automatically attract the protection of section 41, a well-drawn confidentiality clause will be of considerable assistance to the public authority when it is considering an FOIA request.[31]

Clearly, a confidentiality clause will not be compatible with the FOIA if it relates to information which is not, in fact, confidential. In such circumstances, the public authority will be obliged to disclose the information to an applicant (unless, of course, some other exemption applies).

Public authorities will take particular exception to confidentiality clauses which purport to give private bodies a veto over the disclosure of any information, whatever its precise status. Some useful guidance on the way in which section 41 might be approached in practice is provided by a recent decision of the Scottish Information Commissioner. The case of *Sturgeon* v. *Scottish Prison Service* (case 02/04, 24 November 2004) concerned an application by an MSP for details of a contract relating to prison escort services in Scotland. The decision was under the pre-FOIA Code of Practice but the Scottish Information Commissioner made some interesting observations about the future application of the FOIA.

The applicant was provided with a redacted version of the contract. The respondent relied on three exemptions to justify the decision not to release full details of the contract:

- law enforcement and legal proceedings (a provision similar to FOIA, s.31);
- effective management and operations of the public service (a provision similar to FOIA, s.36); and
- commercial confidentiality (a provision similar to FOIA, s.41).

The Information Commissioner was strongly of the view that the first two exemptions had not been made out. The respondent had simply asserted that they were applicable and that the public interest lay in withholding the information, but had not engaged in any proper consideration or analysis.

The confidentiality exemption was less straightforward. The contract contained a clause in the following terms:

> The Parties agree that the Contract may be published by the Authority in accordance with the Authority's policy on access to information. However, the Service Provider shall have the right to require the Authority to remove any sections of the Contract before the Contract is published if the Service Provider considers such sections contain operationally or commercially sensitive information. The Authority shall give the Service Provider at least fourteen days' notice in writing of its intention to publish the Contract following which the Service Provider shall notify the Authority in writing of the sections to be removed in accordance with this Clause 33.1.

As the Information Commissioner pointed out, this effectively gave the service provider a veto over any disclosure. He described this as an 'extraordinarily unbalanced arrangement' (Decision, para.37). However, he took the view that, in the light of the service provider's refusal to allow disclosure, any release of information could found an action for breach of confidence (Decision, para.49).[32]

The Information Commissioner went on to make some comments of potentially general application in relation to confidentiality agreements. He recorded the respondent's position as follows:

> The SPS has justified the inclusion of the clause (giving the company the right to require information to be withheld) on the grounds that their discussion with prospective tenderers and a knowledge of the market in private corrections work has led them to believe that the absence of a similar clause or some other mechanism to prevent disclosure would have an adverse effect on negotiating a best value for money outcome on behalf of taxpayers.
>
> (Decision, para.57)

The Information Commissioner made it clear that he was not impressed with this argument: 'I am bound to say that this is not an argument which I will look favourably upon once the [FOIA (Scotland)] comes into effect' (Decision para.58).

He went on to say:

> My view is that public authorities must resist any suggestion from tenderers that the price of best value is to agree to withhold information which otherwise under freedom of information may be made available. Instead, companies must be made aware that if they expect to be successful in bidding for contracts paid for from the public purse, then they will operate under reasonable terms of scrutiny and openness provided for by the freedom of information legislation.
>
> (Decision, para.60)

He drew attention to the point that, even if (exceptionally) non-disclosure provisions were included in a contract, there should be a proviso that 'information whose disclosure is required on public interest grounds may have to be disclosed regardless of any agreement' (Decision, para.61, relying on the Scottish equivalent of the Section 45 Code).

This decision provides some indication of the approach which is likely to be taken to FOIA requests which may conflict with confidentiality agreements. It confirms the view of many commentators that despite the absolute nature of the section 41 exemption, public interest considerations are likely to have a very important role to play.

In order to provide maximum protection in the context of FOIA applications a confidentiality clause should:

- carefully identify (if necessary by reference to a schedule) the information which is said to be confidential. It is important that the clause is not too widely drawn. The more widely drawn the clause the greater the risk that the public authority will disclose in any event;
- give the reasons why the information is confidential (again, this could be in a schedule) (Section 45 Code, para.34). A provision to this effect is likely to be useful both to the public authority when responding to an FOIA request and to the private body when it is being consulted by the public authority.

It should be noted that the FOIA does not affect the contractual position as between the public authority and a private body. If a public authority agrees that it will not disclose information in a particular category then a disclosure of such information will constitute a breach of contract even if the public authority had an obligation to disclose.[33] The Information Commissioner has pointed out that public authorities risk putting themselves in a dilemma: where they cannot avoid breaching either their statutory or their contractual obligations.[34] This point may be of particular importance in relation to existing contracts with very widely drawn confidentiality clauses.

Consultation provisions

The Section 45 Code suggests that express consultation provisions might be included in public authority contracts (Section 45 Code, para.34). Although there is no English case law on the topic such a clause would plainly be enforceable.[35] The point could be dealt with simply by making it a contractual requirement that the public authority consults with the private body according to an agreed timescale. Bearing in mind the fact that a public authority, in general, has only 20 days to respond to an FOIA request (FOIA, s.10(1)), the timescale must necessarily be a tight one. The following is suggested:

- notification by the public authority of requests within five working days;
- a response by private body within five days;
- notification by the public authority of its disclosure decision within three days.

It may also be useful to include a contractual mechanism for resolving disputes. This could involve, for example, the appointment of an agreed person as adjudicator to decide whether or not a particular exemption applied. However, it is again important to bear in mind the tight timescales laid down by the FOIA, and any adjudication mechanism must be capable of dealing with disputes within a matter of a few days.

If a dispute cannot be resolved by consultation or a dispute resolution mechanism then, in the last resort, it will be necessary to seek an interim injunction to restrain disclosure. This could be sought in the Administrative Court (in the course of an action to challenge the decision to disclose). However, in a section 41 case the most straightforward course will be to seek an injunction in the Chancery Division to restrain a breach of confidence. It should, however, be noted that if the FOIA applicant is a media organisation (or is intending to publish the information sought) the test for granting an injunction will not be the balance of convenience but the higher test of whether the applicant would be likely to succeed at trial.[36]

6.4   PRACTICAL STEPS FOR PROTECTING INFORMATION

6.4.1   Introduction

Against this statutory and contractual background, it is now possible to consider the practical steps which private bodies can take to protect their information from disclosure. It has been suggested that:

> The logical framework for the steps which need to be taken to protect confidential information is based on answers to the following questions:
> - who in the company provides what information to which public authorities?
> - is it clearly recognised which parts of this information are confidential, why and for how long?
> - is confidentiality claimed effectively when or before the information is submitted?
> - has the system been tested to give assurance that the company's information is being treated appropriately by the public authority, and does the public authority have up to date details of who to contact if requests are made for access to it?[37]

These questions can usefully be addressed under two general headings:

- *information audit and other steps:* covering the identification of the commercially sensitive information which has been and is being provided to public authorities, and review of the effectiveness of confidentiality arrangements;
- *co-operation with public authorities:* ranging from informal approaches to ascertain the approach being taken to disclosure to agreed contractual mechanisms for dealing with FOIA issues.

These measures are considered further below.

It should be borne in mind that an essential first step for any private body is to raise awareness amongst its own staff. Staff involved in the provision of information to public authorities, in particular those in sales, marketing and management positions, should be made fully aware of the way in which the FOIA operates and of the detail of the exemptions. They should also be apprised of the way in which information is likely to be handled by public authorities.

6.4.2   Information audit and other steps

Introduction

There are a number of possible steps to be taken in order to protect commercially valuable information from disclosure under the FOIA:

- a review should be conducted of the information given to public authorities in the past;
- clear policies and procedures should be established for the management of information and for claiming confidentiality;
- care should be taken, in particular, to segregate information into that which is confidential and that which is non-confidential, and the basis on which confidentiality is being claimed should be clearly set out.

Past information

Private bodies should begin by reviewing the commercially sensitive material which has been submitted to public authorities in the past. Particular areas of concern include:

- tender documentation;
- supply contracts;
- service performance reports;
- collaborative private/public research results;
- information supplied to regulators – for example, in the context of an investigation or inquiry.

Different public authorities are likely to take different approaches to the disclosure of these types of information. It should, however, be noted that the Office of Government Commerce has produce a draft *Information Disclosure Policy* which deals in detail with information obtained at each stage of the contract process, setting out working assumptions about disclosure.[38]

When material has been identified, an assessment of its continuing sensitivity should be carried out. As a general rule, the older the material the less sensitive it is likely to be. When the sensitive material has been identified then one or more of the following steps can be taken:

- Some material may no longer be needed by the public authority – for example detailed tender documentation where the bid was not successful. In these circumstances, the public authority could be asked to return the material and to confirm that it no longer holds copies.

- Where it is clear that the public authority continues to require the material, it could be asked to provide express confirmation that it recognises that it is confidential (or is a trade secret) and that it would apply the section 41 or section 43(1) exemptions if an FOIA request is made for this information.
- If the material is such that disclosure would cause prejudice to the private body then a written explanation of the prejudice could be given to the public authority and its confirmation could be sought that it would apply the section 43(2) exemption if an FOIA request is made for this information.

In relation to material which is already held, the public authority could be asked to agree a consultation procedure of the type which private sector bodies would wish to include in future contracts (see section 6.3.3, 'Consultation provisions'). Such a procedure would, potentially, be of advantage to both the public authority and the supplier of the information as it would provide informed input into the disclosure decision, and a degree of protection for the public authority against breach of confidence claims.

Future disclosure

In relation to future contracts, an audit can be conducted at the pre-tender stage in order to ascertain what information is likely to be sensitive in the future and how long it is likely to remain sensitive. When this has been done the information could be listed in an appendix to the contract.[39] The Office of Government Commerce has suggested that this approach should be taken and that discussions on this point should be included within general contract negotiations.[40]

A number of practical measures might be taken when preparing and submitting documents to public authorities.

- Sensitive material could be clearly marked and segregated to avoid the risk of inadvertent disclosure. Confidential documents could be watermarked or supplied in a different form or on paper of a different colour from non-confidential ones.
- In some circumstances, documents could be submitted in two versions: one disclosable and one confidential.
- Consideration should be given to whether it is necessary to hand over information to public authorities. In some circumstances, documents could be made available for inspection only.
- Private bodies should avoid providing additional voluntary information to public authorities.
- A record should be kept of all sensitive information supplied, the claims for confidentiality which have been made and the grounds for such claims given to the public authority.

Monitoring

If a private sector body has concerns that a public authority may make inappropriate disclosures of its information then a simple cross-check can be carried out using a third party or surrogate data agency[41] – what has been called the mystery shopper procedure. An FOIA request can be made for the information from the public authority to see whether it will, in fact, be disclosed.

6.4.3 Co-operation with public authorities

It is obviously of central importance for private bodies to establish effective communication with public authorities in relation to FOIA disclosure issues. The aim of such communication is to:

- identify the kinds of information which should be kept from disclosure;
- establish a mechanism for consultation in relation to FOIA requests;
- agree confidentiality provisions and procedures for identifying sensitive material;
- agree policies for document retention and return.

As already discussed, private bodies should take the provisions of the FOIA into account when entering into new contracts with public authorities (see section 6.3.3, 'Confidentiality clauses'). This should be discussed at the tendering stage and properly drawn contracts should contain clear express provision in relation to confidentiality and consultation. Useful general guidance on both is provided by the Office of Government Commerce[42] which has also prepared model confidentiality clauses.[43]

6.5 MAKING USE OF THE FOIA

The FOIA can be an important business tool. A substantial proportion of freedom of information requests in the United States are made by businesses seeking information concerning their competitors and the activities of government. There have been a number of requests by UK businesses aimed at obtaining such information under the FOIA[44] although none have yet been considered by the Information Commissioner or the courts.

A private sector body which believes that public authorities might hold information which is of commercial value to it should carefully target its requests, perhaps engaging the services of a surrogate data agency with experience of making requests. A useful technique is the so-called jigsaw request – seeking by means of a number of co-ordinated requests to identify the missing pieces of the information jigsaw.

The useful information available under the FOIA could include:

- details of previous bids by competitors, including matters such as pricing, personnel levels and competency;
- contract compliance and performance data, which reveal how competitors' contracts have been performed;
- background information relating to procurement decisions and the regulatory climate, for example, working party and consultants' reports;
- clients' evaluation criteria, which show exactly how previous bids have been evaluated and contract decisions reached;
- the health and safety records of competitors or reports of health inspectors.

It should be remembered that not all transactions between the public and private sectors are subject to contracts. Information relating to some of these more informal dealings will generally be less restricted. FOIA requests could be made in relation to subjects such as lobbying of government departments, or hospitality provided by competitors to public authorities.

6.6 CONCLUSION

Although the FOIA has no direct application to the private sector it is likely to have a substantial impact on the activities of any private body which has substantial dealings with the public sector. Suppliers of goods and services to the public sector must carefully consider the information which they have provided, and will in the future provide, in the course of contractual relationships. In the absence of careful protective measures there is a serious risk that sensitive material may become available to competitors and the media. The provisions of the FOIA are complex and, in relation to commercially sensitive material, import complex private law concepts. Public authorities will, inevitably, require careful guidance as to the types of information which they can properly disclose to applicants under the FOIA. Contracts should be drafted to identify the material which is sensitive and the general reasons why it is sensitive. The consultation provisions of the Section 45 Code should be strengthened by express contractual mechanisms.

The FOIA also presents an important opportunity for the private sector to obtain commercially useful information from the public sector. A potentially vast range of material is available in relation to both the activities and approach of government and the activities of commercial rivals.

The issues which the FOIA introduces into the relationship between public and private bodies are complex and difficult and are likely to be the subject of important decisions of the Information Commissioner and the courts over the next few years. Although it is not clear where this journey will take us,[45] nonetheless it is likely to be an interesting and eventful one.

NOTES

1 See, e.g. the headline article in Volume 1, Issue 2 of *Freedom of Information* (**www.foij.com**), 'Private Companies must act on FOI'.

2 The duty to disclose applies to information held at the time when the request was received – it does not matter when the information was provided. In that sense, the FOIA has retrospective effect, covering information supplied to or obtained by public authorities at any time in the past.

3 That is, bodies listed in Sched.1 to the FOIA (to which the Financial Services Authority and a number of others have been added since enactment) and publicly owned companies as defined by s.6. Lord Falconer recently stated that over 100,000 public authorities are subject to the FOIA.

4 Applications can be made by any person and the reason for the application is, in general, irrelevant. Applications can be made anonymously through surrogate data agencies – i.e. agencies which make requests in their own names so that the public authority does not know the identity of the ultimate client.

5 Public authorities can charge for photocopying and postage but will not charge for the costs of locating the information if this is less than £450 (on the basis of £25 per person hour), or £600 in the case of central government.

6 For example, Pernod Ricard have made an FOIA request for information concerning an OFT investigation into Bacardi, see 'Pernod seeks OFT's data on its arch rival Bacardi', *Independent*, 14 June 2005.

7 This is a complex exemption which has some qualified elements and is therefore sometimes described as a hybrid exemption, see Chapter 8 for a full discussion.

8 See generally, Information Commissioner, *Freedom of Information Act Awareness Guidance No.2: Information provided in confidence*.

9 See Lord Falconer, *Hansard* HL, Vol.617, 17 Oct 2000, col.2; see the discussion in P. Coppel, *Information Law* (2004), §25–004.

10 The Office of Government Commerce suggests that if an exemption under s.41 is likely a public authority should seek legal advice, see *FOI (Civil Procurement) Policy and Guidance*, p.6.

11 For the first three, see *Coco* v. *A N Clark (Engineers) Ltd* [1969] RPC 41, 47; *Murray* v. *Yorkshire Fund Managers* [1998] 1 WLR 951; the fourth has traditionally been regarded as a defence (see *Lion Laboratories* v. *Evans* [1985] QB 526) but is now more appropriately treated as an element of the tort, see *Attorney-General* v. *Guardian Newspapers (No.2)* [1990] 1 AC 109, 214 and (in relation to private information), *Campbell* v. *MGN* [2004] 2 AC 457.

12 It should be noted that the position is now slightly different in relation to private information – misuse of private information is developing as a separate tort (see *Campbell* v. *MGN* [2004] 2 AC 457 and *Douglas* v. *Hello! (No.3)* [2005] 4 All ER 128). In the present context breach of confidence is the relevant form of the tort.

13 See the discussion in F. Gurry, *Breach of Confidence* (1984), pp.70–71,

14 See also *R.* v. *Solicitors Complaints Bureau, ex p. Wylde* (6 October 1996), 'information available to the public can nonetheless remain confidential where in practice it is difficult or impractical to obtain information from the public source'.

15 See, e.g. *Melton Medes Ltd* v. *Securities and Investments Board* [1995] Ch 137 (information not confidential if disclosed in court because the transcript can be obtained for a fee).

16 Per Lord Nicholls, *Campbell* v. *MGN* [2004] 2 AC 457, §14: in relation to information about an individual's private life the tort is now better described as 'misuse of private information', see note 12.

17 See the discussion in *London Regional Transport* v. *Mayor of London* [2003] EMLR 4, especially §§57–58 (Sedley LJ).

18 This is the same public interest which renders contracts in restraint of trade void.

19 Contrast the position in Canada, *Air Atonabee* v. *Canada (Minister of Transport)* (1989) 27 CPR (3d) 180, 198, and the United States, *Critical Mass Energy Project* v. *Nuclear Regulatory Commission* (1991) 942 F.2d 799, D.C. Cir, CA, where the definition of confidentiality under freedom of information statutes is less restrictive than at common law.

20 See the discussion of the English law in *Ansell Rubber Co Pty Ltd* v. *Allied Rubber Industries Pty Ltd* [1972] RPC 811.

21 Office of Government Commerce, *FOI (Civil Procurement) Policy and Guidance*, p.9.

22 See the discussion in P. Coppel, *Information Rights* (2000), §25–033.

23 See generally, Information Commissioner, *Freedom of Information Act Awareness Guidance No.5: Commercial Interests*.

24 *Ibid.*, §15–013.

25 This is the approach in Canada, see e.g. *Ottawa Football Club* v. *Canada (Minister of Fitness and Amateur Sports)* [1989] 2 FC 480.

26 See the discussion in P. Coppel, *Information Rights* (2000), §25–037.

27 For a general discussion of the US case law see US Department of Justice, *Freedom of Information Guide and Privacy Act Overview* (May 2004 ed.), pp.268–360, dealing with Exemption 4 trade secrets and commercial or financial information obtained from a person [that is] privileged and confidential.

28 *Trans-Pacific Policing Agreement* v. *United States Customs* (1999) 177 F.3d 1022 D.C. Cir) – the court went on to find that there was a positive obligation to consider whether the information could be segregated.

29 Although, because the first is an absolute exemption it is likely to be the most important in practice.

30 Although there is nothing in the FOIA or the Codes requiring the public authority to keep a consulted information supplier informed of the result of an appeal it is suggested that there would be a public law duty to do so, in order to make consultation rights effective.

31 See generally, Information Commissioner see *Annexe to Awareness Guidance No.5: Public Sector Contracts*, p.3.

32 This conclusion is questionable – a contractual provision cannot exclude the operation of the public interest test in confidentiality cases, see *London Regional Transport* v. *Mayor of London* [2003] EMLR 4.

33 In other words, because no FOIA exemption applied, e.g. even if information is not, in fact, confidential within the meaning of s.41 this will not prevent its disclosure from being a breach of a provision which deems it to be confidential.

34 See Information Commissioner *Annexe to Awareness Guidance No.5: Public Sector Contracts*, p.3.

35 This was accepted by the New Zealand Court of Appeal in *Astra Pharmaceuticals* v. *Pharmaceutical Management Agency Limited* [2000] NZCA 345, para.37.

36 As laid down by s.12(3) of the Human Rights Act 1998, see *Cream Holdings* v. *Banerjee* [2005] 1 AC 253.

37 Amos and Innes, *A Guide for Business to the Freedom of Information Act 2000* (Constitution Unit), 2001.

38 See Office of Government Commerce, *FOI (Civil Procurement) Policy and Guidance*, Annex A, pp.31–35.

39 This approach is suggested by the Information Commissioner; see *Annexe to Awareness Guidance No.5: Public Sector Contracts*, p.2.

40 See Office of Government Commerce, *FOI (Civil Procurement) Policy and Guidance*, p.6.

41 For this term see note 4 above.

42 See Office of Government Commerce, *FOI (Civil Procurement) Policy and Guidance*.

43 See Office of Government Commerce, *Confidentiality and FOIA Provisions*.

44 The most well known being the request by Pernod Ricard mentioned at note 6 above.

45 Readers may wish to keep up to date with developments by taking a subscription to *Freedom of Information* journal – **www.foij.com**.

CHAPTER 7

Freedom of information and the media

Keith Mathieson, Reynolds Porter Chamberlain

7.1   INTRODUCTION

The word 'media' does not appear anywhere in the FOIA. The FOIA does not give the media any kind of preferential treatment. Newspapers, broadcasters and journalists have the same rights of access as everyone else.

Nonetheless, there are at least two good reasons for considering the application of the FOIA to the media.

First, the media collectively will be one of the most frequent, perhaps *the* most frequent, users of the FOIA. Lord Falconer, the Secretary of State for Constitutional Affairs, has said that in the first month of the FOIA's operation about half of the requests made of central government came from people identifying themselves as reporters.[1]

Secondly, the law recognises that the media occupy a unique position in society and enjoy certain special privileges. The courts have recognised the media's function as the eyes and ears of the public and have confirmed the importance of the role discharged by the media, including investigative journalists, in the expression and communication of information.

It would not be going too far to say that if the FOIA fails the media, then it fails the public.

7.2   EXPERIENCE SO FAR

Although the FOIA has, at the time of writing, been in force for only six months, it has already undergone a fairly thorough road test by journalists. Authoritative data concerning the success rates of freedom of information requests by the media is not currently available. Published sources[2] suggest, however, that the experience has been distinctly mixed.

7.3   MEDIA SUCCESSES – INFORMATION OBTAINED

There have been a number of notable instances of the media successfully exercising rights of access to information under the FOIA, as discussed below.

The *Financial Times* (FT) obtained some 300 pages of documents in response to a request of the Treasury for 'details of government studies on the aftermath and lessons to be learnt from Black Wednesday [the day the UK withdrew sterling from the Exchange Rate Mechanism]'. The manner in which the FT's request was handled sheds interesting light on central government's approach to freedom of information requests and will be explored further later in this chapter.

The *Guardian* has published a number of important stories based upon information released pursuant to freedom of information requests. On 23 March 2005 it published for the first time details of EU subsidies received by British farmers and agricultural companies. On 16 March 2005, following 36 simultaneous freedom of information applications, it published national data about the individual mortality rates of cardiac surgeons practising in the NHS. On 4 February 2005, it published a memorandum obtained pursuant to a freedom of information request by a trade union representative showing that the Chief Inspector of Schools had overruled a decision by his own schools inspectors.

Sky TV obtained details of a case in which senior police officers attended a dinner hosted by a man accused of child sex abuse.

Regional newspapers have taken advantage of the FOIA to obtain information from local government and other decentralised bodies as follows:

- The *Eastern Daily Press* obtained and published details of the private finance scheme to build the Norfolk and Norwich University Hospital. The papers had remained secret since 1998.
- The *Birmingham Post* obtained a previously confidential consultant's report which warned that a £1 billion city redevelopment scheme was financially flawed.
- The *Evening Telegraph* in Derbyshire discovered that a total of 17 sites, including a Korean War memorial, had been considered for a controversial arts centre.
- The *Northwich Chronicle* discovered that the local chief fire officer's salary had increased by £33,000 to more than £126,000.
- The *Milford and West Wales Mercury* obtained from its local health trust figures showing that hospital-borne infections were considered a factor in the deaths of six patients at a local hospital last year.
- The *Newark Advertiser* obtained details of a case in which ambulance drivers had disobeyed orders to take a heart patient to a hospital 18 miles

away when they considered a more local hospital was better placed to deal with the patient.

- The *Burton Mail* used information obtained under the FOIA to publish stories about local restaurants and food outlets which had flouted food hygiene standards (*Press Gazette*, 25 March 2005).
- The *Kent Messenger* published details of previously undisclosed foreign trips by local councillors and officials including a trip to a conference in Seattle which cost £20,000 (*Press Gazette*, 25 March 2005).

7.4 MEDIA FAILURES – INFORMATION REFUSED

Of course, by no means all applications by the media for disclosure of information have been successful. Many requests for disclosure have been refused, some of which are highlighted in the following paragraphs.

In a front page article on 2 February 2005 headed 'Is this freedom of information?', the *Independent* listed 10 freedom of information requests it had made together with the answers received:

- *Iraq war: legal advice*

    Q: Please disclose the legal advice given by the Attorney-General on the legality of the war with Iraq.

    A: No. It is exempt as legally privileged information (Attorney-General).

- *Iraq war: legal discussions*

    Q: Please disclose all ministerial and senior military officer correspondence on the subject of the legality of the war/conflict with Iraq.

    A: No. There is no obligation under the Act to disclose this information (Ministry of Defence).

- *Railways*

    Q: Please disclose material concerning Stephen Byers' decision to declare Railtrack insolvent in autumn 2001.

    A: It would not be possible to respond to this request within the appropriate cost limit (Department for Transport).

- *Belmarsh*

    Q: Please disclose all the open evidence against the Belmarsh detainees.

    A: No, this would be too costly. Some of the information might also be exempt (Home Office).

- *Primary schools*

    Q: How many primary schools in England still have outside lavatories?

    A: The department does not hold this information (Department for Education and Skills).

- *Casinos*

    Q: Please provide minutes of meetings held between officials at the Department for Culture, Media and Sport and executives of US gaming companies.

    A: We need extra time to determine if this is in the public interest (DCMS).

- *Smoking*

    Q: Please let us see papers relating to the DTI investigation into BAT.

    A: The department holds such information, [but] the information itself is being withheld as it falls under the exemption in section 44 of the Act (DTI).

- *Olympic bid*

    Q: Please disclose the assessment of the original candidates to head the Olympic bid following interviews that led to the appointment of Barbara Cassani.

    A: No. Interview notes have probably been disposed of (Greater London Authority).

- *Lord Irvine's flat*

    Q: Please disclose documents relating to the redecoration of the Lord Chancellor's residence, including costings, since 1997.

    A: No. The question is almost certain to exceed the appropriate cost limit (Department for Constitutional Affairs).

The *Independent* claimed to have made 70 freedom of information inquiries of which only 10 had been successful. In the newspaper's view, the government's new era of openness more closely resembled a catalogue of obfuscation and evasion.

The *Guardian*, a long-time campaigner for greater access to public information, also requested details of the Attorney-General's advice on the legality of the 2003 invasion of Iraq. Its request was also refused on the ground of being exempt as information subject to legal professional privilege. On 26 January the *Guardian* announced that along with others, it would be appealing the government's refusal to the Information Commissioner.

The *Manchester Evening News* said that, of 15 freedom of information requests put to a variety of local bodies, eight requests had been refused. One refusal concerned a request of Bury Metropolitan Borough Council for details of suspected payments to a teacher suspended over allegations of touching a pupil (refused on the basis that the disclosure would be an actionable breach of confidence). Another concerned a question about the measures in place to deal with a terrorist attack on Manchester (refused on grounds of health and safety as well as confidentiality). Two further requests were refused on grounds of cost.

A newspaper in East Anglia was refused a report held by a district council on car park charges on the basis that its disclosure would harm the effective conduct of public affairs.

The *Observer* asked the Department of Trade and Industry to produce a copy of its 1995 report into Lord Archer's share dealings in Anglia TV, of which his wife had at the time been a director. The request was refused on the basis that 'Information is exempt information if its disclosure by the public authority holding it is prohibited by or under any enactment.' The newspaper remarked that while the FOIA had been hailed as a new charter for investigative journalism, 'it so far seems to have yielded little of real substance' (6 February 2005).

On 19 February 2005, the *Guardian* reported that the Ministry of Defence had refused a request to supply a copy of the staff directory for the Defence Exports Services Organisation (DESO), which is the MoD's arms sales unit. The refusal was surprising as the full directory is apparently given to all commercial organisations and banks who sign up to receive the DESO's publications. The refusal was justified on the basis that civil servants' identities were exempt from disclosure on grounds of data protection, privacy and, in the case of the DESO, that the civil servants could be subject to harassment. The *Guardian* said that it would be asking the Information Commissioner to rule on whether the withholding of public servants' names was permissible.

Similarly, the *Independent*'s request of 10 Downing Street for the names of recipients of Christmas cards from the Prime Minister was refused on the ground that the list was exempt from disclosure as it contained personal information (*Independent*, 8 March 2005).

The *Independent* asked for details of the Rural Affairs Minister's meetings with pro- and anti-foxhunting lobbyists prior to the enactment of the legislation which banned hunting with dogs. The request was refused on the ground that the information relates to the formulation of government policy (*Independent*, 22 February 2005).

A local newspaper, the *Newark Advertiser*, awarded a Sealed Lips award to its local council after the council waited until the final hour of the 20th working day to refuse access to documents about the redevelopment of part of the town centre. The council justified its refusal on grounds of confidentiality owed to a third party. The paper claimed that this could at best justify withholding part only of the information sought.

The in-house lawyer for one national newspaper group has spoken publicly about her group's experience of central government's approach to freedom of information requests.[3] She highlighted the following tendencies:

- unacceptably undifferentiated reasons for refusal, e.g. saying 'all the information falls within one or more of the following exemptions';
- lack of particularity when explaining the basis for reliance on exemptions;
- failure to provide advice and assistance (as required by FOIA, s.15) by, for example, referring the journalist to another government department;
- unexplained redaction of documents;
- identical refusals from different departments in response to slightly different requests, suggesting preprepared and/or centralised responses.

Conversations with editors and journalists suggest that they have low expectations of the FOIA. There is scepticism towards the Prime Minister's and Lord Chancellor's frequent declarations that the FOIA heralds a new era of open government. That scepticism has not been diminished by the government's refusal to disclose the Attorney-General's advice on the legality of war in Iraq, seen by many journalists as an early indication of the effectiveness of the new legislation. There is a strong feeling that the FOIA offers far too many let-outs for public authorities – central government in particular – and that those authorities will not hesitate to take advantage of those let-outs.

7.5   HOW EFFECTIVE IS THE FOIA FOR THE MEDIA?

It would be foolish to base any assessment of the FOIA's effectiveness on the incomplete, and to some extent anecdotal, evidence offered above. A true picture will take time to emerge. Nonetheless, a reading of the FOIA itself reveals serious limitations on its value to the media arising out of:

1. the width and variety of the applicable exemptions;
2. the public interest test;
3. the fee regime;
4. the time for compliance;
5. the cumbersome appeals procedure; and
6. the lack of any specific protection from civil action arising from publication of information released under the FOIA.

This chapter deals with each of these issues in turn and there will also be consideration of the way in which public authorities may seek to limit the impact of freedom of information. Additionally, some practical ways in which the media can make the most of the FOIA are suggested.

7.5.1 The exemptions

The exemptions are explored in detail Chapters 4 and 5. The purpose of mentioning them here is because collectively they constitute the greatest impediment to the flow of information to the media.

It is hard to exaggerate the sheer breadth of the exemptions contained in the FOIA. The scope and complexity of the exemptions are graphically illustrated by the amount of space they take up in the FOIA itself. While the general right of access to information held by public authorities occupies a few lines of one section of the FOIA, the exemptions occupy no fewer than 24 lengthy sections plus an additional section outlining their general effect. The Department for Constitutional Affair's (DCA) guidance notes on the exemptions are voluminous. The guidance notes to section 26 (Defence), for example, which are not untypical, cover 13 printed pages (**www.foi. gov.uk/guidance/exguid/sec26/index.htm**). The *General Guidance on Use of Exemptions* covers 21 printed pages (**www.foi.gov.uk/guidance/exguide/intro/ index.htm**).

The number and scale of the exemptions offer public authorities immense scope for withholding information in response to media, or indeed other, requests. Moreover, the exemptions cover the very areas – crime, immigration, national security, law enforcement, government policy, etc. – in which the media are most interested.

The following categories of exemption are likely to be those most commonly encountered by the media:

Information supplied by, or relating to, bodies dealing with security matters (s.23)

This provision, which confers an absolute exemption, potentially covers a very wide category of information. In the words of the DCA's procedural guidance:

> Insofar as the application of the exemption turns on whether the information 'relates' to the security bodies, it will be capable of covering a wide range of subject matters of a policy, operational or administrative nature. In relation to any particular item of information, it will be a matter of fact as to whether it falls under section 23 or not. However this may sometimes be a question of degree, or indeed be difficult to ascertain if evidence relating to the origin of the information is not available or is inconclusive. Each request that potentially involves sensitive information, has a national security element or relates, even indirectly, to the Security Bodies, will need to be considered on a case by case basis to ensure that a correct response is made. Where there is any doubt, the originator of the document containing the information should be consulted.
> (**www.foi.gov.uk/guidance/exguide/sec23/chap02.htm**)

A further twist is that, if a public authority reveals that it has no information supplied by or relating to a security body, that fact may itself amount to information about the security body:

> Officials should bear in mind that acknowledging that no information supplied by or relating to any of the Security Bodies is held may in itself constitute information about one of the Security Bodies, and that in some circumstances it may be appropriate to apply the 'neither confirm nor deny' provision under section 23(5) *even when no information is held* (emphasis added).
> (**www.foi.gov.uk/guidance/ exguide/sec23/chap03.htm**)

Investigations and proceedings conducted by public authorities (s.30); law enforcement (s.31)

These closely connected categories of exemption are qualified exemptions and are therefore subject to the application of the public interest test.

In outline, section 30 covers (a) information held for the purposes of any investigation conducted by the public authority with a view to criminal proceedings; or (b) information obtained or recorded by the authority for the purposes of various kinds of investigation, including those of a criminal nature, and which relates to the obtaining of information from confidential sources.

As the DCA guidance notes point out, section 30 is plainly directed towards police investigations and also to criminal investigations conducted by a wide variety of other bodies such as HM Revenue and Customs and the Health and Safety Executive (**www.foi.gov.uk/guidance/exguide/sec30/ chap02.htm**). The wording of the section is sufficiently wide to put most information held by police forces and other bodies exercising powers of criminal investigation well beyond reach of the media.

To the extent that section 30 does not apply, section 31 may nevertheless justify the withholding of information.

Section 31 makes exempt information the disclosure of which could prejudice a wide variety of law enforcement interests, including the prevention or detection of crime, the administration of justice, the collection of taxes and the operation of immigration controls. However, the section extends well beyond what most of us would recognise as law enforcement. It makes exempt, for example, information the disclosure of which could prejudice a public authority's investigation into the cause of an accident.

As the guidance note to section 31 makes clear: 'This exemption covers a very large number of aspects of what may generally be termed "law enforcement"' (**www.foi.gov.uk/guidance/exguide/sec31/chap01.htm**).

Between them sections 30 and 31 draw a veil over the work of law enforcement agencies generally.

Court records, etc. (s.32)

Information held by the courts is fully outside the scope of the FOIA because courts are not public authorities for the purposes of the FOIA.

One might nonetheless think that information in court records held by other public authorities might be accessible. Unfortunately this is not the case. Section 32 provides an additional obstacle to media organisations wishing to obtain information deriving from court documents as it provides an absolute exemption for such information if it is held by public authorities only by virtue of being contained in a document filed with a court, served on or by a public authority, or created by a court for the purposes of proceedings in a particular matter. Those proceedings may include inquests and arbitrations.

This wide category of information would cover information contained in all kinds of court documents, including statements of case and witness statements. It is important to note that the exemption applies only where the information is held by the public only by virtue of being contained in a document of the description set out in section 32. If the information is held by virtue of some other reason, the exemption does not apply.

Parliamentary privilege (s.34)

Section 34, which is an absolute exemption, covers an extensive range of parliamentary material.

The DCA's guidance confirms the wide scope of the exemption (**www.foi.gov.uk/guidance/exguide/sec34/chap02.htm**). It says that the exemption is most likely to be relevant to information contained in documents in the following categories:

- committee reports, and drafts thereof;
- memoranda submitted to committees, and drafts thereof;
- internal papers prepared by the Officers of either House directly related to the proceedings of the House or committees (including advice of all kinds to the Speaker or Lord Chancellor or other occupants of the Chair in either House, briefs for the chairmen and other members of committees, and informal notes of deliberative meetings of committees);
- papers prepared by the Libraries of either House, or by other House agencies such as the Parliamentary Office of Science and Technology, either for general dissemination to Members or to assist individual Members, which relate to, or anticipate, debates and other proceedings of the relevant House or its committees, and are intended to assist Members in preparation for such proceedings;
- correspondence between Members, Officers, Ministers and government officials directly related to House proceedings;

- papers relating to investigations by the Parliamentary Commissioner for Standards;
- papers relating to the Registers of Members' Interests;
- bills, amendments and motions, including those in draft, where they originate from Parliament or a Member rather than from Parliamentary Counsel or another government department.

Additionally, the DCA advises public authorities that particular care should be taken in relation to requests for information about or contained in:

- any of the unpublished working papers of a select committee of either House, including factual briefs or briefs of suggested questions prepared by the committee staff for the use of committee chairmen and/or other members, and draft reports: these are most likely to be in the possession of a department as a result of a Minister being, or having been, a member of such a committee;
- any legal advice submitted in confidence by the Law Officers or by the legal branch of any other department to the Speaker, a committee chairman or a committee, or any official of either House (even if s.42 (legal professional privilege) would in any case be likely to apply);
- drafts of motions, bills or amendments, which have not otherwise been published or laid on the Table of either House;
- any unpublished correspondence between Ministers (or departmental officials) on the one hand, and, on the other hand, any member or official of either House, relating specifically to proceedings on any Question, draft bill, motion or amendment, either in the relevant House, or in a committee;
- any correspondence with or relating to the proceedings of the Parliamentary Commissioner for Standards or the Registrar of Members' Interests in the House of Commons.

Personal information (s.40)

Section 40 contains a mixture of absolute and qualified exemptions concerning personal data, the effect of which will be to make exempt a great deal of information of a personal nature.

The relationship between freedom of information and data protection legislation is fully dealt with in Chapter 8. In short, section 40 places serious limitations on the media's ability to obtain personal data about individuals. The general scheme is that personal data about third parties will not be disclosed if disclosure would breach the data protection principles contained in the Data Protection Act (DPA). Even if the data protection principles would not be breached, unless the public interest justifies disclosure, an exemption will still apply if the data subject could not himself access the data under the DPA, or has objected to disclosure under section 10 of the DPA.

It seems likely that the effect of section 40 will be to protect personal privacy at the expense of freedom of information.

Confidential information (s.41)

Section 41 contains an absolute exemption for information the disclosure of which would be an actionable breach of confidence by a third party. A breach of confidence will be actionable not only where a public authority has expressly agreed to keep certain information confidential but also where it has received information in circumstances in which the law has imposed an obligation of confidence even though no specific confidentiality undertaking has been given.

Public authorities receive all kinds of information in confidence and frequently enter into confidentiality agreements, for example in relation to commercial contracts. The scope of the section 41 exemption is accordingly very wide indeed.

As the DCA guidance points out, the application of this exemption is essentially a legal question which calls for the careful interpretation and application of the law of breach of confidence (**www.foi.gov.uk/guidance/exguide/sec41/chap02.htm**). Public authorities are reminded that if the exemption is wrongly applied and information is wrongly disclosed, a public authority may in some circumstances be exposed to legal action for breach of confidence. Public authorities are encouraged to take legal advice on the applicability of this exemption.

In view of the complexity of the law and public authorities' understandable reluctance to expose themselves to the risk of legal action by third parties, it seems highly likely that public authorities will take a cautious view of this exemption, tending to favour non-disclosure. It is likely, therefore, to be difficult – at least in the early days of the FOIA's operation – for journalists to gain access to information which might reasonably be considered to be commercially sensitive.

7.5.2 The public interest test

In relation to information subject to a qualified exemption, the public authority is, of course, required to consider whether the public interest in maintaining the exemption outweighs the public interest in disclosure. As discussed in Chapter 5, this is not a straightforward analysis. Freedom of information law in certain other jurisdictions requires the decision maker to be satisfied, before withholding information, that the disclosure of the information would be contrary to the public interest. Such a test is likely to involve a general assessment of the public interest, enabling a broad range of matters to be considered as part of the balancing exercise. By contrast, the public interest imposed by the FOIA in relation to qualified exemptions is a more focused test. It does not involve consideration of all aspects of the public interest that weigh against disclosure, but instead involves specific considera- tion of the public interest in maintaining the particular exemption under consideration. In other words, the public interest test will vary according to the nature of the exemption: public interest factors favouring disclosure of defence information, for example, will not necessarily be the same factors as those favouring disclosure of economic information.

Helpfully for the media and applicants generally, the DCA's guidance on the public interest test begins as follows:

> The starting point whenever considering the balance of the public interest is that there is a general public interest in disclosure. In contrast, there is no general public interest in public authorities withholding information.
>
> **(www.dca.gov.uk/foi/ guidance/exintro/chap07.htm)**

The guidance invokes Lord Falconer's words during the passage of the legis- lation: 'information must be disclosed except where there is an overriding public interest in keeping specific information confidential' (*Hansard* HL, 14 November 2000, col.143).

As the guidance says, however:

> the assessment of the public interest is a judgment in which policy and legal inter- pretations are both involved to some degree: it is an inherently dynamic concept. The law and practice of the public interest test will develop by decisions made within Government and by the Information Commissioner and the courts.
>
> **(www.dca.gov.uk/foi/guidance/exintro/chap07.htm)**

There will inevitably be concern among media groups that, despite the pro- disclosure rhetoric, public authorities will nonetheless apply the public interest test in a manner that is too restrictive. The DCA's guidance on appli- cation of the public interest test to certain of the exemptions suggests that disclosure will be in the public interest only in exceptional circumstances. For example, in relation to section 24 (national security), the guidance says:

> There is obviously a very strong public interest in safeguarding national security. If non-disclosure is required to safeguard national security, *it is likely to be only in exceptional circumstances* that consideration of other public interest factors will result in disclosure (emphasis added).
>
> **(www.foi.gov.uk/guidance/exguide/sec24/chap03.htm)**

In relation to section 37 (communications with Her Majesty), the guidance says:

It is a fundamental constitutional principle that communications between the Queen and her Ministers and other public bodies are essentially confidential in nature and there is therefore a fundamental public interest in withholding information relating to such communications . . .

Openness in government can increase public trust and engagement. The FOI Act requires the public interest to be balanced before a final decision can be taken about whether or not to disclose. But for the reasons indicated above, *it is likely to be in exceptional circumstances only* that the public interest will come down in favour of disclosure of this information to the extent that it is to any degree confidential or private (emphasis added).

(www.foi.gov.uk/guidance/exguide/sec37/ chap103.htm)

In relation to other qualified exemptions, the advice is less categorical but it still provides much scope for public authorities to resist disclosure. See, for example, the guidance on section 30 (investigations and proceedings conducted by public authorities):

The factors to be taken into account in considering the balance of the public interest will depend upon the circumstances of the particular case. In determining whether the public interest in withholding the information outweighs the public interest in disclosing the information, one or more of the following factors may be of assistance, namely, the extent to which either disclosing or withholding information would:

- promote or diminish the chances of a successful prosecution, bringing future charges, or making arrests;
- promote or diminish the chances of a fair trial taking place;
- be fair, in cases where decisions have been taken not to proceed, to those who have not been prosecuted;
- assist or hamper the gathering of intelligence information from confidential sources (e.g. informants/whistleblowers/calls to Crimestoppers);
- further the interests of justice in the participation of victims, witnesses, informants, suspects or offenders in investigations and proceedings – and either protect or endanger them as they do so;
- assist or impede other on-going or future proceedings;
- prevent or facilitate the commission of crime.

(www.foi.gov.uk/guidance/ exguide/sec30/chap03.htm)

If the public interest test is applied too narrowly, access to information will be unnecessarily and unjustifiably impeded. The responsibility for applying the test properly rests with public authorities in the first instance, but it is up to the media, as collectively the most prominent user group, to satisfy themselves that the test is being applied consistently and conscientiously and to raise with the Information Commissioner all cases in which it appears that public authorities are failing to do so.

7.5.3 The fee regime

Until the DCA clarified matters towards the end of 2004 the media and others had feared that excessive fees would undermine the effectiveness of the FOIA. It has now been announced that freedom of information really means free information. Media experience so far, with a significant number of requests turned down on grounds of cost, suggests that this is an exaggeration.

Any discussion of the FOIA fee regime requires some understanding of the relevant terminology, for which readers are referred to earlier chapters of this book. The appropriate limit of the cost of disclosing information is the limit beyond which a public authority is entitled to refuse a request.

Under current regulations, the appropriate limit is £600 for Parliament and central government (equivalent to 24 working hours) and £450 for other public authorities (equivalent to 18 working hours).[4] In determining the appropriate limit, the only costs to be considered are those of locating, editing and putting the information into a suitable format for disclosure.

If a request would cost less than the appropriate limit, and there is no other basis for refusing the request, the public authority must comply with the request. It is entitled to make a charge but the charge may only relate to the costs of:

- putting the information in the applicant's preferred format, so far as this is reasonably practicable;
- reproducing any document containing the information, e.g. photocopying or printing; and
- postage and other forms of communicating the information.

No staff costs are chargeable, only tangible costs such as copying, postage and fax.

If a request would cost more than the appropriate limit, a public authority is quite simply entitled to refuse to deal with it. This has the ironic consequence that the media may be deprived of access to information on costs grounds in cases of particular size, complexity and importance while getting free access to trivial information on the ground that it is cheap and easy to retrieve.

A public authority is not obliged to comply with a request in a case where the maximum limit is exceeded even if a media organisation is prepared to pay the authority's costs of retrieving the information. Some public authorities may of course choose to comply in these circumstances, in which case they may charge fees representing the total time spent in responding to the request. While it is up to particular public authorities to decide if they wish voluntarily to provide information where the appropriate cost limit is exceeded, they should remember their obligations to provide advice and assistance. In its fees guidance, the DCA advises public authorities planning to turn down a request for reasons of cost or to charge a high fee that they should contact the applicant in advance to discuss whether the scope of the request might be modified so as to bring the costs of responding within the appropriate limit.

There is not much indication so far that public authorities will be willing to provide information in cases where the appropriate cost limit is exceeded. Indeed, the cost limit may well be regarded by some public authorities as a useful means of avoiding disclosure. Some public authorities have already announced that, where requests exceed the appropriate limit, it will be their policy to exercise their legal right not to respond.

7.5.4 The time for compliance

Most journalists do not operate according to the kind of timetable envisaged by the FOIA for compliance with requests for information (20 working days, see FOIA, s.10). In the world of news media, 20 working days is a very long time.

A journalist working on a story is simply not going to be able to wait for a public authority to answer his request. Even if the authority deals with the request promptly, the information is likely to come back weeks after the journalist's copy deadline has passed, particularly if the authority takes advantage of the extension of time permitted by section 10(3) of the FOIA for qualified exemption cases where the public interest needs to be considered. Early indications are that public authorities frequently require further time for this purpose.

If a request is refused, and a review and/or appeal become necessary, the problem is compounded by the additional time taken by that process, explained further below.

It follows that the FOIA may be of limited use to news journalists working against daily or weekly news pressures. Its effectiveness may be restricted to specialist or investigative reporters working to much longer timescales or on specific projects or investigations.

7.5.5 The appeals procedure

If the media are dissatisfied with the manner in which a freedom of information request has been dealt with by a public authority, they can seek to have the matter reviewed. In practice, how effective is the review process likely to be?

In the first instance, a media applicant will normally have to pursue the public authority's own complaints procedures. These will vary between one authority and another. Some public authorities, for example the Foreign Office, have opted for a no frills review; dissatisfied applicants are invited simply to apply for an internal review. Other authorities, for example the Department of Health, have opted for a more formal style of investigation.

It is possible that these complaints procedures may result in the release of information previously withheld. There is, however, a perception by some sections of the media that in most cases this will not happen and that in the majority of cases the need to comply with the public authority's own complaints procedure will simply constitute an unwelcome delay in the prosecution of its appeal to the Information Commissioner.

As fully discussed elsewhere in this book, a person dissatisfied with a public authority's decision has the right, once he or she has exhausted any relevant complaints procedure, to take the matter to the Information Commissioner. From there he or she has the right to appeal to the Information Tribunal and then, on a point of law, to the High Court.

The FOIA does not prescribe time limits for these review steps. In its booklet *Your right to know – how to complain* (obtainable through **www.information commissioner.gov.uk**) the Information Commissioner says that an initial response to a complaint, which will 'outline the steps we will take', will be sent to the complainant within 28 days. It appears that in all cases the Information Commissioner will initially attempt to resolve the matter informally and only if that proves to be impossible will he issue a Decision Notice under section 51. At the same time as issuing a Decision Notice, the Information Commissioner will provide details of the right to appeal to the Information Tribunal.

Further insights into the procedures likely to be employed by the Information Commissioner are to be found in the Memorandum of Understanding (MoU) between the Information Commissioner and government departments (**www.foi.gov.uk/memorandum.pdf**). This provides that where the Information Commissioner receives a complaint, he will send details of the complaint to the relevant department within 10 working days of receipt. The department will then be required to provide all relevant information as quickly as possible and in any event within 20 working days.

The MoU further provides that the Information Commissioner 'will contact both the Department and the Complainant, whenever appropriate, throughout his consideration of a complaint and, in any event, will normally provide progress reports every 28 days.'

In relation to Decision Notices, the MoU says that before issuing a Decision Notice, the Information Commissioner will consider issuing a non-statutory Preliminary Decision Notice and invite the department to comment on it within 28 working days. The Information Commissioner undertakes to consider any such comments before deciding to serve a Decision Notice under section 50.

If the Information Commissioner does decide to issue a Decision Notice, the MoU provides that the Information Commissioner will, following service of the notice on the department and the complainant, give both parties a reasonable period of time to digest the notice before making it publicly available.

It is apparent from the above that any media organisation dissatisfied with a public authority's decision will have to exercise considerable patience in its dealings with both the Information Commissioner and, in all probability, the

Information Tribunal. In many cases, it may be imagined that the media will take the view that by the time any appeal is resolved, the story may no longer be worth publishing and for that reason an appeal is simply not worthwhile.

7.5.6 Civil liability arising from publication of information released under the FOIA

Journalists are, to state the obvious, in the business of publishing information. Under UK law, publication can be a hazardous occupation. The publication of false, defamatory or private information may give rise to various kinds of liability, including defamation, malicious falsehood, misuse of private information, breach of confidence and breach of the Data Protection Act. The publication of someone else's original material may give rise to an action for copyright infringement.

If published material consists of, or is based on, information released under the FOIA, does this afford the media any protection against liability?

The short answer to this question is no: the law does not give any special protection to the publication of information provided under the FOIA.

Section 79 of the FOIA does provide protection to public authorities where information communicated by a public authority contains defamatory matter. In such a case, the publication to the applicant is privileged unless the publication is shown to have been made with malice.

Section 79 plainly does not confer privilege upon the subsequent publication of defamatory matter by the media. The extent, if any, to which privilege will apply to such a publication will depend on an analysis of the nature and occasion of the media publication and the application of the law of defamation to that publication. It appears unlikely that the courts will place much emphasis on the fact that published information was derived from an FOIA request. In assessing the applicability of privilege, the courts will be more concerned with (a) the nature of the information itself; and (b) the circumstances of publication. In relation to *Reynolds* privilege, however, which requires a consideration of the status of the published material, it may sometimes be relevant that the material was considered appropriate for disclosure to the media under FOIA (*Albert Reynolds* v. *Times Newspapers Limited* [2001] 2 AC 127).

In relation to copyright, section 50 of the Copyright, Designs and Patents Act 1988 provides that 'where the doing of a particular act is specifically authorised by an Act of Parliament, whenever passed, then, unless the Act provides otherwise, the doing of that act does not infringe copyright.' While this provision may provide some protection for public authorities who provide copyright material to the media, it offers no protection to any media organisation that may subsequently publish copyright material (though some other defence to copyright infringement may of course apply).

It follows that the media publish information at their own risk. The freedom of information regime confers no protection on them and, while in a great many cases publication will pose little or no risk, that will not be so in all cases. It is important, therefore, that the media understand that the FOIA provides access to information: it does not provide a licence to publish.

7.5.7 Control of communications versus freedom of information

Most governments recognise the importance of controlling the flow of information and, where possible, the message being communicated. How is the desire to control official communications to be reconciled with the liberalisation of access to information inherent in freedom of information legislation?

There is an obvious risk that central government in particular will try to subvert the use of the FOIA by journalists in such a way as to embarrass it. Some indication of the sensitivity of government to the FOIA's potential to generate scoops has been seen in a recent announcement by Lord Falconer in which he made it clear that journalists cannot expect to keep for themselves information generated in response to an FOIA request.

On 29 December 2004 Lord Falconer announced that 'when government departments receive requests under the FOI legislation which are of general public interest, government departments will publish the responses'. On the face of things this is tough to argue against. As Lord Falconer put it:

> It is a fundamental principle of the UK legislation that authorities should treat FOI requests in exactly the same way, regardless of who asks for the information
> . . .
> Some members of the media seem to be taking what might be seen as a more partisan view, arguing that responses to their inquiries made under FOI should be kept secret for them . . .
> I find this response hard to fathom. Surely media organisations, for so long campaigners for open government and for freedom of information, cannot be suggesting that their own commercial interests are of greater importance to them than the public's right to know.
>
> (*Guardian*, 29 December 2004)

Suggesting that the media are more interested in preserving their own scoops than the public's right to know may be clever politics, but it appears to have little to do with furthering the media's role in promoting the FOIA. If the FOIA is to work effectively, it is important that journalists have an interest in using it. If they are to be deprived of stories by the government information machine, there will be little incentive to use the FOIA. As the *Guardian* itself said in response to Lord Falconer's announcement:

> The courts have long recognised that most media companies are commercial organisations as well as providers of news . . . Ferreting information out of Whitehall will often be time-consuming and expensive. Editors will be reluctant to assign reporters

to long and labour-intensive investigations if the fruits of their inquiries will be released to every other journalist before they even have a chance to publish it themselves. This is not a wish to keep information 'secret for journalists'. No editor would object to all the documents being placed in the public domain immediately after publication. It is a simple question of timing. This sly little announcement reeks of Lord Falconer having been nobbled by a Sir Humphrey. He should think again.

(*Guardian*, 30 December 2004)

There are other ways governments can – and do – deal with unwelcome freedom of information requests by journalists. An academic study of the use by journalists of freedom of information legislation in Canada has shown that requests by journalists (and members of opposition parties) are routinely subjected to special vetting procedures (**http://faculty.maxwell.syr.edu/ asroberts/documents/journal/roberts_PA_Spin_2004.pdf**). While there is little evidence to suggest that valid requests by journalists are improperly rejected, there is evidence showing that this so-called 'amber lighting' procedure delays the response to the request, sometimes in such a way as to frustrate the story altogether since by the time the information is released, the matter is no longer newsworthy. Alternatively, the government has in the meantime 'spiked' the story by making a pre-emptive statement of its own or even by taking pre-emptive action such as, in the case of allegations of financial malpractice, organising an independent audit to investigate the matter.

As it happens, there is already some insight into how central government approaches freedom of information requests because the Treasury mistakenly sent to the BBC copies of internal Treasury documents which describe the Treasury's deliberations on a request by the *Financial Times* for information about 'Black Wednesday', the day in 1992 when Sterling withdrew from the European exchange rate mechanism. The BBC duly published the documents on its website (**http://news.bbc.co.uk/1/hi/uk_politics/4250399.stm**).

The documents show that a standard template exists for answering freedom of information requests. The template is divided into three sections as follows:

- Part 1: Detail of question;
- Part 2: Draft reply to questioner;
- Part 3: Background note.

Part 3 is further divided as follows:

- Section A: Summary of information being recommended for disclosure. The template explains that this section should include 'whether or not any exemptions were considered and a brief description as to how the public interest test was applied in the case of qualified exemptions. This is subject to Part C on section 36 exemptions below'.
- Section B: Summary of information not being recommended for disclosure because an exemption applies. The template says: 'Please include an

account of what exemption is being applied, and, in the case of qualified exemptions, how the public interest test was applied. This is subject to Part C on section 36 exemptions below'.

- Section C: Section 36 exemptions. The template says: 'Please highlight whether or not a case for an exemption under section 36 arises. This relates to the effective conduct of public business and needs to be signed off by a Minister. To do this, you should:

    - Attach the paper or specific sections to be considered under Section 36;
    - Attach an analysis of the relevance of the exemption.'

- Section D: Process by which decisions have been reached. The template says: 'To complete this section you should:

    - Give the name of the *Director* who has signed off the draft reply;
    - State that the Information Rights Unit and Treasury Legal Advisers have been consulted;
    - State whether there are any related requests within the Treasury or outside that you know of (for example if it is a round robin);
    - State whether the request has gone to the DCA clearing house.'

The relevant civil servant marked the relevant documents in three colours: pink for those parts he thought should be exempted; yellow for those parts where exemptions were considered but ruled out; and green for those parts which were outside freedom of information exemptions but 'raised potential presentational issues'.

An important reason for disapplying exemptions that might otherwise have applied was the fact that the former Prime Minister, John Major, had discussed aspects of the information sought in his published autobiography. The civil servant noted that certain information – criticism of the French – was potentially embarrassing but there was 'little case' for exempting.

The application of the exemptions in part 3 section B of the document was, broadly, reflected in the draft letter to the *Financial Times* journalist who had requested the information. The exemptions relied on were section 27 (international relations), section 29 (the economy) and section 35 (formulation of government policy). The public interest relied on was partly that disclosure of the information, which included details of conversations with foreign officials, could inhibit the free and frank exchange of information. Further public interest justifications arose from the following considerations:

- references to losses incurred by other central banks as a result of UK borrowings should be excluded as 'it could be more difficult to enter into future financial transactions with these banks and others if they could not be sure if details of their transactions would be made public or not';

- a part of the document which referred to the Bank of England's operational tactics as 'sub-optimal' was redacted on the ground that questioning the way the Bank handled the Black Wednesday episode 'would potentially damage our credibility and effectiveness in future intervention episodes';
- final, but unpublished economic forecasts were withheld even though they were 13 years old. According to the memo: 'Clearly, economic forecasts constitute advice and opinion that are highly important in the setting of economic policy. We recommend that you decide that their disclosure would inhibit the free and frank exchange of views and that disclosure would lower the quality of economic policy advice.'

In relation to the last of the above, the memorandum noted that Treasury lawyers had advised that in view of the age of the forecasts:

> it could be difficult to sustain the argument that they should not be disclosed if [the journalist] complains about their non-disclosure. They consider that the Information Commissioner may well take a different view of the application of the public interest test in this case.

It is revealing that Treasury officials, despite legal advice to the contrary, preferred to recommend non-disclosure. This may suggest that not all civil servants have yet switched their default setting from 'this should be kept quiet unless' to 'this should be published unless'.[5]

It will be noted that the template mentioned provides for special consideration to be given in all cases to the possible applicability of the section 36 exemption (prejudice to effective conduct of public affairs). In the case of the Black Wednesday documents, the civil servant concluded that section 36 was inapplicable because section 35 applied and section 36 can apply only where information is not exempt by virtue of section 35. However, the memorandum still drew attention to a number of comments which were 'potentially excludable' under section 36, though the case was 'not compelling' in view of the passage of time. These comments included such remarks as 'Mrs Thatcher's removal of her veto on ERM membership was determined by her own increasing weakness.' It would surely be hard for even the most freedom of information-resistant of civil servants to argue persuasively that such a comment might have a prejudicial effect on the conduct of public affairs over a decade later.

What is perhaps most striking about the Treasury's approach to the *Financial Times* request is the care it took over how to respond. This may to some extent reflect the fact that the FOIA is still in its infancy and it no doubt also reflects the Treasury's conscientiousness. It would seem also to reflect, though, a certain discomfort with the freedom of information regime and even a degree of fear about what may be let out of the bag and what the media might do with it. Presentational issues are raised more than once and it is interesting that before any documents were released, the former Prime Minister and Chancellor were both supplied with copies of the documents by the Treasury. The purpose of doing so appears to have been to give the former Prime Minister and Chancellor the opportunity to prepare in advance their responses to the inevitable press enquiries. It is difficult to see any objection to that. What would be objectionable would be to provide such documents in order to provide third parties with the opportunity to object to the documents' release. The FOIA contains no provision for third parties to veto the release of information.

The Black Wednesday request was not sent to the DCA clearing house referred to in Part 3 of the template. The clearing house is described in the DCA guidance as 'the central point of expertise, guidance and advice for all FOI requests which raise sensitive issues and have Whitehall-wide implications'. It is envisaged that the clearing house will deal with requests of the following types:

- requests which obviously involve cross-Whitehall issues;
- round robin requests, such as those relating to departmental financial information;
- requests raising difficult issues about the application of sensitive exemptions, for example those relating to the policy-making process (advice to Ministers, ministerial letters), cabinet correspondence or papers, national security or international relations, commercial confidentiality or legal advice;
- requests for which ministerial certificates may have to be considered; and
- particularly difficult mixed requests.

The clearing house is a ready mechanism whereby FOIA requests could be vetted by central government – compare the amber lighting process in Canada referred to above. It is earnestly to be hoped that the clearing house will be used for the purposes envisaged by the guidance and not to subvert the legitimate use of the FOIA by the media.[6]

7.6 PRACTICAL CONSIDERATIONS FOR MEDIA APPLICANTS

- Consider whether the information might be available from other sources before making a freedom of information request: those sources may produce the information more quickly and cheaply.
- Make the request for information as specific as possible.
- If the request is refused as being unclear, or because the public authority claims not to hold the information in question, remind the authority of its duty to provide advice and assistance.
- Anticipate possible objections to the request on grounds of cost. Try to confine the request within reasonable bounds.

- Consider making the request in some other (consenting) person's name if it appears the public authority may treat a request from a media representative differently.
- If the request is refused, consider whether the terms of the refusal satisfy freedom of information requirements. Is it clear why the request has been refused? If not, insist that the authority gives a proper reason for its refusal.
- Be prepared to challenge refusals. Remind public authorities that they have a discretion to provide information despite (a) the availability of exemptions; and (b) the fact that to comply with the request may exceed the appropriate cost limit.
- Where a refusal is based on a qualified exemption, take a critical look at the public interest justification for the refusal. The decision to withhold must be based on sound and specific reasoning.

NOTES

1   Inaugural DCA/Constitution Unit lecture on freedom of information, 25 January 2005: **www.dca.gov.uk/speeches/2005/lc250105.htm**.
2   Information in this section, where not otherwise attributed, is derived from *Media Lawyer*, March 2005.
3   Louise Hayman, address to IBC Media Law Conference, London, 17 March 2005.
4   Freedom of Information and Data Protection (Appropriate Limit and Fees) Regulations 2004, SI 2004/3244.
5   Jack Straw, Home Secretary, HC 7 Dec 1999 340 HC Official Report (6th series) col.174.
6   For further guidance issued by the government on the release of information, see the Working Assumptions for requests for information posted at **www.foi.gov.uk/guidance/index.htm**.

CHAPTER 8

Relationship between freedom of information and data protection

Antony White QC, Matrix Chambers

8.1 INTRODUCTION

At first blush legislation concerned with data protection and legislation concerned with freedom of information would seem to pull in opposite directions. The Data Protection Act 1998 (DPA) is a measure designed to safeguard individual privacy, whereas the Freedom of Information Act 2000 (FOIA) is a measure designed to secure open access to information. They have very different origins and objectives, yet they share a common regulator (the Information Commissioner) and have in many respects a similar enforcement regime (through decisions of the Information Commissioner and the Information Tribunal). They deal with overlapping subject matter so there must of necessity be an interface between the two Acts. This chapter explores the differences between the two pieces of legislation and their interaction.

In this chapter, section 8.2 explains the different origins of the two Acts and the main ways in which they differ. Section 8.3 provides a brief overview of the DPA, drawing attention to the amendments introduced into that Act by the FOIA. Section 8.4 explores the manner in which the two Acts interact through the medium of section 40 of the FOIA.

8.2 LEGISLATIVE HISTORY OF THE TWO ACTS AND THE PRINCIPAL DIFFERENCES

8.2.1 History of the DPA

The political climate of the late 1960s and early 1970s which fostered the introduction of race and sex discrimination legislation also resulted in increasing concern about personal privacy. No fewer than eight Bills concerned with different aspects of privacy were introduced into Parliament during this period but none received government support.[1] In 1972, the government-appointed Committee on Privacy, chaired by Kenneth Younger, produced its report (Cmnd 5012, 1972). The Younger Report set out a series of proposed guiding principles for the use of computers which manipulated personal data. In 1978, the government-appointed Data Protection Committee chaired by Sir Norman Lindop produced a further report recommending data protection legislation (Cmnd 7341, 1978). A government White Paper with proposals for legislation followed in April 1982 (Cmnd 8539, 1982). This led to the enactment of the Data Protection Act 1984. The 1984 Act was novel and complex legislation which had only limited impact.

On 24 October 1995 the European Parliament and the Council of the European Union adopted Directive 95/46/EC on the Protection of Individuals with Regard to the Processing of Personal Data and on the Free Movement of Such Data. As Brooke LJ observed in *Douglas* v. *Hello! Limited* [2001] QB 967 at para.56, this Directive 'was self-avowedly concerned with the protection of an individual's Convention rights to privacy'.[2] This view of the Directive was echoed by Lord Phillips MR giving the judgment of the Court of Appeal in *Campbell* v. *MGN Limited* [2003] QB 633 where he stated at para.73:[3]

> The Directive was a response to the greater ease with which data can be processed and exchanged as a result of advances in information technology. Foremost among its aims is the protection of individuals against prejudice as a consequence of the processing of their personal data, including invasion of their privacy.

The DPA was passed to implement Directive 95/46/EC in domestic law.[4] The DPA largely follows the form of the Directive.[5] It follows that in interpreting the DPA it is appropriate to look to the Directive for assistance. Lord Phillips MR explained in *Campbell* v. *MGN Limited*[6] at para.96:

> The Act should, if possible, be interpreted in a manner that is consistent with the Directive. Furthermore, because the Act has, in large measure, adopted the wording of the Directive, it is not appropriate to look for the precision in the use of language that is usually to be expected from the Parliamentary draftsman. A purposive approach to making sense of the provisions is called for.

In addition to informing its interpretation, the European origin of the DPA means that in applying the DPA the Information Commissioner, the Information Tribunal and the ordinary courts must all be guided by the principle of proportionality. In particular, the principle of proportionality must govern any sanctions applied in the operation of the domestic legislation which implements the Directive.[7] This principle of proportionality is likely to be of particular importance in any situation where competing rights or societal values, enshrined in or recognised by the European Convention on Human Rights (ECHR), are in play – for example competing rights of privacy and freedom of expression,[8] or the competing privacy rights of two different individuals.[9]

8.2.2 History of the FOIA

In contrast to the DPA, the FOIA has no European origin. The European Court of Human Rights has consistently declined to interpret Article 10 of the ECHR as providing a right of access to officially held information.[10] The same approach is evident in domestic cases in which reliance has been placed on Article 10 in an attempt to obtain open access to government inquiries into foot and mouth disease and medical misconduct.[11]

A Freedom of Information Act was a 1997 manifesto commitment of the incoming Labour government. A White Paper (Cm 3818, 1997) proposed radical changes with a view to promoting open government and transparent decision making. Freedom of information legislation had been introduced elsewhere in the common law world at a much earlier stage.[12] The Freedom of Information Bill introduced by the government drew upon experience in other common law jurisdictions, as well as on the values protected by the rights introduced into domestic law by the Human Rights Act 1998. The government recognised that legislation required a delicate balance of the right to know against the right to privacy and confidentiality.[13]

The FOIA was passed on 30 November 2000 but most of its provisions were not brought into force until 1 January 2005. On the day it was brought into force the Secretary of State for Constitutional Affairs, Lord Falconer, stated:

> We have caught up with other countries, and, in many cases, we have overtaken them. We have studied the experience of other countries to enable us to introduce one of the most generous freedom of information regimes in the world. The need to know culture has been replaced by a statutory right to know.

8.2.3 Similarities and differences between the two Acts

The fact that the DPA was passed to implement a Directive, whereas the FOIA has no European origin, might be thought to indicate a significant difference of approach in the two pieces of legislation. However, their difference in origin may not be particularly significant when it comes to their operation and application. Of course the DPA will be interpreted and applied in a manner consistent with the Directive which it implemented, whilst no such interpretative tool is available for the FOIA. However, the European principle of proportionality is rapidly becoming established in the field of English public law,[14] where the FOIA is located, and in the private law of confidentiality,[15] with which the Act is necessarily concerned. In these circumstances the general approach to the interpretation and application of the two Acts is likely to be consistent. A consistent approach to their interpretation and operation is also called for by the fact that the FOIA introduces significant amendments into the DPA, and by the fact that section 40 of the FOIA expressly refers to and incorporates substantial parts of the DPA when dealing with personal information, as explained further below.

Two further important links between the two statutes should be emphasised. First, both Acts have at their core a right of access to information. This is self-evident in the case of the FOIA. In the case of the DPA, the primary right provided to data subjects is the right of access under section 7 of the DPA to personal data of which they are the subject. As Laddie J emphasised in *Johnson* v. *Medical Defence Union Limited* ([2005] WLR 750, para.19), the other rights provided to data subjects under sections 10–14 of the DPA are all dependent upon the data subject being able to discover, through the exercise of the right of access provided by section 7, whether and in what fashion personal data is being processed by a data controller. The right of access under section 7 of the DPA is given special status by section 27(5) of the DPA which provides that it shall have effect 'notwithstanding any enactment or rule of law prohibiting or restricting the disclosure, or authorising the withholding, of information'.[16] Thus both Acts are fundamentally concerned with access to information. Secondly, as already noted, the two Acts share a common enforcement regime, with the Information Commissioner and Information Tribunal established under section 6 of the DPA for the purposes of both Acts.[17]

There are, of course, also significant differences between the two Acts. The most significant of these are as follows:

- The DPA, in general terms, provides for rights against any data controller. A data controller may be a private individual, a small private company, a charitable organisation, a partnership, a large quoted company, or a public authority. By contrast, the FOIA provides rights only against public authorities.
- Under the DPA rights are, in general, provided only to data subjects which are defined as living individuals. By contrast, the rights under the FOIA are conferred upon any person, which will include natural persons, companies, statutory or other bodies, and unincorporated associations.
- The information with which the DPA is concerned is confined, in general, to data relating to a living individual who can be identified from the data. The FOIA is concerned with all kinds of information.
- The DPA is, in general, concerned with information processed on computer equipment or contained in structured filing systems. The FOIA extends to information recorded in any form.[18]

Further, it is apparent that a statute which entitles any person to request from a public authority any information recorded in any form has the potential to interfere with a measure designed to promote informational self-determination[19] for individuals. The manner in which these competing objectives are reconciled through section 40 of the FOIA is considered in section 8.4 below. It is first necessary to have a basic understanding of the operation of the DPA.

8.3 OVERVIEW OF THE DPA

8.3.1 Key concepts

Sections 1–5 of the DPA define a number of key expressions and set the territorial limits of the Act.

Data

Data is defined by section 1(1), as amended by the FOIA 2000, to mean information which:

(a) is being processed by means of equipment operating automatically in response to instructions given for that purpose;
(b) is recorded with the intention that it should be processed by means of such equipment;
(c) is recorded as part of a relevant filing system or with the intention that it should form part of a relevant filing system;
(d) does not fall within paragraph (a), (b) or (c) but forms part of an accessible record as defined by Section 68; or
(e) is recorded information held by a public authority and does not fall within any of paragraphs (a) to (d).

In broad terms, paragraphs (*a*) and (*b*) of this definition of data refer to information which is or is intended to be processed on computer equipment. Paragraph (*c*) of the definition extends to information recorded as part of, or intended to form part of, a relevant filing system. A relevant filing system means any set of information relating to individuals which, although not computerised, is structured either by reference to individuals or by reference to criteria relating to individuals in such a way that specific information relating to a particular individual is readily accessible (s.1(1)). In *Durant* v. *Financial Services Authority* [2003] EWCA Civ 1746; [2004] FSR 28 the Court of Appeal gave a narrow interpretation to the expression 'relevant filing system', concluding at paragraph 48 that 'Parliament intended to apply the Act to manual records only if they are of sufficient sophistication to provide the same or similar ready accessibility as a computerised filing system' (per Auld LJ, with whom Mummery and Buxton LJJ agreed). Paragraph (*d*) of the definition makes specific provision for health records, educational records and the accessibility of public records (see s.68 and Scheds.11 and 12).

Paragraph (*e*) of the definition of data was inserted by the FOIA. It extends the reach of the DPA to cover unstructured manual records held by public authorities (*Smith* v. *Lloyds TSB Bank plc* [2005] EWHC 246 (Ch), Laddie J at para.27), but not other data controllers.

Data subject, personal data and sensitive personal data

Section 1(1) of the DPA also defines a data subject as an individual who is the subject of personal data. Personal data is defined as data which relate to a living individual who can be identified from such data or from such data and other information which is in the possession of, or is likely to come into the possession of, the data controller. It includes any expression of opinion about the individual and any indication of the intentions of the data controller or any other person in respect of the individual.

In *Durant* v. *Financial Services Authority* [2003] EWCA Civ 1746; [2004] FSR 28 the Court of Appeal also gave a narrow interpretation to the expression 'personal data'. It held that the question of whether data referring to an individual amounts to an individual's personal data:

> . . . depends on where it falls in a continuum of relevance or proximity to the data subject as distinct, say, from transactions or matters in which he may have been involved to a greater or lesser degree . . . there are two notions that may be of assistance. The first is whether the information is biographical in a significant sense, that is, going beyond the recording of the putative data subject's involvement in a matter or an event that has no personal connotations, a life event in respect of which his privacy could not be said to be compromised. The second is one of focus. The information should have the putative data subject as its focus rather than some other person with whom he may have been involved or some transaction or event in which he may have figured or have had an interest, for example, as in this case, an investigation into some other persons, or bodies, conduct that he may have instigated. In short, it is information that affects his privacy, whether in his personal or family life, business or professional capacity (per Auld LJ in para.28. Mummery and Buxton LJJ agreed).

Some types of personal data are identified as sensitive personal data in relation to which particularly stringent requirements are applied. Section 2 of the DPA identifies sensitive personal data as personal data in relation to the data subject consisting of information as to:

(a)   his racial or ethnic origin;
(b)   his political opinions;
(c)   his religious beliefs or other beliefs of a similar nature;
(d)   whether he is a member of a trade union;
(e)   his physical or mental health or condition;
(f)   his sexual life;
(g)   the commission or alleged commission by him of any offence; or
(h)   any proceedings for any offence committed or alleged to have been committed by him, the disposal of such proceedings or the sentence of any court in such proceedings.

A noteworthy omission from this list is any reference to finance, taxation or similar matters.

Data controller and data processor

In general the rights provided by the DPA are rights against a data controller, meaning a person who (either alone or jointly or in common with other persons) determines the purposes for which and the manner in which any personal data are, or are to be, processed. A data processor is any person other than an employee of a data controller who processes data on behalf of the data controller.

Processing

The expression 'processing', in relation to information or data, is defined extremely widely. It embraces the obtaining, recording or holding of information or data or the carrying out of any operation or set of operations on the information or data including:

- organisation, adaptation or alteration of the information or data;
- retrieval, consultation or use of the information or data;
- disclosure[20] of the information or data by transmission, dissemination or otherwise making it available; or
- alignment, combination, blocking, erasure or destruction of the information or data.

The special purposes

The special purposes, which are relevant to certain exemptions and remedies, are defined in section 3 of the DPA as any one or more of the following:

(a) the purpose of journalism;
(b) artistic purposes; and
(c) literary purposes.

The data protection principles

Section 4(4) of the DPA sets out the basic statutory duty of all data controllers, which is to comply with the data protection principles in relation to all personal data. The data protection principles are set out in Part I of Schedule 1 to the Act (s.4(1)). Part II of Schedule 1 provides guidance on the interpretation of the data protection principles (s.4(2)). Schedule 2 (which applies to all personal data) and Schedule 3 (which applies only to sensitive personal data) set out conditions applying for the purposes of the first data protection principle (s.4(3)).

The eight data protection principles set out in Part I of Schedule 1 are as follows:

1. Personal data shall be processed fairly and lawfully and, in particular, shall not be processed unless:

   (a) at least one of the conditions in Schedule 2 is met; and
   (b) in the case of sensitive personal data, at least one of the conditions in Schedule 3 is also met.

2. Personal data shall be obtained only for one or more specified and lawful purposes, and shall not be further processed in any matter incompatible with that purpose or those purposes.
3. Personal data shall be adequate, relevant and not excessive in relation to the purpose or purposes for which they are processed.
4. Personal data shall be accurate and, where necessary, kept up to date.
5. Personal data processed for any purpose or purposes shall not be kept for longer than is necessary for that purpose or those purposes.
6. Personal data shall be processed in accordance with the rights of data subjects under the DPA.
7. Appropriate technical and organisational measures shall be taken against unauthorised or unlawful processing of personal data and against accidental loss or destruction of, or damage to, personal data.
8. Personal data shall not be transferred to a country or territory outside the European Economic Area (EEA) unless that country or territory ensures an adequate level of protection for the rights and freedoms of data subjects in relation to the processing of personal data.

Part II of Schedule 1 to the DPA contains important guidance on the interpretation of the first, second, fourth, sixth, seventh and eighth principles. Paragraphs 1 and 2 of Part II of Schedule 1 are of particular significance in that they impose requirements of fairness in relation to the obtaining of data.[21] It is also important to understand how the sixth principle operates. Paragraph 8 of Part II of Schedule 1 provides that a person is to be regarded as contravening the sixth principle only if he contravenes one or more of sections 7, 10, 11, 12 or 12A of the DPA. Such contraventions can only occur if a data subject has invoked the rights provided by those sections.

Schedules 2 and 3 each contain a list of conditions. At least one of the Schedule 2 conditions must be met before the first data protection principle can be satisfied in relation to any processing of personal data. If the personal data in question is sensitive personal data, the first data protection principle will not be satisfied unless, in addition, at least one of the conditions in Schedule 3 is also met.[22]

8.3.2 Territorial limits

Section 5 sets out the territorial limits of the application of the DPA. In general it applies to a data controller in respect of any data only if:

- the data controller is established in the UK[23] and the data are processed in the context of that establishment;[24] or
- the data controller is established neither in the UK nor in any other EEA state but uses equipment in the UK for processing the data otherwise than for the purposes of transit through the UK.

Export of data to a country or territory outside the EEA may contravene the eighth data protection principle. Note, however, that a person does not transfer data to a country or territory outside the EEA simply by loading the data on to an Internet page which may be accessed from other countries.[25]

8.3.3 Part II of the DPA: data subject rights

Part II of the DPA provides for the rights of data subjects and others. These are:

- the right of access to personal data (ss.7–9A);
- the right to prevent processing likely to cause damage or distress (s.10);
- the right to prevent processing for purposes of direct marketing (s.11);
- rights in relation to automated decision taking (s.12);
- rights of data subjects in relation to exempt manual data (s.12A);
- entitlement to compensation for failure to comply with certain requirements (s.13);
- rectification, blocking, erasure and destruction (s.14).

It is a noteworthy feature of the rights provided by sections 7–12A (although not sections 13 or 14) that the first step in enforcing the rights is the service of a written notice by the data subject. In the case of such rights the court can only have a role if such self-help proves ineffective.

Right of access to personal data

As already noted, the right of access to personal data may be seen as the primary right conferred on data subjects by the DPA. The nature of the right was described in the following terms by Laddie J in *Johnson* v. *Medical Defence Union Limited* [2005] 1 WLR 750, paras.20–21:

> . . . Section 7(1)(a) allows the individual to find out whether personal data about him are being processed and Section 7(1)(b) allows him to find out how they are being processed if Section 7(1)(a) is answered in the affirmative. There is no pre-condition that the individual believes or can demonstrate a prima facie case that the data controller has any of his personal data nor is there a pre-condition that, if any such personal data are held, the individual believes or can demonstrate

a prima facie case that they are being processed improperly. Section 7 is not concerned with whether the data controller is acting improperly. Therefore the purpose of these provisions is to make the processing of personal data transparent. Because there is nothing in this to limit applications to cases where the data controller has acted in some way improperly, he may charge a fee for complying with a data request under this section (Section 7(2)(b)). The section also contains provisions which allow the data controller to refuse requests for information, at least in part, where compliance might disclose the identity of third parties.

The right of access to personal data is exercised, in the first instance, by a data subject serving on a data controller a request in writing and, if required, paying a fee up to a prescribed amount (s.7(2)). Unless the data controller reasonably requires further information in order to satisfy himself of the identity of the data subject or in order to locate the information which the data subject seeks, and has informed the data subject of that requirement, the data controller must comply with the request within 40 days (s.7(3), (8) and (10)). Where the data controller cannot comply with the request without disclosing information relating to another individual who can be identified from that information he may be able to refuse to comply with the request, either wholly or in part, if that other person does not consent to the disclosure (ss.7(4)–(6) and 8(7)). A data controller who has previously complied with a request by an individual is not obliged to comply with a subsequent identical or similar request by that individual unless a reasonable interval has elapsed since compliance with the previous request (s.8(3)).

Subject to the matters referred to in the preceding paragraph, a data subject is entitled in response to a request made under section 7(1):

(a) to be informed by any data controller whether personal data of which that individual is the data subject are being processed by or on behalf of that data controller;

(b) if that is the case, to be given by the data controller a description of:

   (i) the personal data of which that individual is the data subject;
   (ii) the purposes for which they are being or are to be processed; and
   (iii) the recipients or classes of recipients to whom they are or may be disclosed;

(c) to have communicated to him in an intelligible form:

   (i) the information constituting any personal data of which that individual is the data subject; and
   (ii) any information available to the data controller as to the source of those data; and

(d) where the processing by automatic means of personal data of which that individual is the data subject for the purpose of evaluating matters relating to him such as, for example, his performance at work, his creditworthiness, his reliability or his conduct, has constituted or is likely to constitute the sole basis for any decision significantly affecting him, to be informed by the data controller of the logic involved in that decision-taking.

Under section 7(9) if a court is satisfied that a data controller has failed to comply with a request in contravention of the provisions of section 7, the court may order him to comply with the request. Under section 15(2) the court may inspect the information which the data subject has requested in order to see whether section 7 has been complied with, but it shall not, unless it determines that question in the data subject's favour, require the information to be disclosed to him. In *Johnson* v. *Medical Defence Union Limited* [2005] 1 WLR 750 Laddie J held that section 15(2) did not prevent a data subject whose application to the court under section 7(9) had failed from obtaining disclosure of documents relating to the processing of his or her personal data in subsequent substantive proceedings for breach of the data protection principles. Section 8 contains supplementary provisions relating to the operation of section 7, and section 9 modifies the operation of section 7 where the data controller is a credit reference agency.

Section 9A, which was introduced by the FOIA, provides an important modification to the operation of section 7 where the information requested by a data subject is unstructured personal data held by a public authority. In such a case the public authority is not obliged to comply with section 7(1) in relation to any unstructured personal data unless the request contains a description of the data (s.9A(2)). Even if the data are described by the data subject in his request, the public authority is not obliged to comply with section 7(1) if it estimates that the cost of complying with the request in relation to those data would exceed the appropriate limit.[26] The effect of section 9A is to increase significantly the right of access to personal data held by public authorities. Whereas other data controllers will only have to search structured manual filing systems which meet the narrow definition of a relevant filing system laid down by the Court of Appeal in *Durant* public authorities will have to conduct much more extensive searches. The burden imposed upon public authorities in relation to unstructured personal data held by them is limited, outside the operation of section 7, by section 33A of the DPA.

Right to prevent processing likely to cause damage or distress

By section 10(1) an individual is entitled by notice in writing to a data controller to require the data controller at the end of a reasonable period to cease, or not to begin, processing any personal data in respect of which he is the data subject, on the ground that, for specified reasons:

(a) the processing of those data or their processing for a particular purpose or in a particular manner is causing or is likely to cause substantial damage or substantial distress to the data subject or another; and

(b) that damage or distress is or would be unwarranted.

The right to serve a notice under section 10(1) does not apply if the data subject has given consent to the processing, or if the processing is necessary for the performance of a contract with the data subject or for the taking of steps at the request of the data subject with a view to entering into a contract, or if the processing is necessary for compliance with any legal obligation of the data controller (other than an obligation imposed by contract), or if the processing is necessary in order to protect the vital interests of the data subject (see s.10(2) and Sched.2, paras.1–4).

The data controller must respond within 21 days of receiving a notice under section 10(1) stating whether he has complied or intends to comply with the request, and if not, why not (s.10(3)). If the data controller fails to comply with the notice, a court may order him to take such steps for complying with it as the court thinks fit (s.10(4)).

Right to prevent processing for purposes of direct marketing

Section 11(1) entitles a data subject to serve a notice in writing on a data controller requiring the latter at the end of a reasonable period to cease, or not to begin, processing personal data for the purposes of direct marketing. If the data controller fails to comply with the notice the court may order him to do so (s.11(2)).

Rights in relation to automated decision taking

Section 12(1) entitles a data subject to serve a notice in writing on a data controller requiring the data controller to ensure that no decision taken by or on behalf of the data controller which significantly affects the data subject is based solely on the processing by automatic means of personal data for the purpose of evaluating matters such as, for example, performance at work, creditworthiness, reliability or conduct. The data controller must respond within 21 days stating whether he intends to comply with the notice (s.12(3)). Certain types of automated decision making are exempt (s.12(4)–(7)). A court may order a data controller who has failed to comply with a notice under section 12(1) to reconsider his decision or take a new decision which is not based solely on automatic processing of personal data (s.12(8)).

Rights of data subjects in relation to exempt manual data

Under section 12A, which applies only until 24 October 2007,[27] a data subject is entitled to serve a notice in writing requiring a data controller to rectify, block, erase or destroy exempt manual data which are inaccurate or incomplete. The expression 'exempt manual data' means manual data held immediately before 24 October 1998 or accessible records within section 68 (s.12A(4)(b) and Sched.8, para.14). If the data controller fails to comply with the notice the court may order him to do so (s.12A(3)). The expressions 'inaccurate' and 'incomplete' are both defined.[28]

Compensation for failure to comply with certain requirements

Section 13 provides that an individual who suffers damage by reason of any contravention by a data controller of any of the requirements within the DPA is entitled to compensation (s.13(1)). An individual who suffers distress as well as damage is entitled to compensation from the data controller for that distress (s.13(2)(*a*)). Even if the individual does not suffer damage, he is entitled to compensation for distress if the contravention of which he complains relates to the processing of personal data for the special purposes (s.13(2)(*b*)). It was under this provision that Morland J awarded damages for distress to Naomi Campbell [2002] EMLR 617.

Rectification, blocking, erasure and destruction

A data subject may apply to the court where personal data of which he or she is the subject is inaccurate, and the court may order the data controller to rectify, block, erase or destroy such data and any expression of opinion which appears to the court to be based on the inaccurate data (s.14(1)). Specific provision is made for situations in which the data controller has obtained the inaccurate data from the data subject or a third party (s.14(2)), and for informing third parties of the court's decision (s.14(3)). The court also has a power, which is not limited to inaccurate data, to require the rectification, blocking, erasure or destruction of data in relation to which there has been a contravention by a data controller of any of the requirements of the DPA which has caused damage to the data subject entitling him to compensation where there is a substantial risk of further contravention (s.14(4)).

8.3.4 Part III – notification and registration requirements

Sections 16–26 of the DPA make provision for the registration of data controllers. Under section 17, processing without prior registration is prohibited. Breach of that prohibition is a criminal offence (see s.21). Supplementary provision is made in relation to fees and other matters.

8.3.5 Part IV – exemptions

The provisions of Part IV of the DPA, read together with Regulations made thereunder and with Schedule 7 to the DPA, provide a number of important exemptions from the requirements of the Act. These provisions are extremely complex and in a work of this nature it is impossible to provide more than a bare summary.

The first point to note is that section 27(1), which introduces the exemptions which follow, explains that the exemptions may relate either to data or to processing. The distinction between exempting data, and exempting the processing of it, was significant in relation to the interpretation of the media exemption in section 32 by the Court of Appeal in *Campbell* v. *MGN Limited* [2003] QB 633.

The various exemptions make either data or processing of different sorts exempt from different provisions or sets of provisions. Throughout Part IV two expressions are used as shorthand formulae for different sets of provisions. These two expressions are:

- 'the subject information provisions', which means (a) the first data protection principle to the extent to which it requires compliance with paragraph 2 of Part II of Schedule 1 (one of the requirements relating to fairness in the obtaining of data from the data subject or other sources); and (b) section 7 (the right of access to personal data);
- 'the non-disclosure provisions', which means (a) the fair and lawful requirement of the first data protection principle; (b) the second, third, fourth and fifth data protection principles; and (c) sections 10 and 14(1) to (3).

Notwithstanding the introduction of these two shorthand formulae, some of the exemptions make data or processing exempt from a wider set of provisions – see for example the exemption in relation to national security under section 28. Other exemptions apply only in relation to section 7 – see for example the exemption in relation to personal data processed for research purposes provided by section 33(4). Other exemptions refer to Part II of the DPA (which includes section 7) without referring specifically to section 7 – see for example section 33A.

The types of data and/or processing of data exempt from some or all of the provisions of the DPA are as follows:

- section 28 – national security;[29]
- section 29 – crime, taxation and unlawful benefit claims;
- section 30 – health, education and social work;[30]
- section 31 – regulatory activity;[31]
- section 32 – journalism literature and art;[32]
- section 33 – research history and statistics;
- section 33A – manual data held by public authorities;[33]
- section 34 – information available to the public by or under any enactment;[34]
- section 35 – disclosure required by law or made in connection with legal proceedings;
- section 35A – parliamentary privilege;
- section 36 – domestic purposes;
- section 37 – miscellaneous exemptions. These are:

- Schedule 7, paragraph 1 – confidential references given by the data controller;
- Schedule 7, paragraph 2 – prejudice to combat effectiveness of the armed forces;
- Schedule 7, paragraph 3 – data processed for the purposes of judicial appointments, the appointment of Queen's Counsel or the conferring of any honour or dignity;
- Schedule 7, paragraph 4 – Crown employment and Crown or ministerial appointments;[35]
- Schedule 7, paragraph 5 – management forecasts and management planning;
- Schedule 7, paragraph 6 – corporate finance information to the extent that information might emerge which would be price sensitive or might damage the economic or financial interests of the United Kingdom;[36]
- Schedule 7, paragraph 7 – negotiations with the data subject;
- Schedule 7, paragraph 8 – examination marks;
- Schedule 7, paragraph 9 – examination scripts;
- Schedule 7, paragraph 10 – legal professional privilege;
- Schedule 7, paragraph 11 – privilege against self-incrimination;

- section 38 – further exemptions made by Order of the Secretary of State. These are:[37]

  - human fertilisation and embryology;
  - adoption records and reports;
  - statement of child's special educational needs;
  - parental orders, records and reports.

8.3.6 Part V – enforcement

Sections 40–50 of the DPA contain provisions relating to enforcement by the Information Commissioner and appeals to the Information Tribunal.

Section 40 empowers the Information Commissioner to serve an Enforcement Notice if satisfied that a data controller has contravened or is contravening any of the data protection principles. An Enforcement Notice may require the data controller to take specified steps or to refrain from any processing of personal data or specified personal data, and may require the data controller to rectify, block, erase or destroy inaccurate data and to notify third parties.

Section 42 provides that any person who believes himself to be directly affected by any processing of personal data may request the Information Commissioner to assess whether it is likely or unlikely that the processing has been or is being carried out in compliance with the DPA. On receiving such a request the Information Commissioner shall decide how to proceed, taking into account, in particular, whether or not the person making the request is entitled to make an application for access to the personal data under section 7. This tends to emphasise again that the right of access under section 7 is the primary right afforded by the DPA.

Section 43 empowers the Information Commissioner to serve an Information Notice on a data controller in order to pursue a request under section 42 or in order to obtain information for the purpose of determining whether the data controller has complied or is complying with the data protection principles. Such an Information Notice will require the data controller to furnish the Information Commissioner with information in such form as may be specified.

Sections 44–46 make specific provision relating to enforcement where the personal data are, or are claimed to be, being processed for the purposes of journalism, art or literature, including provision for service of a Special Information Notice which may be served with a view to ascertaining whether data are being processed only for such purposes.

Section 47 makes a failure to comply with an Enforcement Notice, Information Notice or Special Information Notice a criminal offence.

Sections 48–49 provide that a person served with an Enforcement Notice, an Information Notice or a Special Information Notice may appeal to the Information Tribunal against the Notice. The appeal is a full appeal on facts and law and may involve the fresh exercise of discretion. A further appeal on a point of law lies to the High Court.

Section 50 and Schedule 9 provide the Information Commissioner with powers of entry and inspection, subject to the issue of a warrant by a circuit judge.

8.3.7 Part VI – miscellaneous and general provisions

Sections 51–54 and 58–59 make further provision relating to the functions of the Information Commissioner and the Information Tribunal. Section 51 imposes general duties on the Information Commissioner to promote good practice, disseminate information, give advice and issue Codes of Practice. By Section 52 the Information Commissioner's reports and Codes of Practice must be laid before Parliament. Section 53 gives the Information Commissioner power to grant legal assistance in cases of substantial public importance. Section 54 sets out the Information Commissioner's role in relation to international co-operation and obligations in the area of data protection. Section 58 prevents any enactment or rule of law from prohibiting the provision of information to the Information Commissioner. Section 59 imposes obligations of confidentiality on the Information Commissioner and his staff in relation to information obtained under the DPA or under the FOIA.

Section 55 creates the criminal offence of unlawfully obtaining personal data. It is subject to a public interest defence.

Sections 56–57 render ineffective contractual terms requiring the production by a data subject of certain data which he or she could obtain from a data controller. In essence these provisions are designed to prevent an employer from obliging an employee to disclose criminal records, health records or other details. There is a public interest exemption.

8.4 INTERFACE BETWEEN THE DPA AND THE FOIA: SECTION 40 AND EXEMPTION BY INCORPORATION

8.4.1 The purpose and structure of section 40

Section 40 of the FOIA contains strikingly complex provisions which govern the interaction between that Act and the DPA. The complexity arises as a result of the legislative technique used in section 40 to establish sets of potential exemptions from the duties imposed on a public authority under section 1 of the FOIA by incorporating substantial parts of the DPA.

The key to understanding the provisions of section 40 is to bear in mind three points:

1. Where a living individual makes a request to a public authority for personal data (within the meaning of s.1(1) of the DPA) of which he or she is the data subject (again within the meaning of s.1(1) of the DPA), that request cannot be dealt with by the public authority under the FOIA, but must be dealt with by the public authority under the DPA.

2. Where, however, (a) a living individual requests personal data of which he is not the data subject (i.e. information relating to another living individual); or (b) a request for personal data is made by a person who is not a living individual (e.g. a company, partnership or unincorporated association), the request must be dealt with by the public authority under the FOIA but will be subject to potential exemptions (absolute and/or qualified) arising from the provisions of the DPA which are incorporated by reference into section 40(3) and (4).

3. A separate provision (s.40(5)) provides for exemptions in relation to the public authority's duty to confirm or deny under section 1 of the FOIA. There is an absolute exemption from this duty where a request for personal data is made by a living individual who is the data subject. In other cases the exemption from the duty to confirm or deny is qualified, even if there is an absolute exemption from the duty to communicate the information requested.

Bearing these three points in mind, the provisions of section 40 may be broken down into four component parts as outlined below.

1. Section 40(1) provides:

    Any information to which a request for information relates is exempt information if it constitutes personal data[38] of which the Applicant is the data subject.[39]

    This is the provision which prevents a living individual using the FOIA to request personal data of which he is the data subject from a public authority. It provides for an absolute exemption: section 2(3)(*f*)(i). The policy of the legislation is that such requests are outside the scope of the FOIA and must be pursued under section 7 of the DPA. In furtherance of this policy the definition of data (and hence of personal data) in section 1(1) of the DPA was amended by the FOIA to extend to any recorded information held by a public authority. In practice, in accordance with the requirements of good public administration, any request under the FOIA falling within section 40(1) will be dealt with by the public authority as a data subject access request under section 7 of the DPA. The public authority will be under no duty even to confirm or deny under the FOIA (s.2(1)(*a*) and s.40(5)(*a*)), but will be obliged to respond to the request in accordance with section 7 of the DPA.

2. Section 40(2)–(4) provides as follows:

    (2) Any information to which a request for information relates is also exempt information if:

        (a) it constitutes personal data which do not fall within sub-section (1); and
        (b) either the first or the second condition below is satisfied.

    (3) The first condition is:

        (a) in a case where the information falls within any of the paragraphs (a) to (d) of the definition of 'data' in Section 1(1) of the Data Protection Act 1998, that the disclosure of the information to a member of the public otherwise than under this Act would contravene:

            (i) any of the data protection principles; or
            (ii) section 10 of that Act (right to prevent processing likely to cause damage or distress); and

        (b) in any other case, that the disclosure of the information to a member of the public otherwise than under this Act would contravene any of the data protection principles if the exemptions in section 33A(1) of the Data Protection Act 1998 (which relate to manual data held by public authorities) were disregarded.

    (4) The second condition is that by virtue of any provision of Part IV of the Data Protection Act 1998 the information is exempt from section 7(1)(c) of that Act (data subject's right of access to personal data).

    These subsections contain the absolute and qualified exemptions which may apply where information which constitutes personal data[40] is requested from a public authority by a living individual who is not the data subject (i.e. the person to whom the personal data relates), or by a legal person such as a company, firm or unincorporated association. The operation of these potential exemptions is considered further below. It is, however, worth noting at the outset that where section 40(3)(a)(i) or (b) applies an absolute exemption is conferred (see s.2(3)(f)(ii)), whereas if section 40(3)(a)(ii) or section 40(4) applies, a qualified exemption is conferred.

3. Section 40(5) provides:

> (5) The duty to confirm or deny:
>
> (a) does not arise in relation to information which is (or if it were held by the public authority would be) exempt information by virtue of subsection (1); and
> (b) does not arise in relation to other information if or to the extent that either:
>
> (i) the giving to a member of the public of the confirmation or denial that would have to be given to comply with section 1(1)(a) would (apart from this Act) contravene any of the data protection principles or section 10 of the Data Protection Act 1998 or would do so if the exemptions in section 33A(1) of that Act were disregarded; or
> (ii) by virtue of any provision of Part IV of the Data Protection Act 1998 the information is exempt from section 7(1)(a) of that Act (data subject's right to be informed whether personal data being processed).

This part of section 40 confers a qualified exemption in relation to the duty to confirm or deny. It confers a qualified exemption because section 40(5) is not one of the provisions listed in section 2(3). However, although in general the effect of section 40(5) is to confer qualified exemptions, the combined effect of section 40(5)(a) and section 2(3)(f)(i) is to confer an absolute exemption from the duty to confirm or deny where a request for information falls within section 40(1).

4. Section 40(6) provides:

> (6) In determining for the purposes of this section whether anything done before 24 October 2007 would contravene any of the data protection principles, the exemptions in Part III of Schedule 8 to the Data Protection Act 1998 shall be disregarded.

As noted above, Part III of Schedule 8 to the DPA relates to the processing during the second transitional period[41] of manual data which was held prior to 24 October 1998. The effect of section 40(6) is to reimpose, for the purposes of section 40, restrictions on the processing of such data during the second transitional period which are disapplied by paragraphs 14(2) or 14A of Part III of Schedule 8 to the

DPA. This will not impact on the rights of data subjects under the DPA, but will impact upon the rights of living individuals who are not the data subject or other persons to obtain personal data relating to others under the FOIA.

8.4.2 The operation of subsections 40(2)–(4)

The threshold requirement

The potential exemptions provided by subsections 40(2)–(4) are only engaged where a public authority receives a request for information which constitutes personal data from a living individual who is not the data subject or from a legal person such as a company, firm or unincorporated association. This threshold requirement is set out in section 40(2)(*a*). In simple terms it requires a request for personal data relating to a living individual who is not the person making the request. As was pointed out earlier in this chapter when explaining the operation of the DPA, the expression 'personal data' has been given a narrow interpretation by the Court of Appeal in *Durant* v. *Financial Services Authority* [2004] FSR 28.[42] Information is not personal data simply because it makes reference to a living individual. It must be information which is biographical in a significant sense, which has the data subject as its focus rather than some other person with whom he may have been involved or some transaction or event in which he may have figured or have had an interest (*Durant* v. *Financial Services Authority* [2004] FSR 28, para.28). If the information to which a request relates crosses this threshold, it will be exempt information if either the first condition (set out in s.40(3)), or the second condition (set out in s.40(4)) is satisfied.

The first condition

The first condition, set out in s.40(3) has two limbs, (*a*) and (*b*). Limb (*a*) is itself subdivided into two parts, (i) and (ii). As already noted, part of the first limb (s.40(3)(*a*)(i)) and the second limb (s.40(3)(*b*)) of the first condition confer absolute exemptions. The second part of the first limb (s.40(3)(*a*)(ii)) confers a qualified exemption.

The difference between the two limbs of the first condition is that the first limb (s.40(3)(*a*)) applies where the information requested falls within any of paragraphs (*a*) to (*d*) of the definition of data in section 1(1) of the DPA. This is a reference to the definition of data prior to its amendment by the FOIA. As explained in section 8.3.1, paragraphs (*a*) and (*b*) of the definition of data refer to information which is or is intended to be processed by means of computerised equipment, (*c*) refers to information recorded or to be recorded as part of a relevant filing system,[43] and (*d*) is limited to accessible records defined by section 68 of the DPA.

The second limb of the first condition, contained in section 40(3)(*b*), relates only to information falling within paragraph (*e*) of the definition of data in section 1(1) of the DPA. It will be recalled from section 8.3.1 that paragraph (*e*) of the definition of data was inserted by the FOIA and extended the definition of data to include all recorded information held by a public authority not falling within paragraphs (*a*) to (*d*) of the definition. In essence, paragraph (*e*) covers unstructured manual records held by public authorities.

The first part of the first limb of the first condition (s.40(3)(*a*)(i)), and the second limb of the first condition (s.40(3)(*b*)) confer an absolute exemption (s.2(3)(*f*)(ii)). That absolute exemption applies where the disclosure of the information in question to a member of the public otherwise than under the FOIA would contravene any of the data protection principles. For the purposes of the second limb of condition 1, when assessing whether such disclosure would contravene any of the data protection principles the exemptions contained in section 33A(1) of the DPA are disregarded (s.40(3)(*b*)). For the purposes of the first part of the first limb there is no comparable disapplication of any of the exemptions from the data protection principles contained in the DPA, from which it would appear that the assessment required under that part of the first limb is whether the disclosure to a member of the public would contravene any of the data protection principles insofar as they are applied by the DPA to the kind of data in question.[44]

The data protection principles are contained in Part I of Schedule 1 to the DPA and are set out in section 8.3.1. Guidance on the interpretation of the data protection principles is provided in Part II of Schedule 1 to the DPA. Since the data protection principles cover all aspects of processing of data, and processing is widely defined to include obtaining, recording, holding, organising, adapting, altering, retrieving, consulting or using the data as well as disclosing it, only certain parts of certain of the data protection principles would appear to have an impact on an assessment of whether there should be disclosure of the information in question to a member of the public.

The data protection principles most likely to apply to the first part of the first limb, and to the second limb, of the first condition are those following below.

- *The first data protection principle* – personal data shall be processed fairly and lawfully and, in particular, shall not be processed unless:

    (a)   at least one of the conditions in Schedule 2 is met; and
    (b)   in the case of sensitive personal data, at least one of the conditions in Schedule 3 is also met.

As explained above, the first data protection principle imposes three cumulative requirements: the data must be processed fairly and lawfully; at least one of the conditions in Schedule 2 must be met; and, in the case of sensitive personal data, at least one of the conditions in Schedule 3 must also be met. As to the first of these requirements, although the provisions of section 40 will be capable of rendering disclosure of the information to a member of the public lawful, such disclosure will not be treated as fair unless the data controller complies with paragraph 2 of Part II of Schedule 1 to the DPA. In essence this paragraph requires certain information to be provided to the data subject where the data has been obtained from that data subject, and, with limited exceptions, requires the same information to be provided to the data subject where the information has been obtained from another source. The practical consequence of these requirements is that the disclosure of personal data by a public authority is unlikely to be fair unless the public authority has taken all reasonably practicable steps to contact the data subject and provide him with the requisite information. So far as the second and third requirements of the first data protection principle are concerned, it is thought that conditions 3 and/or 5(b) and/or (d) of Schedule 2 to the DPA will be met, and that, where necessary, condition 7(1)(b) of Schedule 3 to the DPA will be met.[45]

- *The second data protection principle* – personal data shall be obtained only for one or more specified and lawful purposes, and shall not be further processed in any manner incompatible with that purpose or those purposes.

  It is likely that this data protection principle may be contravened by disclosure of information to a member of the public, on the basis that information obtained for one purpose (e.g. medical treatment, social service functions, education or rating) will be disclosed to a stranger in a manner incompatible with that purpose.[46] Paragraph 6 of Part II of Schedule 1 to the DPA suggests that there may be a contravention of the second data protection principle where it is disclosed to a person who intends to use it for a purpose other than that for which the public authority obtained it.

- *The third data protection principle* – personal data shall be adequate, relevant and not excessive in relation to the purpose or purposes for which they are processed.

  The disclosure of irrelevant or excessive personal data would contravene this principle. However, provided a public authority limits the disclosure to that which is relevant and necessary it will not contravene this principle.

- *The sixth data protection principle* – personal data shall be processed in accordance with the rights of data subjects under the DPA.

  This principle might be contravened if the data subject had served a notice on the public authority under section 10 of the DPA requiring it not to disclose personal data relating to him on the ground that such disclosure would be likely to cause the data subject or another person substantial damage or substantial distress which would be unwarranted.

221

- *The eighth data protection principle* – personal data shall not be transferred to a country or territory outside the EEA unless that country or territory ensures an adequate level of protection for the rights and freedoms of data subjects in relation to the processing of personal data.

Although it has been suggested[47] that this principle is unlikely to have particular relevance to disclosure of information under the FOIA, it is not safe to assume this will be the case. In a press release issued on 1 January 2005 to coincide with the coming into force of the FOIA, the Secretary of State for Constitutional Affairs Lord Falconer pointed out that 'anyone, of any nationality, and living anywhere in the world, will be able to make a written request for information'.[48] If a public authority receives a request for personal data from a country outside the EEA, there is no reason why a transfer of the data in question to that person will not be covered by this principle. The public authority must consider the matters listed in paragraph 13 of Part II of Schedule 1 to the DPA when deciding whether an adequate level of protection for the rights and freedoms of data subjects in relation to the processing of personal data exists in the country or territory from which the request was received and to which the data are to be transferred.

The second part of the first limb of the first condition (set out in section 40(3)(*a*)(ii)) confers a qualified exemption where the information falls within paragraphs (*a*) to (*d*) of the definition of data in section 1(1) of the DPA and the disclosure of the information to a member of the public would contravene section 10 of the DPA. Such a contravention could only occur where the data subject had served a notice in writing under section 10(1) of the DPA requiring the data controller to cease, or not to begin, processing of personal data in respect of which he or she is the data subject on the ground that the processing was causing or was likely to cause substantial damage or distress to the data subject or to another which was or would be unwarranted. It should be a simple matter for the public authority to check whether such a written notice has been received from the data subject.

The second condition

The second condition, set out in section 40(4), is that by virtue of any provision of Part IV of the DPA the information is exempt from section 7(1)(*c*) of that Act. This confers a qualified exemption. When considering the provisions of Part IV of the DPA (which are summarised in section 8.3.5) it is important to bear in mind that information is exempt from section 7(1)(*c*) where the relevant exemption refers either (a) to Part II of the DPA (where s.7 appears); or (b) to the subject information provisions (defined in s.27(2) of the DPA) (which includes s.7); or (c) specifically to section 7. The relevant exemptions are:

- section 28 – national security;
- section 29 – crime, taxation and unlawful claims for benefit;
- section 30 – health, education and social work;
- section 31 – regulatory activity;
- section 32 – journalism, literature and art;
- section 33 – personal data processed for research purposes;
- section 35A – parliamentary privilege;
- section 36 – domestic purposes;
- section 37 and the following paragraphs of Schedule 7:

  - (1) confidential references given by the data controller;
  - (2) information prejudicial to the combat effectiveness of the armed forces;
  - (3) judicial appointments/appointments of Queen's Counsel/honours and dignities;
  - (4) Crown employment and Crown or ministerial appointments;
  - (5) management forecasts and management planning;
  - (6) corporate finance;
  - (7) negotiations with the data subject;
  - (8) examination marks;
  - (9) examination scripts;
  - (10) legal professional privilege;
  - (11) privilege against self-incrimination.

- section 38 – miscellaneous exemptions made by Order of the Secretary of State:

  - human fertilisation and embryology;
  - adoption records and reports;
  - statement of child's special educational needs;
  - parental orders, records and reports.

A public authority, even if it acts in perfectly good faith in performing what it understands to be its obligations under the FOIA, may if it errs in its approach to the law, be held liable for infringing the Article 8 (ECHR) rights of affected individuals.[49] It is therefore important for public authorities to adopt a methodical, structured approach to the operation of section 40.

Persons requesting information under the FOIA, and public authorities responding to such requests, may find it helpful to adopt the following step-by-step approach to the operation of section 40.

1. Consider first whether the information to which the request relates constitutes personal data as defined by section 1(1) of the DPA, in the light of the interpretation given to that definition by the Court of Appeal in *Durant* v. *Financial Services Authority* [2004] FSR 28. If the

information requested does not constitute personal data section 40 will not apply.

2. If the information to which the request relates constitutes personal data, consider whether the applicant is the data subject of the data for the purposes of section 1(1) of the DPA. If so, section 40(1) confers an absolute exemption, and there is no obligation on the public authority to confirm or deny or to communicate information. However, the public authority should, consistently with the principles of good public administration, process the request as a subject access request under section 7 of the DPA.

3. If the information to which the request relates constitutes personal data, but the applicant is not the data subject of the data, consider whether either the first part of the first limb of the first condition (set out in s.40(3)(*a*)(i)), or the second limb of the first condition (set out in s.40(3)(*b*)) applies to make the information exempt on the grounds that disclosure of the information to a member of the public otherwise than under the FOIA would contravene any of the data protection principles.

4. If that is not the case, consider whether the second part of the first limb of the first condition (set out in s.40(3)(*a*)(ii)) applies on the grounds that disclosure of the information to a member of the public otherwise than under the FOIA would contravene section 10 of the DPA. If so, consider the usual public interest test required in the case of a qualified exemption.

5. If neither of the limbs of the first condition is satisfied, move on to consider whether the second condition (set out in s.40(4)) is satisfied on the grounds that the information in question is exempt from s.7(1)(*c*) of the DPA by any provision of Part IV of that Act. If so, a qualified exemption is conferred and again the usual public interest balancing exercise must be conducted.

8.5 CONCLUSION

Both the DPA and the FOIA have at their core a right of access to information. In the case of personal biographical information liable to impact on an individual's right of privacy, the individual to whom the information relates has a right of access under the DPA but not under the FOIA. If other individuals or legal persons seek access to information relating to another living individual they must do so under the FOIA, and their right of access to such information is subject to a large number of exceptions which section 40 of the FOIA incorporates by reference from the DPA. In this way, the two Acts seek to balance respect for a living individual's autonomy and dignity by giving access to and control over personal data, against the public interest in the free flow of information held by public authorities with a view to promoting greater participation in the democratic process and transparency of public decision making. The balancing mechanism is complex and a methodical, step-by-step approach to section 40 will be required in practice if the mechanism is to operate in the manner intended by Parliament.

NOTES

1   Zinser, *The United Kingdom Data Protection Act 1998: International Data Transfer and its Legal Implications* [2005] ICCLR 80, note 2.
2   For an analysis of the decision in the *Douglas* case, see *Privacy & Data Protection* (**www.pdpjournal.com**), Vol.5, Issue 6, pp.9–12.
3   In a passage unaffected by the subsequent appeal in that case to the House of Lords: [2004] 2 AC 457.
4   *Douglas* v. *Hello! Limited* [2001] QB 967, para.56; *Campbell* v. *MGN Limited* [2003] QB 633, para.72.
5   *Campbell* v. *MGN Limited* [2003] QB 633, para.72.
6   See note 5.
7   See *Criminal Proceedings Against Lindqvist* [2004] QB 1014, ECJ.
8   As in *Campbell* v. *MGN Limited* [2003] QB 633.
9   As in *W* v. *Westminster City Council* [2005] EWHC 102 (QB), Tugendhat J.
10 See *Leander* v. *Sweden* (1987) 9 EHRR 433, and *Guerra* v. *Italy* (1998) 26 EHRR 357.
11 *R. (Persey)* v. *Secretary of State for Environment etc.* [2003] QB 794, *R. (Howard)* v. *Secretary of State for Health* [2003] QB 830.
12 In the United States there has been a Freedom of Information Act since 1966, and in Australia, Canada and New Zealand freedom of information legislation was enacted in 1982.
13 Hansard, HL (Series 5) Vol.612, Cols.823–30 (20 April 2000).
14 See e.g. Fordham, *Judicial Review Handbook*, 4th ed. (2004) section P58 and cases there discussed.
15 See *Campbell* v. *MGN Limited* [2004] 2 AC 457.
16 Carey in *Data Protection: A Practical Guide to UK and EU Law*, 2nd ed. (2004) observes at p.153 that this gives the subject access right special status.
17 See s.6(1) and (3) of the DPA, as amended by the FOIA.
18 In certain specific situations the FOIA provides that information includes unrecorded information – see e.g. s.51(8).
19 See Professor Ian Lloyd's *Guide to the Data Protection Act 1998*, para.4.6 (1998).
20 In *Campbell* v. *MGN Limited* the Court of Appeal held that publication of data in a newspaper amounted to processing where the information in question had previously been processed on computer equipment: [2003] QB 633, para.106.
21 In *Campbell* v. *MGN Limited* at first instance ([2002] EMLR 30) and again in *Douglas* v. *Hello! Limited (No.3)* [2003] 3 All ER 996 it was held that data obtained by means of surreptitious photography had not been fairly obtained. In each case the Court placed reliance on *R.* v. *Broadcasting Standards Commission ex p. BBC* [2001] QB 885 where the Court of Appeal recognised that surreptitious photography is regarded as objectionable. See also *R.* v. *Loveridge* [2001] EWCA Crim 973.
22 These requirements, together with the requirement of the first data protection principle that personal data shall be processed fairly and lawfully are cumulative: *Campbell* v. *MGN Limited* [2002] EMLR 30, paras.102, 119. The Court of

Appeal did not disagree with this part of the trial judge's analysis – see [2003] QB 633, para.88.

23 See s.5(3). An individual is established in the UK if ordinarily resident here. A company is established in the UK if incorporated under the law of any part of the UK. A partnership or unincorporated association is established in the UK if formed under the law of any part of the UK. Any other person who maintains in the UK an office, branch or agency through which he carries on any activity, or a regular practice, is also established here.

24 This requirement may give rise to difficult questions where data is processed by the UK office of a multinational concern.

25 See *Criminal Proceedings Against Lindqvist* [2004] QB 1014, ECJ at p.1038, paras.69–71.

26 See the Freedom of Information and Data Protection (Appropriate Limit and Fees) Regulations 2004, SI 2004/3244, reg.3. The appropriate limit is £600 in the case of a government department, the House of Commons or House of Lords, the Northern Ireland Assembly or the National Assembly for Wales, or the armed forces of the Crown. In the case of any other public authority the appropriate limit is £450.

27 See Sched.13 – the period between 24 October 2001 and 23 October 2007 is referred to in the DPA as the second transitional period. There were a number of provisions relating to the first transitional period which ended on 23 October 2001. These are no longer of relevance.

28 Inaccurate is defined in s.70(2). Incomplete is defined in s.12A(5).

29 Provision is made for a conclusive ministerial certificate subject to review on administrative law principles by the Information Tribunal. See s.28(2)–(7) and *Baker* v. *Secretary of State for the Home Department* [2001] UKHRR 1275.

30 See the Data Protection (Subject Access Modification) (Health) Order 2000, SI 2000/413; the Data Protection (Subject Access Modification) (Education) Order 2000, SI 2000/414; the Data Protection (Subject Access Modification) (Social Work) Order 2000, SI 2000/415.

31 The definition of relevant regulatory functions in s.31(2) is extremely wide.

32 Under s.32(4)–(5) there is a complete bar on pre-publication injunctive relief. Under s.32(1)–(3) there is a public interest exemption which applies both to pre-publication processing and to publication itself: *Campbell* v. *MGN Limited* [2003] QB 633.

33 In the case of personal data relating to appointments or removals, pay, discipline, superannuation or other personnel matters this exemption extends to all of the provisions in Part II: s.33A(2). In relation to other personal data held in manual form by public authorities the exemption is more limited, and in particular the fourth data protection principle (which requires data to be accurate and up to date) and the sixth data protection principle so far as it relates to the rights conferred by ss.7 and 14, remain in effect: s.33A(1).

34 Such enactments do not include the FOIA. This exclusion is necessary in order to avoid circularity.

35 See the Data Protection (Crown Appointments) Order 2000, SI 2000/416.

36 See the Data Protection (Corporate Finance Exemption) Order 2000, SI 2000/184.

37 See the Data Protection (Miscellaneous Subject Access Exemptions) Order 2000, SI 2000/419.

38 As defined in s.1(1) of the DPA – see s.40(7).

39 As defined in s.1(1) of the DPA – see s.40(7).

40 As defined in s.1(1) of the DPA – see s.40(7).

41 24 October 2001 to 23 October 2007 – see para.1(2) of Part 1 of Sched.8 to the DPA.

42 See also *Smith* v. *Lloyds TSB Bank plc* [2005] EWHC 246 (Ch) at paras.30–31.

43 See section 8.3.1 – in *Durant* v. *Financial Services Authority* [2004] FSR 28 the Court of Appeal gave a narrow interpretation to the expression 'relevant filing system', limiting it to structured filing systems with their own internal indexation or search facility, i.e. manual records only if they are of sufficient sophistication to provide the same or similar ready accessibility as a computerised filing system (para.48).

44 Coppel, *Information Rights*, (2004) at p.627 points out that this has the odd consequence that the applicability of one of the exemptions under the DPA makes it easier to obtain disclosure under the FOIA. This is indeed surprising – the exemptions under the DPA are largely designed to hold the balance between the rights of the data subject and the rights of and burden upon data controllers. It is not self-evident that the same exemptions are apt where access to personal data held by a public authority is claimed by someone who is not the data subject.

45 For a contrary view see Coppel, *Information Rights*, pp.631–2.

46 This appears to be the view of Wadham and Griffiths in *Blackstone's Guide to the Freedom of Information Act 2000*, 2nd ed., (2005) para.10.4.3. A contrary view is adopted by Coppel, *Information Rights*, p.629 where it is suggested that the prohibition on further processing contained in the second half of the second data protection principle is directed to voluntary disclosure rather than disclosure in accordance with a statutory obligation. No authority is cited for this assertion which receives no support from Article 6(1)(*b*) of the Directive upon which the second data protection principle is based.

47 Coppel, *Information Rights*, p.630.

48 Department for Constitutional Affairs Press Release, 1 January 2005.

49 Compare *R. (Robertson)* v. *City of Wakefield Metropolitan Council* [2002] QB 1052 and *W* v. *Westminster City Council* [2005] EWHC 102 (QB).

CHAPTER 9

The Environmental Information Regulations 2004

Professor Brian Jones, Christopher Rees and
Anna-Marie Harty, Herbert Smith

9.1   INTRODUCTION

Although the main focus of this book is the rights of access to information
provided by the Freedom of Information Act 2000 (FOIA), it is important
for readers to note that where the information requested by an applicant is
environmental information the provisions of the FOIA do not apply.

Instead there exists a parallel legal regime of access to information under
the Environmental Information Regulations 2004 (EIR) (SI 2004/3391). As
will become apparent in this chapter, the access regime under the EIR differs
in significant ways from that contained in the FOIA.

The EIR came into operation on 1 January 2005, implementing EU
Council Directive 2003/4 on Public Access to Environmental Information.
They supersede earlier Regulations dating from 1992,[1] themselves imple-
menting an earlier EU measure: Directive 90/313 on Freedom of Access to
Information on the Environment.

In the context of environmental information, rights of access to information are not new (in contrast to rights of access to non-environmental information under the FOIA) and UK and ECJ case law under the earlier
Regulations and Directive remains relevant to the interpretation of the
recently revised rules.

The purpose of this chapter is to describe the main features of the EIR,
and to draw attention to the more important differences between rights of
access to environmental information under the rights of access to other kinds
of information under the FOIA.

9.2   WHY A SEPARATE AND DIFFERENT REGIME?

In relation to rights of access to environmental information the UK is subject
to particular obligations under international law, namely the 1998 Aarhus

Convention on Access to Information, Public Participation and Access to Justice in Environmental Matters;[2] and also under EU law – Council Directive 2003/4 on Public Access to Environmental Information.

Rather than draft the FOIA so that access to all information would be governed by rules equivalent to the Aarhus/EU rules which only apply to environmental information, the approach adopted by the government was to create the two separate legal regimes indicated above.

9.2.1 Mutual exclusivity of the two regimes

In any case where a request for information involves or includes a request for information which is environmental information the rules set out in the EIR will apply to the application. Insofar as the requested information may also include information which is not environmental information the rules within the FOIA will apply to that other information.[3]

9.2.2 How do the two regimes compare?

As the discussion which follows will demonstrate there are many differences between the two regimes. Some provisions within the respective regimes which may seem broadly similar differ quite significantly in terms of detail; and on certain matters the rules differ starkly in content.[4] The purpose of this chapter is to give a clear message that will resonate, bell like, in the minds of our readers long after they have turned this page. The message is: 'never assume that the answer to any particular question will be the same under each of the two regimes'.

Although this basic message will become more apparent as this chapter progresses it may be useful at this point to flag two of the key differences between the two regimes as follows.

- The bodies subject to obligations to disclose information differ significantly as between the two regimes. In particular there are entities not subject to FOIA obligations which do have duties of disclosure of information under the EIR.
- The exceptions to the duty to disclose are broadly similar within the two regimes but are by no means identical. It is essential to look closely at the detailed formulation of each exemption within each regime. In general, however, it may be said that exemptions from the duty to disclose information are more narrowly drawn under the EIR than under the FOIA.[5]

At the same time as stressing significant differences between the FOIA and the EIR it should be noted that some attempt has been made to marry up the procedural and enforcement aspects of the two regimes. So, for example, time periods for disclosure are broadly the same, and jurisdiction in relation to disputes has been conferred in relation to both regimes on the Information Commissioner and the Information Tribunal.

9.2.3   Breadth of the definition of environmental information

The key concept of environmental information is a notably broad one. It extends beyond what might commonly be thought to be environmental information.

Given that different rules about rights of access apply depending on whether the information is, or is not, environmental information the breadth of the definition of this concept may provide a trap for the unwary. As, generally speaking, the EIR provide broader access rights than the FOIA it would seem advisable, wherever a credible case can be made out, for an application for disclosure to be couched in terms of an application under the EIR. Strictly speaking it does not matter whether any request for information makes reference to either the FOIA or the EIR and it is similarly irrelevant whether the request makes reference in the circumstances to the correct one of those two regimes. However, in a credible case there can be no harm in directing the public authority's mind to the EIR; particularly, where the public authority may be one which more usually is asked for information which is not environmental information, and which may accordingly tend to think (incorrectly) of the FOIA as the sole legal regime relating to rights of access to information.

The breadth of the concept of environmental information can best be demonstrated by setting out the definition within the EIR.

This provides that environmental information means:

any information in written, visual, aural, electronic or any other material form on

(a)   the state of the elements of the environment, such as air and atmosphere, water, soil, land,[6] landscape and natural sites including wetlands, coastal and marine areas, biological diversity and its components, including genetically modified organisms, and the interaction among these elements;

(b)   factors, such as substances, energy, noise, radiation or waste, including radioactive waste, emissions, discharges and other releases into the environment, affecting or likely to affect the elements of the environment referred to in (a);[7]

(c)   measures (including administrative measures), such as policies, legislation, plans, programmes, environmental agreements, and activities affecting or likely to affect the elements and factors referred to in (a) and (b) as well as measures or activities designed to protect those elements;

(d)   reports on the implementation of environmental legislation;

(e)   cost-benefit and other economic analyses and assumptions used within the framework of the measures and activities referred to in (c);

(f)   the state of human health and safety, including the contamination of the food chain, where relevant, conditions of human life, cultural sites and built structures inasmuch as they are or may be affected by the state of the elements of the environment referred to in (a) or, through those elements, by any of the matters referred to in (b) and (c).[8]

It seems likely that the scope of this definition will be tested early. As indicated above, if information is environmental information it may be requested of a broader range of bodies than if not environmental information; and if information is environmental information it may be that exemptions which would apply to other kinds of information (so as to protect from disclosure) will not apply. Hence the precise boundary between environmental information and other information will assume some critical importance.

9.2.4 Bodies subject to obligations under the EIR

The definition of public authority under the EIR is based closely on the wording of the EU Directive (see Art.2(2)), which in turn reflects the definition contained in the Aarhus Convention (see Art.2(2)).

Whereas the FOIA has adopted an approach of listing by name the bodies to which the Act's obligations apply, the approach as regards environmental information has been to describe entities not by name but by reference to certain characteristics.

Although the concept of public authority is significantly broader in relation to environmental information than under the FOIA, there is at present a good deal of uncertainty – indeed there are marked differences of opinion – as regards just how broadly the definition within the EIR should be interpreted.

The present differences of view as to the breadth of the concept of public authority under the EIR can probably be explained, at least in part, by examination of the legislative history of the EU Directive which those Regulations purport to implement.

In summary, the legislative history shows that within the European Commission's initial Proposal for the Directive the definition of public authority was substantially broader in scope than that which emerged in the final text of the adopted Directive.

In the initial Proposal the definition suggested was:

Public authority shall mean:

(a) government or other public administration at national, regional or local level;
(b) any legal or natural person having public responsibilities or functions, or providing public services, relating directly or indirectly to the environment under the control of a body or person falling within (a);
(c) any legal person entrusted by law, or under arrangements with a body or person falling within (a) or (b), with the operation of services of general economic interest which affect or are likely to affect the state of elements of the environment.

This Proposal was acknowledged by the Commission to go further than was necessary in order to meet Aarhus Convention requirements. In particular, the Proposal's reference to bodies entrusted 'with the operation of services of general economic interest which affect or are likely to affect the state of elements of the environment' would have produced a Directive which would have been clearly applicable to public utility services generally, across the fields of water, waste, electricity, nuclear power and so on.

When the matter came before the European Parliament's lead Committee on this Directive (its Environment Committee) an amendment to the definition of public authority was immediately proposed with a view to aligning the wording of the Directive more closely with that of the Aarhus Convention. At first reading, the European Parliament adopted this proposed amendment.

At this point the Commission produced an amended Proposal (June 2001) in which it accepted the Parliament's approach that the Directive should adopt the same definition of public authority as contained in the Aarhus Convention. In particular the definition in the amended Proposal no longer referred to bodies whose functions were likely to 'affect' the environment. Rather, the definition was now couched in significantly narrower terms: in terms, that is, of bodies having public responsibilities or functions 'in relation to the environment'.

The definition contained in that amended Commission Proposal was to all intents and purposes the same as that which was adopted in the final Directive.

Given the significant changes which occurred to the definition of public authority during this EU legislative process it is important to be wary of early statements about what the Directive was intended to achieve, since these may better reflect the Commission's original intentions than its intentions when putting forward the amended Proposal.

With these remarks in mind we can turn to the definition of public authority within the EIR.

9.2.5 Meaning of public authority

The EIR define public authority (reg.2(2)) as comprising:

(a) government departments;
(b) certain other public authorities as defined in FOIA, s.3(1) (with some exceptions);
(c) any other bodies or other persons which carry out functions of public administration; and
(d) any other bodies or other persons which are under the control of a person falling within (a), (b) or (c) above and

(i)   have public responsibilities relating to the environment;
(ii) exercise functions of a public nature relating to the environment; or
(iii) provide public services relating to the environment.

What does this mean?

Categories (a) and (b) seem reasonably self-explanatory. They cover governmental bodies which will almost certainly also be listed as bodies covered by the FOIA.

Category (c) serves to bring squarely within the scope of the EIR a variety of entities which perform what may legitimately be regarded as functions of public administration notwithstanding that they may be organisationally independent of governmental entities falling within (a) or (b). This would seem to cover those branches of government which have over past decades been hived off to executive agencies. Note, however, that the functions of public administration performed by these bodies need not be functions which are in any respect environmental.

Category (d) is more controversial. It brings within the scope of the EIR a variety of entities which are not government bodies and which do not perform functions of public administration.

The aim of category (d) appears to be to ensure that private law entities which perform certain functions that at one time may have been regarded as functions of the state shall not, simply as a consequence of the privatisation of that function, fall outside the scope of the EIR.

It is important to note, however, that category (d) does not purport to bring all privatised industries within the scope of the EIR. For an entity to fall within category (d) it must satisfy both of the following conditions:

- it must be under the control of a body which is a public authority within one of categories (a), (b) or (c); and
- it must have public responsibilities relating to the environment, or exercise functions of a public nature relating to the environment, or provide services relating to the environment.

Unfortunately none of the above phrases is defined either in the EIR or in the Aarhus or EU texts. It would appear to be the intention of the Convention, the Directive and the Regulations that companies exercising governmental functions which are essentially environmental functions shall be subject to the duties of disclosure of environmental information in cases where those companies have been afforded only a very limited degree of operational freedom from governmental control.

In contrast, companies which do not perform environmental functions, or which do perform such functions but do so with some substantial operational freedom from governmental prescription do not appear to fall within the EIR.

In interpreting the key phrases it would seem probable that the mere fact that a company's activities have significant impacts on the environment should not be regarded as the same as the company having responsibilities in relation to the environment, providing services in relation to the environment or having public functions in relation to the environment.[9]

Further, the concept of 'under the control of' a governmental body would seem to suggest something rather more than merely that a company operates in a field of activity which is, in the general public interest, closely regulated by government. It would seem to import the notion of government having some rather substantial degree of managerial control over the running of the company.[10]

It will clearly be necessary for companies to consider, limb by limb, whether they fall within the scope of the definition of public authority within the EIR. Where there is room for argument a company may well opt to withhold information requested, putting the onus on the applicant to refer the matter to the Information Commissioner for resolution, with further recourse later perhaps to the Information Tribunal and the courts.

For the moment the message should be that:

- the notion of public authority under the EIR is clearly broader than the equivalent concept under the FOIA;
- the concept certainly extends to a range of companies which might be surprised to find themselves so described;
- the concept does not extend as broadly as intended initially by the European Commission (and some recollections of that original intention may have influenced some of the broader present statements about the EIR);
- each case should be taken on its merits, looking to see how far the characteristics of the company in question match the key statutory tests described above.

9.2.6 Regulations not applicable to public authorities exercising certain functions

The rights of access and the public authority obligations summarised below are expressly stated not to apply in relation to any public authority to the extent that that authority is acting in a judicial or a legislative capacity (reg.3(3)).

9.2.7 The Houses of Parliament

The Regulations do not apply to either House of Parliament to the extent that this is required to avoid an infringement of the privileges of either House (reg.3(4)).

9.2.8 General duty to disseminate information

In addition to duties to respond to particular requests for environmental information, public authorities to which the EIR apply are under a general duty progressively to make the environmental information which they hold available to the public by electronic means which are easily accessible. Further, each public authority must take steps to organise the environmental information relevant to its functions with a view to active and systematic dissemination to the public of that information (reg.4(1)(a) and (b)).[11] This obligation does not, however, extend to any information covered by the exemptions to the duty to disclose information, as set out in regulation 12 (reg.4(3)).

For the purposes of this and other provisions of the EIR environmental information is held by a public authority if the information:

(a) is in the authority's possession and has been produced or received by the authority; or
(b) is held by another person on behalf of the authority (reg.3(2)).

The precise scope of the expression 'held by another person on behalf of the authority' is not clear. Certainly this may be thought to apply where a public authority has provided information to a third party (perhaps for storage, or in relation to some task or function to be performed by that third party). In such case a request made to the public authority will require the public authority to recover the information in order to be in a position to disclose it to the applicant. It is less clear, however, whether information possessed by those who contract with government (which does not emanate from government, and was created by the contractor) should be regarded as held on behalf of government simply because the information may relate directly to the performance of that contract. In this situation a request made to government should probably be met by the response that the public authority does not hold the information sought;[12] and a request to the third party contractor would undoubtedly be met with the response that the contractor is not a public authority and so not subject to the disclosure requirements of the EIR.

The information which is required by the EIR to be disseminated must include at least:

(i) texts of international treaties, conventions or agreements, and of Community, national, regional or local legislation on the environment or relating to it;
(ii) policies, plans and programmes relating to the environment;
(iii) progress reports on the implementation of the items referred to in (i) and (ii) above when prepared in electronic form by public authorities;
(iv) national (and where appropriate, regional and local) reports on the state of the environment published at regular intervals not exceeding four years – such reports to include information on the quality of, and pressures on, the environment;

(v)   data or summaries of data derived from the monitoring of activities affecting, or likely to affect, the environment;

(vi)   authorisations with a significant impact on the environment and environmental agreements (or a reference to the places where such information can be requested or found);

(vii) environmental impact studies and risk assessments concerning the environmental elements referred to within the definition of 'environmental information' (reg.4(4(a))).[13]

There must also be disseminated facts, and analyses of facts, which the public authority considers relevant and important in framing major environmental proposals (reg.4(4)(b)).

9.2.9   The general duty to make environmental information available on request

Regulation 5 imposes a general duty[14] that public authorities should upon request[15] make available to an applicant environmental information which it holds (or which is held by another on its behalf) (reg.5(1)). No obligations apply in relation to information no longer held by the public authority[16] or by any person on its behalf; save in the case where the public authority has passed the information over to a different public authority (see section 9.2.12).

Under the EIR the general duty to make environmental information available on request applies notwithstanding any enactment or rule of law that would prevent the disclosure of information in accordance with the EIR (reg.5(6)). This rule, it should be noted, is directly the opposite of the principle found in the FOIA.[17]

Requests for environmental information may be made by any person,[18] and unless one of the exceptions described below applies, public authorities are required to make requested information available as soon as possible, and no later than 20 working days after receipt of a request. This 20-day period may, however, be extended by the public authority to 40 working days in cases where this is reasonably believed by the public authority to be necessary in light of the complexity and[19] volume of the information requested. The necessity in question may here relate either to the business of actually providing the information requested within the 20-day period, or the difficulty within that period of making a decision that the information should not be disclosed (reg.7(1)). Any decision to extend the 20-day period must be taken by the public authority and notified to the applicant within that 20-day period (reg.7(3)).

Prima facie the public authority must make the information available in such form or format as the applicant requests. However, this presumption is displaced where it is reasonable for the public authority to make the information available in some other form or format or the information is already publicly available and accessible to the applicant in another format (reg.6(1)).[20]

There is also a potentially far-reaching obligation under the EIR that the information 'shall be up to date, accurate and comparable, so far as the authority reasonably believes' (reg.5(4)). It is presently unclear how proactive public bodies must be to ensure on an ongoing basis that information in their possession meets these requirements.

For example, the scope of obligations imposed on a public authority where the authority is aware that its latest information is out of date or inaccurate is not clear. Is it sufficient merely to make these shortcomings clear, or is there an obligation to correct the shortcoming by updating or securing more accurate information?[21]

9.2.10   Charging

In relation to charging for the provision of information, a distinction is drawn in the EIR between recoupment by a public authority of the costs it incurs in providing the information requested by an applicant, and recoupment of costs incurred merely in affording on-site access to that information.

A public authority may not make any charge for allowing an applicant access to any public registers of environmental information which it holds; nor may it make any charge in relation to the examination of requested information at the place which the public authority makes available for that examination (reg.8(2)).

However, outside these two situations a public authority may charge the applicant for making the requested information available to the applicant (reg.8(1)).[22] It is not clear whether the expression 'making the requested information available' relates only to the cost of copying and transmitting retrieved information to the applicant, or whether it also embraces the cost of retrieving that information internally. The matter seems finely balanced as a matter of interpretation. Even if the expression is to be regarded as covering retrieval as well as copying and transmission it is difficult to read the expression as also covering the cost of the deliberative process through which a decision is taken that retrieved information is subject to the duty of disclosure.

Whatever the charge may relate to, it must not exceed an amount which the public authority is satisfied is a reasonable amount (reg.8(3)).[23] The concept of reasonableness of charge is not further defined. In a case in 1999 (*Commission* v. *Federal Republic of Germany*, Case C-217/97 (1999)) the European Court of Justice took the view, in relation to the reasonable charge criterion of the earlier EU Directive, that charges set at a level which would serve to deter persons from seeking access to information would frustrate the main aims of the Directive, and so would not qualify as reasonable. It would seem to follow that public authorities cannot assume that they can necessarily recover all administrative costs incurred in retrieving and relaying requested information. This is of particular significance in the light of the fact that, unlike under the FOIA, there is no provision under the EIR permitting a public authority to refuse to disclose information because of the dispropor-tionate expense likely to be involved.[24] In certain circumstances a request involving a public authority in very substantial expense may fall within the manifestly unreasonable exemption (see further section 9.2.13). However, there may be circumstances where the public interest in the matter being disclosed is sufficiently great to render the request not manifestly unreasonable, despite the fact that disclosure may be at substantial public expense.

Public authorities are required to publish and make available to applicants a schedule of their charges, and also information on the circumstances in which a charge may be made or may be waived (reg.8(8)).[25]

A public authority may require payment of its proposed charge in advance of making the environmental information available to the applicant. Where the public authority opts to do so it must inform the applicant of this fact, and also of the amount of the charge, within 20 working days of receipt of the request for the information (reg.8(4)).[26] In such circumstances the appli-cant has 60 working days from the date of such notification within which to pay the charge, and trigger the duty to disclose the information (reg.6(5)). Although the duty to disclose will lapse if the charge is not paid within this 60-day period there is no reason why a further, albeit identical, request could not be made by the applicant – triggering a new duty to disclose.

9.2.11 Advice and assistance

Public authorities are required to provide advice and assistance to applicants so far as it is reasonable to expect them to do so (reg.9(1)). For example, where the public authority considers that an applicant has formulated a request in too general a manner (so that the 'too general' exemption from disclosure may apply) the authority is required to ask the applicant for more particulars and also to assist the applicant in providing those particulars (reg.9(2)).

9.2.12 Transfers of requests

Where a public authority receives a request for environmental information which it does not hold but it believes that the information is held by another public authority, the former public authority is required either to transfer the request to the other public authority or to supply the applicant with the name and address of the transferee authority (reg.10(1)).[27]

9.2.13   Exceptions to the duty to disclose environmental information

A public authority may[28] refuse to disclose environmental information in circumstances where the following two conditions are satisfied:

- the information falls within one of the categories listed below; and
- in all the circumstances the public interest in non-disclosure outweighs the public interest in disclosing the information (reg.12(11)).

Note that both of the above conditions must be satisfied before a request for disclosure may be refused, and also that in weighing the two facets of public interest within the second bullet point the public authority must apply a presumption in favour of disclosure (reg.12(2)).

A public authority may, applying the above conditions, refuse to disclose environmental information to the extent that[29] such disclosure would adversely affect:[30]

(i)   international relations, defence, national security (in relation to which a ministerial certificate of adverse affect is conclusive) (reg.15(1) and (3))[31] or public safety;

(ii)   the course of justice, the ability of a person to receive a fair trial or the ability of a public authority to conduct an inquiry of a criminal or disciplinary nature;

(iii)   intellectual property rights;

(iv)   the confidentiality of the proceedings of that or any other body where such confidentiality is provided by law;

(v)   the confidentiality of commercial or industrial information where such confidentiality is provided by law to protect a legitimate economic interest;

(vi)   the interests of the person who provided the information where that person:

    (a)   was not under, and could not have been put under, any legal obligation to supply it to that or any other public authority;

    (b)   did not supply it in circumstances such that that or any other public authority is entitled apart from under the EIR to disclose it; and

    (c)   has not consented to its disclosure; or

(vii)   the protection of the environment to which the information relates.

A special rule of some substantial potential significance applies in relation to information which relates to emissions. The exemptions stated in points (iv) to (vii) above do not apply in relation to requests for such information (reg.12(9)). The concept of emissions is not specifically defined in either the Environmental Information Directive or the EIR. It should, however, probably be afforded a meaning consistent with its defined usage in other EU

Environmental Directives. As such it seems likely to be construed as including both direct and indirect releases of substances, vibrations, heat or noise from individual or diffuse sources to the atmosphere, to water, and on to land.

It will be apparent that in any case where it may be sought to justify non-disclosure under grounds (iv) to (vii) above a key issue may be whether the information in question does, or does not, relate to an emission.

In addition to the above, a public authority may refuse to disclose environmental information in circumstances where the public interest in non-disclosure outweighs the public interest in disclosure, and:

- it does not hold the information when the applicant's request is received;[32]
- the request for information is manifestly unreasonable;[33]
- the request is formulated in too general a manner;[34]
- the request relates to material which is still in the course of completion, to unfinished documents or to incomplete data;[35] or
- the request involves the disclosure of internal communications, including communications between government departments.[36]

The last of these exceptions seems, at first glance, potentially very wide in scope. Is it not the case that a high proportion of documents sought from public authorities will fall within the general rubric 'internal communications'? The key point to note, however, is that none of these exceptions is satisfied simply because the request falls within the scope of one of the bullet pointed expressions. The exceptions only apply where the request falls within that ambit, and in addition the public interest in non-disclosure outweighs the public interest in disclosure (with the presumption being always in favour of disclosure). In other words, taking the last example on the list, there is no blanket exception in relation to internal communications; there is simply an exception in relation to internal communications in respect of which a clear case can be made out that in the circumstances of the case the public interest in protecting the confidentiality of that disclosure outweighs the public interest in such disclosure.

9.2.14 Power to neither confirm nor deny

Where a request for environmental information is for information which, if held by a public authority, might fall within one of the various exceptions referred to above, and the public authority holding such information forms the view that the information should not be disclosed under one of the exceptions, the public authority is empowered in certain situations to respond to the request by neither confirming nor denying whether such information exists and is held by the authority. The situations where the refusal to disclose will legitimately incorporate a statement neither confirming nor denying that the information exists and is held by the authority are where such confirmation or denial would itself adversely affect international relations, defence, national security or public safety, and the public interest in such confirmation and denial would be outweighed by the adverse effect in question (reg.12(6) and (7).

9.2.15 Personal data[37]

We noted earlier that the general duty of disclosure under the EIR does not apply to the extent that the environmental information is personal data of which the applicant is the data subject (reg.5(3)). Applications for such data must instead be treated as subject access requests made under the DPA (see, in particular, DPA, s.7).

In contrast, to the extent that the requested environmental information may comprise personal data of which the applicant is not the data subject the information is subject to the provisions of the EIR. Although requests for this category of environmental information do not fall to be governed directly by the DPA, some of the protections afforded by that Act to personal data are replicated in the EIR.

The EIR provide that such requested personal data must not be disclosed where one or other of the two conditions laid down in regulation 13(2) are satisfied (reg.12(3)).

The first of those conditions deals separately with two distinct situations depending on whether or not the information falls within the first four categories of data in section 1(1) of the DPA.[38]

Where the information falls within those categories of data the information must not be disclosed where such disclosure would either contravene one or more of the data protection principles (reg.13(2)(a)(i));[39] or would contravene section 10 of the DPA (i.e. where the data subject has given notice that disclosure would cause unwarranted substantial damage or distress to the data subject), and the public interest in not disclosing outweighs the public interest in disclosing the information (reg.13(2)(a)(ii)).[40]

Where the information does not fall within the first four categories of data in s.1(1) of the DPA[41] the information must not be disclosed where the disclosure of that information would contravene any of the data protection principles (reg.13(2)(b)).[42]

The second condition is that requested information must not be disclosed where the information is exempt from the disclosure requirements of section 7 of the DPA by virtue of any of that Act's exemptions (see Part IV, DPA),[43] and in all the circumstances of the case the public interest in not disclosing the information outweighs the public interest in disclosing it (reg.13(3)).

9.2.16 Reasoned decisions

Decisions by public authorities to refuse to disclose information under any of the various exceptions, or under the personal data provisions, must be communicated in writing and within 20 working days of the receipt of the request (reg.14(1)).[44] The decision must indicate the particular exception(s) relied upon, and must indicate the matters the public authority took into consideration in reaching its decision that the public interest favoured non-disclosure rather than disclosure (reg.14(3)).

The written refusal must also inform the applicant of the right to make representations to the public authority under the regulation 11 internal review procedure, and of the enforcement and appeal provisions applicable to the decision.

9.3 ENFORCEMENT AND APPEALS

At the outset of this chapter it was emphasised that although the new EIR came into force on the same day as the FOIA, their pedigrees are quite different: one a home-grown measure, the other a measure designed to meet requirements set at international multilateral treaty level and at EU level. As such a warning was sounded that in significant ways their substantive breadths of operation are by no means identical.

One area, however, where a close link has been achieved between the two regimes lies in the fields of enforcement and appeals. Regulation 18 provides that, subject only to certain modifications,[45] the enforcement and appeal provisions of the FOIA (Parts IV and V) apply also for the purposes of the EIR.

The relevant provisions of the FOIA are dealt with in Chapter 10. In briefest summary, a person who has made a request may make initial complaint[46] to the Information Commissioner if he considers that the request has not been handled[47] or determined in accordance with the EIR. The Information Commissioner has power to issue an Information Notice as a means of gaining the information the Information Commissioner will need in order to determine the complaint. The Information Commissioner also has powers of entry, search and seizure; and offences exist with respect to any obstruction of the Information Commissioner in the exercise of these functions. Given the ubiquity within the EIR of the need for the balancing of public interests it will generally be necessary for the Information Commissioner to review documents sought in order to decide whether a correct decision has been reached by the public body in question. The Information Commissioner will issue a Decision Notice giving his decision on the merits of the application. From decisions of the Information Commissioner, appeal lies at the suit of the applicant for information or at the suit of the public authority as the case may be, to the Information Tribunal. From the Information Tribunal there lies a further right of appeal on a point of law to the High Court (and beyond).

9.3.1 Offences (reg.19)

Where a request has been made to a public authority for environmental information and that request is one which does not fall within the scope of the above mentioned exemptions (including the provisions restricting access to personal data) an offence is committed by any person[48] who, with the intention of preventing the disclosure of all or part of the information, alters, defaces, blocks, erases, destroys or conceals any record held by the authority.[49]

No proceedings in relation to this offence may be instituted except by the Information Commissioner, or by or with the consent of the Director of Public Prosecutions (reg.19(4)).

NOTES

1   SI 1992/3240, subsequently amended by SI 1998/1447.

2   Ratified by the UK in February 2005. For the text, see **www.unece.org/env/pp/ documents/cep43e.pdf.**

3   This is the practical effect of s.39 of the FOIA, as modified by reg.20 of the EIR. Section 39 renders information which can be required to be disclosed under the EIR (or which could so be required but for an exception within the EIR) exempt information to which the provisions of the FOIA are not applicable.

4   Compare, for example FOIA, s.44 with reg.5(6) (contrary approaches to effect of prior legislation requiring that a public authority shall not disclose information in its possession). Note also that there is no explicit provision in the EIR permitting non-disclosure on grounds of the cost of compliance: cf. FOIA, s.12.

5   But, not always: see, e.g. reg.12(4)(e) protecting internal communications where the exemption under the EIR appears on its face to be broader than any equivalent under the FOIA. But note, as explained later in the chapter, that internal communications of environmental information are only exempt from disclosure where the public interest in protecting the confidentiality of the internal communication outweighs in all the circumstances of the case the public interest in the information being disclosed.

6   For a broad construction of the notion of information relating to the state of land see *R.* v. *British Coal Corporation, ex p. Ibstock Building Products Ltd* [1995] Env LR 277, decided under the earlier Regulations. Harrison J formed the view that information disclosing the identity of persons who claimed to have knowledge of past and potentially contaminative activities in the relation to a site was 'environmental information'. Revelation of the identity of those informants was relevant to an assessment of the credibility of the information they had provided.

7   Note that where information covered by para.(b) is made available, the public authority is required, upon request, insofar as it is possible so to do, to refer the applicant to where information can be found on the measurement procedures used in compiling that information. See reg.5(5). In *R.* v. *Secretary of State for the Environment, Transport and the Regions, ex p. Alliance against Birmingham Northern Relief Road (No.1)* [1999] Env LR 447 applicants sought disclosure of a concession agreement under which a company had contracted with government to construct and operate the M6 toll road. Sullivan J found that this contract could be regarded as environmental information, applying a broad and purposive construction to that term. It involved information on a matter which would

have effects on elements of the environment. Nevertheless, certain exemptions with the 1992 Regulations were applicable, and the agreement was ordered to be disclosed subject to power to withhold certain provisions which fell within the exemption relating to confidentiality.

8　This definition of environmental information is identical to that contained in Art.2(1) of Directive 2003/4; which itself draws closely from that within the Aarhus Convention (see Art.2(3)).

9　DEFRA Guidance on the Environmental Information Regulations includes some conclusions about the scope of these phrases which seem difficult to square with either the wording or the legislative history of the Regulations and EU Directive. For example, para.2.4 states: 'Examples of bodies covered by EIR are private companies or Public Private Partnerships with obvious environmental functions such as waste disposal, water, energy, transport companies (such as the Civil Aviation Authority and port authorities), and environmental consultants. Public utilities, for example, are involved in the supply of essential services such as water, sewerage, electricity and gas fall within the scope of the EIR. Other bodies covered include the Ambulance Service, which carries out a public service and collects statistics in road traffic accidents, and Customs and Excise in dealing with the illegal import of endangered species'. Certain of the bodies referred to certainly do qualify as public authorities under earlier limbs of the definition than the one presently under consideration. However, as regards those bodies referred to within the paragraph which are not government bodies *per se*, nor are bodies exercising functions of public administration, the words quoted reach very broad conclusions which are asserted rather than explained, and in a number of instances may legitimately be doubted. It is suggested that in relation to certain of the examples given there may be a confusion between notions of activities with evident environmental impacts, and activities which genuinely fall within the three phrases in the main text above. Moreover, remember that falling within one of those three phrases is only one part of the test within part (d) of the definition of public authority. Such bodies also have to fall within the control requirement before they may be regarded as public authorities.

10　The DEFRA Guidance suggests: 'Control ... mean[s] ... the possibility of directly or indirectly exercising a decisive influence on a body ... Control may relate not only to the body but also to control over the services provided by the body. It covers financial, regulatory and administrative control' (para.2.4). This suggests an interpretation of control which seems rather broader than that suggested in the text above, and for which no source of authority is provided. DEFRA's broad approach should be noted, but with the caution that ultimately it is for the courts to interpret and apply the unelaborated definitional phrase.

11　By virtue of reg.4(2) the use of electronic means to make information available or to organise information is not required in relation to information collected before 1 January 2005 in non-electronic form.

12　It would not appear that it would make a difference that the public authority has some contractual right to be afforded the information in question by the contractor. If the information is the contractor's it is not held on behalf of the public authority; and unless and until the contractual right is exercised the information is not held by the public authority.

13　Incorporating by reference Art.7(2) of Dir. 2003/4. Note that Art.7(2) also requires that such information 'shall be updated as appropriate'. This requirement does not expressly appear within the EIR. But see further, below, at note 21.

14 The duty does not apply where the environmental information is 'personal data of which the applicant is the data subject' (reg.5(3)). Applications for such data must be made under the procedures of s.7 of the Data Protection Act 1998. For applications in relation to 'personal data of which the applicant is not the data subject', see further section 9.2.15.

15 There is no requirement that such request should be in writing, and certainly the request does not need to be a request explicitly for access under one or other of the statutory access regimes. There appears to be no obligation upon an applicant to reveal his or her identity. However, if the applicant's identity and reasons for wanting the information are not provided it may not be possible for the public authority to form proper assessments of certain matters which may determine whether it has or has not a duty to disclose. For example, it may be difficult to balance the public interest in disclosure against the public interest in upholding an exemption in a case where the identity and interest of the applicant is not known.

16 Where information was not held by the public authority at the time of the request but is acquired by the authority prior to its decision regarding disclosure, the Information Commissioner will regard it as good practice for the public authority to regard that information as disclosable (subject to the operation of an exemption).

17 FOIA, s.44 provides an absolute exemption from disclosure for information that is prohibited from being disclosed by another Act or Community obligation.

18 The applicant is not required to demonstrate any particular interest in the matter.

19 In the draft Regulations put out to consultation in the summer of 2004 this phrase read 'complexity *or* volume'.

20 If the information is not made available in the form or format requested the public authority must explain (in writing if requested) the reason for this as soon as possible and no later than 20 days from the receipt of the request for the information, and inform the applicant of his rights to make representations under reg.11 and to take advantage of applicable appeal and enforcement mechanisms. See reg.6(2).

21 Note that, curiously, the requirement within reg.5(4) is not to be found within EU Directive 2003/4. The nearest provision in the Directive (Art.7(2)) applies to data disseminated by public authorities independently of particular requests. See further, above, at note 13. Has there here been some inadvertent error of transposition?

22 It seems clear that no charge may be made in relation to refusals of information.

23 The wording of Recital (18) to the EU Directive may be instructive in interpreting notions of reasonable charge. It reads: 'Public authorities should be able to make a charge for supplying environmental information, but such charge should be reasonable. This implies that, as a general rule, charges may not exceed actual costs of producing the material in question . . . In limited cases where public authorities make environmental information available on a commercial basis, and where this is necessary in order to guarantee the continuation of collecting and publishing such information, a market-based charge is considered to be reasonable.'

24 Under the FOIA an exception exists where costs will exceed the appropriate limit within the meaning of Fees Regulations made under ss.9, 12, and 13.

25 The DEFRA Guidance recommends that central departments and local authorities should waive charges where costs incurred are less than £600 and £450 respectively. This is to achieve consistency with practice under the FOIA.

26   In calculating the 20 working days within which the public authority must disclose the information the period from the date of such notification and the payment of the advance charge is ignored: see reg.8(6).

27   For the purpose of the 20-day rule the transferee authority has 20 working days from the date on which it receives the transferred request. See reg.10(2).

28   There is no express duty not to disclose information just because an exception applies. However, since for an exception to apply it will be necessary for the public authority to judge that the overall balance of public interest lies in favour of non-disclosure there would not seem to be any scope for seeking that a public authority should volunteer information which falls within one of the exemptions.

29   It is clear that public authorities may not refuse to disclose entire documents in circumstances where by excluding from the disclosure certain parts of the document what remains does not fall within the terms of any of the exceptions. Note here reg.12(8) which states: 'Nothing in these Regulations shall authorise a refusal to make available any environmental information contained in or otherwise held with other information which is withheld by virtue of these Regulations unless it is not reasonably capable of being separated from the other information for the purpose of making available that information.'

30   The phrase 'would adversely affect' seems a more onerous pre-condition than its equivalent under the FOIA: that is, 'would be likely to prejudice'.

31   A Minister may designate another person to certify such matters on his or her behalf: reg.15(2).

32   Note here the duties imposed on a public authority where that body is aware that the requested information is held by another public authority. See section 9.2.12.

33   The Information Commissioner's advice on vexatious requests under the FOIA is likely to be a useful guide also to interpretation of this 'manifestly unreasonable' exception. See *Awareness Guidance* 22.

34   Note here the public authority's obligation under reg.9 to assist the applicant in providing particulars which may render the request less general.

35   Where this exemption is relied upon the written decision refusing disclosure must specify, if known, the estimated time in which the information will be finished or completed. See reg.14(4).

36   Reg.12(4) and (8). The intent here appears to be to provide some protection in relation to communications which do not yet constitute the settled view within government on a particular matter.

37   This concept is defined in the Data Protection Act 1998, s.1(1) as data which relate to a living individual who can be identified (a) from those data; or (b) from those data and other information which is in the possession of, or is likely to come into the possession of, the data controller, and includes any expression of opinion about the individual and any indication of the intentions of the data controller or any other person in respect of the individual. For a restrictive interpretation of the scope of this definition see *Durant* v. *Financial Services Authority* [2003] EWCA Civ 1746.

38   'Data' within the meaning of s.1(1) of the DPA consists of information which (i) is being processed by means of equipment operating automatically in response to instructions given for that purpose; (ii) is recorded with the intention that it should be processed by means of such equipment; (iii) is recorded as part of a relevant filing system or with the intention that it should form part of a relevant filing system; (iv) does not fall within paragraph (i), (ii) or (iii) but forms part of an accessible record as defined by s.68 of the DPA; or (v) is recorded information held by a public authority and does not fall within any of paras.(i) to (iv).

39   The data protection principles are set out in Sched.1 to the DPA and further elaborated in Scheds.2, 3 and 4. They include the principle that 'personal data shall be obtained only for one or more specified and lawful purposes, and shall not be further processed in any manner incompatible with that purpose or those purposes.'

40   The public interest criterion applies only to the s.10 ground, so that where disclosure would contravene one of the data protection principles no such balancing of public interests arises.

41   i.e. it is recorded information held by a public authority not falling within the first four categories of data listed in s.1(1) of the DPA.

42   For these purposes the exemptions from the data protection principles for the fifth category of data in s.1(1) of the DPA, that is, recorded information held by public authorities, should be disregarded. The exemptions referred to, and to be disregarded, are those contained in s.33A(1) of the DPA (added by FOIA, s.70).

43   In other words, generally speaking the non data subject cannot access information under the EIR which the data subject himself/herself could not access under the DPA.

44   For power to extend this period, see section 9.2.10.

45   For example, Part IV (enforcement) does not apply where a certificate has been issued by a Minister under reg.15.

46   This should follow the internal review process provided for by reg.11.

47   The complaint may for example be as regards level of fee charged, or time taken to determine the request.

48   Strictly speaking the offence may be committed only by the public authority, or any person who is employed by, is an officer of, or is subject to the direction of, the public authority. See reg.19(2). Moreover, where the public authority is a government department, the department shall not itself be liable to prosecution (although the offence may in that case be committed by a person in the public service of the Crown, i.e. a civil servant).

49   The offence is triable summarily. The maximum penalty is a fine not exceeding level 5 on the standard scale.

CHAPTER 10

Enforcement and appeals

Jeremy Ison, Clifford Chance

10.1 INTRODUCTION

Ultimately, it is only through the enforcement of the new rights and duties created by the FOIA – especially in cases at the margins – that the full extent of the seismic shift in the democratic life of the nation which it represents will be mapped out. The rulings of the Information Tribunal, together with decisions of the Information Commissioner, create a freedom of information case law, which will help public authorities and applicants alike to better understand the practical implications of the FOIA and will promote consistency and predictability of decision making at all levels. That said, it is worth remembering that merely because an earlier case concerned similar facts, that does not mean that the outcome of the later case will inevitably be the same; time will have moved on and considerations as to the application of the exemptions and the public interest test may well be materially different.

Primary responsibility for enforcement of the FOIA lies with the Information Commissioner, who monitors public authorities and can issue notices directing them to take action so as to comply with their statutory obligations. Failure to comply with the Information Commissioner's notices can be punished as if it were a contempt of court. The enforcement and appeals regime under the FOIA applies also to the EIR.[1] The FOIA applies in England, Wales and Northern Ireland only. In Scotland the enforcement regime under the Freedom of Information (Scotland) Act 2002 and the Environmental Information (Scotland) Regulations 2004 (SSI 2004/520) is broadly similar but there is no equivalent of the Information Tribunal north of the border. The only appeal from the Scottish Commissioner is to the Court of Session, and only on a point of law.

At the heart of the enforcement regime lies the complaints process. This is the route (outlined in Figure 10.1) which an applicant must follow if he considers that his request for information has been turned down or dealt with improperly.

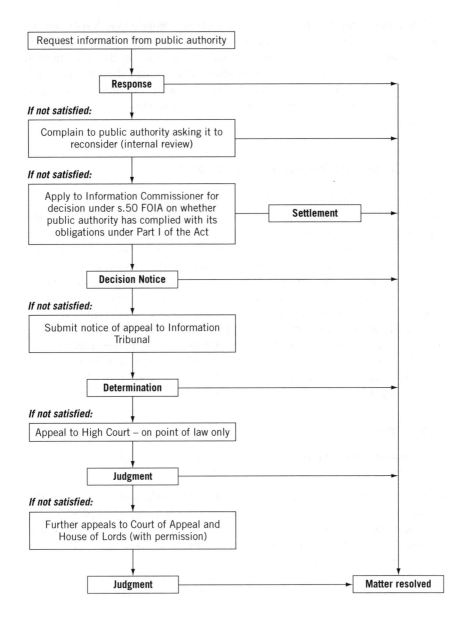

Figure 10.1 The complaints process

This chapter will first review the Information Commissioner's role and the various notices he can serve, before looking in detail at the complaints process at sections 10.5 to 10.8, including appeals to the Information Tribunal. Finally, it will turn to the position of interested third parties (such as private sector companies which do business with the public sector) and their somewhat limited opportunities to restrain disclosure of information which affects them.

10.2 THE INFORMATION COMMISSIONER'S ROLE

Although appointed by the Crown and answerable to Parliament, the Information Commissioner is completely independent of government. As the regulator, he is charged with ensuring that the rights and duties contained in the FOIA and the EIR are widely known about and respected. (He has a similar role in relation to the DPA.) He is supported by a staff of some 250,[2] including two Deputy Commissioners, nine Assistant Commissioners and a legal department. The Information Commissioner's Office is based in Wilmslow, near Manchester, with satellite offices in Cardiff, Edinburgh and Belfast. He investigates complaints and has the power to instruct bodies to disclose information. In practice, his primary focus in this regard is to consider whether the exemptions in Part II of the FOIA have been properly applied by public bodies and to ensure that, in doing so, those bodies have had due regard to the public interest in disclosure.

10.2.1 Duties

The Information Commissioner's duties are outlined as follows under Parts III and IV of the FOIA and under the EIR:

- to promote the following of good practice[3] by public authorities generally, and in particular to carry out his work in such a way as to promote the observance by public authorities of the requirements of the legislation and the provisions of the two Codes of Practice made under the FOIA and the EIR[4] (FOIA, s.47(1); EIR, reg.16(5));
- to publish information about the operation of the legislation, good practice and other matters relating to his statutory functions (FOIA, s.47(2); EIR reg.16(5));
- to lay an annual report before each House of Parliament containing a general report on the exercise of his statutory functions (s.49(1));
- (save in certain circumstances) to determine, when asked to do so by an applicant under section 50(1), whether or not a public authority has complied with its obligations under Part I of the FOIA; or Parts 2 and 3

of the Regulations, in responding to a request for information (FOIA, s.50(2); EIR, reg.18).

10.2.2 Powers

In order to assist him in carrying out these duties, the legislation gives the Information Commissioner the following powers:

- to advise anyone on the operation of the legislation, good practice and other matters relating to his functions (FOIA, s.47(2); EIR, reg.16(5));[5]
- to assess whether a public authority is following good practice, subject to that authority's consent (FOIA, s.47(3); EIR, reg.16(5));
- to issue a written Practice Recommendation to a public authority, specifying the steps which it should take to remedy the situation where he considers that its practice does not conform to the Codes of Practice (FOIA, s.48);
- to charge for certain of his services,[6] subject to consent from the Secretary of State;
- to lay reports before each House of Parliament from time to time as he thinks fit, in addition to the obligatory annual report referred to above (FOIA, s.49(2));
- to approve a public authority's Publication Scheme, or to refuse to approve it or revoke his approval for it (giving reasons); and to approve a Model Publication Scheme, or to refuse to approve it or revoke his approval for it (again, giving reasons) (FOIA, ss.19–20);
- to issue Decision Notices, Information Notices and Enforcement Notices (FOIA, ss.50–52; EIR, reg.18);
- to obtain a warrant to enter and search premises so as to obtain evidence where he suspects a public authority of failing to comply with its obligations under the legislation or the notices referred to in the previous bullet, or where he suspects an offence under section 77 of the FOIA or regulation 19 of the EIR (obstructing disclosure of requested information) (FOIA, s.55 and Sched.3; EIR, reg.18);[7]
- to certify to the court that a public authority has failed to comply with a Decision Notice, an Information Notice or an Enforcement Notice, so that the court can investigate and punish the non-compliance as a contempt of court if appropriate (FOIA, s.54; EIR, reg.18).[8]

It should be noted that the Information Commissioner has no power to impose fines on public authorities for a breach of their duties under the FOIA or the EIR, nor does he have the power to award compensation to complainants or to make costs orders against the parties involved in a complaint which is directed to him for determination. It is also important to be aware that the Information Commissioner is not empowered to adjudicate formally on, and issue Decision Notices about, complaints against public authorities by anyone other than a person who has sought information from them under section 1 of the FOIA or regulation 5 of the EIR.[9]

10.3 THE INFORMATION COMMISSIONER'S NOTICES IN MORE DETAIL

10.3.1 Decision Notices

Decision Notices are only issued in the context of a complaint by someone who is dissatisfied with a public authority's response to his request for information and has applied to the Information Commissioner under section 50(1) for a decision on whether the authority has met its obligations under Part I of the FOIA. Following his determination of the matter, the Information Commissioner must either notify the complainant of his reason for not adjudicating on the complaint or serve a Decision Notice on the complainant and the public authority (s.50(3)). Where he decides that the public authority failed to comply with obligations under sections 1(1), 11 or 17 of the FOIA or regulations 5(1), 6, 11 or 14 of the EIR,[10] the notice must set out the steps he requires it to take to be in compliance and by when they must be taken. There is no bar on the Decision Notice containing such steps in other cases, however. The Information Commissioner may also make reference in a Decision Notice to any provisions of the Section 45 Code of Practice which the public authority has breached and with which it is to comply.[11]

Either the complainant or the public authority may appeal to the Information Tribunal against a Decision Notice under section 57 and notices must contain details of that right of appeal (s.50(5)). The deadline for taking the steps specified in the notice cannot expire before the end of the period within which the public authority is entitled to appeal – namely 28 days from when it is served with the notice.[12] Further, if the authority does challenge the Information Commissioner's decision, it is not obliged to take any action affected by the appeal until the appeal's determination or withdrawal (s.50(6)). Failure to comply with a Decision Notice is ultimately punishable in the High Court as if for contempt of court (s.54). It can also lead to the Information Commissioner obtaining a warrant to search premises to find evidence of non-compliance (s.55 and Sched.3). There is no provision permitting the Information Commissioner to cancel a Decision Notice once issued, as is possible with other notices. A Decision Notice can, however, be overridden by the so-called ministerial veto (see section 10.3.5 below). For details of the Information Commissioner's policies regarding the issuing and publication of Decision Notices see section 10.6.1.

10.3.2 Information Notices

If the Information Commissioner has received an application for a Decision Notice or reasonably requires any information to determine whether a public authority has complied with, or is complying with, any of the requirements of Part I of the FOIA or the Section 45 and Section 46 Codes of Practice, he may serve an Information Notice on the authority requiring any information (which in this case can include unrecorded information (s.51(8))[13] relevant to those matters and he may specify how, and by when, he is to receive it (s.51(1)(*b*)). If the Information Commissioner serves the Information Notice in response to a request for a decision under section 50(1), the notice must say so. Otherwise, the notice must state that the Information Commissioner regards the information sought as relevant for the purposes mentioned above and reasons must be given (s.50(2)).

The public authority (but not a complainant) may appeal against the notice to the Information Tribunal under section 57 of the FOIA and notices must contain details of that right (s.51(3)). The deadline for providing the Information Commissioner with the information he specifies cannot expire before the end of the period within which the public authority is entitled to appeal, which is 28 days from service of the notice.[14] Further, if the authority does challenge the notice, it is not obliged to furnish the Information Commissioner with the information before the appeal's determination or withdrawal (s.51(4)). The Information Commissioner may cancel an Information Notice by written notice to the relevant public authority (s.51(7)). (An authority could thus seek cancellation of the notice where it was for some reason no longer appropriate but the time for appealing had expired.) Failure to comply with an Information Notice is ultimately punishable in the High Court as if it were a contempt of court. The same is true where, in purported compliance with an Information Notice, a public authority makes a statement which is false in a material respect, either with knowledge of its falsity or else recklessly (s.54). Failure to comply with the notice can also lead to the Information Commissioner obtaining a warrant to search premises to find evidence of non-compliance (s.55 and Sched.3).

In responding to the notice, the public authority is under no obligation to provide the Information Commissioner with information in respect of any legally privileged communications containing legal advice on a client's rights, obligations or liabilities under the FOIA or made in connection with, or in contemplation of, proceedings arising out of the Act (s.51(5)).

The Information Commissioner's policies regarding the issuing and publication of Information Notices are discussed in section 10.6.1.

10.3.3   Enforcement Notices

If the Information Commissioner is satisfied that the public authority is in breach of any of its Part I obligations, he may serve an Enforcement Notice requiring it to take particular steps by a particular time to comply with those obligations. An Enforcement Notice cannot be issued purely in relation to a breach of a Code of Practice unrelated to a breach of the FOIA. Code breaches can be the subject of Practice Recommendations (see section 10.3.6).

An Enforcement Notice must specify the Part I obligations with which the Information Commissioner is satisfied the public authority has failed to comply, and his reason for reaching that conclusion. It must also give details of the right to appeal against the notice under section 57 (s.52(2)). Only a public authority may appeal, not any complainant with an interest in the matter. As with the notices considered above, the deadline for taking the steps specified in an Enforcement Notice cannot expire before the end of the period within which the public authority is entitled to appeal – 28 days from when it is served.[15] Again, the authority is not obliged to comply with it pending any appeal's determination or withdrawal (s.52(4)). The Information Commissioner may cancel an Enforcement Notice by written notice to the public authority (s.52(4)). (Again, an authority could thus ask him to cancel the notice where it was for some reason no longer appropriate but the time for appealing had expired.) An Enforcement Notice can also be overridden by ministerial veto (see section 10.3.5). Failure to comply with a notice can be punished in the High Court as a contempt of court (s.54) and can also lead to the Information Commissioner obtaining a warrant to search premises to find evidence of non-compliance (s.55 and Sched.3).

The distinction in practice between Enforcement and Decision Notices is that the latter arise in the context of specific complaints, whereas the Information Commissioner has said he is more likely to issue the former where there have been systemic failures or repeated non-compliance with the FOIA.[16] Rather than rushing to issue Enforcement Notices at the earliest opportunity, the Information Commissioner aims to give public authorities ample opportunity to comply voluntarily. When they are issued it is likely to be either in cases where the public authority has failed to comply with the section 19 obligations regarding Publication Schemes,[17] or where it is guilty of other systemic failures, for instance as follows:

- a number of similar adverse Decision Notices have been issued to the same public authority following unconnected complaints;
- an authority has clearly failed to follow a Practice Recommendation and to provide proper responses to subsequent requests for information under section 1(1);
- an authority clearly indicates it would not accept a Practice Recommendation if issued and fails to respond properly to a request for information under section 1(1);

- non-compliance has come to light as a result of proactive compliance-monitoring by the ICO or information provided by a whistleblower or other complainant;
- an authority subject to the EIR does not have an internal complaints process as the Regulations require.

The Information Commissioner has indicated that his procedure will involve the following steps:

(i)   establishing that the public authority falls under the FOIA;
(ii) asking the public authority informally to explain and correct any apparent non-compliance;
(iii) in the absence of a positive response, considering issuing a Preliminary Enforcement Notice (see section 10.3.4), which will generally give the authority 28 days in which to make representations why a final notice should not be issued (an appropriate response for the authority here might be to give an undertaking – that it will establish a publication scheme within a certain period, for example);
(iv) in the continued absence of a satisfactory response, issuing the public authority with an Enforcement Notice, setting out the steps it must take to comply with the relevant statutory obligations;
(v)   in the absence of compliance, making an application to the High Court to have the authority punished as if guilty of contempt of court.

10.3.4   Preliminary notices

Although there is no provision for them in the FOIA, the Information Commissioner has indicated that he intends to issue Preliminary Decision (or Enforcement or Information) Notices where he considers it likely that this could lead to the satisfactory resolution of the matter and avoid the cost, time and effort involved in an appeal to the Information Tribunal.[18] The thought is that a public authority, seeing what the Information Commissioner is minded to order it to do,[19] may prefer to take the appropriate action voluntarily or will come to some mutually acceptable compromise with the complainant, thus avoiding an official sanction. In such a case, the Information Commissioner will invite the complainant to withdraw his complaint. The Information Commissioner's grounds for considering he has discretion to introduce this extra step into the statutory procedure is that section 50(2)(*d*) allows him not to issue a Decision Notice where the complainant has withdrawn his request for a decision. A similar approach has been approved by the Council on Tribunals in the context of the Information Commissioner's enforcement activity under the DPA. The use of preliminary notices in practice is discussed further in section 10.6.1.

10.3.5 Ministerial veto

Under the controversial section 53 of the FOIA, a Decision Notice or an Enforcement Notice issued by the Information Commissioner (or modified on appeal by the Information Tribunal) and served on a government department, the Welsh Assembly or any public authority designated by the Secretary of State (s.53(1)(*a*))[20] can be overridden by a politician. The notice ceases to be of effect if within 20 working days of its service (or of the withdrawal or determination of any appeal under s.57) an accountable person in relation to the authority in question gives the Information Commissioner a signed certificate stating that he has, on reasonable grounds, formed the opinion that in respect of the request(s) concerned there was no failure:

- to comply with section 1(1)(*a*) of the FOIA in respect of information which falls within any provision of Part II of the Act stating that the duty to confirm or deny does not arise; or
- to comply with section 1(1)(*b*) in respect of exempt information.

What this obscure drafting means is that where the Information Commissioner has decided that the information falls within a qualified exemption[21] but that the public interest requires the authority to disclose the information (or at least confirm whether or not it holds such information), the accountable person can trump the Information Commissioner's view on the public interest analysis (or the Information Tribunal's view) and prevent disclosure.

As soon as practicable after delivering the certificate, the accountable person must lay a copy of it before each House of Parliament, and the Northern Ireland or Welsh Assembly too, if relevant to those bodies. Further, where the certificate overrides a Decision Notice, as soon as practicable after delivering the certificate, the accountable person must also inform the complainant straightaway of the reasons for their opinion but need not, in so doing, provide any exempt information.

An accountable person is in most cases a Cabinet Minister or the Attorney-General but in relation to a Northern Ireland department or public authority would be the First Minister and Deputy First Minister of Northern Ireland acting jointly, or the First Secretary of the Welsh Assembly regarding that body or any designated Welsh public authority.

There is no statutory appeal to the Information Tribunal against such a certificate. The ministerial decision would, however, be subject to judicial review on the application of a party with the requisite standing – the most obvious candidates being the complainant or the Information Commissioner. To succeed in the Administrative court, however, would generally mean showing that the Minister had acted irrationally or in a way that no one in his position reasonably could have done, which will often be a difficult test to meet.[22] The complainant and even the Information Commissioner may in addition be largely ignorant of the relevant detail lying behind the government's decision, as it will no doubt be kept back from them, being allegedly exempt and quite possibly made the subject of a claim to public interest immunity.[23] There would also be the risk of being ordered to pay the government's costs if the application for review was unsuccessful.

It remains to be seen with what frequency the government resorts to the use of this override. The Lord Chancellor has sought to allay fears on this score by indicating that it will only be used very exceptionally and subject to the approval of the entire Cabinet.[24] For his part, the Information Commissioner has expressed the view that it is desirable for the credibility of the FOIA, and indeed likely, that the veto will only be used rarely.[25]

10.3.6 Practice Recommendations

If it appears to the Information Commissioner that the practice of a public authority does not conform to provisions of the codes of practice issued under sections 45 and section 46 of the FOIA and regulation 16 of the EIR, he may give the authority a recommendation specifying the steps which ought in his opinion to be taken for promoting such conformity (FOIA, s.48(1); EIR, reg.16(5)). A Practice Recommendation differs from the notices discussed above as there are no sanctions for non-compliance with it, nor is there any statutory right of appeal against it. This difference is reflected by the fact that the notices are dealt with in Part IV of the FOIA (entitled Enforcement) and Practice Recommendations in Part III, which is concerned with the general functions of the Information Commissioner. A failure to take account of a Practice Recommendation will not be formally sanctioned, yet it could lead to an adverse comment in a report to Parliament by the Information Commissioner or some other negative publicity, albeit that the Information Commissioner has indicated he will not normally publish Practice Recommendations (see section 10.6.1). Also worth bearing in mind is that an authority which receives a Practice Recommendation is by definition at risk of breaching the FOIA, so it serves as a warning that procedures need to be addressed in order to avoid a more formal sanction. In the absence of an appeal mechanism, the Information Commissioner's decision to issue a Practice Recommendation is likely to be amenable to judicial review if one can show grounds, namely, that the decision was unreasonable, unlawful or procedurally unfair, or else a breach of the Human Rights Act 1998.

The purpose of Practice Recommendations is to suggest measures which the authority can take to facilitate dealing with requests for information and hence the exercise of rights under the FOIA. The Information Commissioner has indicated that he will issue Practice Recommendations in order to help public authorities and they will often be made by agreement, following a practice assessment under section 47(3) of the FOIA, for instance. In the case of serious or repeated failings on the part of a public authority which also involve breaches of the FOIA, however, the Information Commissioner is more likely to issue an Enforcement Notice.[26]

The sort of issues likely to be the subject of Practice Recommendations under the Section 45 Code of Practice include internal complaints procedures, the timing and content of refusal notices, and the quality of assistance given to applicants. In the case of the Section 46 Code, Practice Recommendations will probably deal with maintenance of records disposal schedules, indexing, searching, storing and cataloguing. Recommendations can only be made under the Section 46 Code, however, after consultation between the Information Commissioner and the Keeper of Public Records (or the Deputy Keeper in cases concerning Northern Ireland) (s.48(3) and (4)).[27]

10.4 ADDITIONAL SUPPORT FOR THE INFORMATION COMMISSIONER'S ENFORCEMENT POWERS

10.4.1 Non-compliance with notices punishable as if contempt of court

A public authority which has been served with a Decision Notice, Information Notice or Enforcement Notice might, deliberately or otherwise, fail to comply with the steps specified in the notice within the required deadline.[28] Once the time for compliance has expired, and likewise the time for appealing against the notice (28 days from service), or else after an unsuccessful appeal, then assuming that the notice has not been overridden by ministerial veto (see section 10.3.5), the Information Commissioner can take further enforcement action. In many cases the prompt for him to do so will be another complaint from the applicant who is waiting to receive the requested information. The Information Commissioner can certify the non-compliance in writing to the High Court (the Court of Session in Scotland), upon which the Court may inquire into the matter and, after hearing any witness who may be produced against or on behalf of the public authority, and after hearing any statement that may be offered in defence, deal with the public authority as if it had committed a contempt of court (s.53(3)).

The principal sanctions for contempt are an unlimited fine and a fixed-term prison sentence of up to two years (Contempt of Court Act 1981, s.14) but the Court can also order sequestration of assets,[29] or issue an injunction (*Elliot* v. *Klinger* [1967] 3 All ER 141). Committal and sequestration, being drastic penalties, are only imposed in serious cases, where there is an element of fault or misconduct (*Fairclough & Sons* v. *The Manchester Ship Canal Co. (No.2)* (1897) 41 Sol Jo, 225). They will not often feature in the context of the FOIA. The amount of any fine imposed must take account of the seriousness of the contempt and the damage to the public interest.[30] Where a public authority accidentally fails to comply with the Information

Commissioner's notice, the court will often simply make an order for costs against it, although this can be on the indemnity basis (e.g. *Stancomb* v. *Trowbridge Urban District Council* [1910] 2 Ch 190).

In principle, only the party bound by an order can be liable for civil contempt (breach of a court order – in this case the Information Commissioner's notice). As section 54(3) provides that the authority can be dealt with as if it had committed a contempt, it seems unlikely that the Court could sanction the individual officers and employees by whom it acts (and who were in fact responsible for breaching the notice), unless it made a further order requiring named individuals to act or refrain from acting in a certain way and they then breached that order.[31] Arguably, there is an exception to this, however, where the authority is a corporate body, in which case an order for sequestration or committal could be made against any director or other officer aware of the terms of the notice if they wilfully fail to take adequate steps to ensure compliance, by virtue of RSC Order 45, r.5(1), contained in Schedule 1 to the CPR (see *Attorney-General for Tuvalu* v. *Philatelic Distribution Corp. Ltd* [1990] 2 All ER 216, CA). There is perhaps in addition a risk that any employee of a public authority who knowingly assists it in breaching a notice issued by the Information Commissioner could be liable for criminal contempt, on the basis that this constituted an interference with the administration of justice. That could certainly be the case in relation to a breach of any subsequent order from the court to comply with the notice (*Marengo* v. *Daily Sketch and Sunday Graphic Ltd* [1948] 1 All ER 406). An intention to interfere with the course of justice would need to be proved, however, with mere recklessness not sufficing (*R.* v. *Runting* (1989) 89 Cr App R 243, 247, CA, per Lord Lane LCJ). While it is not possible for the Crown to be held in contempt, a Minister can be (*M* v. *Home Office* [1994] 1 AC 377).

Procedure regarding orders for committal is dealt with in RSC Order 52 (Schedule 1 to the CPR) and the accompanying Practice Direction. Even with civil contempt the criminal standard of proof applies, i.e. the case would need to be proved beyond reasonable doubt (*Dean* v. *Dean* [1987] 1 FLR 517, CA). That said, it is not necessary to prove that the authority intended to breach the Information Commissioner's notice (*Stancomb* v. *Trowbridge Urban District Council* [1910] 2 Ch, 190, 194), merely that it knew of its existence (*Z Ltd* v. *A-Z and AA-LL* [1982] QB 558, 580 per Eveleigh LJ) and intended to do the acts or omissions which constituted the contempt (i.e. the failure to comply); an argument by the authority that it was simply negligent in overlooking the notice may well not suffice to avoid liability (*VDU Installations Ltd* v. *Integrated Computer Systems and Cybernetics Ltd* [1989] 1 FSR 378, 394 per Knox J). On the other hand, if breach of the notice is accidental, the authority may well face costs but no additional sanctions (*Fairclough & Sons* v. *The Manchester Ship Canal Co. (No.2)* (1897) 41 Sol Jo, 225). If the Information Commissioner's notice does not express in clear terms what steps the authority must take to comply with it, that might give the authority scope to argue against the making of an order for committal. Any order punishing a contempt (whether civil or criminal) can be appealed to the Court of Appeal.[32]

Public authorities ought to bear in mind that even where contempt proceedings are not brought, an authority which fails to comply with a notice from the Information Commissioner opens itself up to negative publicity and reputation damage beyond that surrounding the publication of the Information Commissioner's determination, as its non-compliance is likely to be included in a report to Parliament, by way of either a special report or the Information Commissioner's regular annual report under section 49 of the FOIA, or both.

10.4.2   Prosecution of offences under section 77 (obstructing disclosure)

Where a public authority has been asked for information, it is an offence under section 77 of the FOIA for the authority or any of its officers, employees or anyone under its direction to alter, deface, block, erase, destroy or conceal any record which it holds, with the intention of preventing disclosure of any information to which the applicant would have been entitled under section 1 of the FOIA (subject to payment of any fee). The offence is punishable in the magistrates court by a fine of up to level 5 on the standard scale (currently £5,000 (Criminal Justice Act 1982, as amended, s.37)).

The Information Commissioner is a prosecuting authority for these purposes and a prosecution under this section can only be started in England, Wales and Northern Ireland by him or by, or with the consent of, the Director of Public Prosecutions. Any investigation into a suspected offence would take place under the rules of the Police and Criminal Evidence Act 1984 and prosecutions are brought in accordance with the Code for Crown Prosecutors. Government departments are not liable to prosecution under this section but a person in the public service of the Crown can be (s.81(3)).

10.4.3   Exchange of information with other ombudsmen

Schedule 7 to the FOIA (which is given effect by s.76(2)) provides that certain ombudsmen[33] can make available to the Information Commissioner any information which they obtain in the exercise of their statutory functions if it appears to them to relate to a matter in respect of which the Information Commissioner could exercise any power conferred by Part IV of the FOIA (which includes the issuing of Enforcement, Information and Decision Notices and the powers of entry and inspection) or section 48 of the FOIA (Practice Recommendations) or the commission of a section 77 offence.[34]

10.4.4 The Information Commissioner's powers of entry and inspection

Where the Information Commissioner has reasonable grounds to suspect that a public authority has failed to comply with any requirement of Part I of the FOIA or of one of his notices,[35] or similarly where he has reasonable grounds to suspect an authority of committing an offence under section 77 of the FOIA (see section 10.4.2), he can apply to a circuit judge[36] for a warrant authorising entry to any premises[37] and search, inspection and seizure of materials which may be evidence of such breaches. The warrant may in addition authorise the Information Commissioner to inspect, examine, operate and test any equipment found there in which information held by the public authority may be recorded. This will give the Information Commissioner access to computer files. These powers are granted under section 55 and Schedule 3 to the FOIA.

Except where urgent or where a warning might prevent seizure of relevant evidence, the judge will need to be satisfied before he grants the warrant that (i) the Information Commissioner gave seven days' written notice to the occupier of the premises demanding access; (ii) either access was demanded at a reasonable hour but unreasonably refused or entry was granted but the occupier unreasonably refused to comply with a request of the Information Commissioner or his staff; and (iii) the occupier has been notified by the Information Commissioner of the application for the warrant and has had an opportunity of being heard by the judge in relation to whether it should be issued or not.

Schedule 3 contains provisions for the manner of execution of such a warrant which include the following: a person executing the warrant may use such reasonable force as may be necessary (para.4); the warrant must be executed at a reasonable hour unless the person executing it considers that he has grounds to suspect that to do so would prevent finding the evidence which is sought (para.5); the warrant must be shown to an officer or member of staff of the occupier of the premises (whether the occupier is a public authority or not), if present, and a copy must be given to them or left in a prominent place (para.6(1) and (2)); the person executing the warrant must on request give a receipt for any item seized (para.7(1)); if requested by the occupier of the premises, and if the person executing the warrant considers it is possible without causing undue delay, he must give a copy of anything seized under the warrant (para.7(2)); anything seized under the warrant can be retained for as long as is necessary in all the circumstances (para.7(2)).

Certain information is exempt from inspection or seizure under the warrant. This applies first to any national security-related information falling within the exemptions in sections 23(1) or 24(1) in Part II of the FOIA (para.8). Secondly, a warrant cannot authorise inspection or seizure of any legally privileged communication held by a client or his legal adviser which contains legal advice relating to the FOIA or is made in contemplation of proceedings under or arising out of the Act (para.9). This does not extend to any material held in furtherance of a criminal purpose or held by a third party. Where the occupier of the premises objects to inspection or seizure on the ground that some of the material contains matters which are covered by these exemptions, he must nevertheless give the person exercising the warrant a copy of the remaining material if the latter so requests (para.10).

10.4.5 Related criminal offences: obstruction of execution of a warrant

The following offences are created by paragraph 12 of Schedule 3 to the FOIA:

- intentionally obstructing a person in the execution of a warrant issued under Schedule 3;
- failing without reasonable excuse to give any person executing a warrant such assistance as he may reasonably require for its execution.

10.5 INTERNAL REVIEW FOLLOWING A COMPLAINT

Where an applicant has requested information from a public authority and is dissatisfied with the result (perhaps because it has been refused or he suspects that there is additional disclosable information which has not been produced or he considers that the authority has not satisfied particular procedural requirements imposed by the FOIA), his first step must in most cases be to complain to the authority itself, asking it to reconsider its decision. The FOIA does not require authorities to have a procedure for reviewing decisions (the EIR does, by contrast: reg.11) but the guidance in the Section 45 Code of Practice is that they ought to (para.36).

Not only is a complaint to the authority in question likely to be the most straightforward way of resolving the matter but it is also virtually required by the FOIA by virtue of section 50(2)(*a*), which permits the Information Commissioner not to entertain a complaint where the complainant has not exhausted any internal complaints procedure which the public authority provides.

From an applicant's point of view, it is worth bearing in mind that the more wide-ranging the request (and the larger the public authority in question), the more likely it is in practice that relevant information will have been missed first time around and thus a different result might be reached when the request is looked at by a fresh pair of eyes, which will often be those of a more senior person, who may have a better or broader view of the work of the organisation.

10.5.1   The Section 45 Code of Practice

The Section 45 Code of Practice contains guidance for public authorities from the Secretary of State for Constitutional Affairs on practice which he thinks it desirable for them to follow in connection with the discharge of their functions under Part I of the FOIA. Breach may result in the Information Commissioner issuing a Practice Recommendation but cannot form the basis of a section 50(1) complaint by an applicant unless it also constitutes a breach of the FOIA. Paragraph 36 of the Section 45 Code of Practice suggests that in the first instance a complaint should, if possible, be resolved informally. If this cannot be achieved swiftly or satisfactorily, however, the public authority ought to give the applicant details of its internal complaints procedure, and of how to contact the Information Commissioner about the matter, should they wish to. Complaints procedures are to be as clear and simple as possible and to encourage prompt determination of complaints (para.39).

Similarly, when communicating a decision to refuse a request on the grounds that an exemption in Part II of the FOIA applies or that the request is vexatious or repetitious or that the estimated cost of complying with the request exceeds the free-provision ceiling, public authorities are obliged, under section 17(7) of the FOIA, to give applicants details of their internal complaints procedure, or else state that they do not have one. In doing so, paragraph 37 of the Code of Practice says they should provide full details of their own complaints procedure and of how to make a complaint, and inform the applicant of his or her right to complain to the Information Commissioner under section 50 if he or she is still dissatisfied following the authority's review.

Applicants wishing to submit a complaint to a public authority should therefore request details of the authority's complaints procedure, if not already provided, and follow it. Details of the complaints procedure will often be published under a public authority's Publication Scheme and may be available on its website.

Applicants should put their complaints in writing or confirm them in writing if made initially by telephone or in person. (Complaints (representations) under the EIR must be made in writing: reg.11(2).) Providing a clear, dated record of the complaint will assist its resolution by the public authority and also any subsequent complaint to the Information Commissioner. It also obliges the authority to deal with it properly because paragraph 38 of the Code of Practice advises authorities to treat as a complaint any written communication from the applicant (which includes faxes and emails) expressing dissatisfaction with its response to a request for information, as well as any written communication from a person who considers that the authority is not complying with its Publication Scheme. Such communications are to be handled in accordance with the authority's complaints procedure, even if the applicant does not expressly state their desire for the authority to review its decision or handling of the request. Nonetheless it would be advisable to mark the envelope or entitle the email, 'Request for internal review under FOIA/EIR', to ensure it is dealt with promptly. In urgent or significant cases which are likely to be appealed to the Information Commissioner it would also be prudent to send any letters by recorded delivery in order to have proof of posting and evidence of receipt by the authority.

10.5.2   Formulating arguments for and against the complaint

Even if not required to by the relevant public authority's complaints procedure, it will usually help an applicant to set out in as much detail as possible the grounds for disputing the authority's notice refusing disclosure of the requested information. Not only is a well argued case more likely to succeed in the first instance but it may well draw out more detailed reasons for any further refusal. This would be of value to the applicant, first in evaluating whether it is worth referring the matter to the Information Commissioner, and second in knowing what issues and arguments to deal with when putting together a complaint to the Information Commissioner.

An applicant requesting an internal review would thus be well advised to consider the reasons for non-disclosure given in the authority's refusal notice against the detail of the exemption provisions in Part II of the FOIA or the exceptions in regulation 12 of the EIR (both available on the Internet via the Information Commissioner's Office (ICO) website (**www.information commissioner.gov.uk**)). Helpful interpretation of how those provisions (and the public interest test) should apply in practice is provided not only in books such as this but also in a series of Awareness Guidance notes (and separate EIR guidance) available on the ICO website, and in guidance for government departments, but of use to other public authorities and applicants too, produced by the Department for Constitutional Affairs (**www.foi.gov.uk/ guidance/**). Similarly, the Department for Environment, Food and Rural Affairs has published guidance on the EIR (**www.defra.gov.uk/corporate/ opengov/eir/guidance/**). The applicant may be able to support the argument for disclosure further by pointing to cases where information was supplied in response to comparable requests, and should consider:

- reported rulings of the Information Tribunal (**www.informationtribunal. gov.uk**);
- published decisions (and related guidance) of the Information Commissioner (**www.informationcommissioner.gov.uk**);
- any disclosure log published by the authority in question, which will show whether it has granted similar requests in the past (see for example, details of information released by DEFRA at **www.defra.gov.uk/corporate/ opengov/inforelease**);
- disclosure logs kept by similar organisations;

- decisions of the Parliamentary Ombudsman (in particular when applying the public interest test) under the non-statutory Code of Practice on Access to Government Information, which was in force from 1994 to 2004 and has been superseded by the FOIA;[38]
- public interest arguments drawn from the freedom of information case law of comparable jurisdictions, as analysed in *Balancing the public interest: applying the public interest test to exemptions in the UK Freedom of Information Act 2000*, a study carried out by the Constitution Unit at the request of the Information Commissioner.[39]

Public authorities would of course also be well advised to have regard to such sources of guidance and authority, and they are likely to find that giving as detailed reasons as they can for turning down requests (supported by reference to any cases from the above list) will be the best way of reducing the number of complaints to the Information Comissioner that they are forced to deal with. As stated in section 10.1, however, and as the Information Commissioner has underlined, 'it would be a mistake to regard one decision as setting a binding precedent in other circumstances'.[40] Public authorities may also wish to note the Information Commissioner's recommendation that only the strongest reasons for turning down a request should be referred to in a section 17 refusal notice (or on a request for internal review) rather than listing every single possibly relevant exemption, as this could give the impression of an over secretive organisation. It will also potentially add delays to any subsequent investigation by the Information Commissioner or appeal to the Information Tribunal.

10.5.3 A fair, thorough and independent review

The Section 45 Code of Practice provides that an authority's complaints procedure should constitute a fair and thorough review of the handling of the request and of decisions taken pursuant to the FOIA, including decisions about where the public interest lies in respect of exempt information (para.39). There should be a full reconsideration of the case and where the complaint concerns a request for information the review should be undertaken, where reasonably practicable, by somebody senior to the person who took the original decision (para.40). The Information Commissioner has glossed this as, 'someone independent of the original decision making process'.[41]

10.5.4 Timescales

No time limit for the submission of requests for internal reviews under the FOIA is specified in the FOIA or the Code of Practice but complainants ought to consult the procedures of the relevant public authority to see what regulations it imposes in this regard (the position is different with complaints under the EIR – see section 10.5.6). If the authority refuses to accept a complaint, saying it is out of time, the applicant should apply direct to the Information Commissioner (but see section 10.6.1 on time restrictions for such complaints).

As for public authorities' responses, the Code of Practice states that complaints should be acknowledged promptly and that the complainant should be informed of the authority's target date for determining the complaint. Where it is apparent to the authority that it will take longer than estimated to deal with, it should inform the applicant and explain the reason for the delay (para.41).

Authorities are encouraged to set their own target times for dealing with complaints but these are required to be reasonable and subject to regular review. They must also be published, together with details of how successful the authority is in meeting them (para. 42). Guidance from the Department for Constitutional Affairs recommends that straightforward complaints be dealt with within two or three weeks of receipt, and complex reviews (for example, those involving a reconsideration of the public interest test) within six weeks. It also says that applicants should be given a new date by which the department will respond if the initial deadline is missed and that every effort must be made to ensure that this is met (**www.foi.gov.uk/guidance/proguide/chap09.htm**).

10.5.5   Outcomes

The Section 45 Code of Practice provides, naturally enough, that the complainant ought always to be informed of the outcome of the complaint (para. 40). Where the outcome of a complaint is a decision that information should be disclosed which was previously withheld, the information in question should be disclosed as soon as practicable and the applicant should be informed how soon this will be (para.44). Where the internal review reveals that the procedures within an authority have not been properly followed, the authority is to apologise to the applicant and take appropriate steps to prevent similar errors occurring in future (para.45).

Where the outcome of a complaint is that an initial decision to withhold information is upheld, or is otherwise in the authority's favour, the applicant is to be informed of the right to ask the Information Commissioner for a determination on whether the request for information has been dealt with in accordance with the requirements of Part I of the FOIA, and is to be given details of how to do so (para.46).

Public authorities are required to maintain records of all complaints and their outcome. They are also supposed to have procedures in place for monitoring complaints and for reviewing, and, if necessary, amending, procedures for dealing with requests for information where such action is indicated by more than occasional reversals of initial decisions (para.43).

10.5.6   EIR

The Section 45 Code of Practice does not apply to requests made for environmental information but largely similar provisions are contained in the code of practice issued under regulation 16 of the EIR. The EIR themselves provide that applications for an internal review of decisions on requests for environmental information must be submitted in writing within 40 working days of the date on which the applicant believes the public authority has failed to comply with a requirement of the EIR. In most cases this will mean within 40 working days of receipt of the refusal notice turning down the original request. The authority cannot charge any fee to consider the complaint and it must reply as soon as possible, within 40 working days in any event. Notification of any revised decision by the authority must include a statement of its failure to comply with the EIR, the action it has decided on in order to comply with the relevant requirement and the period within which that action is to be taken (reg.11). Where the decision is taken to release information this should be actioned immediately (Regulation 16 Code of Practice, para.65).

10.6   COMPLAINING TO THE INFORMATION COMMISSIONER

10.6.1   Complaints about individual requests for information

The term 'complaints' when used in this context is convenient shorthand for what is in fact an application to the Information Commissioner under section 50(1) of the FOIA, by a person who requested information from a public authority, for a decision on whether that request was dealt with by the authority in accordance with its obligations under Part I of the FOIA (or Parts 2 and 3 of the EIR where relevant). An application under section 50(1) cannot be made because a public authority has merely breached a Code of Practice provision.

Those obligations include, most significantly, the obligation under section 1(1) of the FOIA to confirm or deny whether the authority holds information requested by the applicant and to communicate it to him (subject, most importantly, to the exemptions in Part II).[42] However, it also includes many obligations of a more procedural nature, so that a complaint could, for instance, be made to the Information Commissioner where the applicant believes:

- the public authority has charged excessive fees for responding to his request (FOIA, ss.9 and 13; EIR, reg.8);
- the authority took longer to respond to the request than it should have (FOIA, s.10; EIR, regs.5(2), 7 and 14);

- the authority was unreasonable in not complying with his preference for how he wished to receive the information (FOIA, s.11; EIR, reg.6);
- the authority was wrong to say the cost of complying with the request meant that it was not obliged to comply (FOIA, ss.12 and 13; EIR, reg.8);
- the authority was wrong to label the request vexatious or repetitious and refuse to deal with it (FOIA, s.14; EIR, reg.12(4)(*b*));
- the authority failed to offer him appropriate assistance in formulating and submitting his request (FOIA, s.16; EIR, reg.9;
- the authority should have given reasons for claiming that the information sought was exempt (FOIA, s.17(1), (3) and (4); EIR, reg.14(3)).

The typical stages through which a complaint to the Information Commissioner will pass are described below. Certain aspects of this procedure are set out in the FOIA but much of the detail is a matter of discretion for the Information Commissioner. Increasingly that detail is becoming available in ICO publications available on the website, the most significant of which are the following two policy documents: *Regulation under the Freedom of Information Act 2000 and the Environmental Information Regulations 2004* (referred to in this chapter as the *Regulation* paper) and a memorandum of understanding between the Information Commissioner and, effectively, government departments[43] (referred to in this chapter as the MoU).

Formalities

Applications for a decision under section 50(1) should be submitted to the ICO in writing either by post to FOI/EIR Complaints Resolution, Information Commissioner's Office, Wycliffe House, Water Lane, Wilmslow, Cheshire SK9 5AF; or by fax to 01625 524 510. (A complaint could be submitted by email to *mail@ico.gsi.gov.uk* but given the need to send accompanying documents, which an applicant may not have in electronic form, it may be easier to do so by post or fax.) It would be prudent to obtain proof of posting by using the recorded delivery service. (Queries can be made via the telephone helpline on 01625 545 745, the fax number above, or by email to: *foi-enquiries@ico.gsi.gov.uk* or *eir-enquiries@ico.gsi.gov.uk* as appropriate.)

The applicant must be identified, i.e. complaints submitted anonymously will not be considered (this does not preclude the submission of requests by a named person on behalf of another, whose identity is not disclosed). An address of course must also be provided, and it can be helpful for the applicant to give his telephone number and/or email address as well.

Only the person who submitted the original request (or a person acting on behalf of that person) may apply to the Information Commissioner under section 50(1) of the FOIA. (Third parties cannot apply: see section 10.9.)

In order to consider the complaint, the Information Commissioner will expect to receive the following, as appropriate:[44]

- brief details of the issues the applicant wishes the Information Commissioner to consider;
- a copy of the original request for information, or in the absence of that (i) a summary of the request; and (ii) evidence that the request was submitted to the public authority (a recorded delivery receipt, for instance, or an acknowledgement from the authority);
- a copy of the refusal notice issued by the public authority;
- a copy of the applicant's complaint to the public authority concerning that initial refusal of information (i.e. the applicant's request for an internal review); or if no such complaint was made, an explanation why not;
- a copy of the public authority's response following its reconsideration of the request;
- any other information the applicant believes relevant. This could include, for example, the complainant's arguments as to why the information does not fall within the exemptions claimed by the authority, or why the public interest favours disclosure if a qualified exemption is relevant. Although there is no requirement for an applicant to set out any arguments in support of the access request, it may well be in his or her interests to do so, both in order to persuade, and in view of the fact that, in order to make decision making as speedy as possible, against a background of a high volume of complaints, the Information Commissioner's staff will place 'heavy reliance ... on the content of Refusal Notices and on specific allegations of non-compliance as put forward by complainants, though allowance will be made for the needs of "non-professional" complainants'.[45] If the applicant needs the information urgently, it would be relevant to say so and why. There is no guarantee, however, that the complaint will be expedited as a result.

Applications must be submitted without undue delay or the Information Commissioner is entitled not to consider them (s.50(2)(b)). Undue delay is not defined in the FOIA but the Information Commissioner has indicated that he will normally expect complaints to be submitted within two months of receipt of the public authority's final refusal to disclose the information, i.e. following any internal review (para.10 of the *Regulation* paper). Complaints submitted later than this might still be considered if there is a good reason for the delay. On the other hand, the Information Commissioner will not consider complaints submitted before the end of the period which the FOIA allows the authority for complying with a request, or before the extended period (if reasonable) which the authority has said it needs, in a refusal notice under section 17(2), to consider the public interest position regarding the request.

There is no fee to pay on submission and neither the applicant nor the public authority can be ordered by the Information Commissioner to pay the other's costs. In some cases, parties (especially public authorities) will want to obtain expert evidence and/or legal advice in order to argue their case before the Information Commissioner. Such costs will potentially be recoverable only if the matter goes on appeal to the Information Tribunal (see sections 10.7.1 and 10.7.2).

Acknowledgement

On receipt of a complaint, the ICO will send an acknowledgement to the complainant.

The Information Commissioner decides whether to deal with the complaint

A case officer from the ICO's complaints resolution team will be assigned to the complaint and will conduct an initial evaluation to determine whether or not the Information Commissioner has a duty to make a decision on it in accordance with section 50(2) of the FOIA or, if not, whether he will exercise his discretion to do so nonetheless. The duty arises in relation to all applications for a decision by those who have previously applied to a public authority for information, except in the four specific situations listed below.

1. Where the complainant has not exhausted any complaints procedure provided by the public authority in conformity with the Section 45 Code of Practice (see section 10.5.1).

    The Information Commissioner might, however, be prepared to take on such a complaint where, for example, the public authority has simply not responded to the applicant's request for information, or where there is nobody suitable to undertake the internal review because there is no one on the authority's staff who is independent of, and more senior to, the original decision maker.
2. Where there has been undue delay in making the application (in most cases this means anything later than two months after the public authority's final decision – see above, 'Formalities').
3. Where the application is frivolous or vexatious.

    These terms are not defined in the FOIA but the Information Commissioner has outlined his likely approach as follows. He may regard a complaint as vexatious where: it clearly has no serious purpose or value; it is designed to cause disruption or annoyance; its main effect is that it causes disproportionate inconvenience or expense or harasses the public authority or the Information Commissioner, including where it is part of a campaign conducted by different, but linked, individuals; it is made in respect of information which the complainant knows to be exempt from disclosure and, if relevant, not in the public interest to be disclosed; it is made in respect of information which the complainant knows will have to be redacted (blanked out) to such an extent that the material disclosed would be meaningless or of no real use to him; or where it can otherwise be fairly characterised as obsessive or manifestly unreasonable. Abusive, offensive or threatening language may be a strong indicator that a complaint is vexatious but will not be conclusive. A complaint which is so lengthy and rambling as to be impenetrable may be considered vexatious. The Information Commissioner may regard a complaint as vexatious and/or frivolous where it concerns a request that was rejected by a public authority under section 14 as vexatious or a repeated request but is not supported by good evidence of grounds for complaint. The Information Commissioner may regard a complaint as frivolous if it has no reasonable prospect of success or where there is no real interest in its outcome. He may equally regard a complaint as frivolous where the authority had clearly shown that the Information Commissioner, the Information Tribunal or the courts have ruled in the authority's favour in similar cases. In addition, a complaint may be regarded as frivolous where the complaint is so minor that the serving of a Decision Notice would have no purpose, for example where a complainant had received all the information requested within 21 days rather than 20. Although the Information Commissioner has not said so, it is possible that a complaint may be regarded as vexatious or frivolous where a complainant insists on pursuing it even after the public authority has agreed to disclose the requested information during the Information Commissioner's handling of the matter, such as following a Preliminary Decision Notice (see section 10.3.4 and 'The Information Commissioner's policy on preliminary notices' below).

It is important to note that the Information Commissioner must consider whether the complaint is vexatious rather than the complainant. Nevertheless, if the Information Commissioner is aware of previous vexatious conduct by the complainant and considers the current complaint a continuation of that conduct, he may conclude that the complaint itself is vexatious.[46]

4. Where the application has been withdrawn or abandoned.

It is understood that the Information Commissioner will only regard a complaint as withdrawn where the ICO has received a written statement from the complainant confirming that that is the case. Similarly, the Information Commissioner is likely to regard a complaint as abandoned only where the complainant has failed to reply to a minimum of two pieces of correspondence, the latter of which will warn that this is what will happen in the absence of a response within a given period, such as 28 days.[47]

As part of his initial evaluation, the case officer may contact the relevant public authority to establish the basic circumstances of the case. He will contact the complainant usually within 28 days to request any further information necessary to complete his initial evaluation; or to confirm that the Information Commissioner will be investigating the complaint (whether under a duty to do so or otherwise) and to explain what will happen next; or to explain why the Information Commissioner will not be dealing with the complaint, in which case some advice may be given on what the complainant ought to do next, such as applying to the public authority for an internal review.

For the sake of speed and efficiency, the parties will often be contacted by telephone or email, as well as by post. When communicating with the ICO, the parties should always quote the case reference number which they will be given at this initial stage.

An applicant whose application for a decision under section 50(1) is not proceeded with on one of the four section 50(2) grounds discussed above could challenge the Information Commissioner's decision in that regard by way of judicial review – there is no appeal provided under the FOIA. The bar to success would be set high, however, as the applicant would need to show that no Information Commissioner could reasonably have come to the same decision.[48]

The Information Commissioner investigates the complaint

The Information Commissioner will be able to decide a minority of cases with little more than that in the way of investigation but in many others he will need to ask the public authority for information so he can make his assessment. It is worth noting in passing that a public authority cannot refuse to disclose any information to the Information Commissioner or the Information Tribunal which is 'necessary for the discharge of their functions' on the grounds that in doing so it would be making itself civilly or criminally liable (by breaching a confidence, for example).[49] Nor will a claim of legal privilege permit the public authority to withhold information from the Information Commissioner except where it concerns FOIA-related communications between a lawyer and client, or, where proceedings are in contemplation, a third party (s.51(5) and (6)).

The approach which the Information Commissioner is likely to take with public authorities when requesting information is set out in the MoU (see note 43), which contains guideline procedures designed to apply in the majority of cases in relation to his functions under sections 50 and 51, which deal with Decision Notices and Information Notices. Procedures regarding Enforcement Notices are not covered by the MoU. Nor does the document apply where a government department is claiming an exemption under the national security provisions of the legislation (ss.23 and 24 of the FOIA and reg.12(5)(*a*) of the EIR), in which case the separate considerations discussed at Annex 2 to the MoU will apply.[50] Although the MoU applies directly only to government departments, the Information Commissioner will operate to the same standards with the rest of the public sector, and likewise expects all public authorities to follow the principles of the MoU in their dealings with him.[51]

The Information Commissioner will initially make an informal request for information and will normally only issue authorities with Information Notices (see section 10.3.2) where he believes information is being withheld or unreasonably delayed. Where possible, he will warn of his intention to serve such a notice.[52] In general the Information Commissioner will not seek information from public authorities unless necessary to determine the complaint. Specifically, he will not ask authorities to provide information where they claim exemption from the duty to confirm or deny in cases where he can see such a claim is justified without access to any further information (para.12 of the MoU). Other situations where the ICO is unlikely to request information include where a public authority is self-evidently justified in relying upon an absolute exemption or can clearly justify refusal on public interest grounds, or else where the complaint simply concerns a procedural point, such as an inadequate refusal notice.[53]

The Information Commissioner aims to notify public authorities of the details of complaints against them as soon as practicable and certainly within 10 days of receiving them. He will ask for all relevant information and invite the authority to comment on the case, ideally through a single channel of communication (para.7 of the MoU). The Information Commissioner will normally expect public authorities to supply him with the information as quickly as possible and in any event within 20 working days of his request. Any follow up requests for information are to be met within 10 days. Where authorities cannot meet these standard deadlines, they will be expected to give reasons and a date by when they aim to provide the information (para.7 of the MoU and para.24 of the *Regulation* paper). Wherever possible the Information Commissioner and public authorities are supposed to communicate electronically with each other (para.27 of the MoU).

The Information Commissioner will generally request the public authority's record of how it responded to the access request and why, as well as any information that was withheld from the applicant or redacted (blanked out) (paras.23 and 24 of the *Regulation* paper). He is also entitled to ask for relevant unrecorded information, such as what officials know of the relevant matter beyond what is documented.[54] He may also wish the authority to tell him any views on the access request expressed by an interested third party, such as on the potential for prejudice to arise from disclosure or the relative public interests in disclosing or withholding the information. If he judges that any such third party's views are potentially relevant but have not been provided, it is thought that the Information Commissioner will in some cases approach the third party himself and in others invite the public authority to do so.

In sensitive cases and where the security of the public authority's information is a particular issue, government departments (and potentially other public authorities) can ask the Information Commissioner himself or named staff to go and inspect papers *in situ* rather than sending them to the ICO. The Information Commissioner will not refuse such requests unless they significantly obstruct the discharge of his statutory functions (MoU, paras.15 and 16). In other cases, the Information Commissioner may agree it is mutually beneficial for his staff to inspect information at the public authority rather than being provided with it, such as where the papers are voluminous or need technical explanation by officials (MoU, para.17). The Information Commissioner has agreed not to retain papers obtained from authorities for longer than necessary and will liaise over their return or disposal (MoU, para.13).

If the Information Commissioner has not received all the information he requires from a public authority after informal request and service of an Information Notice, he can seek a warrant to obtain access to any premises where he might find such information (see section 10.4.4).

Authorities should take up the Information Commissioner's invitation to comment on the complaint by setting out in writing their arguments against disclosure or in defence of whatever other complaint is levelled at them. In appropriate cases this might include written expert evidence showing why a particular exemption applies. For example, where a public authority is relying on the exemption under section 29(1)(*a*) in respect of disclosures which would be likely to prejudice the economic interests of the UK or part of it, the authority's arguments might be bolstered by presenting the Information Commissioner with a report prepared by a suitably qualified economist or industry expert. Similarly, in the context of the exemption under section 44, an authority may wish to obtain professional legal advice on whether the disclosure of requested material would breach a duty of confidence owed to a third party and whether there would be a defence of public interest or not. (The Information Commissioner has recognised that when considering a complaint he may sometimes need to get his own expert advice on the validity of the arguments presented to him in relation to the exemptions.)[55] The costs of seeking external advice would not be recoverable from the other party by order of the Information Commissioner. Even if the case went to the Information Tribunal the recoverability of costs is limited (see sections 10.7.1 and 10.7.2).

It is worth pointing out that there is nothing to prevent a public authority from arguing to the Information Commissioner that it is entitled to withhold information on the basis of an exemption which it did not rely on when turning down the applicant's request for information originally. It may, however, find in such a case that it is ordered in a Decision Notice to issue an amended refusal letter citing the relevant exemption and grounds.

Where an authority is relying on a qualified exemption, it will clearly need to give the Information Commissioner what it thinks are the public interest arguments against disclosure, but it should certainly consider commenting on the arguments in favour as well. This is a tactical question. Instinctively one might not wish to draw attention to matters which support the opponent; but it may often be advantageous to the authority to do so, thereby showing the Information Commissioner that it has thought carefully about all the issues, and maximising the persuasiveness of its claim that the public interest arguments in favour of maintaining the exemption do indeed outweigh those supporting disclosure.

The Information Commissioner's policy is to contact the complainant and the public authority whenever appropriate during his consideration of the complaint and will usually provide them with a progress report every 28 days (MoU, para.19).

On the question of how far the Information Commissioner will tell the complainant what information he has sought and received from the public authority and whether the complainant can ask for a copy of it, the starting point is that in principle the Information Commissioner will provide all information it receives from each party to the other. This is subject to an important qualification, however: the Information Commissioner will not disclose information (whether to the complainant or a third party) which has been provided to him in confidence without the consent of the supplier. In addition, the Information Commissioner will not disclose information against the wishes of a public authority if the information remains potentially the subject of an appeal to the Information Tribunal or the courts.[56]

Finally, as the Information Commissioner is himself a public authority under Schedule 1 to the FOIA, he has agreed to notify government departments (and probably any public authority) as soon as possible where he has been asked (whether under the FOIA or otherwise) to provide information supplied by a department, or he considers release of such information necessary in connection with any enactment, proceedings, EU-related obligation or otherwise. In addition, the Information Commissioner has undertaken to resist disclosure by all reasonable means, including appeals, where it is reasonable to do so (see MoU, paras.10 and 11).[57]

Hearings

The Information Commissioner may from time to time arrange meetings with one or other party if this would speed the resolution of a complaint but will not generally hold hearings.[58]

Burden of proof and standard of proof

While the Information Commissioner talks at times of the underlying presumption of openness in the FOIA,[59] this is merely a way of describing the fact that the perspective of the FOIA is to start by granting a general right of access and then subjecting that to certain limitations – principally the exemptions, and even the majority of those are circumscribed by the public interest test. There is in fact no express burden on either the complainant or the public authority to prove their case or else know that they cannot succeed.

Ordinarily the burden of proof in administrative matters lies with the party alleging that the decision is invalid,[60] in this case the complainant. Certainly the complainant will need to prove that he submitted the request for information and will help himself by detailing the grounds of his complaint. Rather than his having to go on to show that no exemption applies, though, the structure of the FOIA as just described suggests that the onus will at that point shift to the public authority to establish that a specific exemption does apply and, if appropriate, that the greater public interest lies in withholding the information. It may, however, be inappropriate to speak of a formal burden of proof in the context of cases before the Information Commissioner.[61]

The position differs under the EIR, as public authorities are subject to an express presumption of openness (reg.12(2)), and thus do appear to bear the burden of proving that they are not required to release the environmental information in question. Accordingly, should there be doubt as to whether an exception applies or where the greater public interest lies, the Information Commissioner is likely to rule in favour of disclosure when dealing with complaints under the EIR.

Where the public authority does present evidence, it will need to come up to the normal civil standard, namely that the facts alleged are, on the balance of probabilities, true. This would be the case for example where an authority argues under section 38 that disclosure of the requested information would, or would be likely to, endanger someone's physical or mental health or their safety. Merely asserting harm will not suffice (*Attorney-General* v. *Guardian Newspapers (No.2)* [1990] AC 109, 263, 283).

Exceptionally, the legislation provides five instances where a government minister may serve a conclusive evidence certificate which precludes the Information Commissioner from assessing the evidence himself. For example, under regulation 15 of the EIR a Minister can assert conclusively that disclosure of certain information would adversely affect national security and would not be in the public interest (see section 10.7.2).

Attempt at informal resolution

The Information Commissioner has recognised that particularly while the FOIA is bedding down, applicants and public authorities involved in complaints will be keen to obtain a ruling from him (and the Information Tribunal) in order to obtain clarity on the practical application of the FOIA and establish points of principle. Nonetheless, it is his hope that parties to complaints will, as time goes on, be prepared to settle complaints prior to a formal ruling, so that all involved can enjoy the savings of time, money and effort and the increased regulatory efficiency that that would bring.[62] He has agreed to explore the scope for settlement wherever practicable (MoU, para.20). The Information Commissioner anticipates that in some cases public authorities will be moved to respond to a request which they had previously ignored or they might be more forthcoming as regards the information they are prepared to disclose when they learn that the applicant has sought the Information Commissioner's intervention. In other cases, the Information Commissioner may seek to stimulate such a change of heart by issuing the public authority with a Preliminary Decision Notice (see section 10.3.4 and later in this section) showing his intention to order disclosure of some or all the information previously refused. Where the complainant is content with the steps the authority offers to take (for example to provide all or at least some of the information) the Information Commissioner will invite the complainant to withdraw the complaint. If the complainant agrees, the Information Commissioner no longer has a duty to make a decision on the complaint by virtue of section 50(2)(d). Where appropriate it will be made clear to the complainant that even if he does not withdraw the complaint, any Decision Notice issued will record the Information Commissioner's decision but will not require the authority to take any further steps.[63] If the complainant refuses to withdraw the complaint without good reason, he may be running the risk that the Information Commissioner will not go on to make a decision, on the grounds that the complaint is then frivolous or vexatious because the information requested has been received and there is nothing left to complain about. Before refusing to withdraw a complaint in such circumstances, therefore, a complainant ought to ensure he understands from the Information Commissioner what the consequences of his doing so will be. If the Information Commissioner were to refuse to issue a Decision Notice, there would be no grounds for appeal to the Information Tribunal and the only means of challenge would be by way of judicial review or else by invoking the ICO complaints procedure and then appealing to the Parliamentary Ombudsman (see section 10.6.3).

In most cases, where a complainant does withdraw his complaint, the Information Commissioner is unlikely to issue a Decision Notice.[64] However, even where a public authority suddenly decides to disclose some or all of the requested information, and the complainant is prepared to withdraw the complaint, that will not always guarantee the avoidance of a formal notice and possible attendant negative publicity for the authority. For example, in compliance with his section 47 duty to publish information about the operation of the FOIA and about good practice, the Information Commissioner might decide to issue a Decision Notice in any event, to which he could then give publicity as an example to other public authorities on a point of principle. Again, therefore, prior to agreeing to settle a complaint, an authority may wish to find out whether this is likely.

Any Preliminary Decision Notice will be served on both the public authority and the complainant and they will have an opportunity to make written representations on it. If they do not respond by the time specified in the notice (usually 30 days), the ICO will generally proceed on the basis that the parties are happy with the conclusion set out in the notice.[65]

The MoU says that where a government department indicates it will not comply with steps required of it set out in a preliminary notice, the Information Commissioner will liaise with it over the reasons for its adopting this stance and explore any alternatives. Whether the Information Commissioner follows the same approach with non-governmental public bodies remains to be seen.

The Information Commissioner's policy on preliminary notices

The Information Commissioner sets out his policy on the use of preliminary notices in Annex 1 to the *Regulation* paper. 'The governing principle which will be followed is that preliminary notices will be served in those cases where the Information Commissioner judges that this is likely to lead to a swifter more equitable outcome both for applicants and public authorities' (para.3). Although that comment seems mainly to address a situation where a complaint has been made, the Information Commissioner will use a preliminary stage not only for Decision Notices but also for Information Notices and Enforcement Notices which are unrelated to a section 50(1) application (such as in relation to authorities' obligations regarding Publication Schemes). The decision whether to serve a preliminary notice or not is a matter of judgment but the Information Commissioner will be guided by the rules of thumb he sets out in Annex 1.

It appears that preliminary notices will be issued primarily in the more complex cases (those more likely to generate an appeal) and that a Preliminary Decision Notice is unlikely to be thought suitable where:

- the complaint concerns procedural matters only, such as where a public authority failed to issue an adequate refusal notice or the Information Commissioner regards as insufficient the assistance provided to the applicant;

- there is no practical purpose in specifying steps for the public authority to take, such as where the requested information was provided but later than the 20 days allowed by the FOIA, or where the authority is clearly justified in claiming an exemption;
- a refusal notice or a complaint explicitly reject compromise (it follows that in appropriate cases parties should consider making such views clear to the Information Commissioner).

Where a public authority relies on an irrelevant exemption in refusing an access request, a Preliminary Decision Notice may be issued but will generally not be.

A preliminary notice is far more likely to be issued in the following cases:

- where a correct exemption has been relied on but disclosure has been refused under the public interest test – unless the Information Tribunal has ordered disclosure in similar circumstances;
- where, in complex cases, the Information Commissioner's investigation of the complaint has identified additional exemptions or public interest arguments on which the parties could rely.

Like Decision Notices (see later in this section) a Preliminary Decision Notice might require a public authority to reconsider its response to the original request, perhaps taking account of an exemption not previously applied by it. Unlike a Decision Notice, it may contain a number of alternatives.[66]

The Information Commissioner is likely to issue a preliminary notice prior to a final Enforcement Notice where this might allow the authority to explain that enforcement is inappropriate, because for example it is already in the process of altering its procedures to avoid breaching the FOIA in future; or else where a preliminary stage would enable the Information Commissioner to discuss and agree with the authority a realistic timetable for necessary changes, such as the introduction of a Publication Scheme.

Preliminary Information Notices will be more uncommon and served only where the Information Commissioner anticipates that immediately serving a final notice would be likely to lead to a relatively complex appeal to the Information Tribunal.

It is not yet clear what, if any, information about informally settled complaints will be published by the Information Commissioner, and whether, if it is, that might include the identity of the parties. As a precaution parties should therefore consider notifying the ICO of any preference they may have not to be identified, and giving reasons.

The Information Commissioner's decision

If the matter cannot be resolved informally, the Information Commissioner will take account of any representations made in response to any Preliminary

Decision Notice served and issue a Decision Notice setting out any steps required of the public authority, such as what information is to be disclosed, how soon and by what means. He might order disclosure of all or just part of the requested information or else he might uphold the authority's claim that it is exempt from disclosure. Where he finds that the authority incorrectly relied upon a particular exemption, he would appear to be free to find that the information is nevertheless exempt by virtue of another exemption.

The Information Commissioner has indicated that on occasion he will issue Decision Notices which do not determine whether or not the public authority ought to disclose the requested information but which require the authority to reconsider its response to the original request, possibly in the light of factors or exemptions which the Information Commissioner speci-fies.[67] A complainant who felt that in putting the onus back on the authority, the Information Commissioner had failed to discharge his section 50 duty to decide whether or not the authority had complied with its statutory obliga-tions, could appeal against the Decision Notice to the Information Tribunal.

Served with the Decision Notice but in a separate document (either annexed to it or in an accompanying letter) is a short Statement of Reasons summarising the Information Commissioner's rationale for the decision, which will provide a basis for the parties to consider an appeal.[68] In view of the fact that public authorities may wish to appeal against the decision to the Information Tribunal and that a Statement of Reasons may include refer-ences to or quotations from material which an authority considers exempt, the version given to the applicant will often not be identical to that given to the authority.[69] Decision Notices and Statements of Reasons will be served on parties simultaneously and they will be given time to digest the contents before they are made public (MoU, para.23 and see later in this section). The delay in publication will be a matter of days only. The authority will have 28 days in which to lodge an appeal. In the absence of any appeal, the deadline for taking action ordered in the Decision Notice will often be 30 days from the date of that notice.

As to the requirements in the legislation regarding the content of Decision Notices, their appealability, the potential for ministerial override, and the consequences of non-compliance, see Sections 10.3.1 and 10.3.5.

Publicity

All Decision Notices and Enforcement Notices are publicly available and the Information Commissioner's policy is to post the most significant ones on the ICO website, together with an index of all other cases so that anybody can request a copy of the relevant notice. He also places on the website a summary of all important cases which he considers,[70] excluding any exempt information.[71] The Information Commissioner is prepared to comment on published Decision Notices but without disclosing any information which may be subject to appeal (MoU, para.26). Cases likely to be of particular assistance to other public authorities will receive additional publicity, possibly in the form of a commentary in which the Information Commissioner draws out the lessons to be learned.[72] The public authority which is the subject of the complaint will almost always be identified, whereas complainants' names will generally not be released, unless for example they are journalists who have publicly referred to their complaint.[73] As a precaution, parties (especially complainants) should consider notifying the ICO of any preference they may have not to be identified and giving reasons. Preliminary notices, Practice Recommendations and Information Notices will not normally be published.[74]

The Information Commissioner will also publish the nature and outcome of Information Tribunal cases and prosecutions brought in relation to the FOIA. Information Tribunal decisions are published on the Tribunal's website (**www.informationtribunal.gov.uk**).

Timescales

The time taken to resolve complaints will obviously vary considerably from one case to another, depending on its complexity and the speed and adequacy of response of the public authority and the workload on ICO staff. Procedural cases can be dealt with relatively quickly but cases involving the application of the exemptions take longer. In the first ten months of the FOIA's full operation around 2,000 complaints were lodged with the ICO, of which some 700 had been resolved. Some months earlier the Information Commissioner's informal target had been to issue a decision in 50 per cent of cases within six months of receipt of the complaint.[75]

10.6.2 Complaints relating to a Publication Scheme

A person seeking to obtain information from a public authority which is supposedly available under its Publication Scheme may be concerned at the amount of money he has been asked to pay for it or at the near impossibility of obtaining access to it in practice. In another situation a company or an individual whose reputation has been damaged by information released by a public authority under its Publication Scheme may be irate that they were not consulted prior to the disclosure.[76] An application under section 50(1) for a decision of the Information Commissioner cannot be made, however, in relation to a complaint about a public authority's Publication Scheme. Nevertheless, were these people to bring their grievances to the Information Commissioner's attention, he would be able to investigate the matter under his general duties to promote authorities' observance of the FOIA and the Codes of Practice (ss.47 and 48). The outcome may be that he issues the public authority with a Practice Recommendation or an Enforcement Notice but, unlike a Decision Notice, these are not required to be served on the person who had complained. In some circumstances, it may be open to an aggrieved party to take legal action in respect of disclosures under a Publication Scheme, such as for judicial review, breach of confidence or under the DPA (see section 10.9.5).

10.6.3 Complaints about the ICO

A party dissatisfied with the content of the Information Commissioner's ruling should appeal to the Information Tribunal. However, if a party wishes to complain about the way in which an assessment was conducted, rudeness of staff, for example, they should ask for a copy of the ICO's complaints procedure. The Office will try to respond to complaints with their findings within 28 days. If the complainant remains dissatisfied, he or she can appeal the decision and ultimately complain to the Parliamentary Ombudsman through an MP.[77]

10.7 APPEALS TO THE INFORMATION TRIBUNAL[78]

There are two separate regimes for appeals to the Information Tribunal under the FOIA: the first in relation to appeals brought under section 57(1) or (2) of the Act challenging notices issued by the Information Commissioner; the second concerns appeals brought under section 60(1) or (4) relating to ministerial certificates issued in the context of information which is allegedly exempt as it relates to national security matters. The two regimes are governed principally by procedural rules contained in two different pieces of subordinate legislation. Appeals under the EIR are subject to the same regimes by virtue of reg.18.

10.7.1 Appeals against the Information Commissioner's notices (s.57 appeals)

Under section 57 of the FOIA both the complainant and the public authority may appeal as of right to the Information Tribunal against a Decision Notice served on them by the Information Commissioner. A public authority has a similar right in respect of an Enforcement Notice or an Information Notice, as does a responsible authority in relation to certain Decision Notices or Enforcement Notices regarding materials in the Public Records Office (now called National Archives).[79] An interested third party or a complainant without an automatic right of appeal may ask the Information Tribunal to exercise its discretion to join him to the appeal.

Grounds of appeal

The grounds of appeal are contained in section 58, which provides that the appeal will succeed if the Information Tribunal finds that the notice is unlawful (for example because the Information Commissioner misinterpreted the effect of an exemption on the facts or because he ignored a material fact) or the Information Commissioner should have exercised his discretion differently in dealing with the complaint (for instance, in relation to his analysis of the competing public interests in disclosure of the information and maintaining the exemption). In all other cases, the Information Tribunal is bound to dismiss the appeal. When considering the appeal, the Information Tribunal may review any finding of fact on which the notice was based. In allowing the appeal, the Information Tribunal may issue any notice which the Information Commissioner could have done, in substitution for the original. It is not able to award compensation or impose fines in connection with breaches of the FOIA. As to costs, see later in this section.

The Information Tribunal panel

Appointment to the Information Tribunal in general is governed by section 6 of the DPA, which provides for a legally qualified chairman and one or more deputy chairmen, chosen by the Lord Chancellor, and for members appointed by the Secretary of State for Constitutional Affairs, who do not have to have a legal qualification but who represent the interests of either public authorities or those who make requests for information under the FOIA.

The Information Tribunal panel that hears specific appeals under section 57 of the FOIA is presided over by the chairman or a deputy chairman and an equal number of the members appointed to represent the interests of applicants and of public authorities, thus making a panel of at least (but usually) three. The individual members are nominated by the chairman, or, if he is unable to act, by a deputy chairman.[80] There is an exception in relation to certain appeals against Information Notices, which are heard by the chairman alone (see below). The chairman may also act for the Information Tribunal on matters preliminary or incidental to an appeal under certain rules.[81]

Procedure

The rules governing procedure in appeals under section 57 are principally contained in the Information Tribunal (Enforcement Appeals) Rules 2005, as amended (the 2005 Rules) (see **www.informationtribunal.gov.uk** for Rules and Practice Direction 1).[82] Provision is made for a wide range of procedural steps, some familiar from ordinary court-based litigation but others not. Some are of particular note.[83]

Under rule 5, time for appeal, a written notice of appeal must be served on the Information Tribunal within 28 days of service on the appellant of the relevant Information Commissioner's notice. This time limit can be extended if the Information Tribunal considers it just and right to do so in view of the special circumstances.

A notice of appeal (rule 4) must: (a) identify the decision of the Information Commissioner which is being disputed and the date on which the related notice was served on the appellant; (b) state the following: the name and address of the appellant; the grounds of appeal; whether or not the appellant is likely to want a hearing; the name and address of the public authority to which the disputed decision relates; the special circumstances which justify the Information Tribunal's accepting jurisdiction where the notice has not been served within the ordinary 28-day limit (see above); an address for service of documents on the appellant; and (c) be signed by or on behalf of the appellant.

An appellant may seek the early determination of the appeal by including such a request in the notice of appeal and giving reasons for it.

In an appeal against an Information Notice, the notice of appeal must include any representations the appellant wishes to make as to why it is necessary in the interests of justice for the appeal to be heard by an Information Tribunal panel rather than by the chairman sitting alone as provided by rule 21(2) (see the discussion on hearings (rules 16–24) later in this section).

A notice of appeal form and guidance is available at the Information Tribunal's website. The completed notice of appeal should be sent to: Information Tribunal, Arnhem House Support Centre, PO Box 6987, Leicester, Leicestershire, LE1 6ZX. The fax number is 0116 249 4253. The email address is: *informationtribunal@dca.gsi.gov.uk* and the telephone number is 0845 600 0877. (See the discussion on notices (rule 25) later in this section.) Information Tribunal staff will send the appellant an acknowledgement of service and serve a copy of the notice of appeal on the Information Commissioner and any other party (rule 6(1)(*b*)).

Under rules 8 and 9 the Information Commissioner has 21 days to send the Information Tribunal and the appellant a written reply in which he sets out his grounds for opposing the appeal (or says he will not oppose it). The Information Tribunal may extend this period on the same basis as for the period for service of the notice of appeal.[84] In his reply the Information Commissioner may, giving reasons, apply to strike out the notice of appeal on the grounds that (i) an appeal does not lie to, or cannot be entertained by, the Information Tribunal; or (ii) the notice of appeal discloses no reasonable grounds of appeal. The strike out application may be heard as a preliminary issue or at the start of the substantive appeal. There is no similar express provision for the appellant to strike out the Information Commissioner's reply. An appellant aware of a fundamental flaw in the Information

Commissioner's case could seek to bring it before the Information Tribunal as a preliminary issue (see the discussion about directions (rule 14) later).

Rule 7 gives the Information Tribunal power, should it judge it desirable, to order another person to be joined as a party to the appeal and it may make such an order of its own motion, or on the application of one of the parties, or where a third party has itself applied to the court to be joined to the appeal. The most likely third parties to an appeal would be anyone affected in some way by the information whose disclosure was ordered by the Information Commissioner, or either the applicant for the information or the public authority wishing to support the Information Commissioner in opposing the appeal.

Whether or not it has been contacted first by the Information Tribunal and sent a copy of the notice of appeal or the reply, any third party wishing to participate in the appeal must give notice of this fact to the Information Tribunal by way of a joinder notice. The notice must be in writing and must include: the full name and address of the person seeking to be joined to the appeal; a statement of his interest and whether or not he opposes the appeal, together with any reasons on which he relies in support of his interest; and the name and address of any representative the person appoints, and whether the Information Tribunal should send correspondence and notices concerning the appeal to the representative instead. The notice and any attachments must be provided to the Information Tribunal in triplicate to enable it to send a copy to each of the other parties. The joinder notice will be treated as the third party's reply to the notice of appeal if the Information Tribunal issues an order of joinder making him a party to the appeal. The Information Tribunal may give directions in relation to the joining of a third party to an appeal.

By rule 10, after considering the notice of appeal and the reply, the Information Tribunal may of its own motion dismiss the appeal summarily if it considers it proper to do so but it must first notify the appellant of its intention and give him an opportunity to make written representations and request a hearing. There is no express provision for the Information Commissioner to apply for summary disposal (but we have seen above that he can apply to strike out the notice of appeal), nor for the appellant to seek summary determination in its favour.

The Information Tribunal may, of its own motion or on application by a party, give any directions which it thinks proper to enable the parties to prepare for the hearing or to assist the Information Tribunal to determine the issues (rule 14).[85] These include directions for disclosure and inspection of relevant documents (subject to the ordinary rules of privilege); the exchange of witness statements and statements of expert witnesses; the preparation of lists of agreed matters, chronologies and skeleton arguments; and (in particular) a direction that a specific matter be dealt with as a preliminary issue and that there be a pre-hearing review. The purpose of the pre-hearing review is not made clear but it seems that it might not be merely for administrative efficiency in preparing for the hearing but could be used as an opportunity to hear argument on a preliminary issue. This supposition arises from the fact that the Information Tribunal is expressly permitted to treat a pre-hearing review as the hearing of the appeal, and rule accordingly, where it considers that its decision therein substantially disposes of the whole appeal.

The parties may ask the Information Tribunal to vary or set aside any direction, or extend any time limit. A party that fails to comply with a direction of the Information Tribunal risks having their appeal/application, or their reply, wholly or partially struck out. The Information Tribunal is prepared in principle to hold hearings for directions by telephone or video conference (Practice Direction 1, paras.3 and 5). Any information or material provided under directions (such as in witness statements or in disclosure of documents) may only be used for the purposes of the appeal.

By rule 15 the Information Tribunal can make an order requiring the occupier of any premises, on seven days' notice, to permit the Information Tribunal (accompanied by the parties and Information Tribunal staff) to enter the premises at a specified time and inspect, examine, operate or test any equipment there which is used (or intended to be used) in connection with the storage or recording of information, and to inspect, examine or test any documents or other material on those premises connected with the same. Privileged documents are immune from inspection, examination or testing. The occupier can apply to have the order set aside.

The appellant must seek permission from the Information Tribunal if he or she wishes to amend the notice of appeal or deliver supplementary grounds (rule 11). If leave to amend is granted, this triggers a right for the Information Commissioner (and any other party which has been joined to the appeal) to amend their replies and serve them on the Information Tribunal and the other parties within 21 days. There is also provision for the Information Commissioner to seek the Information Tribunal's permission to amend his reply in any event, although this does not trigger an express right for the other parties to amend their notice/reply in consequence. There is no express provision for a third party to seek leave to amend its reply spontaneously. In view of the Information Tribunal's wide power to give directions, however, a party wishing to take steps which are not expressly provided for in the rules should apply to the Information Tribunal to give an appropriate direction on the grounds that it would assist that party (and the others) to prepare for the hearing or that it would assist the Information Tribunal to determine the issues.

Hearings are covered by rules 16–24. Unless the appellant or Information Commissioner requests a hearing, or the Information Tribunal orders one, the appeal will be determined without one. Where a party does request a hearing, the Information Tribunal shall grant the request unless it is satisfied that the appeal can properly be determined without one (rule 16). Any hearings which do take place are to be in public, subject to concerns of the parties or the Information Tribunal relating to the desirability of safeguarding commercially sensitive information or any allegedly exempt information (rule 22). The Information Tribunal indicate that hearings will generally be held in London but may be held elsewhere if requested and clearly shown to be more suitable.

Upon the application of a government Minister, the Information Tribunal has power to exclude any party from the appeal if it is satisfied that this is necessary for reasons of substantial public interest (rule 23). Such applications are made without notice to the other parties.

In the absence of specific requirements in the 2005 Rules, the Information Tribunal is free to conduct proceedings in any way it thinks fit and is to avoid formality so far as is appropriate (rule 24(4)). The Information Tribunal may compel a person anywhere in the UK to appear at an appeal hearing, answer any questions and produce any relevant documents under his or her control as it specifies. Parties (including the Information Commissioner) may appear in person or be represented by anyone they choose (legal aid is not available). Provision is made for examination and cross-examination of witnesses, followed by representations on the evidence and on the appeal generally.

Where a party fails to appear at a hearing without good reason, the Information Tribunal can simply dismiss the appeal if that party is the appellant or, in any case, hear and determine the appeal, or any particular issue, in the party's absence and may make such order as to costs as it thinks fit.

Appeals against Information Notices, and any related issues, are heard or determined by the chairman sitting alone unless it appears to him that the Information Tribunal must, in the interests of justice, sit as usual in a panel of (at least) three, taking into account any representations made by the appellant in the notice of appeal or the Information Commissioner in his reply (rule 21).

Any evidence may be adduced even if not admissible in a court (rule 27). Hearsay and documentary evidence is therefore admissible (but would potentially carry less weight than direct oral evidence). The Information Tribunal can require evidence to be given on oath or affirmation.

The Information Commissioner has the burden of satisfying the Information Tribunal that the disputed decision should be upheld in appeals by a public authority (or the responsible authority (see FOIA, s.53)) against an Information Notice or an Enforcement Notice (rule 26, as amended by rule 6 of SI 2005/450). That is not the case however with appeals brought against Decision Notices under section 57(1), where neither one side nor the other appears to shoulder a burden of proof.

Rulings are covered by rule 28. Once the Information Tribunal has determined the appeal,[86] the chairman certifies the outcome in writing, and includes, to the extent possible without disclosing exempt information, any material finding of fact and the reasons for the decision. The Information Tribunal's determinations are published on its website, subject to any amendments necessary to safeguard commercially sensitive information and information which is exempt under the FOIA.

The Information Tribunal has power to award costs on any appeal (rule 29)[87] but only as follows:

- against the appellant and in favour of the Information Commissioner where it considers that the appeal was manifestly unreasonable;
- against the Information Commissioner and in favour of the appellant where it considers that the disputed decision was manifestly unreasonable;
- against any party, and in favour of any other, where it considers that party was responsible for frivolous, vexatious, improper or unreasonable action, or for any failure to comply with a direction or any delay which with diligence could have been avoided.

A party will not receive an adverse costs order without first having an opportunity to make representations to the Information Tribunal against the making of the order. The Information Tribunal has power to award a specific sum in respect of the costs incurred by the beneficiary in connection with the proceedings, or all or part of such costs as taxed (if not otherwise agreed) by county court taxation.

Rule 25 covers notices. Documents required or authorised by the 2005 Rules may be served by registered or recorded post, hand delivery or electronic communication (i.e. fax or email). Although there is no express wording stating that other methods of communication – such as by ordinary post – are invalid, it would be prudent to assume that is the case. Parties are however not obliged to accept service of documents sent electronically unless they have agreed to do so.

Obstruction effectively contempt

Acts or omissions of a person involved in proceedings before the Information Tribunal which would, in court, constitute a contempt can be certified to the High Court by the Information Tribunal, investigated by the High Court and then punished as if for contempt of court (DPA, Sched.6, para.8). (For the penalties the court can impose for contempt see section 10.4.1.)

10.7.2 Appeals against national security certificates (s.60 appeals)

There is a special procedure for challenging ministerial conclusive evidence certificates issued under sections 23(2) and 24(3) of the FOIA and regulation 15 of the EIR in relation to national security matters.[88] (As to the nature of those certificates, see Chapter 4 (the s.23 exemption), Chapter 5 (the s.24 exemption) and Chapter 9 (the EIR)). An applicant wishing to challenge such certificates will bypass the Information Commissioner, as the appeal lies direct to the Information Tribunal. The Information Commissioner may also appeal against the certificate.

Section 60(2) provides that a certificate issued under section 23(2) can be quashed if the Information Tribunal finds that the information referred to in the certificate was not in fact exempt under section 23(1). Similarly, the Information Tribunal may, under section 60(3) (modified where the EIR is concerned by reg.18(7)) allow an appeal and quash a certificate issued under section 24(3) of the FOIA or regulation 15(1) of the EIR where it finds that the Minister (or his designate where the EIR is concerned) did not have reasonable grounds for issuing the certificate. In determining this question, the Information Tribunal is required to apply the principles applied by the court on an application for judicial review (as to which, see the comments on the difficulties of judicial review applications in section 10.3.5).

If a public authority claims that a certificate issued under section 24(3) of the FOIA or regulation 15(1) of the EIR which describes the information to which it applies in general terms applies to certain information specifically, any other party to the proceedings may appeal to the Information Tribunal on the ground that the certificate does not apply to that information. Unless the Information Tribunal determines that the certificate does not apply to the information in question, it will conclusively be deemed so to apply (s.60(4) and (5)).

The Information Tribunal panel

Appeals relating to national security certificates can be heard only by people designated for the role by the Lord Chancellor from among the Information Tribunal chairman and deputy chairmen. In most cases there must be a panel of three such people, presided over by whichever of them the Lord Chancellor designates. Certain proceedings may be heard by just one such person (or more than one), however.[89] In addition, the designated president may act alone on behalf of the Information Tribunal on certain preliminary or incidental matters.[90]

Procedure

The relevant procedural rules are principally contained in the Information Tribunal (National Security Appeals) Rules 2005 (SI 2005/13, the 2005 National Security Appeals Rules).[91] The provisions of the 2005 National Security Appeals Rules are largely similar to those governing appeals under section 57 (see section 10.7.1) but they have some important differences, which are now highlighted.[92]

Rule 6 covers time allowed for appeal. For appeals brought under section 60(1) of the FOIA (or that section as applied to the EIR by reg.18), a notice of appeal may be served on the Information Tribunal at any time during the currency of the disputed ministerial certificate to which it relates. For appeals under section 60(4) of the FOIA (or that section as applied to the EIR by reg.18), the notice must be served on the Information Tribunal within 28 days of the claim constituting the disputed certification (i.e. the disputed claim by the public authority that a ministerial certificate applies to particular information). This period may be extended if the Information Tribunal considers it just and right to do so in view of the special circumstances. If sent in accordance with the notices provisions in rule 31 (similar to those for s.57 appeals above) a notice of appeal will be treated as having been served on the date on which it is received for dispatch by the Post Office.

The notice of appeal (rule 5) must: (a) identify the certification which is being disputed; (b) state the following: the name and address of the appellant; the grounds of appeal; the name and address of the public authority from which the disputed certification was received; the name and address of the appellant's representative, if he has appointed one; an address for the service of notices and other documents on the appellant; and (c) be signed by or on behalf of the appellant.

For appeals under section 60(4) of the FOIA (or as applied to the EIR) the notice of appeal must also state: the date on which the public authority made the claim constituting the disputed certification; an address for service of notices and other documents on the public authority; the special circumstances which justify the Information Tribunal's accepting jurisdiction where the notice has not been served within the ordinary 28-day limit (see above).

An appellant may seek the early determination of the appeal (brought under either subsection) by including such a request in the notice of appeal and giving reasons for it. A blank notice of appeal form is available on the Information Tribunal website.

Information Tribunal staff will send the appellant an acknowledgement of service and serve a copy of the notice of appeal on the Information Commissioner (where he is not the appellant).

The Information Tribunal is placed under a general duty (rule 4) to secure that information is not disclosed contrary to the interests of national security. The point is expressly made that a disclosure which would merely indicate the existence or otherwise of any material can itself be contrary to the interests of national security.

The Minister who signed the disputed certificate has 42 days from receipt of the notice of appeal to send to the Information Tribunal the following (rule 8): a copy of the relevant certificate, and a written notice stating:

(i)   (regarding appeals under s.60(1) of the FOIA, or as applied to the EIR) whether or not he intends to oppose the appeal and, if so, setting out a summary of the circumstances relating to the issue of the certificate, the reason for its issue, his grounds for opposing the appeal and the evidence in support of those grounds;

(ii) (regarding appeals under s.60(4) of the FOIA, or as applied to the EIR) whether or not he wishes to make representations in relation to the appeal and, if so, stating the extent to which he intends to support or oppose the appeal, his grounds for supporting or opposing it and his evidence in support of those grounds; and

(iii) (in either case) a request for early determination of the appeal, if he so wishes, supported by reasons.

The Minister may apply to strike out the notice of appeal either in his notice in reply or otherwise. The provisions are, *mutatis mutandis*, the same as under the 2005 Rules (section 10.7.1).

When he submits his notice in reply the Minister can enclose a written objection to his notice being copied to the other party (or the Information Commissioner) on the basis that disclosure of the information would be contrary to the interests of national security. He must give reasons and if possible supply a version of the notice which can be disclosed. The Information Tribunal must consider this application as a preliminary issue before disclosing the material in question and must consider it in the absence of the parties (but with the Minister present if he so wishes, whether a party or not). He must be allowed to make oral representations where the Information Tribunal is minded to overrule his objection or to order him to prepare a notice of reply in a version different from that which he submitted.[93]

The Information Tribunal will send the Minister's notice in reply to the other party and the Information Commissioner unless it decides to dismiss the appeal summarily[94] or where the Minister has objected to disclosure.

Under rule 17, the Information Tribunal must notify the relevant Minister in advance of giving (or varying) any directions, issuing a witness summons or publishing or certifying a determination, and must allow him 14 days to make an application to the Information Tribunal requesting it to reconsider, on the basis that to go ahead would result in disclosure of information which is exempt under the FOIA. Where such an application is made, the Information Tribunal may consider it as a preliminary issue or at the start of the hearing of the substantive appeal but in either case it must be in the absence of the parties (but with the Minister present if he so wishes, whether a party or not) (rule 18).

Rules 19–25 cover hearings. An individual issue or the entire appeal can be determined without a hearing where the parties agree in writing, or the Information Tribunal considers that the issues raised on the appeal have been determined on a previous appeal brought by the appellant on the basis of facts which did not materially differ from the current case and the parties have had an opportunity of making representations to the effect that the appeal ought not to be determined without a hearing (rule 19).[95]

Hearings are to take place as soon as practicable, on at least 14 days' notice and with due regard to the convenience of the parties and to any request for an early hearing (rule 20). Witnesses may be summoned by the Information Tribunal or at the request of the parties (in which case the summoning party must pay the witness's reasonable travel expenses and an allowance for attending the hearing) (rule 21). The Minister may attend and be represented, as can the other parties (rule 22). If the appellant or the Minister does not intend to attend or be represented at a hearing, he or she must inform the Information Tribunal of this intention and may send the Information Tribunal additional written representations in support of the appeal (rule 22(3)).

All hearings under the 2005 National Security Appeals Rules take place in private unless the Information Tribunal, with the consent of the parties and the relevant Minister, directs that the hearing or any part of it take place in public (rule 24(1)). Even where it sits in private, the Information Tribunal can admit individual non-parties to the hearing where the parties and the Minister agree. The Information Tribunal has a duty to exclude any party from some or all of the proceedings (other than the relevant Minister) where it considers this necessary to secure that information is not disclosed contrary to the interests of national security. Any person excluded in this way has the right to have the reasons explained and given to him in writing, so far as this is possible without disclosing information which would prejudice national security (rule 24(3)).

Once the Information Tribunal has determined the appeal,[96] the chairman certifies the outcome in writing, and includes, to the extent possible without disclosing exempt information, any material finding of fact and the reasons for the decision (rule 28). The Information Tribunal's determinations are published, subject to any amendments to the text which are necessary to safeguard commercially sensitive information and information which is exempt under the FOIA, and national security.

Provision is made as to the conduct of proceedings at a hearing (rule 25), powers of the president to act for the Information Tribunal (rule 26), and evidence (rule 27).

The Information Tribunal can award costs (rule 29) in a wider set of circumstances in national security certificate appeals than on section 57 appeals, as follows:

(a) in an appeal under section 60(1) of the FOIA (or as applied to the EIR):

- against the appellant and in favour of the relevant Minister where it considers that the appeal was manifestly unreasonable;
- against the Minister and in favour of the appellant where it allows the appeal and quashes the disputed certificate, or does so to any extent;

- against the Minister and in favour of the appellant where, before the Information Tribunal has made a determination, the Minister withdraws the certificate to which the appeal relates;

(b) in an appeal under section 60(4) of the FOIA (or as applied to the EIR):

- against the appellant and in favour of any other party where it dismisses the appeal, or dismisses it to any extent;
- in favour of the appellant and against any other party where it allows the appeal, or allows it to any extent;

(c) in an appeal under either section: against any party, and in favour of any other, where it considers that party was responsible for frivolous, vexatious, improper or unreasonable action, or for any failure to comply with a direction or any delay which with diligence could have been avoided.

A party will not receive an adverse costs order without first having an opportunity to make representations to the Information Tribunal against the making of the order. The Information Tribunal has power to award a specific sum in respect of the costs incurred by the beneficiary in connection with the proceedings, or all or part of such costs as taxed (if not otherwise agreed) by county court taxation.

10.8 APPEALS FROM THE INFORMATION TRIBUNAL

10.8.1 Appeals to the High Court

Any party to an appeal to the Information Tribunal under section 57 (including a joined third party) may, under section 59, appeal against the Information Tribunal's decision to the High Court (the Court of Session if the public authority's address is in Scotland) – but only on a point of law. An appeal on a point of law includes an appeal on all judicial review grounds, (*Nipa Begum* v. *Tower Hamlets London Borough Council* [2000] 1 WLR 306, CA), therefore covering situations where, for example, the Information Tribunal misunderstands or misapplies the law, makes an order which it has no power to do, comes to a conclusion which is irrational, makes findings of fact without any evidence, does not provide adequate reasons for its decision, fails to take account of a material consideration or has regard to an irrelevant one, makes a procedural error, or acts incompatibly with the European Convention on Human Rights as domesticated by the Human Rights Act 1998.

Permission to appeal is not required. An appellant's notice would need to be filed at the High Court within 28 days of the Information Tribunal's decision (or receipt of its statement of reasons, if later) and served on the other parties and the Information Tribunal chairman (CPR Pt 52 PD 17.3–5) as soon as practicable and within seven days in any event (CPR 52.4(3)). On determining the appeal, the Court has power to: affirm, set aside or vary any order or judgment of the Information Tribunal; refer any claim or issue back to the Information Tribunal; order a new trial or hearing; make orders for the payment of interest; and/or make an order for costs (CPR 52.10(2)).

Unlike the case of appeals to the Information Tribunal, the FOIA does not provide that the effect of the Information Commissioner's notice (as modified or substituted by the Information Tribunal) is suspended pending appeal to the High Court or above. In practice however, the Information Commissioner is most unlikely to seek to enforce it under section 54(1) (see section 10.4.1) until any appeal is disposed of.

In relation to national security certificate appeals brought under section 60 there is no similar provision permitting any further appeal to the courts. That being the case, however, the Information Tribunal's rulings in such appeals are likely to be subject to judicial review in the High Court. (Remedies available on judicial reviews go wider than the traditional prerogative orders now known as quashing, prohibiting and mandatory orders, and include damages, injunctions and declarations, and costs orders can also be made.) Nevertheless, the reviewing court would extend a considerable degree of deference to the Minister, as the courts regard decisions on matters of national security as largely the province of the executive rather than the judiciary (see, e.g. Lord Steyn in *Secretary of State for the Home Department* v. *Rehman* [2001] UKHL 47, [2003] 1 AC 153 at [31]).

10.8.2 Further appeals

An appeal from the High Court lies to the Court of Appeal but only with the permission of the Court of Appeal, which will not be given unless the appeal raises an important point of principle or practice or there is some other compelling reason for the Court of Appeal to hear it (CPR 52.13). A final possible appeal lies to the House of Lords, subject to leave from the Court of Appeal or the House of Lords.[97]

10.9 THIRD PARTIES

10.9.1 Limited rights of intervention under the FOIA

In the context of the FOIA a third party is anyone other than the applicant requesting access under section 1(1) and the public authority to which he addresses that request. A third party might have an interest in an access request (or in information which an authority proposes to publish under its Publication Scheme) because it supplied that information, is its subject, or it would in some way be affected by its disclosure. It could be another public authority, an individual, or a private sector company providing services to the authority under contract. There are many reasons why that person or entity might be reluctant to see the information disclosed: to protect their confidential or commercially sensitive trading information or their reputation, to name but the most obvious. To an extent, their interests are protected by the exemptions under the FOIA but they are still dependent on the public authority choosing to invoke the exemption (the FOIA does not prohibit authorities from disclosing exempt material but doing so may of course bring criminal or civil consequences under other laws such as the Official Secrets Act 1989 or the law of confidence). They also face the risk that the public authority may not appreciate that the requested information is exempt, or may disclose it without meaning to. The third party will often have knowledge which puts them in a better position than the public authority to know, for example, that certain information is a trade secret or that its disclosure would prejudice their commercial interests or the national or regional economy, or to appreciate the relevant public interest arguments in favour of maintaining the exemption and withholding information. More generally, a third party may well have a stronger impulse to shield information which concerns it from public view than the public authority which has been asked to disclose it.

In spite of all this, it is a notable (and in the eyes of many, lamentable) difference between the FOIA and freedom of information regimes in many other countries that in the UK (the position under the Scottish Act is the same) interested third parties have no statutory right to be notified about requests made for information which affects them, nor is there an effective procedure under the FOIA by which they can maintain an objection to its disclosure.[98] They have no standing to apply to the Information Commissioner under section 50(1) to complain about the authority's proposed or actual disclosure of information.

10.9.2 Participation in appeals before the Information Tribunal

The only legislative provision that third parties can directly make use of is their entitlement to apply to be joined as a party to an appeal to the Information Tribunal under section 57 against a notice of the Information Commissioner.[99] It should be noted, however, that it is not open to a third party to lodge the appeal in the first place: that must be done by the applicant or the public authority. In practice, third parties may be prevented from taking advantage of this right because they will not be aware that the appeal is taking place: there is no obligation on the parties to the appeal to notify them that it is, nor to notify the Information Tribunal of the existence of an interested third party. Nevertheless, it is to be hoped that in general third parties will become involved in appeals wherever appropriate. The parties to the appeal, one of which will be the Information Commissioner, are entitled to ask the Information Tribunal to order that an interested third party be joined to the appeal, and the Information Tribunal may decide to make such an order of its own volition. The problem is that in many cases this right of participation in the complaint comes too late in the day, in that disclosure might have occurred at an earlier stage, following a decision of the public authority or the Information Commissioner.

10.9.3 Rights to be consulted when request first made

Interested third parties have a limited entitlement to be consulted by a public authority when it receives a request for information. This is provided by the non-statutory guidance in part IV of the Section 45 Code of Practice, whose provisions are not binding obligations but constitute practice which, in the opinion of the Secretary of State, is desirable for public authorities to follow in connection with the discharge of their functions under Part I of the FOIA. Even where consultation takes place, however, ultimate responsibility for deciding whether or not to disclose the information requested lies with the public authority. An authority is thus not bound to withhold information simply because a relevant third party asks it to or argues that it should.

It is worth pointing out in passing that the Code of Practice provisions on consultation with affected third parties appear to be applicable also in the context of information which a public authority is proposing to release under its Publication Scheme, even though the Code makes no express reference to Publication Schemes in the section on consultation.[100] Although the Information Commissioner encourages public authorities to devise Publication Schemes which entitle them to withhold information covered by an exemption,[101] they are not prevented by the FOIA from releasing such material if they so wish. They may also not always realise that, or be certain whether, the information in question is exempt. Consultation may well be required in such cases under the Code of Practice. There is no mechanism in the FOIA for the making of complaints about Publication Schemes but see the comments in section 10.6.2 above.

The Code of Practice indicates first that consultation with an interested third party will in some cases be necessary, either for the public authority to know whether the information requested is covered by an exemption or to determine whether the obligations in section 1 of the FOIA arise in relation to it (para.27). This last phrase seems likely to mean that it may also be necessary for a public authority to consult a third party on how the public interest test should be applied where information is potentially exempt. (It could also mean such consultation may be necessary to know whether the authority is even required to confirm or deny that it holds the information requested.) However, this begs the question: when will consultation be necessary for those purposes? The word 'necessary' in this context is assumed to mean:

practically needed in order for the public authority to form a view on whether an exemption applies or on the relative public interests at stake, rather than required by law. It is arguable, however, that consultation could be required in some cases because of a public authority's obligations under public law (see section 10.9.5).[102] In addition, any contract between the authority and the third party may require consultation in certain circumstances. Some help with deciding when consultation is necessary can perhaps be drawn from what was paragraph 37 of the original text of the Code of Practice even though it has been removed from the current edition,[103] which explained that consultation would *not* be necessary where: (i) the authority proposes to oppose disclosure on other grounds; (ii) the third party's views could be of no effect, for instance because disclosure is required or prevented by other legislation; and (iii) where no exemption is relevant (which presumably meant, where none was even potentially relevant).

A second category of cases which the Code of Practice contemplates is those where consultation is not necessary but would still be good practice. This applies 'in a range of . . . circumstances' and it gives the example of where an authority proposes to disclose information which relates to a third party or which is likely to affect its interests. Here, though, the Code does not appear to be recommending consultation in the ordinary meaning of the word: authorities are merely to take 'reasonable steps . . . where appropriate, to give [third parties] advance notice, or failing that, to draw it to their attention afterwards' (para.28).

Thirdly, public authorities are advised that in some cases, it may also be appropriate to consult interested third parties about other sorts of question, such as whether the applicant ought to be given any explanatory material or advice, such as any copyright (or other) restrictions as there might be on the applicant's further use of the material (para.29).

The requirement to consult in all three categories of cases appears to be further qualified where the information to be disclosed relates to or affects a number of third parties. Where these share a representative organisation, the authority may consider whether it would be sufficient to notify or consult with that organisation or, in other cases, to notify or consult with a representative sample of the third parties (para.30).

The Section 45 Code, in addition, highly recommends that public authorities ensure that third parties are made aware of the authorities' duties of disclosure under the FOIA (para.26). An authority could comply with this, however, by making a general statement to this effect on first dealing with a particular person or entity rather than in connection with a specific request for information. In summary, the position as to when consultation is required or will take place is uncertain and third parties can take only limited comfort from the provisions of the Section 45 Code of Practice. In the context of the EIR, the Regulation 16 Code of Practice puts even less of an onus of consulting with interested third parties prior to disclosure. Interestingly, the position is made (slightly) clearer where both the public authority and the third-party information provider are government departments:

> No decision to release information which has been supplied by one government department to another should be taken without first notifying, and where appropriate consulting, the department from which the information originated (para.29).

Even where a third party is consulted, there is no provision in the Code of Practice requiring the public authority to notify it of its final decision, or of any request for internal review or of any subsequent complaint to the Information Commissioner. Further, nothing in the FOIA or the Code of Practice obliges the Information Commissioner to consult an interested third party when considering a complaint under section 50 (but see section 10.9.5).

Except in the very clearest of cases, however, where there can be no chance that the public authority has failed to take account of some relevant issue, public authorities would be well advised to do all they reasonably can to consult an interested third party in advance of disclosing information. If they do not, then not only will they risk breaching the Code of Practice (and potentially receiving a Practice Recommendation from the Information Commissioner) but they may find themselves involved in legal proceedings with financial consequences potentially far more severe that a breach of the FOIA or the Code of Practice (see section 10.9.5). Liaising co-operatively with third parties will often of course be fundamental to maintaining good relationships with important suppliers.

Under the legislation, then, interested third parties are essentially left to hope that public authorities and the Information Commissioner will consult them at each stage and that authorities will resist requests with the same zeal and effectiveness as they themselves would at the outset, on any internal review and before the Information Commissioner and that they will, if necessary, appeal to the Information Tribunal.

10.9.4 Maximising the third party's chances of being consulted

A third party can improve its position in advance of any particular request being made by its negotiations and relationship development with the public authorities it deals with. As well as ensuring it has an open channel of communication with such authorities, it should look to insert confidentiality undertakings in relevant agreements, as well as terms requiring the public authority to notify and consult with it promptly and adequately in relation to any request for information which it receives that relates to or affects the third party in any way. It might also look for a commitment to be consulted in the wake of any Decision or Enforcement Notice of the Information Commissioner requiring disclosure of information affecting the third party, so that it and the public authority could consider the scope for appealing against the notice to the Information Tribunal. Similarly, it can review any information it provides, or has in the past provided, to public authorities and draw their attention to which elements it considers as confidential or engaging any of the other exemptions under the FOIA, and it should mark the documents accordingly. With regard to a third party prompting the Information Commissioner to consult, see section 10.9.5.

10.9.5 Are there options for direct action open to third parties?

Yes, there are but each has difficulties and limitations and although some may in theory be used to obtain an injunction to prevent the disclosure of material, the value of such a remedy is severely limited by practicalities: where a public authority has ignored the Code of Practice's provisions on consultation, the first that the third party hears of the request will be after the information has already been disclosed and they receive a call from an interested journalist, for example. Even where the third party is on notice of the request, the window for action may be very narrow because public authorities are under an obligation to respond to requests promptly and in any event within 20 working days. There is the further difficulty that if disclosure has already taken place or cannot be stopped, the right of action, or its value to the third party, may fall away because there are no quantifiable damages to be compensated. Information cases (such as breach of confidence cases) tend to be all about the injunction application, for preventing disclosure is the only valuable remedy to the claimant. Lastly, taking legal action can be costly and exposes the litigant to a court order to pay the other side's legal costs if they lose.

Enforcing the Code of Practice provisions on consultation

Where the third party had negotiated a term in an agreement that the public authority would notify and duly consult them over any request for information in which the third party had an interest, it could seek to enforce the contract by applying for an injunction prohibiting disclosure and requiring consultation, in the unlikely event that it discovered this in time.

Alternatively, a third party could look to public law for a remedy as it is certainly arguable that in certain circumstances public authorities will have a duty at public law to take proper account of the views of interested third parties when deciding how to respond to a request for access under section 1(1) of the FOIA. It is a fundamental principle of public law that a decision maker must have regard to all relevant considerations. Furthermore there is an obligation on decision makers to take reasonable steps to acquaint themselves with relevant material, which can include consulting third parties (*R. v. Secretary of State for Education, ex p. London Borough of Southwark* [1995] ELR 308 at 323C). The potential relevance of third parties' views is reflected within the FOIA regime by: (i) the requirement in section 45(2)(*c*) for the Secretary of State's Code of Practice to include provision on public authorities consulting with interested third parties over requests for information which affect them; (ii) the resultant Section 45 Code of Practice, which makes such provision; (iii) the obligation on the Information Commissioner in section 47 of the FOIA to act in a way which promotes the observance of the Section 45 Code of Practice; and (iv) the provision for third parties to be joined to appeals before the Information Tribunal (see section 10.7.1). One could add that the essence of procedural fairness in public law is that a person who will be affected by a decision should be given prior notice of what is proposed and an effective opportunity to make representations. Equally, consultation may be judged to be all the more important where the public authority's decision in favour of disclosure (or that of the Information Commissioner where he is considering a section 50(1) complaint, or the Information Tribunal on appeal) could affect the third party's reputation or financial interests. More generally, third parties will have what public law terms a 'legitimate expectation' that public authorities will adhere to provisions of the Section 45 Code of Practice.

Failure to consult by the authority (or the Information Commissioner or the Information Tribunal) may therefore render a decision, or an order, to disclose unlawful and liable to be quashed by the Administrative Court on the third party's application for judicial review. (Whether it does or not will of course depend on the circumstances of the case.)

It is important to add in this context that the requirements of proper consultation have been established by the courts:

- consultation must take place at a time when the proposals are still at a formative stage;
- the proposer (in this context, the public authority) must give sufficient reasons for the action it proposes to take to permit intelligent consideration and response;
- adequate time must be given for consideration and response;
- the product of consultation must be conscientiously taken into account in finalising any proposals (*R.* v. *North and East Devon Area Health Authority, ex p. Coughlan* [2001] QB 213).

The duty to consult does not imply a duty to obtain agreement before acting (*R. (on the application of Smith)* v. *East Kent Hospitals NHS Trust* [2002] EWHC 2640, LTL 9.12.2002. per Silber J at [61]), nor will a different outcome necessarily be reached where the reviewing court orders the public authority to reconsider its decision in light of the third party's views.

Even if an interested third party has been consulted, there may be other grounds for judicial review entitling it to challenge the decision of a public authority or the Information Commissioner, including where such decisions are flawed by errors of law or fact, by substantive unfairness or unreasonableness, by unjustifiable inconsistency with earlier decisions, by being supported by inadequate reasons, or by involving a breach of the Human Rights Act 1998.

Pre-action injunctions are available ancillary to an application for judicial review and the Administrative Court may also grant declaratory relief and award damages (Supreme Court Act 1981, s.31(2) and (4)). The procedure on judicial review applications is set out in Parts 8 and 54 of the CPR and the Pre-Action Protocol under Part 54. As a matter of discretion, the courts will not normally make the remedy of judicial review available where there is an alternative remedy by way of appeal (*R.* v. *Chief Constable of the Merseyside Police, ex p. Calveley* [1986] QB 424).

Finally, the third party should consider drawing the authority's failure to consult in accordance with the Code of Practice to the Information Commissioner's attention. (This could not be done by means of a s.50(1) complaint, which is only available to applicants for information.) The Information Commissioner might look into the matter and issue the authority with a Practice Recommendation for a breach of the Code. That will be of no immediate benefit to the third party but it might stimulate a more co-operative response from the authority in relation to future requests. (Third parties with no direct interest in the requested information are similarly free to contact the Information Commissioner to share with him concerns they have that an authority is not meeting its obligations under the FOIA.)

Protecting confidential information

A third party could apply for an injunction restraining a public authority from disclosing its confidential information (or to restrain an applicant who had received it from the authority, or anyone who had received it from them, from making any further disclosure).[104] Damages are available to compensate losses where disclosure has already taken place, as is an account of the profits made from the disclosure. It is a defence for the public authority to show that the material was already in the public domain or that there is a public interest in disclosure.[105] It would seem to be necessary for the integrity of the enforcement regime under the FOIA that an authority which makes a disclosure required of it by a Decision Notice of the Information Commissioner (or such a notice as modified by the Information Tribunal) will be able to argue that it is in the public interest that the Information Commissioner's notices (or the determinations of the Information Tribunal) are complied with. The authority would thus, it is thought, have a defence to any subsequent breach of confidence action, despite the possibility that on appeal the Information Tribunal or the courts might have ruled that the Information Commissioner/ Information Tribunal was wrong and the information was confidential and hence exempt from disclosure.[106] This again shows up the shortcomings of the FOIA from the point of view of third parties, particularly as they are not able to institute complaints to the Information Commissioner or lodge appeals to the Information Tribunal. Where proceedings to restrain a breach of confidence have been issued in parallel with the Information Commissioner's investigation of a complaint which concerns the section 41 confidentiality exemption, it may be that he will decide to defer his decision until after the court has determined that issue.

It is important for third parties to appreciate that although a public authority may be under a *contractual* duty to keep certain information confidential, that will not necessarily mean the authority can avoid disclosing it to an applicant making an access request. Public authorities cannot contract out of the FOIA and the information will only be covered by the exemption in section 41 where its disclosure would constitute an actionable breach of confidence at common law (i.e. a claim to which the public authority would not have a good defence).

Copyright

A third party affected by information to which access has been requested will in some cases have provided that information to the public authority and will own the copyright in the underlying document or work. However, whether third parties are entitled to seek an injunction against public authorities on the grounds that disclosure would constitute an infringement of their copyright is, as yet, unclear. The FOIA is silent on whether the duty of public authorities to provide access to information is subject to the laws of copyright or not. Guidance from the Department for Constitutional Affairs, however, states that a public authority will not be infringing copyright by responding to a request for information.[107] Such guidance is perhaps given in view of section 50(1) of the Copyright, Designs and Patents Act 1988 (CDPA), which provides a defence to infringement where 'the doing of a particular act is specifically authorised by an Act of Parliament . . . unless the Act provides otherwise'. The similar common law tort defence of statutory authority may also apply.[108]

If these defences are available in respect of disclosures by public authorities, third parties will not be able to bring proceedings against authorities to prevent a disclosure which would otherwise constitute an infringement of copyright. The defence would only be likely to apply to disclosures of non-exempt information, however, as it would be hard to characterise the FOIA as authorising disclosure of exempt information. Yet there is uncertainty over whether these defences do apply to the FOIA, which does not expressly authorise the disclosure of copies of documents but of information. It may often be possible (though time-consuming) for a public authority to convey information from a document to an applicant without falling foul of copyright protection of the original document, such as by summarising it in different words or simply granting applicants the right to inspect the information. (These two options are specifically referred to in s.11(1) as means by which an applicant is entitled to have information communicated to him as an alternative to receiving a copy of the information, if reasonably practicable.) In addition, there is a separate argument that the FOIA does in fact prohibit disclosures of material which would constitute copyright infringement, by virtue of the absolute exemption in section 44(1)(*a*), which applies to information whose disclosure is prohibited by or under any enactment, which could be taken to include the CDPA.

Were third parties able to rely on these arguments to prevent (or recover compensation for) disclosure of their copyright material, however, the effectiveness of the FOIA as a means of promoting freedom of information could be significantly undermined. The courts may therefore not look favourably on such arguments and rule that public authorities can indeed rely on the section 50(1) defence.[109]

Regardless of these issues, the third party would need to prove its case in the normal way, including showing that what was copied was a substantial part of the copyright work. Equally, the authority might be able to rely on any of the other normal defences to such actions, which include consent (express or implied), public interest and – of specific relevance to many public authorities – the CDPA defences in sections 47 (copying of material which is open to public inspection under statute), 48 (the issuing to the public of material communicated to the Crown in the course of public business), and 49 (copying of materials which are public records under the Public Records Act 1958).

What is not in doubt is that even assuming that a public authority is authorised to make disclosures which would otherwise infringe copyright, a third party would be entitled to prevent the applicant who receives the mater-ial from making any further infringing use of it. (Again, this would be subject to any defences, and where the media is concerned it might have a defence of fair dealing for the purpose of reporting current events (CDPA, s.30(2)).) Technically, the public authority itself could take such action in respect of its own copyright materials, although this would be unseemly and could perhaps be countered by the courts extending the public interest defence to such applicants.[110] For the present, however, applicants will need to obtain the consent of rights-holders before reusing material obtained under the FOIA, including from the public authority releasing it. Public authorities may wish to consider protecting their position by marking disclosed third party materials with a clear warning that reproduction without appropriate consent could lead to liability in damages and that the authority is not to be taken as authorising any such further disclosure. Otherwise, the authority could potentially be liable in respect of the applicant's subsequent infringements, by virtue of section 16(2) of the CDPA.

Data protection

Personal data (information about a living person which identifies them) is exempt from disclosure under section 40 of the FOIA. Nevertheless, a third party concerned that a public authority was going to disclose information containing personal data about him (or had already done so), could serve notice on the public authority under section 10 of the DPA requiring it to stop processing such data if disclosure (which would constitute processing for these purposes) would be likely cause him damage or distress. Alternatively he could apply to the court under section 14 of the DPA for erasure of the data concerned. For a discussion of the interaction between the two Acts, see Chapter 8.

Defamation

A public authority could potentially be liable to a third party for disclosing information which contained a statement that identified the third party and would have made ordinary, right-thinking people think less of that person or organisation. However, where that information was supplied to the authority by another party and the authority is required to disclose it in response to a request under section 1 of the FOIA, the third party would not succeed in an action in defamation unless the authority acted maliciously in doing so (see FOIA, s.79). An authority will be acting maliciously where it knows the defamatory information is untrue or is reckless as to whether or not it is true. Malice will be particuilarly difficult to prove in the context of a statutory duty to disclose the information. By contrast, where the defamatory material is exempt from disclosure but the authority releases it anyway (perhaps not realising that it is not exempt), the authority will not enjoy the protection of this statutory privilege. In general where defamation is concerned an interim injunction to restrain publication is very difficult to obtain.[111]

It is worth noting however that the section 79 defence will not protect a public authority where the defamatory allegations were contained in papers generated internally, so authorities could be sued in defamation by third parties in respect of such material. In addition, there is no protection in the FOIA for applicants republishing (i.e. communicating to any third party) defamatory information which they have received from public authorities and thus a third party which was the subject of such allegations could sue the applicant (and anyone else) in respect of any such republication. In any claim, the defendant will have various further defences open to it, such as that the allegations were substantially true, or amounted to fair comment, or were made on a privileged occasion (and a media defendant may be able to rely on the extended qualified privilege defence under the *Reynolds* case (*Albert Reynolds* v. *Times Newspapers Ltd & Others* [2001] 2 AC 127) where there is a public interest in publishing the allegations) or else that the third party had consented to their disclosure.

As a public authority could be liable for subsequent disclosures where these were reasonably foreseeable, authorities might wish to consider disclosed materials with a clear warning that republication or reproduction without appropriate consent could lead to liability in damages and that the authority is not to be taken as authorising any such further disclosure.

Negligence/breach of statutory duty

Even where a public authority is flagrantly in breach of duties imposed on it by or under the FOIA, it is not open to applicants or third parties to bring a civil action against the authority for damages or an injunction or any other remedy, as a result of the bar in section 56(1). The position is the same under the EIR (regs.18(1) and 18(4)(e)).

Action on section 50(1) complaints to the Information Commissioner

Where an interested third party becomes aware that an applicant is seeking an adjudication from the Information Commissioner on whether the authority's refusal to disclose the information is justifiable, the third party could write to the Information Commissioner with its views on the questions at issue. He would arguably be obliged under public law to take account of them when reaching his decision, and were he not to do so, he could be open to a challenge from the third party by way of judicial review.

As a separate possibility, where no appeal to the Information Tribunal is made by the applicant or the authority, an interested third party would potentially be able to seek judicial review to challenge a decision of the Information Commissioner's contained in a Decision Notice issued in response to a complaint under section 50(1) of the FOIA.

NOTES

1   The enforcement provisions of the FOIA (contained in Part IV of the Act, including Sched.3) and its appeals provisions (contained in Part V) are applied to the EIR (SI 2004/3391), with the necessary modifications, by reg.18 of the EIR. Similarly, the Information Commissioner's powers and duties under ss.47 and 48 (the latter dealing with Practice Recommendations) are applied, as modified, to the EIR by reg.16(5) and (6). References in this chapter to the FOIA are to be taken to include a reference to the EIR and references to exemptions include a reference to exceptions under the EIR – unless clearly inappropriate in the context. See Chapter 9 for a full discussion of the EIR.

2   About 70 of these are dedicated to freedom of information, the balance to data protection.

3   Good practice in this context is stated not to be limited to following the provi-
     sions of the FOIA and the Codes of Practice made under ss.45 and 46 of the
     FOIA.
4   Two codes of practice have been issued under the FOIA: the code issued by the
     Secretary of State for Consitutional Affairs under s.45 giving guidance to public
     authorities on the practice which he judges it desirable they should follow in
     order to satisfy their obligations under Part I of the Act (sometimes referred to
     as the Access Code), and the Lord Chancellor's code under s.46 of the FOIA
     containing guidance for public authorities on record management. Under reg.16
     of the EIR the Secretary of State for Environment, Food and Rural Affairs
     issued a code of practice in February 2005 for public authorities in respect of
     their obligation under the EIR.
5   By virtue of this section anybody (including public authorities or applicants for
     information) can contact the ICO for advice on the operation of the FOIA or the
     EIR, including on compliance issues, such as an authority's obligations with
     regard to access requests or the effect of particular exemptions. They will be
     advised by staff in a separate section of the ICO from those dealing with
     enforcement or complaints handling. Advice will be generalised, however, and
     staff will not advise on particular cases. Information supplied by those seeking
     advice will not ordinarily be disclosed outside the ICO but it would be prudent
     nevertheless to specify that all such information is to be treated in confidence.
6   Only those under s.47 (s.47(4)) and reg.16(5) of the EIR.
7   The power does not arise in cases of breach of the terms of the Codes of Practice
     or of a Practice Recommendation.
8   Again, this power does not arise in cases of breach of the terms of the Codes of
     Practice or of a Practice Recommendation.
9   As to how third parties can take action where they have complaints about an
     authority's conduct under the FOIA, see section 10.9.
10   FOIA, s.1(1) requires public authorities to provide information requested (or to
     confirm or deny that they hold such information), and EIR, reg.5(1) requires
     authorities to make environmental information available on request. FOIA, s.11
     and EIR, reg.6 require an authority to give effect to an applicant's preferred
     means of receiving the information where reasonably practicable, or to say why
     it is not. FOIA, s.17 and EIR, reg.14 contain the requirements for the sending
     and content of refusal notices, such as explaining why an exemption applies or
     why the greater public interest lies in withholding the information. EIR, reg.11
     requires an authority to review its decision following representations from the
     applicant.
11   Foreword to the Section 45 Code, para.9.
12   Information Tribunal (Enforcement Appeals) Rules 2005, rule 5.
13   Access requests under s.1(1) can only be made in respect of recorded information
     (s.84).
14   Information Tribunal (Enforcement Appeals) Rules 2005, SI 2005/14, rule 5.
15   *Ibid.*
16   Comments on the Information Commissioner's policy on the use of Enforcement
     Notices are drawn from *Regulation under the Freedom of Information Act 2000
     and the Environmental Information Regulations 2004* (ICO, 2.3.05), paras.14–21.
17   On Publication Schemes see Chapter 2, and for the slightly different position
     regarding routine publication under the EIR, see Chapter 9.
18   *Regulation under the Freedom of Information Act 2000 and the Environmental
     Information Regulations 2004* (ICO, 2.3.05), Annex 1.

19 Preliminary notices are generated within the ICO at the same level of sign-off as final notices; in other words they are not less authoritative than final notices as to the Information Commissioner's view (source: personal communication from the Assistant Information Commissioner with responsibility for complaints resolution (April 2005)).

20 Before designating any public authorities in this regard, the Secretary of State is required to consult (a) the Welsh Assembly if the authority to be designated is Welsh; (b) the Presiding Officer of the Northern Ireland Assembly if that body is to be designated; and (c) the First Minister and deputy First Minister in Northern Ireland if the authority to be designated is in Northern Ireland (s.53(5)).

21 That is, any exemption in Part II of the FOIA other than those listed in s.2(3).

22 A more intensive scrutiny of the Minister's decision would be required if it could be argued that it had human rights implications. The Information Tribunal would then need to adopt the approach in *R. (Daly)* v. *Secretary of State for the Home Department* [2001] UKHL 26, [2001] 2 AC 532, where the doctrine of proportionality would make it necessary to consider how the Minister weighed up the various competing interests at stake. Human rights are unlikely to be engaged in many cases, however, as freedom of information is not (yet) regarded by the courts as a right falling within the scope of Article 10 (freedom of expression) of the European Convention on Human Rights (*R. (Persey)* v. *Secretary of State for the Environment, Food and Rural Affairs* [2002] EWHC 371 (Admin), [2003] QB 794 at [52]–[53] (per Simon Brown LJ)). In some cases a right to information could be part of a claim under Articles 2 (the right to life; see *Öneryildiz* v. *Turkey* (2004) 39 EHRR 12) or 8 (the right to respect for private and family life; see *Gaskin* v. *UK* (1989) 12 EHRR 36). The Minister's conclusive determination of the matter would seem not to be open to attack either on the basis of Article 6 (right to a fair hearing) as the Strasbourg court would regard an applicant's claim under the FOIA as a public law right, not falling within the guarantees of Article 6 regarding the determination of civil or criminal obligations (see Blackstone's *Guide to the Human Rights Act 1998* (3rd ed., 2003) by J. Wadham, H. Mountfield and A. Edmundson, at 8.6.4).

23 Government departments have indicated they may not provide the Information Commissioner with information he requests, even where he serves an Information Notice, where it concerns matters of national security (see Annex 2 to the Memorandum of Understanding between the Secretary of State for Constitutional Affairs and the Information Commissioner dated 2 March 2005).

24 See his comments in an interview with the *Guardian* on 1 January 2005 (**www.guardian.co.uk/uk_news/story/0,,1381649,00.html**).

25 Comment at a conference on the FOIA on 21 January 2005 held at the offices of law firm Clifford Chance.

26 The Information Commissioner's policy regarding Practice Recommendations is set out in paras.27–30 of *Regulation under the Freedom of Information Act 2000 and the Environmental Information Regulations 2004* (ICO, 2.3.05).

27 Such consultation will take place in accordance with Memoranda of Understanding between the Information Commissioner and the Keeper and Deputy Keeper of Public Records.

28 In the case of an Information Notice, non-compliance includes cases where, in purported compliance with the notice, a public authority makes a statement which is false in a material respect either knowingly or recklessly (s.54(2)).

29 RSC Order 45, rule 5, contained in Schedule 1 to the CPR.

30   *Re Agreement of The Mileage Conference Group of The Tyre Manufacturers'
     Conference Ltd* [1966] 2 All ER 849 at 862, [1966] 1 WLR 1137 at 1162–3, per
     Megaw P; *Re Supply of Ready Mixed Concrete* [1991] ICR 52 at 70–72, RPC, per
     Anthony Lincoln J (affirmed [1995] 1 AC 456, [1995] 1 All ER 135, HL).
31   On an application for committal brought by the Information Commissioner over
     Allerdale Borough Council's failure to adopt a Publication Scheme and to
     respond to an Enforcement Notice, the court ruled that the contempt proceed-
     ings should have been instituted against the council rather than its CEO, as they
     had been (2004, Chester Crown Court, unreported).
32   Administration of Justice Act 1960, s.13(2)(*b*), as amended by Courts Act 1971,
     s.56(4), Sched.11 Part II. See also CPR 52.3(1)(*a*)(i).
33   The Parliamentary Information Commissioner for Administration, the
     Information Commissioners for Local Administration in England and Wales, the
     Health Service Information Commissioners for England and Wales, the Welsh
     Administration Ombudsman, the Northern Ireland Information Commissioner
     for Complaints and the Assembly Ombudsman for Northern Ireland.
34   Similarly, s.76 of the FOIA provides that the Information Commissioner may
     disclose to those same ombudsmen (plus the Scottish Parliamentary Information
     Commissioner for Administration, the Information Commissioner for Local
     Administration in Scotland and the Scottish Health Service Information
     Commissioner) any information which he has obtained under the FOIA or the
     DPA if it appears to him that it relates to matters investigable by them in accor-
     dance with their functions under the statutes tabulated in s.76 of the FOIA.
35   This does not apply to Preliminary Notices or Practice Recommendations.
36   Sheriff in Scotland and County Court judge in Northern Ireland.
37   Not only premises owned or occupied by the public authority in question but any
     premises at which the Information Commissioner reasonably suspects there to be
     relevant evidence (FOIA, Sched.3, para.1). The term also applies to any vessel,
     vehicle, aircraft or hovercraft, in which case references to the occupier of the
     premises mean the person in charge of that vehicle (FOIA, Sched.3, para.13).
38   The Information Commissioner has said he expects public authorities to
     consider decisions made by the Ombudsman in applying the public interest test
     under the Code (see *Awareness Guidance no.3; The Public Interest Test*, ICO). A
     very useful resource in this context is the Ombudsman's first report to Parliament
     for the 2005–6 session, which looks back at the 10 years of decision making
     under the Code, provides summaries of the landmark cases (section 4),
     comments in general on the public interest test and refers to relevant cases
     (section 5), provides links to several volumes of case reports (Appendix 5), lists
     all the cases decided under each exemption (Appendix 4), and sets out the text of
     the Code (Appendix 1). The report, entitled *Monitoring of the Non-statutory
     Codes of Practice 1994–2005 (Access to official information)* and dated 26 May
     2005, is on the web at: **www.ombudsman.org.uk/improving_services/special_reports/
     aoi/aoi_1994_2005/**. Cases not available on the Internet can be obtained in hard
     copy from the Stationery Office.
39   Available in hard copy, priced £15, from the Constitution Unit, University
     College London, 29–30 Tavistock Square, London WC1H 9QU (email:
     constitution@ucl.ac.uk). The Information Commissioner has said (in
     Awareness Guidance no.3) that until the FOIA case law develops, this analysis
     of foreign cases will provide valuable guidance, albeit that there are some
     significant differences between the FOIA and the equivalent legislation
     abroad. This publication also contains an analysis of decisions by the
     Parliamentary Ombudsman under the Code of Practice on Access to
     Government information.

40 *Regulation under the Freedom of Information Act 2000 and the Environmental Information Regulations 2004* (ICO, 2.3.05), para.41.
41 *Ibid.*, para.10.
42 The equivalent (though slightly different) provision under the EIR is reg.5(1); see Chapter 9.
43 *Memorandum of Understanding between the Secretary of State for Constitutional Affairs (on behalf of government Departments) and the Information Commissioner, on co-operation between government Departments and the Information Commissioner in relation to sections 50 and 51 of the Freedom of Information Act 2000 (including ss 50 and 51 as applied, as amended, by Regulation 18 of the Environmental Information Regulations 2004)* (2.3.05).
44 See *How we will handle your complaint – Information for Complainants* (ICO leaflet).
45 *Regulation under the Freedom of Information Act 2000 and the Environmental Information Regulations 2004* (ICO, 2.3.05), para.12. For sources of guidance and authority on formulating arguments to support (or resist) such applications, see section 10.5.2.
46 These examples of what constitutes a frivolous or vexatious complaint are derived from para.10 of *Regulation under the Freedom of Information Act 2000 and the Environmental Information Regulations 2004* (ICO, 2.3.05) and the Information Commissioner's document entitled *Awareness Guidance 22* (see the ICO website). The latter provides guidance for public authorities on the application of s.14 of the FOIA, under which they are exempted from having to comply with any request for information which is vexatious or substantially repeats an earlier request. The Information Commissioner states in *Awareness Guidance 22* that his interpretation of the terms 'frivolous or vexatious' in s.50(2)(c) will be consistent with the considerations set out in that document. The Information Commissioner's approach has been influenced by the case of *Attorney General* v. *Paul Evan John Barker* (2000) 1 FLR 759, LTL 16/2/2000, *The Times*, 7 March, 2000.
47 According to unpublished ICO policy papers supplied by the Assistant Information Commissioner with responsibility for complaints resolution (April 2005).
48 See note 22 above.
49 Para.18 of Sched.2 to the FOIA, which imports s.58 of the DPA.
50 In such cases government departments will not automatically provide the Information Commissioner with the information he requests and they hope that complaints can be resolved through dialogue. The Information Commissioner is generally to give advance notice if he intends to serve an Information Notice, as is the government department if intending to use the Ministerial veto.
51 See paras.24 and 38 of *Regulation under the Freedom of Information Act 2000 and the Environmental Information Regulations 2004* (ICO, 2.3.05).
52 See para.25 of *Regulation under the Freedom of Information Act 2000 and the Environmental Information Regulations 2004* (ICO, 2.3.05) and para.8 of the MoU.
53 According to unpublished ICO policy papers (April 2005).
54 Section 51(8) allows the Information Commissioner to serve an Information Notice requiring a public authority to provide him with unrecorded information. This can be contrasted with the fact that applicants for access to information under s.1(1) are only entitled to information held by a public authority which is recorded (in any form) (s.84).

55 See *Awareness Guidance No.15* (on the exemption under s.29 of the FOIA), page 4 (ICO website).
56 According to a personal communication from the Assistant Information Commissioner with responsibility for complaint resolution (April 2005); see also para.9 of the MoU.
57 It is very likely that the Information Commissioner will be able to resist disclosure by relying on one or more of the exemptions for investigations (s.30), law enforcement (s.31), effective conduct of public affairs (s.36) and information provided in confidence (s.41). Where he has agreed to inspect an authority's sensitive document *in situ*, he will not be 'holding' such information should an applicant request it under FOIA, s.1(1).
58 Personal communication from the Assistant Information Commissioner with responsibility for complaint resolution (April 2005).
59 See, e.g. para.6 of *Regulation under the Freedom of Information Act 2000 and the Environmental Information Regulations 2004* (ICO, 2.3.05).
60 *Minister of National Revenue v. Wrights' Canadian Ropes Ltd* [1947] AC 109 at 122; *Associated Provincial Picture Houses Ltd v. Wednesbury Corporation* [1948] 1 KB 223 at 228; *Fawcett Properties Ltd v. Buckingham County Council* [1959] Ch. 543 at 575, affirmed [1961] AC 636.
61 Compare the position in planning appeals: *JA Pye (Oxford) Estates Limited v. West Oxfordshire District Council and the Secretary of State for the Environment* [1982] JPL 577, cited by Coppell in *Information Rights* (Sweet & Maxwell, 2004) p.374.
62 For the Information Commissioner's policy on informal resolution, see *Regulation under the Freedom of Information Act 2000 and the Environmental Information Regulations 2004* (ICO, 2.3.05), para.10 and Annex 1, and see later in this section.
63 According to unpublished ICO policy papers (April 2005).
64 Personal communication from the Assistant Information Commissioner with responsibility for complaint resolution (April 2005).
65 *How we will handle your complaints – Information for Complainants* (ICO, as at April 2005). The MoU in fact states that the period for allowing responses to preliminary notices will be 28 working days (para.21).
66 Personal communication from the Assistant Information Commissioner with responsibility for complaint resolution (April 2005).
67 See comments in Annex 1 to *Regulation under the Freedom of Information Act 2000 and the Environmental Information Regulations 2004* (ICO, 2.3.05) para.5 (third bullet point). This might happen where a public authority failed to recognise a request for information or where it had mistakenly understood that an exemption gave it no power to make a disclosure (examples cited in a personal communication from the Assistant Information Commissioner with responsibility for complaints resolution, April 2005).
68 See para.13 of *Regulation under the Freedom of Information Act 2000 and the Environmental Information Regulations 2004* (ICO, 2.3.05).
69 Unpublished ICO policy document (April 2005).
70 Para.41 of *Regulation under the Freedom of Information Act 2000 and the Environmental Information Regulations 2004* (ICO, 2.3.05).
71 MoU, para.26. Note that although this same paragraph of the MoU indicates that it was the Information Commissioner's policy not to publish case summaries while an appeal was still pending, that seems no longer to be the case – see e.g. the summary of case ref: FS50063478 of 20.6.05 concerning a complaint against the National Maritime Museum.

72 After the FOIA had been fully in force for six months, for example, the Information Commissioner produced a list of top 10 tips to assist public authorities in responding to requests for information in ways likely to cut down the number of complaints (see ICO website).

73 Personal communication from Assistant Information Commissioner with responsibility for complaints resolution (April 2005).

74 Para.40, *Regulation under the Freedom of Information Act 2000 and the Environmental Information Regulations 2004* (ICO, 2.3.05).

75 Unpublished ICO policy document (April 2005). Contrast the position in Scotland where, under s.49(3)(*b*) of the Freedom of Information (Scotland) Act 2002, the Information Commissioner must reach a decision within four months of receiving the application or such other period as is reasonable in the circumstances.

76 On consultation of third parties, see sections 10.9.3 and 10.9.4. On Publication Schemes, see Chapter 2.

77 For information on this avenue see **www.ombudsman.org.uk/make_a_complaint/**.

78 Formerly known as the Data Protection Information Tribunal (the name change was effected by s.18(2) and (4) of, and Sched.2, para.1(2) to, the FOIA), it deals primarily with appeals under the FOIA and the DPA.

79 Namely, any such notice which concerns (i) information which is contained in transferred public records but has not been designated open information by the responsible authority for the purposes of s.66 of the FOIA; and (ii) the issue of how the public interest test in s.2 applies to that information. Broadly, transferred public records (defined in s.15(4)) are those which have been transferred to the Public Records Office and the responsible authority in relation to them is the Minister who appears to be primarily concerned (s.15(5)).

80 These provisions are contained in Sched.6 to the DPA as amended by para.4 of Sched.4 to the FOIA.

81 Rule 25 of SI 2005/14 (as amended by SI 2005/450, rule 5). See below.

82 The 2005 Rules, SI 2005/14, are amended by the Information Tribunal (Enforcement Appeals) (Amendment) Rules 2005, SI 2005/450. The 2005 Rules revoke the Data Protection Tribunal (Enforcement Appeals) Rules 2000, SI 2000/189 as amended, and the Information Tribunal (Enforcement Appeals) (Amendment) Rules 2002. The 2005 Rules also apply to appeals under s.48 of the DPA. Appeal proceedings are also governed by Sched.6 to the DPA as amended by Sched.4 to the FOIA.

83 Aside from what is mentioned here, the 2005 Rules also provide for the consolidation of appeals where a common question of law or fact arises in both or all of them, or where it is desirable for some other reason to hear them together, subject to the parties' having the chance to make representations.

84 The Information Commissioner may also seek expedition of proceedings, say whether he thinks a hearing is desirable if the appellant has indicated he will not want one, and indicate whether he thinks it might be necessary in the interests of justice for the appeal to be heard and determined otherwise than by the chairman sitting alone if it is an appeal against an Information Notice (see rule 21).

85 Directions may be made in the parties' absence but a party may always apply to have a direction varied or set aside.

86 Its decisions are taken on a majority of those hearing the appeal (DPA, Sched.6, para.5). As to how quickly the Information Tribunal processes appeals, several months is the likely minimum. The first appeal under the FOIA was lodged on 1 June 2005 but had not been determined as at 1 November 2005, nor had the

other six appeals lodged in June and July. Parties opting for a paper hearing can expect a speedier process than those requesting an oral hearing.

87   This includes appeals which are withdrawn by the appellant under rule 12 of the 2005 Rules, which can be done by written notice to the proper officer of the Information Tribunal at any time before the appeal has been determined.

88   By contrast, the FOIA does not provide for any appeal against the conclusive evidence certificates issued under s.34(3) in respect of parliamentary privilege or s.36(7) in respect of prejudice to effective conduct of public affairs resulting from disclosure of information held by Parliament. In the absence of a statutory appeal, the only remaining avenue of challenge to these certificates would be by way of a judicial review but the courts are most unlikely to intervene, both because of the way the clauses are drafted and out of reluctance to interfere with parliamentary privilege.

89   This applies only to a hearing of an appellant's representations against summary dismissal of the appeal under rule 12 of the Information Tribunal (National Security Appeals) Rules 2005 (see para.6(1) of Sched.6 to the DPA and rule 4(3) of the Information Tribunal (National Security Appeals) Rules 2005).

90   See rule 26 of the Information Tribunal (National Security Appeals) Rules 2005.

91   These rules revoke the Data Protection Information Tribunal (National Security Appeals) Rules 2000, SI 2000/206). Appeal proceedings are also governed by DPA, Sched.6 as amended by FOIA, Sched.4.

92   The following rules are similar: amendment of notices (save that the Minister has 28 days to amend his notice in reply – rather than the 21 days allowed to the Information Commissioner on s.57 appeals – where the appellant is granted leave to amend his notice of appeal) (rule 10); application for strike-out by the Minister (rule 11); power of Information Tribunal to dismiss the appeal summarily (rule 12); withdrawal of an appeal (rule 14); consolidation of appeals (rule 15); the giving of directions by the Information Tribunal, including for a preliminary issue and pre-hearing review (rule 16); time and place of hearings (rule 20); summoning witnesses to attend a hearing (rule 21); representation at a hearing (rule 22); Information Tribunal's powers in default of party's appearance at hearing (rule 23); conduct of hearings (rule 25); evidence (rule 27); irregularities (rule 30); notices (rule 31). The potential liability of the parties to be punished as if for contempt of court is also the same (see section 10.7.1).

93   If the Information Tribunal does overrule the objection or order the Minister to provide a different version of his notice in reply, the Information Tribunal must not disclose or order disclosure of any material which was the subject of the unsuccessful objection if the Minister chooses not to rely upon it in opposing the appeal (rule 18(6)).

94   The grounds (rule 12) are the same as under the 2005 Rules – see earlier in the chapter.

95   Before determining a matter without a hearing under this rule the Information Tribunal can direct any party to provide in writing further information about any matter relevant to the appeal (subject to the Minister's right of objection discussed above) (rule 19(2)).

96   Its decisions are taken on a majority of those hearing the appeal (DPA, Sched.6, para.5).

97   See s.1 of the Administration of Justice (Appeals) Act 1934 and CPR Pt 52 PD 15.19.

98   The possibility for third parties to challenge disclosure under freedom of information regimes abroad is known colloquially as 'reverse FOI'.

99 Information Tribunal (Enforcement Appeals) Rules 2005, rule 7. (This rule is made under para.7(2)(*aa*) of Sched.6 to the DPA, as inserted by para.4(3) of Sched.4 to the FOIA.) With regard to such appeals, see section 10.7.1.

100 See the second bullet point under para.25 of the Section 45 Code.

101 See paras.6.8–6.10 under the section on guidance in *Guidance and Methodology for Publication Schemes* (ICO, April 2003, ICO website) and section 4 of *Publication Schemes: A Practical Guide: Part 1 'Classes'* (ICO, April 2003, ICO website). Publication Schemes are discussed in detail in Chapter 2.

102 Consultation would also be required under the general law in order to obtain the third party's consent to disclosure if an authority wished to disclose information in breach of a legal obligation of confidence (albeit exempt under s.41) without facing liability. Notification of an intention to disclose the third party's personal data will also often be necessary so that the public authority does not breach the DPA requirement that such data be processed fairly and lawfully (processing includes disclosing in this context).

103 Last revised November 2004. Original Code issued November 2002.

104 To obtain an interim injunction, a claimant may well have to show it is more likely than not to succeed at trial. This is a higher test than that ordinarily required on injunction applications, where the claimant must show it has a 'real prospect of success' or there is a 'serious question to be tried' (*American Cyanamid Co.* v. *Ethicon Ltd* [1975] AC 396). This is because of the effect of s.12(3) of the Human Rights Act 1998 where an injunction is sought in a claim for breach of confidence to prevent the exercise of the Article 10 (ECHR) right to freedom of expression (*Cream Holdings Ltd & Others* v. *Banerjee & Another* [2005] 1 AC 253). A government claimant will in addition have to show that there is a public interest in keeping the information confidential (*A-G* v. *Jonathan Cape Ltd and others* [1976] QB 752 at 770–771). For a fuller discussion of what constitutes confidential information, see the section on the s.41 exemption in Chapter 4.

105 Despite the public domain defence, where there has been only a limited degree of disclosure the courts might still be prepared to grant an injunction preventing further disclosure (see e.g. *Franchi* v. *Franchi* [1969] RPC 149).

106 Until there is legal authority on this point, the safer course for public authorities would be to appeal the Information Commissioner's decision to the Information Tribunal, enabling the third party to defend their own interests directly (see section 10.9.2).

107 See *Procedural Guidance, Chapter 8: 'Responding to the request'* DCA, October 2004 (**www.dca.gov.uk/foi/guidance/proguide/chap08.htm#top**).

108 No liability in tort can arise from acts done in pursuance, and within the scope, of statutory powers where the powers are exercised in good faith, reasonably, without negligence, and for the purpose for which, and in the manner in which, the statute provides (*Halsbury's Laws of England*, 4th ed. reissue 1999, vol.45(2) para.365).

109 For arguments in support of such a position, see the article, 'Could copyright be an obstacle to an efficient and effective Freedom of Information regime?' by Julia Apostle and Mark Lawry in *Freedom of Information*, Vol.1, Issue 4, March/April 2005.

110 See Griffiths J, 'Recapturing Liberated Information – The Relationship between the UK's Freedom of Information Act 2000 and Private Law Restraints on Disclosure', Chapter 4 of *Copyright and Human Rights: Freedom of Expression, Intellectual Property, Privacy* (Kluwer Law International, 2004) edited by Paul L.C. Torremans.

111 Due to the rule against prior restraint in *Bonnard* v. *Perryman* [1891] 2 Ch 269 (which the Court of Appeal held in *Greene* v. *Associated Newspapers Ltd* [2004] EWCA Civ 1462, [2005] 1 All ER 30, [2005] EMLR 10 remained unaffected by s.12 of the Human Rights Act 1998), under which a court will not normally grant an injunction where the defendant publisher of the allegedly defamatory statement indicates an intention to prove it is true, or would be subject to some other substantive defence, unless the claimant can clearly show that none of these defences will succeed at trial.

FOI Resources

For general freedom of information guidance and assistance:

The Information Commissioner
Wycliffe House
Water Lane
Wilmslow
Cheshire
SK9 5AF
Tel. 01625 545 700
Fax. 01625 524 510
www.informationcommissioner.gov.uk

To subscribe to *Freedom of Information* journal and for freedom of information training courses training courses:

Freedom of Information Journal
5 Shelgate Road
London
SW11 1BD
Tel. 0845 226 5723
Fax. 0870 137 7871
www.foij.com
www.foij.com/training

For updates and guidance on Freedom of Information:

Department of Constitutional Affairs
Information Rights Division
6th Floor, Selborne House
54 Victoria Street
London
SW1H 6QW
Tel. 020 7210 8034
Fax. 020 7210 8388
www.dca.gov.uk

For enquiries relating to the Environmental Information Regulations:

Department for the Environment, Food and Rural Affairs
Environmental Information Unit
1E Whitehall Place West
3–8 Whitehall Place
London
SW1A 2HR
Tel. 020 7270 8887
www.defra.gov.uk

For information on the Annual Freedom of Information Conference & Workshop Series:

Freedom of Information Conference
60 Battersea Business Centre
London
SW11 5QL
Tel. 0845 226 5723
Fax. 0870 137 7871
www.foiconference.com

Index

I HA

I HAVE
BEEN HERE BEFORE

A Play in Three Acts

by

J. B. PRIESTLEY

I have been here before
But when or how I cannot tell:
I know the grass beyond the door
The sweet keen smell,
The sighing sound, the lights around the shore.
—D. G. ROSSETTI

SAMUEL FRENCH

FRENCH

LONDON
NEW YORK SYDNEY TORONTO HOLLYWOOD

I HAVE BEEN HERE BEFORE

Produced at the Royalty Theatre, London, on Wednesday, September 22nd, 1937, with the following cast of characters :

(In the order of their appearance)

SALLY PRATT	*Eileen Beldon.*
SAM SHIPLEY	*William Heilbronn.*
DR. GÖRTLER	*Lewis Casson.*
OLIVER FARRANT	*William Fox.*
JANET ORMUND	*Patricia Hilliard.*
WALTER ORMUND	*Wilfrid Lawson.*

The Play produced by LEWIS CASSON.

The SCENE throughout is the sitting-room of the Black Bull Inn, Grindle Moor, North Yorkshire, at Whitsuntide.

ACT   I.—Friday.

ACT II.—Saturday.

ACT III.—Sunday.

For some of Dr. Görtler's theories of Time and Recurrence, I gratefully acknowledge my debt to P. D. Ouspensky's astonishing book, *A New Model of the Universe*. It must be understood, however, that I accept full responsibility for the free use I have made of these borrowed ideas, and that it does not follow because I make use of them that I necessarily accept them.

J. B. P.

To face page 7 — I have been here before

I HAVE BEEN HERE BEFORE

ACT I

SCENE.—*The sitting-room of the Black Bull Inn, Grindle Moor, North Yorkshire, a moorland inn of the farmhouse type that serves as the local " pub " and also takes a few guests.*

The room is simply furnished in the style of a North Country farmhouse sitting-room. On the L. is a long low window, deeply set, through which the sunlight is streaming. At the back, on the L., is a door that serves as an entrance to the inn to the people staying there, but not to people who merely go for a drink or a meal. On the R. at the back is the door that leads to the dining-room, the bar and the rest of the inn, including two of the guest bedrooms. Through this door a passage can be seen. Down stage R. is a slighter door, leading to two bedrooms ; it opens directly on to a steep flight of stairs. Through the main door, when open, can be seen a distant glimpse of high moorland. The fireplace of the room is presumed to be in the fourth wall.

(See Photograph of Scene.)

It is an evening in June, about eight o'clock.

The room is empty at the rise of the CURTAIN, *and only the tick of the clock can be heard, but immediately afterwards* SALLY PRATT *enters up* R.C., *bringing in two bowls of flowers. She is a pleasant-looking country-woman in her middle thirties and is nicely dressed, but wears an apron as if she were still busy with household work. She speaks in a rather loud tone and with a North Country accent, but not too broad. After a moment or two,* SAM SHIPLEY *enters up* R.C. *He is a stout, humorous, contented Yorkshireman in his sixties. He is in his shirt-sleeves and is smoking a pipe. His accent is broader than his daughter's, but not very broad.*

SALLY *puts one of the bowls on the table* C. *and the other on top of the desk* L., *upstage end.*

SALLY (*as she finishes her task*). That looks a bit better.

SAM. Ay.

SALLY (*sharply, but not unpleasantly*). Father—get your coat on.

SAM (*moving to above* L. *of the table*). What for ?

SALLY (*going up to* SAM). You know what for, I've told you

7

often enough.   Landlord o' the Black Bull in his shirt-sleeves like a barman !

SAM.   Long as folk pay me what they owe me—they can tak' me for a barman if they like.   I'm not a particular chap.

SALLY (*commencing to dust*).   Now go on.   We'll have somebody here in a minute.   I don't want Miss Holmes and her friends marching in, catching you in your shirt-sleeves.

SAM.   If they never see worse nor that, they'll be lucky. (*Moving slowly to the door* R.C.)   When's Mr. Farrant getting back ?

SALLY.   Any time.   He only wanted some cold meat and salad and cheese left for his supper.   I wish they were all as easy to please.   (*She goes to the desk to rearrange the flowers.*)

(SAM *wanders out during this speech, leaving the door open behind him.   Then he pops his head back.*)

SAM.   Butcher's here.

SALLY.   An' he's rare an' late.

(*As she is going up* R.C., *there is the sound of a car.   She hears it and shouts.*)

Father, I believe there's somebody here.   (*She goes quickly to the window* L.)

SAM (*off*).   I'm coming.

(SALLY *hurries out* R.C.   *In the empty room we hear the clock ticking.   A moment's pause.   Then there is a quiet knocking on the outer door up* L. *and it opens slowly.*   DR. GÖRTLER *enters.   The clock chimes the quarter past.   He is a man about sixty, in well-worn darkish clothes of a foreign cut.   He has a slight foreign accent, and speaks with precision.   Although his appearance and manner suggest the quiet detached scholar, he has a good deal of assurance and authority.   He puts his hat on the table* C. *and looks about him with eager interest and curiosity, and when he has taken the room in, consults a small notebook, as if comparing its appearance with some notes there.   Finally, he nods.*   SAM *now returns, wearing his coat.   The two men look at each other for a moment, then play their scene slowly.*)

(R.C.)   Good evening, sir.   (*He comes down* R.)

DR. GÖRTLER (L.C.).   Good evening.   You are the landlord ?

SAM.   That's right.   Sam Shipley.

DR. GÖRTLER.   You let rooms to visitors ?

SAM.   A few.

DR. GÖRTLER.   Three or four, perhaps ?

SAM (*slightly surprised*).   Yes.

(SALLY *bustles in, then stops short in surprise when she sees* DR. GÖRTLER.)

SALLY (*up R. of the table*).   Oh !——good evening.

DR. GÖRTLER (*smiling*).   Good evening.

SALLY.   Were you wanting a room ?

DR. GÖRTLER (*slowly*).   I am not sure.

SALLY (*who does not like this*).   Oh !——well, it doesn't matter, because I'm afraid we can't oblige you.

DR. GÖRTLER.   You have no room ?

SALLY.   We've only four bedrooms and they're all taken for this Whitsuntide.   There's a gentleman in one already, and the other three are coming to-night.

DR. GÖRTLER.   So.   These three who are coming to-night—you know them ?

SALLY (*surprised*).   Yes.

DR. GÖRTLER (*gently, tentatively*).   Two of them—perhaps—are married people—the man older than his wife—he might be rich—and then—perhaps—a younger man——?

SALLY (*who has listened to this with some surprise*).   No.   We're expecting three ladies.

DR. GÖRTLER (*rather taken aback*).   Three ladies ?

SALLY.   Teachers from Manchester.

DR. GÖRTLER.   Oh !   Perhaps there is another inn here, eh ?

SAM.   Nay, this is t'only one.   There's t'Lion at Dale End, but that's eight mile from here.

SALLY.   But there's one or two here that lets rooms.   You might try Lane Top Farm—Mrs. Fletcher—it's just a bit further on.

SAM.   Not five minutes in a car—if you've come in a car.

DR. GÖRTLER (*still showing signs of disappointment*).   Yes, I have a little car.   I will try this farm, but I do not think it will be any use.   (*He picks up his hat and goes to the door, then turns and smiles rather forlornly.*)   This must be the wrong year.

SAM.   Don't you know what year your friends are coming ?

DR. GÖRTLER (*with a slight smile, turning back to L.C.*).   They are not my friends.   (*He goes to the door again.*)   How do I find this farm ?

SAM (*following him towards the door up L.*).   When you get out o' t'yard here, turn sharp to your right, and she has a sign up—you can't miss it.

(*By the time he has said this, DR. GÖRTLER is outside and SAM is at the door.   SAM closes the door and comes in.   Meanwhile SALLY has gone to the window.*)

There'll be no rain this week-end.   We'd have had a smell of it by now.

SALLY.   Just fancy !   Creeping in like that and asking questions !

SAM (L.C.).   What, yon chap ?   Well, he's a foreigner o' some sort, you see.

SALLY (*by the desk*). What's that got to do with it ?

SAM. Well, happen it's foreign style o' doing things. (*He begins to chuckle.*) Nay, what tickled me was him saying he must ha' come at wrong year. Now that's as good as aught I've heard o' some time. If he's going round asking for people —not friends of his, mind you—and he doesn't know where they are nor what year they'll be there—I reckon he's got his work cut out. I must tell that to some of 'em in t'bar.

SALLY. You and your bar !

(*The telephone rings.* SALLY *crosses below* SAM *to answer it.*)

(*At the telephone.*) Yes, this is the Black Bull. Yes, well I *am* waiting. . . . Oh, Miss Holmes, yes—this is Mrs. Pratt—we were wondering what had become of you. . . . Oh dear dear ! . . . Well, I never did ! . . . No, if your friend's so poorly I don't suppose you could. . . . No, well it can't be helped. . . . Yes, we're sorry to. . . . Oh, we'll manage to get somebody . . . that's right . . . good-bye. (*She puts down the telephone and turns to* SAM.) Miss Holmes—ringing up from Manchester—to say they can't come.

SAM. Nay !

SALLY. One of the other two's been suddenly taken poorly, and they don't like to leave her.

SAM. Oh !

SALLY (*indignantly*). And I should think it is " oh ! " That's all three rooms going begging, at very last minute, an' we could have let 'em four times over. (*Moving down* R.) Here we are— Friday night—Whit Saturday to-morrow—an' now only one room taken. We ought to do what everybody else does, an' charge 'em a deposit when they book rooms in advance, and then if they do give backword we're not clean out o' pocket.

SAM (*moving over to* SALLY). Well, it's happened afore.

SALLY. Does that make it any better ?

SAM. Yes, 'cos we know we'll fill 'em up easy. Black Bull's nivver had rooms empty o' Whitsuntide. There'll be some motorists coming. Ay, and happen some business chaps who'll spend more nor them three women teachers. All they want is cups o' tea, an' they'd nivver put their noses into t'bar.

(OLIVER FARRANT *enters up* L. *He has been walking and wears a tweed jacket and flannel trousers, and is rather dusty. He is about twenty-eight to thirty, good-looking, with something of the boy left in him and something of the intellectual man. He has a decisive, slightly donnish manner, which shows itself least with these two, with whom he is on pleasant easy terms. He has more personal charm than would appear from his actual lines, and though he suffers from the rather priggish conceit of the successful intellectual, there is more of this in the matter than in the manner of his talk.*)

FARRANT. Any sherry left, Sam ?

SAM. Yes, Mr. Farrant.

(*He goes out* R.C. *to get it.* FARRANT *shuts the door up* L.)

SALLY (*who obviously likes him*). Your supper'll be ready when you are.

FARRANT. Good ! (*Sitting down in the chair* L. *of the table and relaxing.*) The last few miles were becoming a bit grim. (*Remembering, with whisper and slightly droll manner.*) Oh !—— have the three females from Manchester arrived yet ?

SALLY (*down* R.). No, they're not coming. One of 'em's poorly.

FARRANT. Well, I can't say I was looking forward to them— but I'm sorry. It's bad news for you, isn't it ?

SALLY. It's a nuisance, but we'll fill up to-morrow all right. I only hope whoever we do have, you can get on with 'em, Mr. Farrant.

FARRANT. Now you're not going to suggest I'm hard to get on with ?

SALLY (*earnestly*). No, I don't mean that, Mr. Farrant, but you know what it is. If we take people at last minute, we can't be too particular, and when you've all got to sit in here together, it might be a bit awkward.

FARRANT. Oh, don't worry about me. I don't suppose I shall be in much this week-end, anyhow, and if the worst comes to the worst, I can always go up to my room and read.

(SAM *enters with a glass of sherry on a tray.   He comes to above the table and puts the tray down.*)

SALLY. I'll see if you've everything you want in there.   Do you like Wensleydale cheese, Mr. Farrant, 'cos I've got some ?

FARRANT. I don't know.   I'd like to try it.

(SALLY *goes out up* R.C., *shutting the door after her.*)

SAM. Bit o' nice Wensleydale tak's some beating. (*Moving down* L.) Have a good walk, Mr. Farrant ?

FARRANT (*sipping his sherry*). Yes, thanks, Sam. I must have done about sixteen miles. Down the dale, then across by the church, up the moor and back over Grindle Top.

SAM. Ay, that'll be all o' sixteen mile. Did you find a bit o' bog again at the Top ?

FARRANT. No, I'm getting artful, Sam. I dodged it this time —worked well over to the right. The ordnance map's all wrong about Grindle Top. (*He sips his sherry, and talks easily.*) You know, Sam, there must have been three or four times as many people living in this dale two or three hundred years ago.

SAM. I've heard 'em say that.

FARRANT. Look at all those old ruins of byres and barns and sheep pounds—and the miles of old walls on the moor.

SAM. Ay, they built them afore folk went into the towns. I remember me grandfather talking about that when I wor a little lad.

FARRANT. Somebody ought to try and find the old records of these dales. Why, in the Middle Ages, what with all that old moorland farming life, and the abbeys and a castle or two, the whole place must have been humming with people.

SAM. I'll bet it worn't humming wi' folk to-day.

FARRANT. Didn't see a soul this afternoon over the Top except a couple of shepherds.

(He finishes his sherry, rises, and begins moving towards his bedroom. SAM takes the glass and puts it on the tray. The telephone rings. SAM puts the tray on the sideboard and rather dubiously prepares to answer it. FARRANT hurries out through the door down R., through which he can be seen going upstairs to his room, the stairs being immediately behind the door.

As SAM takes hold of the telephone, SALLY hurries in up R.C.)

SAM. Yes, this is Black Bull. That's right. . . .

SALLY *(impatiently, L. of him)*. Here, I'll answer it, Father.

SAM *(into the telephone)*. Hold on a minute.

(SALLY takes it from him, pushing SAM down R.)

SALLY. Yes, who is it ? . . . Yes—Mr. Ormund. . . . Well, it just happens we have two rooms because somebody's just given us backword. . . . Yes, they're both ready, you can come up as soon as you like. Straight away ? . . . Will you be wanting supper to-night ? Oh, I see. . . . Well then, you turn to your left just outside Marlingset, and then straight up and you can't miss it. . . . That's right. *(She puts down the telephone and is rather excited.)* Now would you believe it ? *(She comes to above the table C.)*

SAM *(humorously)*. I don't know till you tell me.

SALLY *(excitedly)*. That's a Mr. and Mrs. Ormund. They rang up from Marlingset to see if they could stay over the week-end—they want a bedroom each—and they're coming straight away—they've just had their dinner at the White Hart—and d'you know what I think ?

SAM. No, I don't.

SALLY *(moving close to SAM)*. I believe this Mr. Ormund is one o' them big Ormunds—y'know—Ormunds Limited.

SAM *(down R.)*. Nay, he wouldn't come here if he wor.

SALLY. How do *you* know ? And he sounded as if he'd plenty o' money. Wanted two rooms and didn't ask price or anything. I'll bet you he's one of Ormunds Limited. Him and his wife— they'll be company for Mr. Farrant.

SAM (*moving up* R.).   I told you we'd have them rooms let i'
no time.   (*He opens the door, then stops.*)   I wonder if that
foreign chap's fixed up at Lane End ?

SALLY.   He didn't even know whether he wanted to stay or
not.

SAM (*casually*).   No, but happen it'ud suit him here now.   We
have a married couple for him, if that's what he wants.

(FARRANT *enters down* R., *having changed his shoes and tidied
himself, and crosses to beyond the chair* L. *of the table.   He is
carrying a book.*)

You're having company *to-night*, Mr. Farrant.

(*He grins and goes out* R.C., *closing the door after him.*)

SALLY.   There's a Mr. and Mrs. Ormund coming to-night, to
stay the week-end.

FARRANT (*interested*).   Ormund ?

SALLY.   Yes, an' I fancy it's one o' them big Ormunds—
Ormunds Limited—manufacturers—I expect you've heard o'
them ?

FARRANT.   I ought to.   They put up most of the money for
my school.

SALLY.   Well, I'm sure this is one o' 'em.

(*Footsteps are heard outside,* SALLY *goes* L. *to the window.*)

FARRANT.   Here already ?

SALLY.   No, they couldn't have come from Marlingset so soon.

(*She moves towards the door up* L., FARRANT *watching idly.   Before
she can open it,* DR. GÖRTLER *knocks and enters slowly, carrying
an old-fashioned bag.   He looks at* SALLY, *then sees* FARRANT
and appears to recognize him. SALLY *looks at him, then at*
FARRANT, *rather bewildered.   The door is left open.*)

DR. GÖRTLER (*to* FARRANT, *with some eagerness*).   You are
staying here ?

FARRANT (*below the desk*).   Yes.

(DR. GÖRTLER *takes his hat off.   There is something decisive in his
manner.* SALLY *crosses to* R.C.)

DR. GÖRTLER (L.C.).   I am Doctor Görtler.

FARRANT (*rather puzzled*).   My name's Farrant, Oliver Farrant.

DR. GÖRTLER.   A schoolmaster, I think ?

FARRANT.   Yes, I'm head of Lamberton.

DR. GÖRTLER.   I am now an exile from my own university
—and my country, Germany—and I have been doing some little
work for the University of London.   (*He turns to* SALLY.)   And
still you have no room for me ?

(SALLY *gives* FARRANT *a quick questioning look. He nods reassuringly.*)

SALLY. Well, as a matter of fact we have now, because those three ladies aren't coming and we've a room to spare——

DR. GÖRTLER. I should very much like to stay here.

SALLY (*businesslike*). We charge twelve-and-six a day—all in. That's for this holiday time, and really we ought to charge more because we could easily get it—but——

DR. GÖRTLER (*simply*). But you do not like to be greedy, eh ?

SALLY (*rather taken aback*). No.

DR. GÖRTLER. I will stay. (*He puts his bag down.*) The car will be all right there for a time, eh ? (*He moves to the chair* L. *of the table.*)

SALLY (*moving* R. *a little*). Yes. My father can put it away.

DR. GÖRTLER. And my room ?

SALLY (*pointing to the door down* R.). It's up there.

FARRANT (*smiling*). Next door to me. (*Moving to* DR. GÖRTLER.) I'm just going to have some supper, Doctor Görtler. You'd better join me.

DR. GÖRTLER (*taking* SALLY *in too*). Thank you, yes. I should like something to eat. Anything. (*He sits in the chair* L. *of the table.*)

SALLY. I'll see to it. My father can show you your room.

(*She hurries out up* R.C., *closing the door.*)

FARRANT (*moving round above the table to* R. *of it*). It's a simple, unpretentious little place—but they're nice people—and I think you'll be comfortable.

DR. GÖRTLER. Thank you.

FARRANT. What's your subject ? Science ?

DR. GÖRTLER. It *was* physics and mathematics.

FARRANT. Not now ?

DR. GÖRTLER (*with a slight shrug*). I still teach these subjects. But for myself—I go further——

FARRANT. Research, eh ?

DR. GÖRTLER. You might say—exploring.

FARRANT (*with a smile*). I know. Spherical geometry. Two parallel lines meeting. Two angles of a triangle no longer greater than the third angle. Poor old Euclid turned upside down and inside out. I have a maths. master who talks like that—for his own amusement—not ours—— (*He pauses, then looks hard at* DR. GÖRTLER.) You know, I must have seen your photograph somewhere.

DR. GÖRTLER. No, I do not think so. I am not an Einstein.

FARRANT (*hesitantly*). I thought I—seemed—to recognize you.

DR. GÖRTLER (*calmly*). We often seem to recognize people—and places.

FARRANT. I don't.

DR. GÖRTLER. You have been ill ?

FARRANT. I was ordered a short rest. (*He pauses, moves down* R. *a little, then resumes, rather hastily.*) They say that it's when you're nervously exhausted that the two halves of your brain don't synchronize. Then they play that recognition trick on you. Isn't that the explanation ?

DR. GÖRTLER. Yes. But do not believe it. We are not as simple as bicycles.

(SAM *enters up* R.C.)

SAM. Supper's ready, Mr. Farrant.

(FARRANT *moves up and* SAM *holds the door open for him.*)

FARRANT (*to* DR. GÖRTLER *as he goes*). You'll join me in the dining-room, eh ?

(*He goes.*)

SAM (*heartily, coming down to above the table*). Now then, sir, you're here, after all. And you'd like to see your room ?

DR. GÖRTLER. Please.

(SAM *goes up* L.C. *for* DR. GÖRTLER'S *bag, talking as he moves. He takes the bag and crosses below the table towards the door down* R.)

SAM. Ay, not five minutes after you'd gone, them three ladies rang up to say they couldn't come, so we'd room after all for you. Just the one left.

DR. GÖRTLER. But the other two rooms ?

SAM (*at the door down stage* R.). Oh—we got rid o' them all right. There's a Mr. and Mrs. Ormund coming to-night into them.

(DR. GÖRTLER *rises and crosses to* SAM.)

DR. GÖRTLER (*triumphantly, with a touch of wonder, really to himself*). So ! So ! Ich bin glücklich.

SAM (*opening the door*). What language is that, sir ? German ?

DR. GÖRTLER (*off*). Yes. It means " I am fortunate."

(*They go out and their voices die away. The stage is empty. The light has been fading slowly, but there is a last glow in it. There is a pause of a moment or two, then* DR. GÖRTLER *and* SAM *return, talking as if they had never stopped.* DR. GÖRTLER *crosses over below the table to above the chair* L. *of it and stands with his back to* SAM. SAM *comes* C. *below the table.*)

You say that because you have been happy here ?

SAM. Yes, I can't grumble at all. I've never made much out o' this place, but I've had all I want. I'd ask for naught better —if I had my time over again.

DR. GÖRTLER (*turning—interested*).   Do you often say that ?
SAM.   Say what ?
DR. GÖRTLER (*slowly*).   If you had your time over again.
SAM (*surprised*).   Well—no—not specially.   I mean to say—
it's just a way—like—o' putting it.   Everybody says it.

(SALLY *enters up* R.C., *holding the door open behind her.*)

SALLY (*not very cordially*).   Your supper's ready, Doctor—
er——
DR. GÖRTLER.   Thank you.

(*He goes over towards the door, then stops.   SAM follows him round
to above the chair* L. *of the table.*)

(*Turning, rather mischievously, to* SAM.)   My friend—perhaps
you *will* have your time over again.
SALLY (*at the door*).   In here, that's right.   And if you don't
find everything you want, just ring the bell.   (*She watches him go,
then comes in, closing the door behind her.*)   If four of 'em's going
to sit in here, it wants changing round a bit.

(*Throughout the following dialogue* SALLY *is now busy, with some
small assistance from* SAM, *slightly re-arranging the furniture of
the room.   She brings the chair from up* L.C. *to above the table
and the chair from down* R. *to* R. *of the table.   In between her
remarks, she is looking the place over, then going to move a chair
back or forward, to put an ornament in another place, and so on.*)

What was that Doctor Görtler talking about ?
SAM.   Nay, I just happened to say " If I'd my time over
again "—you know how you do ?—and he seemed right taken
up with it.   (*Repeating it speculatively.*)   " If I'd my time over
again."   Nay, it's a common enough saying.
SALLY (*in a slow, grumbling tone, as she changes the tablecloth for
one in the sideboard*).   Yes, it's common enough.   An' it's silly
enough an' all.   A lot of use it is you or anybody else saying
what they'd do if they had their time over again.   A fat chance
they have, haven't they ?   Time moves on and it takes you with
it, whatever you say—as I know only too well.   (*She is by the
chair* R. *of the table.*)
SAM.   Ay.   Though it's only same for you as for onnybody
else, lass.
SALLY.   Well, I'm not so sure about that.
SAM.   We all go on getting older, Sally.
SALLY.   I didn't mean just that.   (*Leaning on the table.*)
Y'know, Father, it's only four years since Bob and I were staying
here with you over Whitsun.   And Charlie was still a little lad.
The three of us here . . . laughing and talking and going on
day long . . . and nothing to tell us it was nearly all over. . . .
(*She moves up to turn on the lights at the switch by the door* R.C.)

SAM (*disturbed and affectionate*). Ay—I know—lass—but don't think about it.

SALLY (*crossing over* L. *above the table to draw the curtains—upstage one first*). It's not so long since, but time's run on. . . . It's taken Bob from me . . . even Charlie's growing up and doesn't need me like he used to. . . . I almost might be an old woman wondering where they're going to bury me. . . . (*She draws the downstage curtain.*)

SAM (*moving to her and trying to pat her shoulder*). Now then, Sally lass, it's not so bad as it might be.

SALLY. I might have thirty years to live yet—and I'd swop the lot for just that week we had here, four years ago. . . . But what's the use ? (*She crosses to the sideboard and picks up the tray with the sherry glass.*)

SAM. Ay—but give it a chance. You'll forget.

SALLY. I know I'll forget. I'm forgetting now. I can't hear Bob's voice as plain as I could a year or two since. It's taking even that from me now. . . . That's what time does to you . . . and if it's God's idea, He'll get no thanks from me. . . . (*She looks critically at the room.*) Well, I don't think I can do any better with it as it is. I've sometimes had an idea we might do better to bring the big table in and make this the dining-room—I mean, just for people who's staying here. But it's too far from the kitchen.

(*She is silent a moment, and then is heard the horn of a very large car.*)

It'll be Mr. and Mrs. Ormund.

(*She looks towards the window, and at the same time the clock chimes the half-hour.*)

Here, I must nip upstairs and see if their rooms look all right. Go and see to their luggage.

(*She hurries out up* R.C. SAM *goes to the outer door, leaving it open as he goes through. Voices are heard outside. A pause. Then* JANET ORMUND *enters slowly. She is an attractive, sensitive woman about twenty-eight, and is dressed for the country in a simple but expensive style. She enters the room with a slow indifference, leaving a book she is carrying on the* L. *end of the sideboard, then suddenly stiffens, frowns, looks incredulous, then examines it eagerly, without much movement. It is clear that there is some recognition, mixed with incredulity. A sudden uprush of emotion makes her feel almost faint, and she sinks into the chair above the table, exhausted, breathing heavily.*

Her husband, WALTER ORMUND, *enters. He is a biggish man in his early forties, whose manner alternates between alert, sharp command, on the one hand, and a gloomy brooding, on the other. He is dressed in quiet tweeds, the kind a man might wear at an*

B

*office before leaving for the country. He carries a much-used
dispatch-case. He has no eyes for the room, only for his wife.*)

ORMUND (*going to* L. *of her*). What's the matter, Janet?
JANET. I felt rather faint.

(*She takes charge of herself. He would like to help but doesn't know
how, so remains large and helpless, still holding the case. She
looks about her, then at him.*)

ORMUND. Probably tired.
JANET. No. . . . I'm not . . . really. (*She looks about her
again, then at him.*) I had—a sort of feeling—this room—
(*She gives it up.*)
ORMUND. We needn't stay here, y'know.
JANET. No.
ORMUND. We can push on. There's plenty of time.
JANET. Yes, of course we can.
ORMUND. I can simply say " Sorry, not our kind of place,"
give them something for their trouble, and off we go.
JANET. Quite simple. And—I think—rather comforting.
ORMUND (*with touch of burlesque*). You mean—one of us hasn't
been taken ill—the car hasn't suddenly and mysteriously broken
down—there isn't a fog or a flood or a landslide—none of those
sinister compulsory things—— ?
JANET (*with a smile*). No, not one. (*Then with sudden serious-
ness.*) We're quite free. We can choose. We're not being
compelled. (*She rises.*)
ORMUND. Not in the least. We can go now. Just say the
word.
JANET. Why don't you say it?
ORMUND (*marching to the door*). All right. I'll say it. Let's
go. (*He moves to the door up* L.)
JANET (*hesitating, then with a slight laugh*). No. We'll stay.
(*She moves to* R. *of the chair above the table.*)

(ORMUND *puts his hat and dispatch-case on the sideboard, then
closes the door and comes to* L. *of* JANET.)

ORMUND (*with a touch of bitterness*). Anything for a change,
eh?
JANET. Walter—is that one of the remarks you promised not
to make?
ORMUND (*rueful*). Oh—I hope not.
JANET. It sounded like the beginning of one. Remember—
you promised. Play fair.
ORMUND (*who would like to play fair*). I'm trying, Janet.
I'm trying hard. Only—I do seem to be in the one situation in
the world where it's impossible for a man to be fair. You've no
idea what a devil of a job it is.

JANET. I know, Walter.

ORMUND (*not sharply, going* L.). You don't.

JANET (*rather sadly*). No—that's the trouble, I suppose—I don't. (*Looking at him with a touch of wistfulness and pity.*) But —just to be easy and friendly—for once, no arguments, no reproaches—that'll be something, won't it ? (*She has moved down* R. *of the table.*)

ORMUND. Yes, it'll be—something.

JANET (*half-laughing, half-vexed*). Oh—Walter ! The very way you said that——!

ORMUND (*moving back to the table*). No, no, I didn't mean it that way. I'm really doing my best.

(*They meet* C. *below the table.*)

You're right. God knows you're right. It'll be something.

JANET. I'll do my very best.

ORMUND. And I'll do better still. You'll see. Nice. Easy. Friendly. All according to plan.

(*He looks about him, moving down* L. *and whistling softly. She looks at him, and he breaks off and gives her a careful reassuring smile. She returns it, but nevertheless looks troubled.* SALLY *enters up* R.C., *with an obvious sense of the importance of the occasion.*)

SALLY (*rather breathless, as she comes down* R.). Good evening. Mr. and Mrs. Ormund, isn't it ?

JANET (*who has moved up* R. *of the table again*). Yes. (*She sits in the chair above the table.*)

SALLY. You did say you wanted both rooms, didn't you ?

ORMUND (*humorously*). Yes. I have to have a room to myself because sometimes I waken up in the middle of the night and begin scribbling figures on bits of paper—and then—I have to smoke. Yes, smoke. Are you insured against fire ?

SALLY. Yes, we are that.

ORMUND. It's all right then. (*He crosses over to the telephone.*) I shall smoke a lot—and burn holes in your best sheets.

SALLY (*entering into this*). I'll make you pay for 'em if you do, Mr. Ormund. (*To both of them, as she goes to the door up* R.C.) I expect you'd like to see your rooms, wouldn't you ?

ORMUND. You have a look at 'em, Janet. I must telephone to Sykes.

(JANET *rises and goes out* R.C. *with* SALLY. ORMUND *telephones.*)

Trunks. . . . Is that Trunks. . . . This is—(*he looks at the number on the 'phone*)—Grindle five. I want Brensham six-seven. . . . Yes, Brensham six-seven. . . . All right. . . .

(*He waits, telephone to ear.* SAM *enters up* R.C.)

SAM. Your bags are upstairs, sir, and the car's in the garage.
ORMUND. Thanks. Bring me a large whisky-and-soda, will
you? MacFarlane's Old Liqueur, if you've got it.

(SAM *goes out and shuts the door.*)

(*Telephoning.*) Hello, Brensham? Oh—that you, Sykes?
Walter Ormund here. We're fixed up in a little pub on the moors
—the Black Bull, Grindle Moor. 'Phone number's Grindle five.
. . . Yes, get me here any time—shan't be going far. . . .
Yes, well, you work out the marketing costs, and I'll do the rest.
. . . I've got all the information here, including Orgenbaum's
report. . . . Who? Pensfield? . . . No, he won't make any
trouble. I'll offer him a seat on the board. That'll keep him
quiet. . . . Not he! I know too much about him. . . .

(SAM *comes in up* R.C. *with a large whisky-and-soda. He stops in
the doorway as he sees* ORMUND *is still telephoning, then tiptoes
towards the table. As he is passing,* ORMUND *reaches out and
takes the whisky, to* SAM'S *surprise, and has a long drink while
still listening.* SAM *gives him a droll look and goes out and shuts
the door after him.*)

Yes . . . nothing in that, Sykes. . . . Add two and half per
cent to the overhead then. . . . I'll ring you up before Monday
morning. . . . Well, work all night then—put a wet towel
round your head and a bottle of whisky on your desk. . . . Nonsense! Holidays are for boys and girls, not men. . . . I know
all about your children, but they can get on without you. . . .
All right. I'm depending on you. 'Bye.

(*He puts down the telephone, takes his drink to the table, and pulling
an old envelope out of his pocket, makes a few quick notes on it.
Then he looks at what he has written, so absorbed that he does not
notice the entrance of* JANET, *who comes in quietly up* R.C.,
*shutting the door. She watches him take an absent-minded pull
at his drink.*)

JANET (*coming down to the back of the chair* R. *of the table*). You
know, Walter, you'd several whiskies at that place where we
had dinner.
ORMUND. I know. And I'd several before that. And now
I'm having another. And what I say is this. If the only way
I can find dividends for several hundred shareholders and wages
for several thousands of employees is by drinking several whiskies,
then I must drink several whiskies. (*He sits in the chair above
the table.*)
JANET (*moving up to* R. *of him*). But you're not going to do
any work this week-end?
ORMUND (*now sitting with his notes*). I must.

(JANET *moves away a little.*)

I've just been telephoning Sykes. We've a whole big scheme to work out before Wednesday.

JANET (*coming back to beside him*). This isn't going to be much of a change for you, is it ? More work—more whisky.

ORMUND. A change is too much to hope for. Let me just keep ticking over—just ticking over—that'll do.

JANET (*at once sorry and protesting*). I can't blame you for being bitter, Walter, but it isn't going to help us.

ORMUND (*sincerely*). Bitter ! I'm not being bitter, my dear. Not in the least. (*He takes a good drink.*)

JANET (*getting a whiff, perhaps, as she passes behind him to the chair* L. *of the table*). Loathsome stuff ! I can't think how you go on and on drinking it.

ORMUND. There's a good reason why the distilleries are working at full blast. They're busy giving us Old Highland Blended Courage by the case. Faith and Hope at twelve-and-six a bottle. Love seven years in bond.

JANET. And in another minute, Walter, you'll be attacking me again.

ORMUND. No, no, I'm not attacking you, I'm defending whisky. It's dependable. It doesn't change its mind, think it's in love with you and then know better. It may have a little more fusel oil in it this year than last, but that's all the difference. That's why people all over the world now are steadily pickling themselves in it.

JANET (*going to the window*). If it made you silly-drunk, I don't think I'd object.

ORMUND. My dear Janet, you'd walk straight out on me.

JANET. No. The trouble is, it only makes you gloomy.

ORMUND. No, if I pour enough down into the darkness inside, they begin to floodlight things down there. Beautiful images begin to shine. Venuses rise from the sea of Scotch and soda, glorious smiling kind wenches, all looking rather alike—— (*He breaks off suddenly as* JANET *turns to look at him.*) Rooms all right ?

JANET (*grateful for this, moving in a little*). Yes. Queer little windows and a heavenly country smell.

ORMUND. Any spotted china beasts ?

JANET. Yes. Dogs with long necks. They've blue spots in my room, red spots in yours.

ORMUND. Good ! I haven't seen any of those beasts for years and I'm fond of 'em.

JANET (*hopefully, going to* L. *of him*). I believe you're going to like it here.

ORMUND (*with sudden change of mood*). No. (*He finishes his drink, rises and moves down* R.) I can't help feeling it was a mistake coming here.

JANET (*mildly*). It was your idea.

ORMUND. A lot of my ideas are bad. This is too small, too quiet. It throws us straight back on to ourselves——

JANET. That's a good thing.

ORMUND. It's a good thing when people are all right with one another. But when they're trying to be easy and friendly and one of 'em has died on the other, as if he were last year's worst hat—then if they've any sense they want to go and stay at some large damn silly place screaming with jazz bands where you can't possibly think. Here you can't help thinking.

(JANET *goes up to the sideboard to get her book.*)

I've started already. . . .

(FARRANT *enters up* R.C., *leaving the door open. He still has his book. He stops short, and he and* JANET *look at each other. The clock chimes the three-quarters. Then* ORMUND *looks too, and the clock joins in with its tick and chime, as if it had been expecting this. An odd tenseness for a moment.*)

FARRANT (*with a certain effort*). We'd better introduce ourselves. My name's Farrant.

ORMUND (*his bewilderment over*). That's it, of course. You're Oliver Farrant, Head of Lamberton. I'm Walter Ormund. My wife.

FARRANT (R. *of the table*). I didn't expect to meet one of the school governors here.

(JANET *sits in the chair* L. *of the table.*)

ORMUND (*not importantly*). I've been too busy to go and see the school yet, but I was one of the governors who put you in there. Thought we ought to have a young man.

FARRANT (*smiling*). You were quite right.

ORMUND. But what are you doing here ? Term time, isn't it ?

FARRANT. I was told to knock off and have a rest.

ORMUND. Overworking ?

FARRANT. That's what they said. I feel rather a fraud—I'm walking miles and miles every day, and eating like a horse——

ORMUND (*looking hard at him*). Look a bit nervous, though.

JANET. How did you find your way up here ?

(ORMUND *works spasmodically throughout the next scene.*)

FARRANT. Mrs. Pratt—that's the landlord's daughter—has a boy, Charlie, who's at Lamberton. He told me about it.

JANET. Mrs. Pratt was telling me all about her boy. Is he clever ?

FARRANT (*not at his best*). Yes, he's got brains. He's the kind of boy who makes me feel glad I'm a schoolmaster. Ought to be fairly certain of an Oxford scholarship later on. We've a good many boys of his kind.

JANET.   Do you mean—clever ones or from this sort of home ?

FARRANT (*rather deliberately*).   I mean—boys with brains from this class. A lot of them have brains, y'know.

JANET (*who does not like his manner*).   Yes, it never occurred to me that they wouldn't have. (*She opens her book.*)

FARRANT.   And it's part of our policy at Lamberton to encourage them.

ORMUND (*dryly*).   Yes, it was part of *our* policy when we built the school.

FARRANT.   Sorry, I was forgetting.

ORMUND.   That's all right. Have a drink ?

FARRANT.   No, thanks. Too soon after supper.

ORMUND.   There's a bar in there, isn't there ?

FARRANT.   Yes. But the talk's not very amusing.

ORMUND (*almost giving him up as a bad job*).   Anybody else staying here ?

FARRANT.   Yes, a Doctor Görtler.

ORMUND.   German ?

FARRANT.   Yes, Professor of mathematics taking refuge over here. Judging by his talk at supper, he seems to have wandered a long way from mathematics now. I don't quite make him out.

JANET.   Why ?

FARRANT.   Oh—he seems to be turning mystical. Probably seen too much trouble. The German intellect doesn't always stand the strain. (*After a pause.*) I'll be down later, if you want to talk about the school.

(*He nods and goes out down stage* R., *closing the door behind him.* ORMUND *and* JANET *look at each other.*)

ORMUND (*quietly*).   Without having seen him, purely on his record—*and* against considerable opposition, I had that young gentleman appointed Head of Lamberton.

JANET (*rather grimly*).   My dear, I know you did.

ORMUND.   Well ?

JANET (*with irony*).   Oh—very nice, friendly, modest sort of young man—not the least little bit conceited and dogmatic— very charming—humph ! (*She laughs.*)

ORMUND (*starting to collect his papers*).   Yes, most extraordinary thing. Thought I'd take to him. Took to him at once on paper. And he *looks* all right. (*He rises and takes his papers to the sideboard.*) Ought, in fact, to be a very attractive fellow. But—well—there you are——

(*He now turns to the door up* R.C. *leading to the dining-room and bar. This brings him face to face with* DR. GÖRTLER, *who has just entered.* DR. GÖRTLER *looks curiously at the* ORMUNDS, *especially at* JANET, *and is then ceremonious.*)

DR. GÖRTLER (R.C., *with a little bow*). Doctor Görtler. Mr. and Mrs. Ormund ?

ORMUND. Yes, good evening.

JANET. Good evening.

DR. GÖRTLER (*politely*). And a very beautiful evening.

JANET. Yes, hasn't it been ?

ORMUND. Would you like to join me in a drink ?

DR. GÖRTLER. No, thank you.

ORMUND. Janet ?

JANET. No, thank you, Walter.

ORMUND (*gravely*). Then—I think—I shall try the bar. (*As* JANET *makes a murmur of protest*—" Oh, Walter ! ") No, no. Shan't be long.

(*He goes out up* R.C. DR. GÖRTLER *shuts the door after him, then goes to the sofa* R. *and, after a slight bow, sits at the downstage end and looks in a friendly but very deliberate fashion at* JANET, *who smiles in return.*)

JANET. Have you been up here before, Doctor Görtler ?

DR. GÖRTLER (*watching her*). No. Have you ?

JANET (*frowning a little*). No—I haven't—really.

DR. GÖRTLER (*with a slight smile*). You do not seem very certain.

JANET (*slowly*). I've been wondering——

DR. GÖRTLER (*as she hesitates*). Yes ?

JANET (*rather quickly*). I was only wondering if I could have been here when I was a very small child.

(*She breaks off, and looks at him, and then away from him. There is a pause.*)

DR. GÖRTLER. Mrs. Ormund, I am a student—a very old one now. Sometimes we students do not seem to have very good manners. I do not wish you to think I am—inquisitive, impertinent.

JANET (*with a slight smile*). It didn't occur to me that you were—or might be.

DR. GÖRTLER. Lately I have been enlarging my studies—to include the human mind. So I go about asking questions.

JANET. If this means you want to ask me some questions, you can. But I don't think you'd find me much use. I've always thought the psycho-analysts monstrously exaggerated everything. I can't believe that all the little fears and fancies one has are of any real interest or value.

DR. GÖRTLER. Even a few years ago, I would have agreed with you. But now I see that we do not understand ourselves, the nature of our lives. What seems to happen continually just outside the edge of our attention—the little fears and fancies, as you call them—may be all-important because they belong to a profounder reality, like the vague sounds of the city outside that we hear sometimes inside a theatre.

JANET (*startled*). Oh! (*She stares at him, almost terrified.*)

DR. GÖRTLER. What is it?

JANET (*hesitantly and with wonder*). You see . . . suddenly I felt . . . I could have sworn . . . you'd said all that to me before. . . . You and I—sitting, talking, like this . . . and then you said " because they belong . . . to a profounder reality . . . like the sounds of the city . . . we hear sometimes inside a theatre. . . ." (*She dismisses the mood—then hastily.*) I'm so sorry. I must be tired.

(There is a pause.)

DR. GÖRTLER. Mrs. Ormund, what made you come here?

JANET. Oh—pure chance. We wanted to spend this week-end somewhere in the country. A man at the hotel we dined at —to-night—not an hour ago—suggested this place. I'd never heard of it before.

DR. GÖRTLER. It was all quite dull, ordinary?

JANET. Yes . . . until we were driving from Marlingset up here. . . .

DR. GÖRTLER (*as she hesitates*). Yes?

JANET. I find this—rather difficult—— (*She breaks off, and then, with urgency.*) Quite suddenly, I began to feel excited. . . . About nothing, it seemed. . . . My heart was beating terribly. . . . We stopped once . . . only a moment, to make sure about the way. . . . At the roadside there were some white harebells . . . just some white harebells. . . . Of course they looked lovely there . . . white and fragile and perfect, at the edge of the great dark moor. . . . It must have been—just that . . . anything else—is silly.

DR. GÖRTLER (*slowly*). There has not been in your life so far a moment of crisis that you associate with these flowers?

JANET (*slowly, and staring at him*). No. But that's exactly the feeling I had about them.

(DR. GÖRTLER rises.)

DR. GÖRTLER (*prompting her*). And then—you arrived here?

JANET (*rather slowly*). Yes.

(*There is a distinct pause, during which* DR. GÖRTLER *goes nearer to her, to below the chair* R. *of the table.*)

DR. GÖRTLER. You have met Mr. Farrant?

JANET. Yes. But only for a few minutes.

DR. GÖRTLER. He is very young for such a responsible post.

JANET. Yes.

DR. GÖRTLER (*leaning his hands on the table*). But that does not matter, of course. He is fortunate, but he deserves to be.

Very clever—and very charming, very good-hearted too, I think
—— (*He looks at her questioningly.*)

JANET (*rather stiffly*). I'm sure he must be, Doctor Görtler.
(*As he stares at her speculatively.*) Why do you stare at me like
that ?

DR. GÖRTLER (*with a slight smile*). I beg your pardon. I was
thinking. (*After a pause.*) Mr. Ormund—does he feel any of
these things to-night ?

JANET (*with a slight smile*). I think you'd better ask him
that yourself.

DR. GÖRTLER. Yes, I will. (*He sits in the chair* R. *of the table.*)

JANET (*rather hastily, with a resumption of more social manner*).
You may find him—a little difficult. I mean—you mustn't mind
if he seems rather brusque—odd.

DR. GÖRTLER. Why should I ? I am—brusque and odd—
myself.

JANET (*hastily*). He's really very kind and considerate, when
you know him, but he's got the most tremendous responsibilities.
I thought he was going to have a rest this week-end, but he's
brought a lot of work with him. He works far too hard.

DR. GÖRTLER (*calmly*). Yes, I think he is an unhappy man.

JANET (*shocked, reproachful*). Doctor Görtler——! (*Then
dropping the social manner.*) Why do you say that ?

DR. GÖRTLER. I have seen enough unhappiness now to
recognize it.

(FARRANT *enters from down stage* R., *still with the book under his
arm. He shuts the door behind him. He and* JANET *take a
quick look at each other.* DR. GÖRTLER *watches them both.
Then* FARRANT *crosses below the table to the door* L. *to look out,
then comes in and sits down in the desk-chair with his book, first
turning the chair to face down stage. You feel the silence.* JANET
obviously does not like it. DR. GÖRTLER *is interested, watchful.*)

JANET (*who must break this horrible silence*). What are your
special subjects, Mr. Farrant ?

FARRANT (*rather too carefully keeping his place open in the book*).
History and economics.

JANET (*not wistfully, not too brightly*). I don't care about
economics. It never seems to me to be true. But I wish I knew
more history—real history, not the dreary stuff they still taught
us when I was at school. I'm always meaning to learn more
about it.

FARRANT (*with a suggestion of the schoolmaster*). Well, it's
going on all round you, y'know. It's not something that's dead
and done with. We're making it all the time.

JANET (*with a shade of irony*). I don't feel I'm making very
much.

FARRANT. No, but once you realize you're *in* history, helping

to make it, you see the whole thing differently. That's how we
try to teach it now. I show them how completely interdependent
we are.

DR. GÖRTLER (*who has been missing nothing*). Yes, we are like
threads in a pattern.

FARRANT. There's a pretty example of mutual dependence—
quite a nice little pattern—here in this pub. Sam and Mrs. Pratt
are devoted to this boy of hers, Charlie——

DR. GÖRTLER. He is at your school. So they depend upon
you.

FARRANT. Yes. But the school partly depends on the
Ormunds, and especially on your husband, Mrs. Ormund——

(*He is interrupted by the entrance of* SALLY *up* R.C., *who is followed
after a moment by* ORMUND. SALLY *is carrying a tray.*)

SALLY (*coming to above the table*). Excuse me, Mrs. Ormund.
But I just wanted to tell you that we have breakfast at half-past
eight, if that's not too early.

JANET. No, I'd like it then, Mrs. Pratt.

SALLY. And is that all right for you, Doctor Görtler ?

DR. GÖRTLER. Yes, thank you.

(ORMUND *now enters and closes the door.*)

SALLY. And would you like a cup of tea earlier on, Mrs.
Ormund ?

JANET. Not to-morrow morning, thank you. What about
you, Walter ?

SALLY (*turning, as he is behind her*). Oh—I'm sorry.

ORMUND (*coming forward*). No tea. And no breakfast either.
Just a pot of strong coffee for me—about half-past nine. (*He
crosses down below the table to* L.)

SALLY. All right, Mr. Ormund.

FARRANT (*a shade peremptorily*). I'll be out all day again
to-morrow, so can I have some sandwiches in the morning,
please ?

SALLY. Yes, Mr. Farrant.

ORMUND (*to* FARRANT). Going striding over the moors all
day ?

FARRANT. I'll be out all day, I don't know about striding.

ORMUND (*to* JANET). That's what you want, isn't it ? Better
go along with him. (*He comes close to* JANET'S *chair.*)

JANET (*dismayed*). But what are you going to do ?

ORMUND. Oh—I'll do a bit of work—and then slack round.
You'd better join up with Farrant here. (*To* FARRANT.) She
can walk, you know.

FARRANT (*plainly without enthusiasm, after a look at* JANET).
Well—it might be rather rough going—but of course—if you'd
like to come along——

JANET (*furious with both men—shortly*). No, thank you. I may want some sandwiches, Mrs. Pratt. I'll let you know in the morning.

(ORMUND *goes up to the door* L. *and stands looking out.*)

SALLY. Yes, Mrs. Ormund. I've a long day to-morrow— Whit Saturday—an' folks wanting lunches and teas—so I thought I'd get to bed in good time to-night.

JANET. Yes, of course.

SALLY (*somewhat embarrassed*). We're very proud to have you and Mr. Ormund here. Nearly all the money father and I have between us—that we saved to help our Charlie later on—is in Ormunds Limited.

JANET. Do you hear that, Walter ? You're among share-holders, so be careful.

ORMUND (*half-turning, with mock groan*). I know, I know.

DR. GÖRTLER. You see. More dependence.

SALLY (*distrusting this*). What's that ?

JANET. It sounds like an insult, but it isn't. We've been discovering how much we depend on one another. You're in it because your boy's at Mr. Farrant's school.

SALLY. And very lucky he is to be there, too—with Mr. Farrant looking after him.

JANET. And now you say you've money in Ormunds Limited.

FARRANT. And the school partly depends on Ormunds too. Which brings me in.

JANET. And I'm certainly one of the dependants. Walter, you're the only really great one, the giant Atlas himself. We all depend upon you, but you don't depend upon anybody.

DR. GÖRTLER (*quietly, but with startling effect*). *Nein !*

(*They all stare at him.*)

Mr. Ormund depends very much upon somebody. (*To* JANET.) He depends upon you—his wife.

ORMUND (*quietly, with cold anger, coming down to* JANET'S *chair*). That's not the kind of remark we appreciate from a stranger in this country, my dear sir.

JANET (*protesting*). Walter !

DR. GÖRTLER (*rising*). I am sorry. I am—as you say—a stranger—in a foreign country. (*He goes towards the door down stage* R.)

JANET. It's all right, Doctor Görtler.

DR. GÖRTLER. Good night.

ORMUND (*crossing below the table to him*). No, Doctor. I shouldn't have spoken like that. Now don't be offended.

DR. GÖRTLER (*with a slight smile*). I am not offended. Only tired. So please—no apologies. Good night.

(The others say " Good night " and watch him go out, closing the door behind him.)

SALLY *(dropping her voice, dubiously).*   I hope it's going to be all right.

JANET.   Why, Mrs. Pratt, what's wrong ?

SALLY.   I mean—him being here.

ORMUND.   Yes, of course.   Why not ?

SALLY *(in a normal voice now).*   Well, Mr. Ormund—only that he seems to be upsetting you.

FARRANT *(sharply).*   Now, Mrs. Pratt !   Just because he's a foreigner.

SALLY.   No, it isn't that, Mr. Farrant.   Though I'll admit I'm not used to foreigners.   But what's he doing here ?

ORMUND.   Well, what are we all doing here ?

SALLY.   No, that's different, Mr. Ormund.   Why should he come here looking for you ?

ORMUND *(puzzled).*   For me ?

SALLY.   No, for you three.

(This linking of the three of them together—for the first time—has its immediate effect, as if it chimed with some deep obscure feeling each of them knew.   There is a pause, before SALLY resumes.)

He comes here—looking about him—and when I tell him we've no room to spare because I'm expecting three visitors—he looks at me and asks if two of 'em are a married couple with the man older than his wife, and the other a younger man.   And when I say No, we're expecting three ladies from Manchester, he seems disappointed and says something about it being the wrong year. So off he goes, and then the three ladies say they can't come, and you ring up for rooms, and when he comes back, there's a room for him too, and you're all here, and it's just what he expected.

ORMUND.   Oh—he was looking for somebody, and then gave it up.

SALLY.   And then upsetting you like that !   He makes me feel right uneasy.

(She moves L. and closes the door.   There is a short pause.)

Nothing more you'll be wanting, Mrs. Ormund ?   *(She puts the empty whisky glass on the tray.)*

JANET.   No, thank you, Mrs. Pratt.   Good night.

SALLY.   Good night.

(The two men say " Good night " as she goes out up R.C., closing the door after her.   ORMUND gets some papers from his dispatch-case on the sideboard and sits in the chair above the table, preparing to work.   FARRANT is going back to his book.)

JANET *(who has obviously been thinking about it all).*   How could he have been looking for us ?

ORMUND (*busy with his papers*). He couldn't.

FARRANT (*looking up—in a light easy tone*). The arrival of a mysterious foreigner, plus a coincidence, has obviously been too much to-night for poor Mrs. Pratt. And Görtler's prophetic manner has only made it worse.

ORMUND. Yes, he rather asks for it.

JANET (*rising*). Well, I'm tired, Walter. (*She turns L. and moves round to the door up R.C., patting ORMUND as she passes.*) Your room's the far one.

FARRANT (*casually*). I thought I'd met him before somewhere.

(*The clock makes a whirring noise preparatory to striking the hour, which it is presumed to do after the fall of the CURTAIN.*)

JANET (*turning at the door—sharply*). You did! Where?

FARRANT. That's the trouble. Can't remember.

JANET (*tentatively*). Has it . . . worried you?

FARRANT (*slightly surprised*). Yes . . . a little. Why?

JANET. I . . . wondered.

(*There is a pause. Then JANET comes down to R. of ORMUND.*)

(*With decision.*) Walter, will you stop working just one minute ——?

ORMUND (*looking up from his work, first at JANET, then at FARRANT, then back to JANET—coolly and humorously*). You want me to tell you all about it? Quite simple. We're all three a bit off our heads. Farrant says he's been overworking and the doctor sent him away. I've been half-dotty for years. And as for you, Janet, you're just a young woman, always ready to have your fortune told and your horoscope read, always longing for marvels and miracles, not even wanting to be sane.

JANET (*with a smile*). Yes, that's quite simple—and quite silly. (*She moves to the door.*) Good night.

(*She is now in the doorway. The two men stand up and say " Good night." She looks at them a moment, then nods and goes. ORMUND sits down again to resume work, but FARRANT remains standing.*)

FARRANT (*after a pause, making a slight move towards ORMUND*). Ormund—I hope—you'll let me talk to you about the school sometime.

ORMUND (*who is filling a pipe*). Yes, of course. Not now, though, not now.

FARRANT (*after another pause, with a touch of nervous diffidence*). I'm—rather worried—— (*He pauses, and ORMUND looks at him.*) I feel—I haven't—somehow—created a very good first impression.

ORMUND. On me—or on my wife?

FARRANT. On both of you.

ORMUND. I don't think you have, altogether.

FARRANT (*above the chair* L. *of the table*). Do you mind—telling me why ?

ORMUND. My dear chap, I honestly haven't the least idea. So let's forget it. (*Breaking it off.*) What's your book ?

FARRANT. " New Pathways in Science." You might like to look at it afterwards. It answers a lot of questions that have been puzzling me.

ORMUND (*easily, but with an undercurrent of despair*). Yes, but does it answer the questions that have been puzzling *me* ? Who or what are we ? What are we supposed to be doing here ? What the devil is it all about ?

FARRANT. I'm afraid it doesn't.

ORMUND. I thought not.

(FARRANT *crosses slowly below the table with his book to down stage* R.)

Turning in ?

FARRANT. Yes, I think so. Good night.

ORMUND (*back at his work*). Good night.

FARRANT *goes off down stage* R. ORMUND *tries to settle down to his work, but cannot concentrate and looks as if some despairing thought is haunting him. He looks queerly at the wall in front of him, the one he can't see. He rises slowly, and in his distress he snaps the fountain-pen he is holding in two, and as he looks down at the broken pen—*

The CURTAIN *falls.*

ACT II

SCENE.—*The same. Saturday evening. It is still daylight, but though the light is still good, it is that of a clear twilight.*

ORMUND is discovered sitting at the desk in the window, smoking and doing some work, making notes and calculations. After a moment or two, SAM enters with a tray with bottle of whisky, syphon and glass. He closes the door. Finding ORMUND busy, he comes quietly down below the table and puts the tray at L. end. ORMUND looks up.

ORMUND. Sam, you have the noble instincts of a good land-lord. Thank you.

SAM (*moving to below R. of the table*) Well, t'bar's still pretty full and I thought you'd like it handy in here.

ORMUND (*rising and going over to the table to below the chair L. of it*). Quite right. (*He takes up the bottle.*) But not much in this bottle, Sam.

SAM (*with a grin*). It's one you started on at tea-time, Mr. Ormund.

ORMUND. Then I must have had a very good tea. (*He pours out a whisky and soda.*)

SAM (*grinning*). Ay, you didn't do bad.

ORMUND. It looks to me, Sam, as if I drink too much.

SAM. Well, that's not for me to say, Mr. Ormund——

ORMUND Never mind, Sam, say it, say it. (*He sits L. of the table.*)

SAM. I haven't seen monny as could shift it better.

ORMUND. Nor carry it better. Admit that, Sam.

SAM I do, Mr. Ormund. There's one or two as comes here— owd Joe Watson, farmer down t'dale, for one—who's got a head on 'em for liquor, but—by gow !—I'd back you, Mr. Ormund, against best of 'em. You'd have 'em under table i' no time.

ORMUND. Yes, Sam, and sometimes it's useful to have 'em under table. But it won't do. (*Rising.*) If I ask for another bottle to-night, remind me that I drink too much. (*He takes his drink back to the desk and sits.*)

SAM (*going up towards the door, then stopping*) You've had your supper, haven't you, Mr. Ormund ?

ORMUND. Yes. Had it with Doctor Görtler. We got tired of waiting for the other two.

SAM. Ay, they're making a long day of it. Let's hope they haven't got lost.

ORMUND. Not much chance of that, is there ?

SAM. No, not on these light nights. It's easy enough i' winter, if you stop too long on t'moors.

(DR. GÖRTLER *enters up* R.C. *and comes and stands behind* C. *chair above the table.*)

I've known a few daftheads that did. But don't you worry. Mr. Farrant's a good head on his shoulders.

ORMUND. I don't think my wife's with Mr. Farrant. They went out separately.

SAM. Oh—well—happen she's gone a few mile further than she thought. But she'll be all right, Mr. Ormund.

(SAM *goes out up* R.C. DR. GÖRTLER *moves to the door* L.)

ORMUND (*after a pause*). Have a drink, Doctor Görtler ?

DR. GÖRTLER (*who has opened the door* L. *and looked out*). No, thank you. (*He shuts the door and comes down* L.C.)

ORMUND (*indifferently*). Don't like too much drinking, eh ?

DR. GÖRTLER (*coolly, not priggishly*). It is a kind of escape, and I do not need it. I am not afraid.

ORMUND (*with more attention*). Not afraid of what ?

DR. GÖRTLER. I am not afraid of thinking, of reality. (*He sits in the chair* L. *of the table.*)

ORMUND (*considering him, after a pause*). I wonder what you think you're doing here ?

DR. GÖRTLER (*with a smile*). I am asking questions. (*A pause.*) This drinking, it is an escape—from what ?

ORMUND (*really dodging the question*). Well—as you see—not from responsibility—and work.

DR. GÖRTLER. No, I think you work very hard.

ORMUND. I work like hell.

DR. GÖRTLER. And that too is a kind of escape.

ORMUND (*not liking this*). Is it ? But don't forget, my dear professor, I've great responsibilities. Even these people here— and their precious boy—would be badly let down if I failed 'em. I have to keep on.

DR. GÖRTLER. No, you give yourself these tasks so that you must keep on. You dare not stop.

ORMUND (*with an effort*). All right. I dare not stop.

(*He turns to his notes and looks as if he wanted to be done with this talk, yet cannot bring himself to break it off definitely. There is a pause.*)

DR. GÖRTLER (*with a shade of irony*). And yet—you are rich.

ORMUND (*turning*). Have you ever been rich, Doctor Görtler, or lived among the rich ?

DR. GÖRTLER (*who has his own irony—rising*). No, I have only

c

been poor, and lived among the poor. But that is quite an experience too. (*He moves above the table to* R.)

ORMUND. I've no illusions about that. But being rich isn't simply the opposite of being poor. It's not really worth much— being rich. Half the time there's a thick glass wall between you and most of the fun and friendliness of the world.

(DR. GÖRTLER *moves back above the table to* L.C. *again.*)

There's something devilishly dull about most of the rich. Too much money seems to take the taste and colour out of things. It oughtn't to do, but it does—damn it !

DR. GÖRTLER (*leaning on the back of the chair* L. *of the table*). But power—you have that, haven't you ?

ORMUND. Yes, and that's a very different thing.

DR. GÖRTLER. Ah !—you like power.

ORMUND. Well, you get some fun out of it. I don't mean bullying a lot of poor devils. But putting ideas into action. And not being at the end of somebody else's bit of string.

DR. GÖRTLER. And yet that is what you always feel, and that is why you try to escape.

ORMUND (*sharply—rising*). What do you mean ?

DR. GÖRTLER. That you are—as you say—at the end of a bit of string.

ORMUND (*facing* DR. GÖRTLER). Nonsense ! Do I look like —a puppet ?

DR. GÖRTLER (*calmly*). No. But I say you feel like one. (*He pauses, then with calm force.*) You are rich. You are successful. You have power. Yet all the time you try to escape, because deep down you feel that your part in this life is settled for you and that it is a tragic one. So all the time you are in despair.

(ORMUND *crosses below the table to up* R.C.)

(*As* ORMUND *does not reply.*) Is that not true ?

ORMUND (*half-wondering and half-angry—his back to* DR. GÖRTLER). Yes—damn your impudence !—it is. (*He moves restlessly.*)

DR. GÖRTLER (*moving round the chair to* L.C.). Now please tell me why you—who have so much—should feel this despair.

(*After a pause* ORMUND *turns, looks at* DR. GÖRTLER, *then moves to upstage* R. *corner of the table.*)

ORMUND (*speaking more freely than before*). I suppose—in the last resort—you trust life—or you don't. Well—I don't. There's something malicious . . . corrupt . . . cruel . . . at the heart of it. Nothing's on our side. We don't belong. We're a mistake.

DR. GÖRTLER (*sitting in the chair* L. *of the table*). But you have known—good things ?

ORMUND (*looking down now at the sitting* GÖRTLER). Yes.
When you're young, you snatch at 'em and then find they're bait
in a trap. Cheese for the mice. One nibble, you're caught and
the wires are boring through your guts. I can feel 'em there.

DR. GÖRTLER. No. It is something in yourself, something
that hates life.

ORMUND. All right, it's something in me. (*He moves up
towards the door, then turns and comes down* R.) Something that's
waiting to blot out the whole bloody business. (*He moves restlessly, finally sitting in the chair* R. *of the table and speaking with
more freedom.*) Görtler—when I was a boy I watched my mother
die—of cancer. For two years she was tortured . . . she might
as well have been put on the rack and broken on the wheel . . .
and when she couldn't suffer any longer . . . when there was
nothing left to feel any more devilish bloody torment . . . she
was allowed to escape, to die. You see, there wasn't any more
fun to be had out of her. Let her go.

DR. GÖRTLER (*after a pause*). Yes, that was bad. But did
she complain ?

ORMUND. No, she didn't complain much. She was a very
brave woman. I remember—when she could bear it no longer
and screamed in the night, she'd apologize next morning. (*With
terrible irony.*) She was sorry if she'd disturbed us, Görtler, she
was sorry if she'd disturbed us. . . . (*He pauses.*) No, *she*
didn't complain—but—by God !—I complain.

DR. GÖRTLER. Yes, I understand. (*Pause.*) You feel too
much and do not know enough.

ORMUND (*grimly*). I know too much.

DR. GÖRTLER. No. You are like a child who thinks because
it rains one morning, he will never play out of doors again. You
believe we have only this one existence ?

ORMUND. Of course.

DR. GÖRTLER (*with irony*). Of course. We all know that now.
It is so obvious. But what a pity—if we are brutes that perish—
we have not the dim feelings of brutes that perish. To have this
one short existence and to spend it being tortured by cancer—
to be given delicate nerves and consciousness only to feel pain—
that would be a terrible cruelty. It would be better that nobody
should be born at all.

ORMUND. I've thought so many a time.

DR. GÖRTLER. Because you do not understand the long drama
of the soul. To suffer like that, then to die young, that is not
easy nor pleasant, but it is a rôle, a part—like any other brief
appearance here——

ORMUND (*harshly, as he rises and moves down* R.). I'm sorry,
Doctor. That may mean something to you. It means nothing
to me. (*Moving up* R.C.) Just so many fine useless words.

DR. GÖRTLER (*rising and speaking with authority and dignity*).

You will please remember, Mr. Ormund, that all my life I have been a man of science, and then a philosopher.

(SALLY *has entered up* R.C. *with letters in her hand. She hears the men speaking and goes out again.*)

I am not a political orator. My fine words mean something. (*He pauses.*) You were in the War ?

ORMUND (*moving down* R.). Yes. I went all through it. My brother was killed. And before the lunacy stopped, I'd found half a dozen fellows who were nearly as good as brothers, but they never lasted long. . . .

(DR. GÖRTLER *sits* L. *of the table again.*)

I came out of it to find the whole world limping on one foot and with a hole in its head. . . . Most of us are really half crazy. I know I am.

DR. GÖRTLER. But when you began to forget about the War, things were better, eh ?

ORMUND. No. I didn't forget, and things were worse. They were very bad indeed—when—I met my wife, Janet. Then things looked different for a time—— (*He breaks off, then resumes in a more normal tone.*) Well, that's how it's been. Not very cheerful. But I don't suppose *you've* had a rollicking time. (*He sits at the upstage end of the sofa.*)

DR. GÖRTLER (*quietly and with great dignity*). I lost my only son in the War—a young boy. I saw all my family and friends ruined by the economic collapse of Germany. I think it was the worry, the shame, of that period which killed my wife. And now I have seen my pupils taken away from me, and have been turned out of my university and out of my country.

ORMUND. I'm sorry, Doctor Görtler.

DR. GÖRTLER. Yet I do not hate life. I accept it all. Because, you see—there is no traitor—here—— (*He touches his chest.*)

ORMUND. You think there is—in me ?

DR. GÖRTLER. I do not know. I can only guess.

ORMUND (*after a pause, more freely*). Görtler, I'll tell you something I've never told anybody. All my life, I've had a haunted sort of feeling . . . as if, just round the corner, there'd be a sudden blotting out of everything. During the War I thought it meant I was going to be killed, so I didn't give a damn what I did and they thought I was a brave fellow and pinned medals on me. But when it was all over, I still had the same feeling. It's getting stronger all the time.

DR. GÖRTLER. And then, last night, when you arrived here

ORMUND. How did you notice that ? I didn't know I gave myself away.

DR. GÖRTLER. What did you feel?

ORMUND. I felt like a man staring into his grave.

DR. GÖRTLER. When you entered this room?

ORMUND. Yes, yes.

DR. GÖRTLER. When you saw your bedroom?

ORMUND (*rather impatiently*). Yes, yes.

DR. GÖRTLER. But it was worst in the garage?

ORMUND (*surprised*). The garage? I haven't been in the garage. Sam put my car away last night and I haven't looked at it since—(*He stops, stares at* DR. GÖRTLER *suspiciously, then rises and makes a rapid movement to the back of the chair* R. *of the table and speaks with urgency*)—How did you know I kept it there?

DR. GÖRTLER. Where?

ORMUND. In the car.

DR. GÖRTLER. Kept what in the car?

ORMUND. My revolver.

DR. GÖRTLER (*significantly*). So!

ORMUND. I keep a revolver in a side pocket of the car. How did you know that?

DR. GÖRTLER. I did not know.

ORMUND. Then why did you ask me about the garage?

DR. GÖRTLER. I wanted to know what you had felt there, that is all.

ORMUND (*after staring at him a moment, calls*). Sam. Sam.

DR. GÖRTLER. Be careful.

(SALLY *enters up* R.C.)

SALLY. Father's busy in the bar, Mr. Ormund. Can I get you anything?

ORMUND. Is the garage open?

SALLY. Yes, Mr. Ormund, straight across the yard.

(ORMUND *makes for the door* L. SALLY *follows him to* C. *above the table.*)

DR. GÖRTLER (*rising and moving up* L.C.). Do you want me to come with you?

(SALLY *gives them a sharp look.* ORMUND *goes out up* L., *leaving the door ajar.* DR. GÖRTLER *looks anxiously after him.* SALLY *looks at* DR. GÖRTLER, *curiously and dubiously.*)

SALLY. Oh—Doctor—er—(*as he turns*)—I don't think you said how long you wanted your room, did you?

DR. GÖRTLER (*puzzled by this*). Yes. I said it last night, when I came here.

SALLY (*coldly*). I don't remember. It wasn't said to me.

DR. GÖRTLER. I said I wanted it over the week-end. I could not tell, exactly.

SALLY. Well, folks who come here usually know how long they're staying.

DR. GÖRTLER. Yes, but I could not say. I have something to do here.

SALLY (*eyeing him*). Something to do ?

DR. GÖRTLER (*still anxious about* ORMUND, *not bothering about her*). Yes, yes, something very important.

SALLY (*hostile*). Oh, I see.

DR. GÖRTLER (*really attending to her now*). There is no need to talk to me in this way. I have done you no injury. I am quite a harmless person, even though I am a foreigner—and was once a professor.

SALLY. And so you want to know what's the matter ?

DR. GÖRTLER. Yes, there is evidently something. What have I done ?

SALLY (*sturdily*). Well—seeing you've asked me, Doctor—er—I'll tell you. You make me feel uneasy in my mind. That wouldn't be so bad, but I've noticed you've a trick of upsetting other people too. And I don't like it.

(*She is about to turn away, when a revolver shot is heard from outside. It is a startling report. She and* DR. GÖRTLER *give a cry.*)

DR. GÖRTLER (*urgently*). Ormund !

(*He hurries to the door and goes out.* SALLY *stands, a hand pressed to her side, breathing rapidly.* SAM *comes in hastily up* R.C. *and crosses to the door up* L. *You feel all these people are unusually nervous to-night.*)

SAM (*hastily*). What was that, Sally ? Who's playing about wi' a gun so near t'house ?

SALLY (*breathlessly*). I don't know. (*Moving right up to* SAM.) Go and see.

(*As* SAM *is about to go,* ORMUND *enters, followed by* DR. GÖRTLER. ORMUND *looks pale and shaken, but tries to be hearty and genial.*)

ORMUND (*loudly, as he comes* L.C.). That's all right. Hello, Sam, did it bring you out ? Sorry, Mrs. Pratt. Silly thing to do—very silly.

SALLY. But whatever happened, Mr. Ormund ?

(SALLY *is now* R. *above the table,* SAM C. *above the table,* ORMUND L. *above the table, and* DR. GÖRTLER *up* L.)

ORMUND. Went to the garage to have a look at my car and remembered I had a revolver in the side pocket. Took it out to see if it was all right, and nearly got to the door when something went scampering past, making me jump.

SAM. A rat, eh?

ORMUND. Yes. Big brute. And I've always hated rats ever since they used to come snuffling over me in the trenches. So I had to have a pop at him.

SAM. Ay. Did you get him, Mr. Ormund?

ORMUND. Didn't even get him, Sam. (*He gets his empty glass from the desk, comes to the table and pours out another good drink.*) Just made a noise and frightened you all. Sorry, Mrs. Pratt. Won't occur again.

(DR. GÖRTLER *shuts the door.*)

SAM. Ay, well, I don't know why it should ha' bothered me so much—but——

SALLY (*cutting him short*). All right, Father, they'll be wanting you in the bar.

(*She pushes him out up* R.C., *follows and shuts the door.* ORMUND, *no longer bothering to keep up appearances, drops into the chair* L. *of the table, takes a huge drink, then rests his head in his hands and rubs his forehead, as if both baffled and depressed.*)

DR. GÖRTLER (*moving down* L.C.). I am sorry.

ORMUND (*suddenly jumping up, with passion*). Sorry, sorry! Yes, I went into the garage. Now what do I do next? You must have some more amusing ideas. (*Going close to* DR. GÖRTLER.) Who the devil are you to come here and take the lid off my head and stick pins into my guts and say you're sorry?

DR. GÖRTLER. I am not amusing myself with you, Mr. Ormund.

ORMUND (*laying a hand on him, glaring at him*). No? Well, what *are* you doing here? What's your game?

DR. GÖRTLER (*with authority*). It is not a game.

(*He looks steadily at him.* ORMUND *drops his hand, moves away below the table to up* R.C. *and stands with his back to him.*)

Tell me what happened. (*As* ORMUND *does not reply.*) Please.

ORMUND. What I told them about the rat was true. (*He turns.*) But of course that wasn't all.

DR. GÖRTLER. No, I knew that.

ORMUND. It wasn't so bad until I took out the revolver. And I had to take it out—irresistible impulse. But as soon as I stood there with that gun in my hand, I seemed to be falling into black night, and I felt the only thing left for me to do on earth was to put that revolver to my head. How I struggled to the door I don't know, but then I had to pull the trigger. Luckily there was the rat to fire at. At least, I suppose there was a rat. Perhaps not. I'm crazy enough to invent a rat or two. (*Leaning over the table, above the chair* R. *of it.*) *Was* there a rat?

DR. GÖRTLER. I do not know.

ORMUND (*rather wildly*). Thank God, there's something you don't know. (*He grabs the bottle across the table and finds it empty.*) Damn! Look at that. (*He moves up to the door* R.C. *and calls :*) Sam, Sam.

(*Enter* SALLY.)

Oh—Mrs. Pratt—I want a drink and this bottle's dead and done with.

SALLY (*taking it*). Bar's quieter now, Mr. Ormund, if you'd like to go back there.

ORMUND. I would.

(*He nods to* DR. GÖRTLER *and goes out up* R.C., *leaving the door open.* SALLY *comes round above the table to get the tray,* ORMUND'S *glass and syphon.* DR. GÖRTLER *crosses below the table to down* R. SALLY *stops, tray in hand, above the table and looks at* DR. GÖRTLER *in an unfriendly manner, but hesitating to speak. He has been thinking, but now catches her eye.*)

DR. GÖRTLER. Is there something you wish to say to me?

SALLY (*with an effort*). Yes—there is. There seems to have been a misunderstanding about your room, Dr.—er——

DR. GÖRTLER (*deliberately*). Görtler—Gört-ler. And I think the misunderstanding is not about my room, but about me, Mrs. Pratt.

SALLY (*heavily*). I said nothing about you.

DR. GÖRTLER. No.

(*While they are looking at each other, they are interrupted by the entrance of* JANET *at the door up* L. *She closes the door after her. She is dressed for walking and looks tired. She is carrying some wild moorland flowers.*)

SALLY (*glad of this interruption*). Well, you *have* had a long day, Mrs. Ormund. But I thought Mr. Farrant would be with you.

JANET. No. But he'll be here soon. (*She flops into the chair* L. *of the table.*) Oh—I'm tired.

SALLY. I expect you are.

(*There is a pause.*)

Well, I'll see about your suppers. (*She moves up* R.C.)

JANET. I don't want very much, Mrs. Pratt.

SALLY (*turning at the door*). What! after being out all day! That's no way of going on. You want a good meal.

(*She nods, smiles, and goes out* R.C., *closing the door.*)

DR. GÖRTLER (*smiling, as he moves from down* R. *round above the table to* L. *of her*). For once, I think, Mrs. Pratt is right. You must eat plenty of supper. And it is good, too. These people here—not like so many of the English now—they still have good food.

JANET (*lazily*). Yes—when I see it—I'll probably be quite greedy. But, you know how it is, sometimes when you're feeling tired, the idea of enormous platefuls of food . . . isn't . . . very attractive. . . .

DR. GÖRTLER (*moving* L. *towards the desk*). You walked a long way ?

JANET. Further than I meant to.

DR. GÖRTLER. But it was a good walk ? (*He sits in the chair at the desk.*)

JANET (*dreamily*). Heavenly . . . across the moors nearly all the way. . . . I found a sort of tiny secret glen . . . with a little waterfall . . . and mossy rocks . . . carpets of grass . . . harebells. . . .

(*The clock chimes the three-quarters.*)

DR. GÖRTLER. White harebells again ?

JANET. Yes . . . white harebells again. . . . You remember things, don't you, Doctor Görtler ?

DR. GÖRTLER. Only sometimes. My wife used to say I remembered nothing. But that was because I always forgot anniversary days or what to take home from shops. (*He pauses and smiles across at* JANET.) It was peaceful up there ?

JANET. Yes . . . no people . . . just larks and curlews . . . very peaceful, very innocent. . . . I think there's something—almost startling—in the innocence one feels about this sort of country——

DR. GÖRTLER. In these high wastelands ?

JANET. Yes. You must have felt it, haven't you ?

DR. GÖRTLER (*with great tenderness*). Yes. Every summer I used to walk on the Thuringian mountains—with my family and my friends. Ah !—we did not even know how happy we were, to be together and have such summer days—— (*His voice drops ; he is greatly moved.*) I think it would have broken our hearts then to know how happy and fortunate we were——

JANET (*moved with him*). Doctor Görtler—I'm so sorry——

DR. GÖRTLER (*with an innocent natural pedagogic sense, half pathetic and half comic*). These high places have never been settled by men, so they are still innocent. There is not about them any accumulation of evil. Where men have lived a long time, the very stones are saturated in evil memories. Cruelty and suffering remain in the world, and I think the earth cries out under its load of evil.

JANET. But the past has gone.

DR. GÖRTLER. Gone where ?

(*There is a pause.* JANET *looks out to the audience.*)

So Mr. Farrant was not with you ?

JANET. No. . . . I was alone, all day. I was glad to be.

DR. GÖRTLER (*smiling*). To think ?

JANET. No . . . you wouldn't call it thinking . . . almost a sort of day-dreaming. . . .

DR. GÖRTLER (*after a pause*). You—did not see Mr. Farrant to-day, then ?

JANET. Yes. . . . I saw him. . . .

DR. GÖRTLER. Of course. You told Mrs. Pratt he would be here soon.

JANET. Yes. . . . I saw him . . . following . . . behind me.

DR. GÖRTLER. And he couldn't catch up to you ?

JANET. He didn't catch up to me. . . . I saw him somewhere behind me . . . usually a long way off . . . several times . . . half the day, I suppose. . . .

DR. GÖRTLER. You were glad he stayed behind ?

JANET. Yes, very.

(*There is a pause.*)

(*Changing to a more normal, social tone.*) I suppose Walter—my husband—is in the bar ?

DR. GÖRTLER. Yes, he has just gone there. (*He rises and moves round above the table to* R. *of the chair* R. *of the table.*) Before that we were talking. (*He pauses.*) He is a man of force, of character, such as most women admire, eh ?

JANET. Yes, he is.

DR. GÖRTLER (*slowly*). Also, he is a man with deep secret weaknesses, and I think such weaknesses in such a man arouse a woman's pity.

JANET. Yes, I think they might.

DR. GÖRTLER (*after a pause*). There is much to love in him. (*He is now at downstage* R. *corner of the table.*)

JANET. Very much.

DR. GÖRTLER (*softly*). Then why, Mrs. Ormund, do you love him no longer ?

(JANET, *both socially offended and really wounded, rises slowly, obviously giving* DR. GÖRTLER *to understand he has been offensive, though she does not say anything. She gets her book from* L. *corner of the sideboard.*)

(*Moving away a little to* R.C.) You are offended. I am sorry.

(JANET *controls herself, then speaks in a lighter, social tone, itself a rebuke though not a strong one.*)

JANET. Is it true, Doctor Görtler, that time is curved ? I read somewhere the other day that it is. (*She returns and sits* L. *of the table again.*)

DR. GÖRTLER (*moving to the top* R. *corner of the table*). Yes, it is.

But time is not single and universal. It is only the name we give to higher dimensions of things. In our present state of consciousness, we cannot experience these dimensions spatially, but only successively. That we call time. But there are more times than one——

(SALLY *has entered up* R.C., *and one might detect a certain pleasure she has in interrupting* DR. GÖRTLER. *She is carrying a vase of water. She leaves the door open.*)

SALLY. It's all ready when you are, Mrs. Ormund.

JANET. Right, thank you, Mrs. Pratt.

(DR. GÖRTLER, *rather annoyed at being interrupted and not very comfortable now with* SALLY, *crosses to the door up* L., *opens it and looks out.* JANET *gives a rather mischievous look at his back, then at* SALLY, *who is putting* JANET'S *flowers in water at the downstage* R. *corner of the table.*)

Doctor Görtler is trying to explain to me what time really is.

SALLY. I can tell him what time is. It's a woman's greatest enemy—that's what it is.

JANET. It takes a lot away from us.

SALLY. It does that, and I'm not thinking about the pleasure of looking at yourself in the glass. (*She now straightens the chairs, tidies the table and rearranges the flowers in the bowl.*) It can take your man away, turn your baby into a little lad and then into a big lad, off on his own and forgetting you, and soon nothing's the same, except what you go on feeling, right down in your heart. Time doesn't take what you feel right down in your heart, Mrs. Ormund. If it did, it'ud be kinder than it is. But it leaves you behind—to suffer.

DR. GÖRTLER (*turning and coming to above the table*). No. All that is an illusion. Nothing has really gone, nothing is really lost.

SALLY (*above the chair* R. *of the table—impatiently*). Isn't it, indeed ? You wouldn't talk like that if you'd lost as much as I have.

DR. GÖRTLER (*with dignity*). I have lost more than you have. I have lost everything except the love of knowledge—and faith and hope.

(*He turns to go up* L., *and almost bumps into* FARRANT, *who enters looking dusty and tired and strained. There is a quite definite sense of strain in his manner.* DR. GÖRTLER *smiles at him.*)

So—Mr. Farrant, you have had a good walk, eh ?

FARRANT. Not bad.

(*He passes* DR. GÖRTLER *to* C. *above the table without a smile or a look. The effect is that of a snub.*)

Get me a glass of sherry, please, Mrs. Pratt.

(SALLY *moves up to the door* R.C., *but stops as* DR. GÖRTLER *speaks.*)

DR. GÖRTLER (*sharply*). Mr. Farrant.

FARRANT (*turning*). Yes?

DR. GÖRTLER (*rather sadly*). It does not matter.

(*He goes slowly out up* L., *closing the door. The other three look after him.*)

FARRANT (*moving* L.C.). What's wrong with Görtler?

JANET (*coldly*). Perhaps he didn't appreciate your very curt manner. (*She rises and crosses below the table to the door up* R.C.)

FARRANT (*rather dryly*). Sorry about that. Didn't mean to offend him.

SALLY (*going to the door* R.C.). Never mind about him, Mr. Farrant.

(*She exits, leaving the door open.*)

JANET (*with emphasis*). Thank you for not trying to catch up to me.

FARRANT (*confused by this attack*). Oh—were you——

JANET (*cutting in as she goes*). Yes, and you know I was.

(*He stares after her, then sits in the chair* L. *of the table and mechanically takes out a cigarette and lights it.* SALLY *enters with a glass of sherry on a tray.*)

SALLY. And your supper's all ready, Mr. Farrant. (*She puts the sherry on the table beside him.*)

FARRANT. Thanks. I'll come along in a few minutes.

(*He sips his sherry;* SALLY *looks at him.*)

SALLY. You don't think you're overdoing it a bit, do you, Mr. Farrant? I mean, walking too much.

FARRANT (*off-handedly*). I'm rather tired to-day. I slept badly last night.

SALLY. Yes, well, you were sent here for a rest, y'know, and you don't want to go and overdo it. You're looking done up to-night, if you don't mind me saying so.

(*It is now much darker, and* SALLY *begins to switch on the lights and draw the curtains and tidy up a little, doing this slowly as she talks, and continuing until* SAM *enters.*)

FARRANT. Don't worry, Mrs. Pratt. I've always been a lot better than I looked. (*He finishes his sherry.*)

SALLY. Well, you mustn't think I'm fussing at you——

FARRANT (*teasing her, nicely*). Of course you are. And don't pretend you're not.

SALLY (*drawing the curtains*). Yes, but I know what it is

when folk first comes up here. They do too much. And we can't have you making yourself poorly again, I don't know what our Charlie would say to us. He's depending on you to see him through and so are we. And he thinks the world of you I'm sure.

FARRANT (*as he rises and goes slowly below the table to the door down* R.). And we'll see him through. We'll have you nearly bursting with pride over him one day. I must wash.

SALLY. Shall I get you some hot water ?

FARRANT. No, thanks.

(*He goes out.* SALLY *finishes tidying up the room.* SAM *looks in up* R.C. *and comes to above the table. He leaves the door open.*)

SAM. Well, lass ?

SALLY. What was all that commotion just now in t'bar ?

SAM (*grinning*). Oh—that wor only Mr. Ormund having a bit of a game wi' owd Watson and Joe.

SALLY (*dropping her voice*). Is he drunk ?

SAM (*dropping his*). Who ? Mr. Ormund ? Well—amount he's taken to-night he ought to be silly drunk or unconscious— I know I'd be—but you can't say he's more nor a bit wild like. By gow, he can shift it, that chap.

(SALLY *tidies the desk and sets the chair to it.*)

SALLY. And I call it a silly way o' going on. Can't you stop him ?

SAM. Course I can't. It's not as if he wor daft with it. He's nobbut a bit wild.

SALLY. Well, I don't like it, Father.

SAM. No, happen not. Still——

SALLY (*continuing, unhappily*). I'm right sorry now Miss Holmes and her friends couldn't come. (*She moves round below the table to the door up* R.C., *picking up the tray with the sherry glass on the way.*) I can understand them sort o' folk. I've felt uneasy in my mind ever since last night. And I put most of it down to this Doctor Görtler. (*Turning to* SAM.) He's got everybody's back up.

SAM. Nay, it's only 'cos he's a sort of foreigner and a professor and what not, and talks so queer. He means no harm, Sally.

SALLY (*with sudden anger*). Harm or no harm, he leaves here in t'morning. We'll get on better without him. And I'm going to tell him so.

SAM. Now steady on, lass, steady on.

SALLY (*angrily*). What's use of saying " steady on " when we're all getting on edge——

(*She is interrupted by* ORMUND, *who enters up* R.C. *a trifle unsteadily, a glass of whisky in his hand. He has obviously had a lot to drink, but is not conventionally drunk.   He crosses over to* Sam *and puts an arm round his shoulders.*)

Ormund.   Sam, Sam, you're deserting us.   And you've not told me yet what's going to happen to you in the next world.

Sally (*hastily*).   Mrs. Ormund's back, Mr. Ormund.   She's gone to get her supper.

Ormund (*perching himself on the table, his back to the audience*). See that she has a beautiful supper, Mrs. Pratt.   Including your gooseberry pie.   Don't stand any high-brow nonsense from her on that subject.   She must take her share of gooseberry pie. See to it !

(*He waves at* Sally, *who nods, smiles faintly, and goes out* R.C.)

Now, Sam, what's going to happen to you in the next world ?

Sam.   Nay, he didn't say t'next world——

(Farrant *enters from down* R.   *He is tidier than he was, but still looks pale and strained.   He goes up towards the door* R.C.)

Ormund.   Hello, Farrant.   Did you show my wife the moors to-day ?

Farrant (*stopping, and speaking rather shortly*).   No.

Ormund.   Weren't you together ?

Farrant.   No.   I saw her.   But we weren't together.

Ormund.   Why didn't you join up ?

Farrant (*rather stiffly*).   I don't know.   I suppose we both preferred our own company.

Ormund.   That's not very complimentary of you.

Farrant.   Sorry.   I didn't mean to sound offensive.   Actually, I was feeling—rather dreary, and thought I'd better keep it to myself.

Ormund (*pleasantly*).   Well, well.   Sam's just going to tell me what our friend Doctor Görtler says will happen to him when he dies.

Farrant (*going on up to the door* R.C.).   Well, you know what to expect.   (*He stops and turns.*)   I believe Görtler's turning mystical, like so many Germans when things go wrong.

Ormund.   He's had a packet, you know.

Farrant.   Yes, and I think it's a rotten shame.   But even that doesn't excuse a man of science who's begun to talk bosh.

Ormund.   I suppose it is bosh.

Farrant.   From one or two things he said to me last night, I'm afraid it will be.   (*He comes down to the back of the chair* R. *of the table.*)   Perhaps I'm too impatient with that easy, optimistic half-thinking, but it does seem to me to be poor stuff in itself and to get in the way of real thought.   We shan't get out of the muddle we're in except by thinking hard and realistically. Don't you agree ?

ORMUND. We shan't begin to get out of it until we really *want* to get out. What sort of thinking is going to make us *want* to get out, that's the point.

FARRANT. Well, it won't be Görtler's Teutonic mistiness, will it ? I must go and eat.

(*He nods and goes out up* R.C., *shutting the door. After he has gone,* ORMUND *beckons to* SAM, *who joins him at the table.*)

ORMUND (*in a whisper*). Sam, believe it or not, it was I who voted him into that headmastership at Lamberton. And now having met the young man, I don't like him, and he doesn't like me.

SAM (*stoutly*). Nay, Mr. Ormund, Mr. Farrant's a grand young chap when you get to know him. Before you came, he was great company, but this last day or two, he's happen been a bit short and sharp. I fancy he's not so well again.

ORMUND (*rising and crossing* R.). Perhaps that's it. (*He sits on the sofa.*) But now then, Sam, let's hear what's going to happen to you—let's have some bosh.

SAM (*moving over to above* R. *of the table*). Well, it started with me saying last night : " If I'd my time over again," which seemed to right tickle Doctor Görtler. Because he comes to me this afternoon and tells me I'm going to have my time over again. He started on about time going round i' circles an' spirals, an' i' two minutes, what with his dimensions and eternities and what not, he had me dizzy. He says we all go round and round like dobbyhorses.

ORMUND. God forbid !

SAM. Nay, don't say that, Mr. Ormund, 'cos I'm all for this arrangement. He says I'm one o' them that'll go on and on wi' t'same life an' nivver change. When I die, I'm born all ower again, down at Marlingset, same house, same parents, go to t'same school an' have t'same fights wi' t'other lads, just t'same as before.

ORMUND. But you wouldn't like that, Sam, would you ?

SAM. I ask for naught better. It's champion. I wor telling him about day I wor wed. We wor wed early an' then I took her down to Leeds—eh, an' it wor a grand day an' all—Wharfedale shining an' smiling all t'way down—an' Yorkshire wor playing Surrey at Headingley, an' so o' course we went—an' Brown an' Tunnicliffe an' F. S. Jackson knocked them Surrey bowlers silly —an' then we went back to big high tea at Queen's Hotel. Eh, what a day !

ORMUND. Yes, that would be worth having again.

SAM. Well, I says to him, " Nah, is that day coming round again ? " An' he says, " Yes, it's on its way. Same bright morning," he says, " same blushing girl," he says, " same sun on t'same fields—everything." " That'll do me," I says.

ORMUND (*half amused, half serious*). Lucky for you, Sam. But does he seriously think we all just go on and on with the same life ?

SAM. Ay, I think so. That's what he told me.

(DR. GÖRTLER *enters up* L. *They turn and see him.*)

Doctor, didn't you tell me we all went on wi' t'same life round an' round an' round ?

DR. GÖRTLER. I said you might live the same life over and over again. But not all.

SAM. Well, what happens to t'others then, Doctor ?

DR. GÖRTLER (*coming to above the chair* L. *of the table*). Some people, steadily developing, will exhaust the possibilities of their circles of time and will finally swing out of them into new existences. (*Working round the chair to down* L.C.) Others—the criminals, madmen, suicides—live their lives in ever-darkening circles of their time. Fatality begins to haunt them. (*Walking up and down* L.C.) More and more of their lives are passed in the shadow of death. They gradually sink——

ORMUND (*rising—passionately*). For Christ's sake—stop it, can't you !

(*He goes towards the table, then controls himself and swings away, muttering.*)

I don't want to hear any more of that stuff to-night. It's getting on my nerves.

(*He goes out up* R.C., *shutting the door.* SAM *looks reproachfully at* DR. GÖRTLER.)

SAM. You've gone and put your foot in it again, Doctor.

DR. GÖRTLER (*staring after* ORMUND *thoughtfully*). Yes. Perhaps I was wrong to come here. Or wrong to speak at all of these things.

(*Enter* SALLY *purposefully up* R.C.)

SALLY (*decisively*). Just a minute, Father.

SAM (*moving to* L. *of her and lowering his voice*). Now, steady on, Sally.

SALLY (*getting rid of him*). All right, all right.

(SALLY *gets him out and shuts the door on him, then comes* C. *to above the table.* SALLY *and* DR. GÖRTLER *look at each other.*)

DR. GÖRTLER. Yes ?

SALLY (*moving down to below* R. *of the chair* R. *of the table*). Doctor Görtler, there's been a misunderstanding about your room. I thought you were just staying last night and to-night and—well—I promised somebody that room for to-morrow and Monday—and it's somebody who's stayed here many a time—so—you see——

DR. GÖRTLER.   You mean, that you want me to go ?

SALLY.   I didn't say so.   I said we wanted that room.

DR. GÖRTLER.   Yes, but you have nobody coming for it to-morrow.

SALLY (*sturdily*).   No, but we soon can have.   I said that because I didn't want to hurt your feelings.

DR. GÖRTLER.   You have already hurt my feelings.   But tell me the real reason why you wish me to leave.

SALLY (*with force*).   Well, if you want to know, it's because I feel there's something wrong here.   I don't know what it is, but I can feel it all the time.   And so can other people.

DR. GÖRTLER.   Perhaps there *is* something wrong here.

SALLY.   Well, there wasn't before you came.   And you arrived in a queer sort of way—asking who was staying here and all that. And you've got a way of talking and looking at folk that puts 'em on edge.   You may not mean it, and then again you may.   But I do know we'd all be a deal more comfortable if you were gone. And we think a lot o' Mr. Farrant, and Mr. and Mrs. Ormund are folk o' some standing——

DR. GÖRTLER (*with sad irony*).   And I am a stranger, a foreigner.

SALLY.   Well, if you want to put it like that, you can do.   But that's how it is.

(DR. GÖRTLER *moves up towards the door* L.)

We don't expect you to go to-night, y'know.

DR. GÖRTLER (*with sudden passion, moving to above* L. *of the table*).   I will go when I please.   You want to be rid of me— that is enough.   I will pay you now.

SALLY.   Up to to-morrow morning it'll be just two days. We'll call it a pound.

(*He gives her a pound note across the table and, turning away, goes to the door up* L., *opens it wide and stands looking out.*)

(*Uncomfortably.*)   I'm sorry—but we only want to do what's right for everybody——

DR. GÖRTLER (*half turning, curtly*).   I am sorry too—for you.

SALLY (*shortly*).   You needn't be sorry for me.

(*She goes out up* R.C., *closing the door.* DR. GÖRTLER *looks out of the door up* L. *a moment longer, then leaving it wide open, turns and stamps across the room to the door down* R. *and exits. The clock chimes and strikes ten.   During the sixth stroke,* ORMUND *enters up* R.C., *followed by* SAM, *leaving the door open behind them.*)

ORMUND.   He's not here.

SAM (*indicating the open door up* L.).   Must ha' gone out.   (*He calls off* R.C.)   Sally, Sally.   (*He comes down* R.)

(SALLY *appears, looking a trifle upset.*)

D

Has Doctor Görtler gone out, 'cos Mr. Ormund wants him !

ORMUND (*above the chair* L. *of the table*). I want to apologize to him.

SALLY (R.C., *sulkily*). He must have gone out. He's off in the morning.

ORMUND. Going ? What for ?

SALLY (*defiantly*). Because I asked him to go.

SAM. Nay, Sally, you didn't.

SALLY. Well, you wouldn't. You shuffled out of it. (*She turns to go.*)

ORMUND (*with authority*). Just a minute, Mrs. Pratt. Did you really ask Doctor Görtler to leave this inn ?

SALLY (*defiantly, coming to* C. *above the table*). I did. And I'm not sorry. He's made everybody feel uncomfortable. I heard you complaining and shouting at him yourself, Mr. Ormund.

ORMUND (*ruefully*). Yes, God help me !

SALLY. So I think I did right.

ORMUND. No, you did wrong.

SALLY. Why did I ?

ORMUND. Because he's a stranger, a foreigner, who's had to leave his own country. Even if he says things we don't understand, even if he makes us feel uncomfortable at times, we ought to be courteous. God knows I haven't been. But I was hoping *you* were being considerate to him. My fault probably. I could kick myself.

SAM. Why, Mr. Ormund, I can't see it matters much.

ORMUND (*broadly*). It does, Sam, it does. All over this rotten world now, they're slamming doors in the faces of good men. But we've still a door or two open here. We can't bang one of them in the face of this man, who's done none of us any harm. (*He glances at the door up* L.) He can't have gone far. I'm going to tell him I'm sorry and ashamed.

(*He goes out hastily up* L.   SAM *looks after him dubiously, then at* SALLY.)

SAM. You shouldn't ha' done it, Sally.

SALLY. Why not ? We've got our living to earn—and work hard enough to earn it—and we're the best judge of our own business. It's all right Mr. Ormund talking so grand now. (*She shuts the door up* L.) And how much whisky has *he* had ?

SAM (*apologetically*). I know. But he's far from being nasty-drunk, so I can't interfere. Only one as could is his wife, and it beats me she doesn't.

SALLY (*lowering her voice*). Happen she's given him up as a bad job.

(*She does not say any more because* JANET *enters up* R.C. *and comes down* R.C. *There is a slight, awkward pause.*)

Did you enjoy your supper all right, Mrs. Ormund ?

JANET (*who has a strained look*). Yes, thank you.

SALLY (*motioning* SAM *out*). You won't be wanting anything else to-night ?

JANET. No, thank you. (*She sits in the chair* R. *of the table.*)

SAM (*rather awkwardly, as he moves up*). Mr. Ormund's just gone out.

(JANET *nods. As* SAM *is going out* R.C., FARRANT *appears.* SAM *steps aside for him, then exits.*)

SALLY. You won't be wanting anything else, will you, Mr. Farrant ?

FARRANT (*crossing to the chair at the desk* L.). No, thank you.

SALLY. What about to-morrow ? Will you be going out all day again ?

FARRANT (*hastily, as he sits*). I don't know yet. I haven't made any plans.

(*They all say* " Good-night," *and* SALLY *goes out up* R.C. JANET *and* FARRANT *are left silent, not looking at each other. The sense of strain is definitely felt. At last* JANET *can endure it no longer.*)

JANET. Mr. Farrant.

FARRANT (*rather startled*). Yes ?

JANET. This afternoon you walked just behind me for several hours. We've just sat through the whole of supper without exchanging a word. I'm sorry, but I can't stand any more of it. If you're going to sit in here, then I'll either go out or up to my room.

FARRANT (*rising and moving up towards the door* R.C.). Please don't trouble. I'll go.

JANET (*watching him—with a touch of irony*). Thank you.

(*He stops above the table and stands awkwardly, looking doubtfully at her, and not moving.*)

Yes ?

FARRANT (*jerkily*). Would you mind—telling me—how long you're staying up here ?

JANET. I really don't see why I should. (*Pause.*) Why do you ask ?

FARRANT. Because if you're not leaving, then I must leave.

JANET (*rising*). I didn't realize you disliked me as much as that.

FARRANT (*moving to* L. *of the chair* L. *of the table*). I don't dislike you. It isn't that. I'd better clear out in the morning.

JANET. But you've no right to talk as if I'm driving you out.

FARRANT. No, I don't mean that, Mrs. Ormund.

JANET (*moving a step or two down, to be level with the downstage end of the table*). I'm not trying to be difficult. It's simply that I find these long silences intolerable.

FARRANT (*coming down to below the chair* L. *of the table*).   I know they are.   I feel just the same.   And I do assure you—it's quite unusual for me.   I'm often accused of talking too much.   But —you see—last night I never slept at all——

JANET (*moving away* R.).   Neither did I, for that matter.   But that doesn't excuse us——

FARRANT.   No, no, I know.   But then, you see, all to-day when I was out, of course I felt fagged.   (*He moves to below the table.*)   You must have done too.

JANET.   I did.   And when I came back, I felt absolutely worn out.   I couldn't possibly make any effort at supper.   Still, I think you might have done——

FARRANT (*moving to below the chair* R. *of the table*).   I tried, y'know, tried all the time.   I kept—you know how one does— kept forming words——

JANET (*taking a step forward*).   Yes, I did that too.   But couldn't bring them out.

FARRANT.   Exactly.   And then when I came in here, the silence had gone on so long, it seemed—y'know—absolutely indestructible——

JANET.   It was nearly.   I had to take a hammer to it.

FARRANT (*moving a step nearer*).   I'm glad you did, because I wanted to explain.   You must think me a fool——

JANET (*quicker than before, taking another step towards him*).   No.   Of course I felt you disliked me, but then with not sleeping last night and being so tired to-day, you see——

FARRANT (*eagerly, very quickly*).   Yes, well, probably I'm imagining I'm fitter than I am, y'know——

JANET (*she is quite close to him now*).   You look rather nervously tired——

FARRANT (*looking at her, his hands behind him*).   Perhaps we're both—y'know—not quite—our usual selves.

JANET.   No.

(*Involuntarily she steps into his arms and he holds her to him. The clock chimes the quarter past a little softer than usual. They are down below the chair* R. *of the table.   A tremendous inevitability rather than a sudden gust of passion is felt here.   They remain in this embrace for a few moments.   They only draw their faces away to speak.*)

FARRANT (*dazed*).   I didn't know. . . . I didn't know.

(*There is a pause.*)

JANET (*whispering*).   What shall we do ?

(*He now does definitely hold her close.   They are quite ecstatic. Then before they have time to separate,* ORMUND *has entered up* L., *clearly taking in the situation.   JANET sees him and backs down*

R. *a little.* FARRANT *turns* L. *and steps up to beside the chair* R.
of the table.)

ORMUND (*from just inside the door*).   There may be a storm.
And it's nearly Whit-Sunday—the Feast of Pentecost—the Day
of the Spirit, they used to call it.   And—curiously enough—they
didn't mean motor spirit—quick-starting, anti-knock petrol.
They didn't know about that.   They didn't know anything.
We know it all.   Farrant knows it all and is passing on our
knowledge to our lucky boys——

(*He breaks off and comes forward to above* L. *end of the table, looking
at the other two, who are still dumb.*)

And now what ?

(*They are silent.*)

Come on then—damn you !—talk, talk, let's hear all about it.

(*They are silent.*)

I suppose you arranged to meet here.   No ?   Then if you've
got as far as this in twenty-four hours, I ought to congratulate
you.   It's wonderful how everything's being speeded up.

(*There is another pause.* ORMUND *comes down to below* L. *end
of the table and knocks the chair over.* FARRANT *moves up* R.C.
ORMUND *looks at him.*)

Come on, Farrant.   Good God, aren't you man enough to stand
up for what you're doing ?
    FARRANT.   Ormund—I wish I could explain——
    ORMUND.   I can do that.
    JANET.   No, Walter, please.   We've got to try and understand
what's happening——
    ORMUND (*bitterly*).   No difficulty about that.   In one day,
while the pair of you were pretending to dislike each other,
you've suddenly decided you're in love—or in want of amusement
—and couldn't even wait——
    JANET (*with force, going up to* FARRANT).   No, Walter, can't
you see it's not like that ?
    ORMUND.   How can I see what it's like ?
    FARRANT.   Ormund, it's—simply—happened, that's all.   Be-
yond that, we can't explain.

(JANET *is* R. *of the chair* R. *of the table ;* FARRANT *is just above* L.
of her. ORMUND *walks away up* L.C., *then turns in a quieter
mood.*)

ORMUND.   All right, all right.   You're neither of you in any
fit state to talk, and I know I'm in no fit state to listen.   You've
fallen in love.   You don't know why.   You can't help it.   That
it ?

FARRANT. Yes.

JANET. Can't you see we're quite bewildered and helpless ? (*She pauses, then with more urgency.*) You remember what I felt last night when we arrived here, and I didn't want to stay.

ORMUND (*at upstage* L. *corner of the table*). You think you felt then that—this—was about to begin ?

JANET. Yes.

ORMUND (*crossing to them above the table*). But you don't know how it's going to end. (*Looking at both of them.*) How does it end ? We'd better ask Doctor Görtler.

JANET (*moving back a little—urgently*). Why do you say that ?

FARRANT (*quickly*). He's not serious.

ORMUND. I'm in a state of mind when I've stopped considering whether I'm serious or not. Ask Görtler. Ask the devil. (*He looks towards the door* L.)

FARRANT. But Görtler doesn't come into this at all.

ORMUND. Don't be too sure, Farrant.

JANET (*as if making a tremendous discovery*). He knew it had happened before.

FARRANT (*quickly*). He couldn't have done.

JANET. He came to find us here.

ORMUND (*almost in a whisper*). My God !—I'd hate to think that.

JANET. Why, what do you mean ?

ORMUND. I've had one grim session with him to-night. What *does* Görtler know ?

FARRANT (*with quick contempt*). Nothing about this.

JANET (*suddenly sinking on to the sofa, exhausted, then speaking slowly*). I believe he knows everything about us all.

(*There is a pause.*)

ORMUND (*harshly, stepping up to* FARRANT). Well, what do we do now ?

JANET (*in a whisper*). I'm frightened.

(*As they look at each other in silence—*DR. GÖRTLER *crosses the stage from the door down* R. *to the door up* L., *in a curiously detached, almost mechanical fashion, carrying his bag. He does not look at them, but they watch him in silence, staring in fascination and amazement at him. They only speak when he is nearing the door.*)

(*In a terribly alarmed tone.*) Doctor Görtler !

ORMUND (*in alarm and despair*). Görtler !

But he ignores them and walks straight out of the door, banging it behind him, and they remain motionless, staring after him, and then slowly turning their eyes to one another, while the CURTAIN *rapidly descends.*

CURTAIN.

ACT III

SCENE.—*The same. Sunday night. Late evening light.*
The room is empty. Both doors are closed. The clock chimes
the three-quarters. After a moment, SALLY *comes in up* R.C. *and*
goes to L. *of the telephone.*

SALLY. No! I was sure I heard it. (*Over her shoulder to*
SAM, *who is following her.*) Come in, Father, there's nobody here.
Surely they can't be much longer getting that call through. It's
past his bedtime now.

SAM. Well, if t'lad's in bed, he's all right.

SALLY (*sharply, she is worried*). Unless he's poorly. And
how do I know he's safe in bed?

SAM. Why shouldn't he be?

SALLY (*irritably*). I've told you before, Father—I don't know.
I expect I'm making a fool of myself. But I can't help it.

SAM. All right, lass, I'm not blaming you.

SALLY (*moving restlessly*). I'm sorry, Father, I didn't mean
to be short with you. And if it were anybody else but our
Charlie, I'd laugh at myself for getting into such a state.

(*The telephone rings sharply.* SALLY *hastens to answer it.* SAM
is up R.C.)

Yes, yes. . . . Well, this is Mrs. Pratt speaking . . . (*Eagerly.*)
Oh, is he? Thank you very much, though I didn't mean to get
poor lad out o' bed. . . . (*With a marked change of tone.*) Oh,
Charlie, this is your mother. . . . Are you all right, lad? . . .
(*With great relief.*) Well, I'm glad to hear it. I've been right
worried about you. . . . Nay, I don't know. . . . I must be
doting. . . . Yes, it's been nice here, except for a bit of a storm
late last night. . . . That's good. . . . How many runs did
you make? . . . Never mind, better luck next time. . . . Yes,
well—look after yourself, Charlie. . . . God bless you, lad!
(*She puts down the telephone and gives a great sigh.*) He's all
right.

SAM (*moving to her* R.). I didn't expect aught else. How
many runs *did* he make?

SALLY (*half laughing*). You're as bad as he is. Three.

SAM (*moving down to above the chair* R. *of the table*). Tch! tch!
tch! tch! He will try and hit across, instead o' coming forward—left foot. I've told him.

55

SALLY. I've been worrying and worrying about that lad all day. (*She moves down* R. *behind* SAM.) Well, that's *one* load off my mind.

SAM. One load ? (*Moving to* L. *of her.*) How many more have you ?

SALLY. Well, I've this.

(*She produces a rather worn, fairly large notebook, bound in black leather.* SAM *looks at it in astonishment.*)

SAM. Whose is it ? (*He takes it.*)

SALLY. That Doctor Görtler's. I found it in his room this morning. It had slipped down inside the armchair.

SAM (*offering her the book*). Well, you'll have to send it to him.

SALLY. How can I when he didn't leave his address ? And another thing. I feel bad about sending him away like that.

SAM. I told you. (*He still has the notebook.*)

SALLY. I never thought he'd leave last night, without another word. I meant to tell him this morning to stay on, if he wanted to—after what Mr. Ormund said—he'd made me sort o' feel ashamed—and I was right upset when I found he'd gone. I think that started me off.

SAM (*with awkward tenderness*). Never mind, lass. We all mak' mistakes.

SALLY. But don't think I'm the only one who's feeling upset here. There's some worse than me—yes, here in this house.

SAM. Aye. I've hardly seen 'em to-day.

SALLY. Neither have I. But I know.

(FARRANT'S *and* JANET'S *voices are heard outside the door up* L. SAM *looks that way.* JANET *and* FARRANT *enter, looking very serious.* JANET *comes down* L.C. FARRANT, *after shutting the door, moves* C. *to above the table.*)

SAM (*showing the notebook*). Mr. Farrant, Doctor Görtler left this behind. It had got down side of his chair, way my tobacco-pouch has done monny a time. I wor just wondering whether it wor of any importance. It's i' German, I reckon.

FARRANT (*taking the notebook*). I'll see. (*He looks at the first page, curiously.*)

JANET (*very curious*). What does it say ?

FARRANT (*puzzling over it*). *Wiederkehr und Dazwischenkunft.* That's Return or Recurrence and—Interference or Intervention. This notebook, it says, is for problems and instances of Recurrence and Intervention. (*He flicks the pages carelessly.*) Yes —— (*He hands it back casually to* SAM.) He's sure to want that back. (*He comes down* L. *to* JANET.)

JANET (*who has been thinking*). What could he mean by problems and instances of Recurrence and Intervention ?

FARRANT (*on her* R., *shrugging*). God knows ! But as I've told you before, I don't think Görtler had quite retained his mental balance. It often happens when an elderly scholar suddenly has a lot of trouble. (*He turns, rather sharply, to* SALLY *and moves back to above the table.*) Mrs. Pratt, I'm leaving to-night, so can I have my bill, please ?   And—Sam—would you mind getting my car out ?

SAM (*surprised*).   All right, Mr. Farrant.

(*He puts the notebook down beside the telephone and goes out up* R.C.)

FARRANT (*to* JANET).   I'll pack now.

(*He crosses down* R. *below the table and exits.* SALLY *looks after him in astonishment, then moves to above the table and looks at* JANET.)

JANET.   Do you know where my husband is, Mrs. Pratt ?

SALLY (*gravely*).   He was up in his room, Mrs. Ormund. I went in about quarter of an hour since, and he was there, writing letters. (*She breaks off, then, looking hard at* JANET, *moves a step nearer to her.*)   Mrs. Ormund, are *you* going to-night, as well as Mr. Farrant ?

JANET.   Yes, we're going together.

SALLY.   You're leaving your husband ?

JANET.   Yes.

SALLY.   Leaving him for good ?

JANET.   Yes.

SALLY (*very earnestly*).   But that's a terrible thing to do, Mrs. Ormund.

JANET (*steadily*).   I know it's a very serious thing, Mrs. Pratt. But it happens to be the only possible—the only fair thing—to do—in the circumstances. You'll have to believe that.

SALLY (*going over to* JANET).   But have you thought, Mrs. Ormund ?

JANET (*with a rather wan smile, as she sits in the desk chair*).   I've been doing a lot of thinking.

SALLY.   Yes, but I mean—have you thought about what'll happen to Mr. Ormund ?   He's your husband. And what will he do, left to himself ?   He seems such an unhappy sort o' gentleman with all his drinking and what not.

JANET.   I'm afraid he is unhappy.

SALLY.   You're not leaving him—surely—because he's taken to drinking too much——

JANET (*cutting in*).   No, Mrs. Pratt. My husband always has been unhappy. There was a time when I tried very hard to make him happy, but somehow I couldn't. It was my fault, not his, probably. I just couldn't feel what I ought to have felt for him. (*After a pause.*)   No, it's no use.

SALLY (*very earnestly*).   But Mr. Farrant, too !   Have you

thought what might happen to him—with his school and everything ?   That's where my Charlie is, you know.   And if anything
did happen to Mr. Farrant !

JANET (*a trifle less sympathetically*).   You can be sure I've
thought about that too.   We both have.

SALLY.   Oh—I knew there was something wrong.   Mrs.
Ormund, please—I've lost my own man, and I've only this lad
of mine—and I'm older than you—listen to me a minute.   Don't
go snatching at what you think might be happiness, when you
don't really know.   And please—please—don't rush off and do
something you might regret all the rest of your life.   We haven't
just ourselves to consider, y'know, and the older you get, the more
you see that.   Mrs. Ormund—please—give yourself a bit more
time—think it over—for all our sakes——

(*She is disturbed by the entrance of* ORMUND *up* R.C., *looking rather
pale.   He is completely sober, and comes down* R.C., *leaving the
door open.*   SALLY *gives him one look and then hurries out
up* R.C., *shutting the door after her.*   ORMUND *waits until she has
gone.*)

JANET (*quietly, but not without emotion*).   I've just told Mrs.
Pratt that Oliver and I are going away.

ORMUND (*above the chair* R. *of the table*).   When ?

JANET.   We're going to-night.

ORMUND (*hopelessly*).   I see.   (*He sits in the chair* R. *of the table.*)

JANET.   It's the fairest and wisest thing to do, Walter—to
make a clean break now, so that none of us has any more of
this agony.

ORMUND (*in the same tone*).   I've no doubt you're right.

JANET (*rising to* L. *of the chair* L. *of the table*).   We've talked it
all out.   We've faced the worst that might happen—even lost
the school because of possible scandal.

ORMUND.   You mean—you've talked about facing the worst
that might happen—you haven't actually faced it yet, y'know.

JANET.   Well, we've realized all that this might involve.
We're not going away with our eyes closed.

ORMUND.   I wonder.

JANET.   Why do you say that ?

ORMUND.   Because I wonder how you know what the worst
is that might happen.   When we decided to come here together,
I thought the worst that could happen would be that we'd have
another of our rows.   But now something much worse has
happened.   I'm losing you altogether.   You see, we don't know.

JANET (*rather wearily*).   I realize that, Walter.   I only said
that we tried to face the possible consequences.

(ORMUND *rises and moves round below the table to* R. *of her.*)

ORMUND (*looking curiously at her*).   You're going away.   But
you're not happy, are you, Janet ?

JANET (*with great sincerity, as she crosses round above the table to the door up* R.C.). No, I'm not. I'm miserable—and rather frightened. And perhaps it's a good thing I am.

ORMUND. Why ?

JANET (*turning and facing* ORMUND—*very seriously*). Because if I were all excited and feeling gay, I might be doing something foolish going away like this. As it is, I know what I feel for Oliver Farrant is absolutely real—now and for ever. I believe it's always existed, always been part of me.

ORMUND (*rather wearily*). Perhaps it has. Who knows ? We know so little that's worth knowing about ourselves. We're like children groping about in the dark.

(*There is a pause.* FARRANT *enters down* R. *carrying a suitcase, raincoat and hat. He stands stiffly when he sees* ORMUND.)

All right, Farrant, all right. Only put that damned gear of yours outside. (*He moves up to the sideboard.*)

FARRANT. My car should be there.

(*He crosses below the table to the door up* L., *puts his things outside and returns immediately, closing the door.*)

ORMUND. I was asking Janet if she was happy. She says she isn't.

FARRANT (*stiffly*). I didn't suppose she would be. (*He is* L., *above the desk chair.*)

ORMUND. What about you ?

FARRANT. No, of course I'm not. This is a hateful business. If I'd thought my clearing out would settle it, I'd have cleared out. But I knew it wouldn't.

JANET (*now by the chair* R. *of the table*). And I knew it wouldn't. We've talked it all out and we've agreed on that.

ORMUND (*to* FARRANT). You're doing the only possible thing, you feel——

FARRANT. Yes.

ORMUND. You're both deeply in love. I hope I'm not over-stating it.

FARRANT (*curtly*). You're not.

ORMUND. And yet you're feeling miserable about it. Why ?

FARRANT (*shrugging*). I suppose it's a bad case of conscience.

ORMUND (*with irony*). Conscience ? Come, come.

FARRANT. I believe that a man and woman, feeling as Janet and I do, have a perfect right to do what we're doing. But somewhere at the back of my mind, I've still to contend against centuries of belief that what we're doing is wrong. I'm being worried by my ancestors, as we are all the time. That's about all it is.

JANET (*impulsively*). No, Oliver. I'm sure it isn't that.

FARRANT (*surprised*). Well, what is it. then ?

JANET (*sitting in the chair* R. *of the table—struggling with her thought*). I don't know. I wish I did. But there's something —some sort of influence—behind all that we do and say here— something compelling—and tragic——

FARRANT (*moving down* L.). No, that's simply being fanciful, Janet.

ORMUND (*with savage irony, crossing down* R.). No—for God's sake—don't let's be fanciful, not when we live in such a nice, simple, straightforward little world as this.

FARRANT (*with force*). There's no sense in bewildering our-selves with mysteries of our manufacture. People have done that too long. The point is, we're acting rationally and according to our own code, but our so-called consciences were made for us —during childhood—before we could make our own code. There-fore we can know we're doing right and yet still feel, obscurely but quite strongly, that we're doing wrong. And that's what's the matter with us.

ORMUND (*moving up to above* R. *end of the table*). And I don't believe that's the half of it, Farrant. It's all too damn simple, like a lot of your explanations.

FARRANT. But perhaps things are really much simpler than you like to think they are.

ORMUND. I suspect they're even more complicated than I think they are. (*Going nearer to* FARRANT, *with a marked change of tone*.) I don't suppose I'll ever see you again, Farrant. Let me give you one last word. (*He moves away again above the table to up* R.C.) Don't be too sure you know it all. Don't think you've got it all worked out. You bright young men, with your outlines of everything, are going to be horribly surprised yet. (*As* FARRANT *moves up* L.C. *and begins to protest*.) No. Another word and I've finished. Don't think you know it all, and she knows nothing. She knows more about what's going on in this crazy universe than you or I do. She doesn't get it out of books, because it isn't in books. But she can guess right, now and then, and we can't.

FARRANT. But you're not going to blame me for preferring knowledge and judgment to guesswork ?

ORMUND. No, but I'm not going to have you gassing about knowledge and judgment when you can't really account for a single thing that's happened to you these last two days. (*He moves away* R.) You can give us nice bright simple outlines of everything under the sun, but the minute something really important happens to you, you can't make head or tail of it, and wonder if you're going mad. (*He comes back to above* R. *of* JANET'S *chair*.)

JANET (*urgently*). That's true, at least, Oliver.

(FARRANT *goes up to the sideboard*.)

You know we're all equally bewildered. And there's something more—something that hasn't been accounted for yet—something that perhaps can never be explained—like so many things——

(*She breaks off, and looks across to the doorway up* L. ORMUND *and* FARRANT *look too. It has rapidly been growing dimmer in the room.* DR. GÖRTLER'S *figure—he does not wear a hat or carry a bag—stands very dark in the doorway.*)

ORMUND (*coming forward to above* R. *end of table*). It's Görtler.
DR. GÖRTLER (*still in the doorway*). Yes. It is dark in here.

(ORMUND *goes to the door up* R.C. *and turns on the light.* DR. GÖRTLER *comes forward, leaving the door open, gives a little bow to the three of them, and then speaks rather casually.*)

Thank you. But I am not staying——
ORMUND (*gravely*). Just a minute, Doctor. (*He opens the door up* R.C. *and calls.*) Mrs. Pratt, Mrs. Pratt.
SALLY (*off*). Just coming, Mr. Ormund.
ORMUND (*to* DR. GÖRTLER, *moving down slightly*). You see, you didn't give us a chance last night to say how sorry we were that you—a stranger, an exile in this country—had been treated with such discourtesy.

(SALLY *appears in the doorway up* R.C. FARRANT *moves to the window* L. *and draws the curtains.*)

Mrs. Pratt, I'm apologizing to Doctor Görtler.
SALLY (*coming forward to* C. *above the table—speaking humbly and with feeling*). Yes, Doctor Görtler, I want to beg your pardon. I shouldn't have asked you to leave. You'd done nothing wrong. I was blaming you just because you're a foreigner. I'm sorry.
DR. GÖRTLER (*rather embarrassed and touched*). No, please, please. I lost my temper too—that has always been my trouble —a bad temper—and so I behaved foolishly.
SALLY. I hope you'll stay, now you've come back.
DR. GÖRTLER (*taking a step or two towards her*). No, I cannot do that. I only came back because I have lost something—something very important—and I am hoping that I may have left it here——

(SALLY *gets the notebook from beside the telephone.*)

SALLY (*holding up the notebook*). Is this it ?
DR. GÖRTLER (*taking it eagerly*). Yes. Thank you. That is all I want.

(*He glances at the notebook, then looks up at* SALLY, *and gives her a smiling nod of dismissal. She looks at him hesitantly, then turns and goes out up* R.C.)

I would not like to have lost this. There is a great deal of valuable work here. (*He turns, smiling, and makes a move in the direction of the door up* L.)

ORMUND (*moving towards him*). Görtler! You're not going?

DR. GÖRTLER. Yes. Why not?

(*He looks at* ORMUND. ORMUND *looks from him to the other two.*)

JANET (*impulsively, rising*). Doctor Görtler, you know something, don't you? Something that we don't know.

FARRANT (*quietly, not superciliously*). That's quite impossible, y'know, Janet.

ORMUND. Is it though? I'm not so sure.

JANET (*to* DR. GÖRTLER). You know, don't you?

FARRANT (*protesting*). Janet, really it's——

JANET (*cutting him short*). Please, Oliver! (*To* DR. GÖRTLER.) You believe that something happened here before, don't you?

DR. GÖRTLER. I know it did.

FARRANT. How could it, seeing that not one of us has ever been here before?

DR. GÖRTLER. Are you sure you haven't?

FARRANT (*very decidedly*). Of course I am. I'm quite capable of remembering exactly where I've been.

DR. GÖRTLER (*shutting his notebook and turning to go*). Then there is nothing more to be said.

JANET. Yes, there is. Please! What do you know about us?

FARRANT. Wait a minute, Janet. We can't possibly drag Doctor Görtler into our private affairs.

DR. GÖRTLER. I have no wish to be dragged into them. (*He looks at him with a slight smile.*) Have you and Mrs. Ormund planned to leave here to-night together?

FARRANT. How did you guess?

DR. GÖRTLER. It is not guessing.

ORMUND (*moving up* C. *to above the table*). Görtler, I don't blame you for losing your temper. You were badly treated. But we've apologized. And things are serious here now——

DR. GÖRTLER (*coolly*). They always were—*very* serious.

ORMUND. All right, then. Now—the truth, as simply as you can state it, please. You had some definite purpose in coming here, hadn't you?

DR. GÖRTLER. Yes.

ORMUND. What was it?

DR. GÖRTLER. I came to verify an experiment, and, if possible, to make a further experiment.

ORMUND. But you didn't do anything?

DR. GÖRTLER. Yes. Everything happened as I thought it would. (*He comes down* L.C. *a little.*) I verified my experiment. But then, last night, I suddenly lost patience, because I felt I was being badly treated, so I did not try the further experiment. That does not matter very much. I can try that other experiment with some other example.

(*He turns back to the door.* ORMUND *shuts it before he gets there.*)

JANET (*urgently*). Doctor Görtler, you mean it doesn't matter to you or to your theory or whatever it is. But what about us ?

FARRANT (*impatiently*). How *can* it matter to us, Janet ?

(DR. GÖRTLER *looks at them indifferently. There is a pause.*)

ORMUND (*very forcefully*). Doctor Görtler, last night you asked me a good many unusual questions—you remember ?— and I told you things I had never told anybody else——

DR. GÖRTLER. Yes, that is true. You were very helpful, Mr. Ormund.

ORMUND. Now I am asking you something. It is your turn to be helpful. Why did you come to this inn ? What was this experiment of yours ?

DR. GÖRTLER (*after a short pause*). Very well. (*He pauses, comes* L. *of the table, then begins in the brisk impersonal tone of the scientist.*) In this notebook are some records of very unusual states of mind and feats of memory. Some of them came to me like clear dreams. They are quite vivid little scenes.

(*He rapidly turns the pages of the notebook to a place he wants, then glances at it.* FARRANT *sits at the desk.* ORMUND *has moved back to* C. *above the table.* JANET *is standing above the chair* R. *of the table.*)

In the best of them, I remember not only what I have seen, but also what has been said. I was fortunate enough to have a very good example about three months ago. I put down all the details here. (*He moves to below the chair* L. *of the table, looks at the notebook a moment, then at his listeners.*) In this memory— this dream if you prefer it—I found myself a year or two older than I am now, but situated as I am now, an exile living in London. I was in rooms—cheap rooms not unlike those I am in now—but here the rooms above mine, very poor rooms, were occupied by two people, a man and his wife, still quite young, but very shabby, very poor, and very unhappy. They had been quarrelling bitterly and I had heard them, and because I was sorry, I went up to see what I could do. Then, I learned their history.

(*He stops and turns up* L. *to the door.* JANET *stirs and draws a sharp breath.*)

This was not the woman's first husband. She had been the wife of a rich man, older than herself, with whom she had fallen out of love.

(JANET *sits in the chair* R. *of the table.*)

But they had gone on a little holiday together, at Whitsuntide, to a small inn, which they described.

(ORMUND *moves away down* R.)

There she had instantly fallen in love with a younger man—the one now her husband—and they had run away.

(*He pauses and sits in the chair* L. *of the table.* JANET *draws a sharp breath again and looks at* FARRANT. *He shakes his head impatiently.*)

JANET. Doctor Görtler——

DR. GÖRTLER. Then there came, out of this, as they now realized, the ruin of many innocent lives. A great business collapsed, and many people, simple people—like this landlord and his daughter here—lost their money. Not only that, but there had been a great scandal, so that this young man had been driven out of his profession, and both of them had to endure poverty and loneliness. But what made them so bitter was that though their love for one another had compelled them to take this course, had made them poor and lonely and neglected, it had given them nothing in return. This love of theirs, it had died.

JANET (*rising—very sharply, painfully*). No, it couldn't have done that.

DR. GÖRTLER. Yes. They admitted that. There were too many shadows between them, too many reproachful faces. They could no longer be happy together, yet they could not be indifferent to one another, having suffered so much, so now they were quarrelsome, bitter——

JANET (*with a heartbroken cry*). Oh—God—no—not that——

FARRANT (*angrily, rising and moving towards the table*). But—Janet——

JANET. It was us he saw, Oliver, of course it was us. (*She turns away.*)

FARRANT (*angrily*). It's only some fantastic dream of his.

JANET. No. You recognized us here, didn't you ?

DR. GÖRTLER. Yes. At once.

JANET (*to* FARRANT). You see, I knew all the time, there was something—— (*She sits in the chair* R. *of the table again.*)

FARRANT (*almost savagely*). Wait a minute. (*Turning on* DR. GÖRTLER.) How did you induce these dreams of yours ?

DR. GÖRTLER. They weren't dreams. They were actual memories.

FARRANT. Memories of what ?

DR. GÖRTLER. Of past cycles of my own life.

FARRANT. You're contradicting yourself—on your own ridiculous theory. You said you were then as you are now, an exile living in London.

DR. GÖRTLER.   Why not ?   I have been an exile in London in past cycles of my life.   We repeat our lives, with some differences, over and over again.

FARRANT (*moving away* L. *a little*).   You can't expect us to believe that.

DR. GÖRTLER.   My friend, I do not care whether you believe it or not.   You asked me to explain and I am explaining.

FARRANT (*turning to him*).   Yes, but you're not merely airing a fantastic theory now, you're interfering in our affairs.   How did you induce these states of mind ?

DR. GÖRTLER.   By a certain method I have developed.   We have to change the focus of attention, which we have trained ourselves to concentrate on the present.   My problem was to drift away from the present—as we do in dreams—and yet be attentive, noticing everything——

FARRANT (*with savage intensity*).   Yes, yes, but how did you do it ?   By doing without food, I suppose ?

DR. GÖRTLER.   Yes, to some extent.

FARRANT.   I thought so.   And did you use drugs ?

DR. GÖRTLER.   A German colleague found a certain narcotic for me——

FARRANT (*triumphantly to* JANET).   I knew it.   (*He strides up and down* L.)   You see.   I suspected that all along.   He's starved himself and drugged himself and let himself be hag-ridden by a completely illogical fantastic theory of life, and then comes here with a story of some ridiculous dream he had——

ORMUND (*cutting in, quietly but sharply*).   Then what are we all doing, playing such convincing parts in it ?

(*There is a silence.* FARRANT *turns.* ORMUND *moves nearer the door up* R.C.)

DR. GÖRTLER (*quietly, rising*).   I expected this.   But it was you who asked me to explain.   I have given you my explanation.   (*He picks up the notebook from the table and puts it in his pocket.*)

JANET (*with a sort of quiet despair*).   I believe it's true.

FARRANT (*angry and resentful*).   Janet, you can't.

JANET.   Yes.   It accounts for so many things.   (*To* DR. GÖRTLER.)   But afterwards—when you had made your notes —— ?

DR. GÖRTLER (*now above the chair* L. *of the table*).   That was three months ago.   I soon found that these things had not yet happened in this cycle of your lives—because I discovered at once that Mr. Oliver Farrant was still the headmaster of Lamberton School——

JANET.   You had our *names* ?

DR. GÖRTLER.   Yes, of course.

FARRANT.   What proof have we of that ?

E

DR. GÖRTLER. I think you read German ? My handwriting is not good, but you can read enough, I hope, to convince you.

(*He hands over the notebook, open, to* FARRANT, *who takes it, sits in the desk chair and stares at it in amazement.* ORMUND, *after watching* FARRANT'S *face a moment, slips out quietly by the door up* R.C.)

You will see I had not the actual name of the inn—only an idea of the sort of place it was and its situation among these hills.

FARRANT. I don't understand this. Must be some sort of clairvoyance, clairaudience. I believe there are instances—— (*He hands the notebook back.*)

(DR. GÖRTLER *shakes his head, with a little smile, and moves to above the table.*)

DR. GÖRTLER. So I came here for this Whitsuntide holiday. At first, when two of you were not even expected here, I thought I had chosen the wrong year. But no. I was fortunate.

JANET. That's why—you asked those questions——?

DR. GÖRTLER. Yes. I also found that you were all closely interdependent. And I saw also that two of you were so instantly and fatally attracted that you were superficially resentful of one another. (*He smiles.*) It was like watching a performance of a play that one has first read carefully.

JANET (*wildly*). You're talking as if we were marionettes, with no minds and wills of our own.

FARRANT (*resentfully*). Going round and round. It's a monstrous, hellish theory.

DR. GÖRTLER. Yet—what have you felt these last two days ? Have you felt you had minds and wills of your own ?

JANET. No. (*Then with a sort of despairing energy.*) But— Doctor Görtler—we're not really like that. I know—I *know* we're not. We *can* make our own lives, can't we ?

DR. GÖRTLER. Once we know, yes. It is knowledge alone that gives us freedom. I believe that the very grooves in which our lives run are created by our feeling, imagination and will. If we know and then make the effort, we can change our lives. We are not going round and round in hell. (*He looks at* FARRANT.) And we can help each other.

JANET. How ?

DR. GÖRTLER. If I have more knowledge than you, then I can intervene, like a man who stops you on a journey to tell you that the road ahead is flooded. That was the further experiment I had hoped to make. To intervene.

JANET (*pointing to the notebook*). Recurrence and Intervention.

DR. GÖRTLER. Yes. That seemed possible too. I discovered some things I did not know before. Two of you, troubled by memories, were instantly attracted to each other. That I expected. But the third——

JANET. You mean Walter ?

DR. GÖRTLER. Yes. The one I had not met before, I soon
discovered that he was a man who felt he had a tragic destiny
and was moving nearer and nearer to self-destruction——

JANET (*startled*). Suicide !

DR. GÖRTLER. Yes, that was why the great business collapsed,
why so many were ruined, why everybody knew the story. You
told me when you left him, ran away, your husband went into
the garage here and shot himself——

JANET (*looking round*). Walter ! (*She sees he is not there.*)
Where did he go ?

FARRANT (*rising and pointing to the door up* L.). Not that way.

JANET (*urgently*). Doctor Görtler, he keeps a revolver in one
of the pockets of his car. Will you go and get it for me, please ?

DR. GÖRTLER (*gravely*). Yes, that would be better. (*He
moves towards the door, opens it and then turns.*) That is one thing
to do, but there are others, more important.

JANET (*quietly*). Yes, I understand.

(DR. GÖRTLER *goes out, shutting the door after him.* FARRANT
turns eagerly to JANET.)

FARRANT (*with passion, crossing to upstage* L. *end of the table*).
Janet—you're not going to let that fantastic stuff of his make any
difference to us ?

JANET (*urgently*). But—you see, Oliver, I believe it. It
explains so many things I couldn't understand before. (*At the
chair* R. *of the table.*) It explains *us*—why it's all happened so
quickly between us. And it explains why I've never felt happy
about it, why there's been a great shadow over it all. (*She sits
in the chair* R. *of the table, then announces quietly.*) So you must
go. But I must stay.

FARRANT (*moving to upstage* R. *end of the table*). Janet, if you'd
told me to go last night, I'd have gone without a word. But after
what we've said to one another to-day, I can't go without you, I
can't.

JANET. You must, Oliver.

FARRANT (*pleading*). But nothing's been really changed.
We're exactly the same people that we were an hour ago. If it
was impossible for you to stay here with Ormund then, it's
impossible now. We still feel the same about each other. Can't
you see, Janet, everything's just the same ?

JANET (*distressed*). No it isn't, because now we know
more.

FARRANT (*moving away to upstage* L. *end of the table*). We know
nothing. (*Turning to her again.*) My God, Janet, you're not
going back on everything we've said, everything we've planned,
because of this old German's mystical rubbish ?

JANET. Oh—my dear—I must. I feel it's true—here——

(*She puts a hand over her heart.*)   Just as I feel the truth of my love and yours.

FARRANT (*coming closer again*).   But now it means tearing our lives in two.

JANET.   But it's better to do that than tear so many other people's lives in two—only to find in the end we'd lost one another.   And this can't be for ever, you know.

FARRANT (*bitterly*).   It can for me.   (*He sits in the chair c. above the table.*)   I happen to know I've only one life, not dozens of 'em like the rest of you.   Only one, and now it's in bits—— (*Almost breaking down.*)   Oh—Janet—and you'll do nothing to mend it——   (*This is almost inaudible.*)

JANET (*very quietly, rising and moving to* R. *of him*).   No, my dear, if this wasn't the beginning, then this can't be the end of it all.   (*She kneels beside him.*)   There must be somewhere—our own place, our own time.   (*Taking his face between her hands.*)   Let me look at you.

FARRANT (*almost mumbling*).   Why ?   What does it matter now ?

JANET.   I'm trying to make myself remember every single line of your face.   And I know I shan't.   Very soon I shall try to see it again, and there'll be nothing but a blur while hundreds of faces that mean nothing will come between us.   It's a hard world for love, Oliver.   Even the memory of its face won't stay to comfort us.

(DR. GÖRTLER *enters up* L., *leaving the door open.   He comes down* L.   JANET *and* OLIVER *have risen and are now apart again.*)

DR. GÖRTLER.   The revolver is not there now.   And it was there yesterday.

JANET (*hurriedly, moving round below the table to* DR. GÖRTLER).   Will you please find my husband—tell him I am saying good-bye to Oliver—and stay with him until I come in again ?   (*She goes upstage* L. *and stretches out her left hand to* FARRANT.)   Oliver——

(DR. GÖRTLER *watches* FARRANT *and* JANET *go through the door up* L., *the latter closing the door after her.   When they have gone he moves up above the table to the door* R.C. *and calls.*)

DR. GÖRTLER.   Ormund.   Ormund.

(*After a moment* ORMUND *enters, looking rather wild.*   DR. GÖRTLER *closes the door.*)

ORMUND (*coming down to above the chair* R. *of the table*).   Where are they ?

DR. GÖRTLER.   Out there—but they are saying good-bye.

ORMUND.   Good-bye ?

DR. GÖRTLER (*moving down to* R. *of* ORMUND).   He is going. She will stay with you.   (*He pauses.*)   She sent me to find your revolver, but it was not there.

ORMUND. No, because it's here. (*He pulls it out of his pocket.*)

DR. GÖRTLER. It would be better to give that to me.

ORMUND (*moving away to upstage* L. *end of the table*). If I'd
any sense I'd use it. No more questions that can't be answered,
twisting like knives in your guts. Sleep, a good sleep, the only
good sleep.

DR. GÖRTLER (*crossing below the table to down* L.). I am afraid
you will be disappointed. It will be a sleep full of dreams—like
this. And the questions will be still there. You cannot blow
them to bits with a pistol. But why should you want to try
now ? It is all different.

ORMUND. I don't see any difference.

DR. GÖRTLER. Your wife will not leave you now. And perhaps she will be changed a little—with a new kindness.

ORMUND (*harshly*). I don't want her kindness. Let her go.
(*He moves to upstage* R. *end of the table.*)

DR. GÖRTLER. But now she does not want to go.

ORMUND. Yes, she does. But she's afraid to. And I've lost
her, whether she goes or stays, so there's no difference. She
can't keep me alive simply by staying by my side.

DR. GÖRTLER. No one can keep you alive but yourself.

ORMUND. And I don't want to go on living.

DR. GÖRTLER (*dryly, turning away* L.). I am not going to cry
over you, my friend.

ORMUND (*angrily*). Who the devil asked you to ?

DR. GÖRTLER (*turning up to him*). But I must remind you—
there's no escape.

ORMUND. No ? I suppose because you believe that if I take
the jump into the dark, I'll find myself back again on the old
treadmill. Well, I don't believe it. I can find peace.

DR. GÖRTLER. You can't. Peace is not somewhere just waiting for you.

ORMUND. Where is it, then ?

DR. GÖRTLER. You have to create it.

ORMUND. How could I ? You've some idea of what's gone
on in my head these last twenty years. Where's the peace
coming from ?

DR. GÖRTLER (*sternly*). If you must talk and act like a child,
then at least be as humble as a child. If you cannot create your
own peace, then pray for it. Go down on your knees and ask
for it. If you have no knowledge, then have faith.

ORMUND. Faith in what ? Fairy tales ?

DR. GÖRTLER (*with authority and passion*). Yes, my friend—
if you will—in fairy tales.

ORMUND. I've lived too long—and thought too much—to
begin now——

DR. GÖRTLER (*with great authority*). I have lived longer than
you. I have thought more, and I have suffered more. And I

tell you there is more truth to the fundamental nature of things in the most foolish fairy tales than there is in any of your complaints against life.

ORMUND. Rubbish! Why?

DR. GÖRTLER. Because all events are shaped in the end by magic——

ORMUND (*scornfully*). Yes, I thought we'd come to that. Magic!

DR. GÖRTLER. Yes. The creative magic of our feeling, imagination and will. These are the realities—our feeling, imagination and will—and all our histories are their dreams.

ORMUND. All very easy!

DR. GÖRTLER (*with passion*). It is not easy. Life is not easy. It provides no short cuts, no effortless escapes. Peace and ecstasy are not laid on like hot and cold water. (*He has worked his way to* C. *above the table.*)

ORMUND (*with savage irony*). You needn't tell me that. I know it. (*He is* R. *of the chair* R. *of the table.*)

DR. GÖRTLER. Yes, but you do not know—you will not understand—that life is penetrated through and through by our feeling, imagination and will. In the end the whole universe must respond to every real effort we make. We each live a fairy tale created by ourselves.

ORMUND. What—by going round and round the same damned dreary circle of existence, as you believe?

DR. GÖRTLER. We do not go round a circle. That is an illusion, just as the circling of the planets and stars is an illusion. We move along a spiral track. It is not quite the same journey from the cradle to the grave each time. Sometimes the differences are small, sometimes they are very important. We must set out each time on the same road, but along that road we have a choice of adventures.

ORMUND. I wish I could believe that, Görtler.

DR. GÖRTLER. What has happened before—many times perhaps—will probably happen again. That is why some people can prophesy what is to happen. They do not see the future, as they think, but the past, what has happened before. But something new may happen. You may have brought your wife here for this holiday over and over again. She may have met Farrant here over and over again. But you and I have not talked here before. This is new. This may be one of those great moments of our lives.

ORMUND. And which are they?

DR. GÖRTLER (*impressively*). When a soul can make a fateful decision. I see this as such a moment for you, Ormund. You can return to the old dark circle of existence, dying endless deaths, or you can break the spell and swing out into new life.

ORMUND (*after a pause—staring at* DR. GÖRTLER, *then with a*

certain breadth and nobility of manner). New life! I wish I could
believe that.

(DR. GÖRTLER *sits in the chair* L. *of the table.* ORMUND *moves
up to the sideboard.*)

They've never told me yet about a God so generous and noble
and wise that He won't allow a few decisions that we make in
our ignorance, haste and bewilderment to settle our fate for ever.
Why should this poor improvisation be our whole existence ?
Why should this great theatre of suns and moons and starlight
have been created for the first pitiful charade we can contrive ?

DR. GÖRTLER. It was not. We must play our parts until the
drama is perfect.

ORMUND (*very slowly, coming down to the table*). I think what
I've resented most is that the only wisdom we have is wisdom
after the event. We learn, but always too late. When I was no
longer a boy, I knew at last what sort of boy I ought to have
been. By the time we are forty, we know how to behave at
twenty. Always too late. So that the little wisdom we get is
useless to us.

DR. GÖRTLER (*very quietly*). In your world. Not in mine.

(ORMUND *stands erect, but with his head bowed for a moment.* DR.
GÖRTLER *watches him in silence, without moving. Finally*
ORMUND *looks up, obviously having arrived at decision.*)

Well ?

ORMUND (*very quietly*). At least we can improve on this
Whitsuntide drama of yours. I'll live. (*He puts the revolver on
the table.*) But on nobody's self-sacrifice. Ask my wife to come
in here for a moment. And please tell Farrant to stop out there.

(DR. GÖRTLER *nods, rises and goes out up* L. ORMUND *takes up
the revolver and begins unloading it, then pockets it as* JANET
*slowly enters, shutting the door after her. She looks anxiously
at him.*)

JANET (*quietly*). I was just saying good-bye to Oliver. (*She
remains up* L. *by the door.*)

ORMUND. Yes.

JANET. You understand—I'm not leaving you now.

ORMUND. You love him. He loves you. You are certain of
that ?

JANET. Yes, absolutely certain.

(*He looks at her gravely for a moment, turns away restlessly, then
swings round, almost savagely.*)

ORMUND. Go on, then. Go with him.

JANET (*suddenly lighting up with great hope*). Walter ! (*Then
she realizes it could not work, and the eagerness and light go.*) I
couldn't—you see—not now when I know——

ORMUND (*harshly*). You don't know. How could you ?

JANET (*moving in to above the chair* L. *of the table*). Doctor Görtler said——

ORMUND (*cutting in sharply*). These are our lives, not his. Go, I tell you. There'll be no suicide, no scandal, no disasters. Everything'll go on. You can depend on me.

JANET (*with growing excitement and eagerness*). Oh—Walter —are you sure ? If only I could——

ORMUND (*with a touch of impatience, as he moves upstage and then back to* R. *of the table*). I tell you it's all right. Farrant's only got to take you away now for a little time, perhaps abroad, and then go quietly back to his work. And whatever happens I'll see he's not howled out of his school.

JANET (*she is radiant now, and speaks confusedly*). Walter—I can't—is it really true ?—oh, I can't talk—I'm too happy——

ORMUND (*with a touch of bitterness, moving up to above the table*). Yes, I never remember seeing you so happy before.

JANET (*eagerly*). It's not just for myself—or even for Oliver —but for you too, Walter. You've changed everything now.

ORMUND (*with a slight effort*). All right, keep on being happy then, Janet. You were meant to be happy, to be radiant. I always wanted you to be—but somehow it didn't work. Now— it seems—it's working.

JANET (*looking at him, then speaking slowly and with great affection*). Walter—something tremendous has happened to you

ORMUND. I wonder. (*He looks at her, then slowly smiles.*)

JANET. Yes. You're suddenly quite different. And yet— as you always ought to have been. I know now—you're bigger than I am—bigger than Oliver. I think—now—you'll be a great man, Walter.

ORMUND. Not a chance. I'll never be a great man. There aren't many of them, and you have to stand a long way off to see their true size. No, Janet, perhaps I'm at last—a man—a real man—and not a mere bundle of fears and self-indulgences.

JANET. That's not how I shall think of you. (*After a pause.*) What will you do now ?

ORMUND (*crossing to the sofa and back again*). Stay here to-night, probably to-morrow night too. And try and think. I've never done much real thinking. I've always been afraid to.

(SALLY *enters up* R.C., *hesitantly and anxiously.* ORMUND *turns and sees her.*)

Oh—Mrs. Pratt—ask Sam to put Mrs. Ormund's things in the car outside.

SALLY. Your car ?

ORMUND. No, Mr. Farrant's. (*As she stops and looks troubled and anxious, he adds gently.*) Everything will be all right, Mrs.

Pratt. And stop worrying about that boy of yours. He'll have
his chance. Nobody's going to let you down.

Sally (*relieved*). Thank you, Mr. Ormund.

(*She goes out again, up* R.C., *closing the door.*)

Ormund (*quietly, moving close to* R. *of her*). I'll say good-bye
now, Janet. I won't come out.

Janet. There seem to be a thousand things I want to say now,
Walter.

Ormund. Then don't forget them. Because some day, soon,
I want to hear them.

(Dr. Görtler *appears at the door up* L.)

Good-bye, Janet. Keep on being happy.

(*He holds out a hand, but as she takes it she moves forward and kisses
him.*)

Janet (*whispering*). Dear Walter—good-bye—God bless you !

(*She hurries out,* Dr. Görtler *holding the door open for her.*
Ormund *watches her go. There is a slight pause after she has
gone.*)

Ormund (*very quietly*). Close that door, Doctor.

Dr. Görtler (*after closing the door*).   I, too, must be going now.

Ormund (*with a slight smile*). Having concluded the experiment. (*After a pause.*) I am still wondering whether I believe
a word of it.

Dr. Görtler. It is very difficult at first, like all new knowledge. (*He is staring curiously at* Ormund.)

Ormund. You look at me as a doctor looks at his patient.

Dr. Görtler (*calmly*). Yes, because if my theory is correct,
you are now in the unusual and interesting position of a man
who is moving out on a new time track, like a man who is suddenly
born into a strange new world——

Ormund (*raising his hand as the sound of* Farrant's *car going
off is heard*). Just a minute, Doctor.

(*They listen a moment until the sound of the car dies away—*Ormund
listening with a painful intensity.)

Like a man who's suddenly born into a strange new world, eh ?
Well, that's not altogether fanciful, Görtler. I feel rather like
a new-born creature. Rather cold, small, lonely. (*He shivers a
little.*)

Dr. Görtler (*with a little smile*). Yes, it may be hard at first.
But it will pass. There are a million suns waiting to keep you
warm and to light your way.

(*He goes towards the door up* L. Ormund *follows him slowly.*)

Perhaps we shall meet again. So I will say *Auf Wiedersehn*.
ORMUND. Yes, we'll meet again. Good-bye.

*(They shake hands. DR. GÖRTLER goes, and ORMUND stands at
the door looking out into the night, which faintly lights him with
moonlight. As he stands there, he mechanically brings out his
pipe and pouch and begins to fill the pipe. SAM enters hesitantly
—pipe in hand—through the door R.C., and looks doubtfully and
sympathetically across at ORMUND. He shuts the door and, as he
clears his throat, ORMUND turns and sees him.)*

Well, Sam ?
SAM *(with awkward kindness)*. I just wondered—like—Mr.
Ormund—whether there might be aught I could do for you—
like——
ORMUND. Well, you can sit down and smoke your pipe, Sam.
(He shuts the door up L. and moves in to L.C.)
SAM. Ay.

*(He sits in the chair R. of the table. ORMUND sits in the chair L.
of the table. When they are both seated SAM speaks.)*

I hear them shepherds t'other side o' Grindle Top's been having
a bit o' bother.
ORMUND *(slowly)*. Yes, I heard something about that, Sam.
SAM *(slowly, philosophically)*. Folks thinks shepherds has a
quiet life, but they have their bits o' bother, them chaps, like
onnybody else.
ORMUND. Yes, I suppose they do, Sam.

They are smoking away companionably, in silence, as—

The CURTAIN *slowly falls.*

PROPERTY PLOT

(For setting of Furniture, etc., see Photograph of Scene.)

ACT I

Set best tablecloth in sideboard drawer.

Off Stage R.
Two bowls of flowers and duster for SALLY.
Glass of sherry on tray for SAM.
Large book for FARRANT.
Whisky and soda on tray for SAM.
Empty tray for SALLY.

Off Stage L.
Old-fashioned bag for DR. GÖRTLER.
Well-worn dispatch-case with papers for ORMUND.
Library book for JANET.

Personal.
Notebook for DR. GÖRTLER.
Fountain-pen and old envelope for ORMUND.

ACT II

Open curtains at window.
Open flap of desk.
Strike bowl of flowers from table C.
Set papers and second fountain-pen on desk for ORMUND.
Set JANET'S library book on L. end of sideboard.

Off Stage R.
Tray with almost empty bottle of whisky, syphon and glass, for SAM.
Letters for SALLY.
Glass of sherry on tray for SALLY.
DR. GÖRTLER'S bag.

Off Stage L.
Small bunch of wild flowers for JANET.

Personal.
Cigarettes and matches for FARRANT.
Pound note for DR. GÖRTLER.

ACT III

Open curtains at window.
Set DR. GÖRTLER'S notebook by telephone.

Off Stage R.
Suitcase, raincoat and hat for FARRANT.
Revolver loaded with blanks for ORMUND.

Personal.
Pipe, pouch and matches for ORMUND.

76

EFFECTS

Car engine.
Car horn.
Clock chime.
Clock tick.
Revolver shot.
Telephone.

Definite cues for the Clock Chimes are given amongst the stage directions in the text. It will be found that these do not occur at regular intervals, but await a suitable dramatic moment in the play.

Very few cues are given for the Ticking of the Clock, which is more a matter for the producer's judgment. The ticking should be brought up louder when the stage is empty, also at suitable passages in the play when the actors are pausing for effect or otherwise creating little competitive noise.

After the clock chime at the rise of the curtain on Act III the audience should no longer be conscious of the clock.

LIGHTING

It will be noticed that at the opening of each Act there is some modicum of afternoon daylight which after a while gradually fades until there comes a time when the lights have to be switched on and the curtains drawn at the window.

Act I opens much earlier in the evening compared with Acts II and III, and hence there will be more daylight outside when the curtains are drawn than on the other two occasions.

The following are the cues used in the London Production for the commencement of each fade :

ACT I.   1st Check.   Page 14.
      SALLY.   It's up there.
    2nd Check.   Page 15.
      DR. GÖRTLER.   *So! So! Ich bin glücklich.*

ACT II.   1st Check.   Page 36.
      ORMUND.   I'm sorry, Doctor Görtler.
    2nd Check.   Page 42.
      JANET. . . . I suppose Walter—my husband—is in the bar.

ACT III. 1st Check.   Page 57.
      SALLY.   You're not leaving him—surely—because he's taken to drinking too much——
    2nd Check.   Page 59.
      ORMUND. . . . We're like little children groping about in the dark.
    3rd Check.   Page 60.
      FARRANT.   But you're not going to blame me for preferring knowleage to judgment and guesswork ?